Learning Perl 6

Keeping the Easy, Hard, and Impossible
Within Reach

brian d foy

Beijing · Boston · Farnham · Sebastopol · Tokyo

Learning Perl 6
by brian d foy

Copyright © 2018 brian d foy. All rights reserved.

Published by O'Reilly Media, Inc., 1005 Gravenstein Highway North, Sebastopol, CA 95472.

O'Reilly books may be purchased for educational, business, or sales promotional use. Online editions are also available for most titles (*http://oreilly.com/safari*). For more information, contact our corporate/institutional sales department: 800-998-9938 or *corporate@oreilly.com*.

Editor: Jeff Bleiel
Production Editor: Nicholas Adams
Copyeditor: Rachel Head
Proofreader: Kim Cofer

Indexer: Lucie Haskins
Interior Designer: David Futato
Cover Designer: Karen Montgomery
Illustrator: Rebecca Demarest

September 2018:   First Edition

Revision History for the First Edition
2018-08-24:   First Release

See *http://oreilly.com/catalog/errata.csp?isbn=9781491977682* for release details.

978-1-491-97768-2

[LSI]

Table of Contents

Preface

Welcome to the first edition of *Learning Perl 6*, a book title that sounds similar to others you may have read and I may have written. This one, however, is my first book about the language called "Perl 6." I know the name is a bit confusing; I'm not in charge of that part. I'm just the book writer.

Okay, I can see you're not satisfied with that.

Here's the short answer you probably want: if you need to learn Perl because someone made that choice for you, you're probably looking for my other book, *Learning Perl*, that covers the widely used Perl 5. That's the stable ol' workhorse that's been around virtually forever. This one is about the new language that's still growing up and isn't in wide use yet.

Here's the longer answer for those of you who are still reading. You either know that you want Perl 6 or you don't really care which one you get as long as you learn a new language.

The Backstory of Perl 6

At the Perl Conference in 2000, a group of Perl people got together in a hotel conference room in Monterey, California. It was a Tuesday. Later that day the Perl 5 Porters would meet to talk about the immediate future of Perl. Chip Salzenberg had organized this mostly secret pre-meeting to come up with some ideas. Somehow he dragged me into the pre-meeting.

We started chatting about the roadblocks Perl 5 was facing at the time: the developers hated each other, the source code was intractable, and Perl was losing the popularity contest.

Chip had tried a complete rewrite of Perl in C++ (a project he called Topaz) but had hit some brick walls. That was part of his motivation for the meeting.

We prattled on about small potatoes stuff until Jon Orwant, publisher of *The Perl Journal*, started throwing coffee mugs against the wall. He wanted to shake things up because we were all being annoyingly polite. We weren't thinking big enough. I think he underestimated the violence of the gesture, but it got our attention. We started thinking big. Infinitely big.

And that's when Perl 6 was born. Perl's creator, Larry Wall, announced it the next day in his State of the Onion (*http://www.perl.com/pub/2000/10/23/soto2000.html*) address. Most notably, he said "Perl 6 is going to be designed by the community." Everyone thought that Perl 6 would be the version after the just-released Perl v5.6. That didn't happen, but that's why "Perl" was in the name "Perl 6."

For a few months people submitted comments (*https://perl6.org/archive/rfc/*) about what they wanted in the new language. Larry digested those comments into a series of "Apocalypse" documents and formed a response for each one. He let those suggestions shape his own thoughts as chief designer. Eventually he put together the "Synopses" to unify all of his ideas. Damian Conway explored those ideas in the "Exegeses." You can find all of them at *https://design.perl6.org*. They're a bit dated, but that's how it goes.

The Perl 6 developers invented a new interpreter named Parrot that was intended to handle multiple languages and make it easy to transpile code and do many other nifty things. It didn't quite work out that way.

At the same time, another group revitalized Perl 5 development. Jarkko Hietaniemi released Perl v5.8 in 2003. That version stuck around for a bit, and people then expected *that one* to be the last version of Perl 5.

In 2005, Audrey Tang implemented Perl 6 on top of the Glasgow Haskell Compiler (GHC). She called it Pugs (*https://github.com/perl6/Pugs.hs*)—the Perl 6 User's Golfing System. People finally had something that would run Perl 6, and they started to get excited. They began to fill out the feature list and the canonical tests an implementation must pass. But development stalled again.

Perl v5.10 came out in 2007. It had new features—some stolen from Perl 6. The Perl 5 Porters developed some formal policies and processes. Perl 5 got back on track. People started to clean up the internals. Core developers got excited about Perl 5 again. Instead of dying, Perl 5 surged. As I write this, the current version of Perl 5 is v5.26 and v5.28 is only a few months away.

This left Perl 6 with competition from what people had thought it would replace. That's where the confusion in the name comes from. Some people want to rename it to avoid the "Perl" part, but the universe has resisted that effort.

Perl 6 kept plodding away until the developers got to the "Christmas" release. They decided that whatever was working by Christmas 2015 would be the first official release. They hit that target, and the development has been consistent since then.

What You Should Already Know

I assume that you know how to create plain-text files using a code editor (not a word processor) and how to run basic commands in a terminal (Unix-like or Windows).

These are basic skills that you'll need as a programmer, but I understand that you might be working on those at the same time you are learning to program. I suggest a few online code runners in the next section that allow you to avoid terminals and files. Don't rely on these, though.

I try to gently introduce programming, but that could be a long book on its own. Perl 6 is an object-oriented language and I mostly ignore the theory and practice of that to focus on the language itself. Sadly, this book can't teach you to be a programmer—take heart, though. Many programmers learned their craft by struggling through books that didn't teach them programming.

You aren't going to learn everything about Perl 6 or programming in this book. You're never done learning, though, so don't be discouraged.

Getting Rakudo

Perl 6 was designed from the start to run on multiple implementations even though no one knew what those would be at the time. There's an effort to compile Perl 6 to the Java Virtual Machine (JVM), and another one to run it on top of JavaScript. There's also MoarVM (*http://www.moarvm.org*) ("Metamodel On A Runtime"), which is the one furthest along and the one I use in this book.

The version of Perl 6 is defined by the version of the test specification and what that covers; as I write this that's v6.c (with v6.d on the horizon). Rakudo 2018.04 is Perl 6 on top of Moar 2018.04, but it's still v6.c. You can see this when you ask for the version:

```
% perl6 -v
This is Rakudo Star version 2018.04 built on MoarVM version 2018.04
implementing Perl 6.c.
```

For the purposes of this book "Rakudo" and "Perl 6" are the same thing, even though that's not really true. If you know how that isn't true you're probably fine choosing your own implementation.

You can try Perl 6 without installing it. Glot.io (*https://glot.io/new/perl6*) and Try It Online (*https://tio.run/#perl6*) have Perl 6 browser-based environments. You can run single-file programs; that should get you through most of this book.

There's also a Perl 6 Docker container (*https://hub.docker.com/_/rakudo-star/*) if you're into that sort of thing:

```
% docker run -it rakudo-star
```

Your local package manager might have it; look for something like *perl6*, *rakudo*, or *rakudo-star*. If you use Chocolatey on Windows you can install it with a package I maintain:

```
C:\ choco install rakudo-star
```

You can also download source or binaries from Rakudo.org (*http://www.rakudo.org/*). That's how I get my macOS packages.

Once you have Rakudo installed you should have a *perl6* binary. Give it a go to ensure that it works. The -v switch tells you some information about your *perl6*:

```
% perl6 -v
This is Rakudo Star version 2018.04 built on MoarVM version 2018.04
implementing Perl 6.c.
```

Without an argument *perl6* drops you into the *REPL* (Read-Eval-Print-Loop). At the > prompt you can type some text between single quotes and the REPL will echo that to you:

```
% perl6
To exit type 'exit' or '^D'
> 'Hello Camelia!'
Hello Camelia!
```

You can also inspect the values of variables. There are special variables that tell you about your setup and might be useful if you have to report a problem:

```
% perl6
To exit type 'exit' or '^D'
> $*VM
moar (2018.04)
> $*PERL
Perl 6 (6.c)
```

If you have gotten this far you have a working Perl 6!

How to Use This Book

This is a tutorial book. My job is to find the parts of the language that you need to understand so you can teach yourself the rest. This isn't a reference book, and there's more that I'll leave out than I include. It's not laid out by topic and the chapter titles only roughly describe the contents. I'll introduce new topics as soon as I can; most of them need a little buildup though.

Sometimes the terminology can get a bit heavy. I've included a glossary toward the end. If you forget what something means try looking for it there.

Along the way you'll find exercises. Do them! Practice what you just read as you encounter the exercises, then read my answers (Appendix A); there's additional information in them. I don't hide information from you but I let you wrestle with some concepts so you can have some fun. Part of the practice is the struggle. Let's do an exercise right now to see how it works.

Exercise 0.1

Install Perl 6. Use the REPL to find the version of Perl 6 you have.

How did that work for you? Let's try another one. This is a bit easier but requires you to download a few things from this book's website. I'll put interesting things and exercise aids at *https://www.learningperl6.com/downloads/* and *https://github.com/briand foy/LearningPerl6_Downloads*. I'll note when something is useful for an exercise.

Exercise 0.2

In the Downloads section of LearningPerl6.com, find the *Preface/find_moth_genera.p6* program and the *DataFiles/Butterflies_and_Moths.txt* data file. Run that program with that data file. Assuming you have them in the same directory, that would be:

```
% perl6 find_moth_genera.p6 Butterflies_and_Moths.txt
```

It's the same on Windows, although your prompt will be different.

I've designed this book for you to finish in a couple of weeks. Go through the chapters in order because they build on each other. With some exceptions, anything I use in a later chapter I should have explained earlier. Some concepts may show up in chapters with a different major topic or even in an exercise answer. Do the exercises! Try a chapter, go through its exercises, and take a break. Don't try to do too much at once.

How to Get Help

If you can't quite figure out your Perl 6 issue, you have a few options. The official website, *https://www.perl6.org (https://www.perl6.org/community/)*, lists several ways you can interact with other Perl 6 users. I tend to like Stack Overflow (*https://stacko verflow.com*) as a question-and-answer site.

Conventions Used in This Book

The following typographical conventions are used in this book:

Italic
> Indicates new terms, URLs, email addresses, filenames, and file extensions.

`Constant width`
> Used for program listings, as well as within paragraphs to refer to program elements such as variable or function names, databases, data types, environment variables, statements, and keywords. Also used for commands and command-line options.

`Constant width bold`
> Shows commands or other text that should be typed literally by the user.

`Constant width italic`
> Shows text that should be replaced with user-supplied values or by values determined by context.

This element signifies a tip or suggestion.

This element signifies a general note.

This element indicates a warning or caution.

Using Code Examples

Supplemental material (code examples, exercises, etc.) is available for download at *http://www.learningperl6.com/*.

This book is here to help you get your job done. In general, if example code is offered with this book, you may use it in your programs and documentation. You do not need to contact us for permission unless you're reproducing a significant portion of the code. For example, writing a program that uses several chunks of code from this book does not require permission. Selling or distributing a CD-ROM of examples from O'Reilly books does require permission. Answering a question by citing this book and quoting example code does not require permission. Incorporating a significant amount of example code from this book into your product's documentation does require permission.

We appreciate, but do not require, attribution. An attribution usually includes the title, author, publisher, and ISBN. For example: "*Learning Perl 6* by brian d foy (O'Reilly). Copyright 2018 brian d foy, 978-1-491-97768-2."

If you feel your use of code examples falls outside fair use or the permission given above, feel free to contact us at *permissions@oreilly.com*.

O'Reilly Safari

 Safari (formerly Safari Books Online) is a membership-based training and reference platform for enterprise, government, educators, and individuals.

Members have access to thousands of books, training videos, Learning Paths, interactive tutorials, and curated playlists from over 250 publishers, including O'Reilly Media, Harvard Business Review, Prentice Hall Professional, Addison-Wesley Professional, Microsoft Press, Sams, Que, Peachpit Press, Adobe, Focal Press, Cisco Press, John Wiley & Sons, Syngress, Morgan Kaufmann, IBM Redbooks, Packt, Adobe Press, FT Press, Apress, Manning, New Riders, McGraw-Hill, Jones & Bartlett, and Course Technology, among others.

For more information, please visit *http://oreilly.com/safari*.

How to Contact Us

Please address comments and questions concerning this book to the publisher:

O'Reilly Media, Inc.
1005 Gravenstein Highway North
Sebastopol, CA 95472
800-998-9938 (in the United States or Canada)
707-829-0515 (international or local)
707-829-0104 (fax)

We have a web page for this book, where we list errata, examples, and any additional information. You can access this page at *http://bit.ly/learning-perl-6*.

To comment or ask technical questions about this book, send email to *bookquestions@oreilly.com*.

For more information about our books, courses, conferences, and news, see our website at *http://www.oreilly.com*.

Find us on Facebook: *http://facebook.com/oreilly*

Follow us on Twitter: *http://twitter.com/oreillymedia*

Watch us on YouTube: *http://www.youtube.com/oreillymedia*

Acknowledgments

I've tried to write this book several times since 2000. The first try involved my frequent coauthor Randal L. Schwartz, who taught me most of everything I know about writing about programming. Even though he didn't take part in this book he's been immensely helpful throughout the years.

Audrey Tang got a hold of my laptop and changed all my Perl 6 slides before my first ever Perl 6 talk. Things had changed overnight. Even during the talk things changed, and Damian Conway would yell out "Not anymore!" They were committing code during the talk. Sometimes you run your fastest and still can't keep up.

Wendy Van Dijk and Liz Mattijsen got serious about a Perl 6 tutorial book a couple of years ago. They put their money where their mouths were. We talked about doing the book as a Kickstarter project with them as the major contributors. Their generosity guided so many other people to help—and thanks to everyone who contributed through my fundraising campaign.

Brian Jepson was an O'Reilly editor at the time I was running my Kickstarter campaign and saw what I was doing. He helped me turn it into a proposal that ultimately turned into this book. He imparted many great ideas before he moved on to a new job.

Allison Randal, my editor on *Mastering Perl*, had many encouraging things to say early in the process. She also had many words of wisdom for the inevitable discouraging things she knew I'd encounter. My good friend Sinan Ünür provided great insights into the workings of non-Perl languages and helped me sort out the structure of the book. He was especially helpful with issues related to Windows. David Farrell, the publisher of PerlTricks.com and now Perl.com (*https://www.perl.com/*), had many interesting insights and angles. Chris Nandor was a constant source of reason and sanity.

I asked many, many questions on Stack Overflow (*https://stackoverflow.com/questions/tagged/perl6*). Some of those were just for me, but many were for the people who will search for the same answers. Many people were quite helpful, including

Christopher Bottoms, Brad Gilbert, Moritz Lens, Liz Mattijsen (again), JJ Merelo, Timo Paulssen, Stefan Seifert, Jonathan Worthington, and numerous others.

Other people were helpful along the way. I filed several bug reports and documentation issues, and many people worked on those. They've all made the world a slightly better place.

## CHAPTER 1

Introduction

This chapter is the big picture view of the language; don't worry if you don't understand everything that's going on just yet. Worry if you get to the end of the book and you still don't! There's much going on, so you'll spiral around some topics, revisit others, and with some practice see how it all fits together—it really is all about the practice.

Why Perl 6?

For starters, you have *Learning Perl 6*. You might as well get your money's worth by using the language!

But what makes this an attractive language? The Perl family has always been fond of *DWIM*—Do What I Mean. Things that you do frequently should be easy to do, and the hardest things should still be possible. The usefulness of any programming language is measured by the extent to which it solves your problems.

Perl 6 is a great text processing language—possibly even better than Perl 5. The *regular expressions* (Chapter 15) have many new and exciting features that make it even easier to match and extract bits of text. The builtin *grammar* (Chapter 17) features allow you to easily write complex rules to handle and react to text.

Gradual typing (Chapter 3) allows you to annotate variables with restrictions about what you can store there. For example, you can specify that a number must be a whole number, or a positive number, or between two other numbers. You don't have to use it (that's the gradual part). You'll be able to annotate what a *subroutine* accepts and what it should return. That can quickly reveal bugs at data boundaries.

Builtin *concurrency* (Chapter 18) features allow you to decompose problems into parts that you run separately and perhaps simultaneously. The language handles most of that for you.

Lazy lists and infinite lists allow you to process sequences without excessive copying or even having the entire list at one time (Chapter 6). You can easily create your own infinite lazy lists.

I could keep going, but you'll run into more amazing features as you work your way through this book.

There will be times that you won't want to use Perl 6. No language is the right tool for every job. If you like something else better or can finish a task faster with a different tool, more power to you! I hope, though, that this book helps you do what you need to do quickly and efficiently in Perl 6.

First Steps with the REPL

The REPL is a Read-Evaluate-Print-Loop tool that provides an interactive prompt. The REPL evaluates the code you type, shows you the result, then prompts you again. It's a quick way to try out small snippets. When you run *perl6* without arguments it starts its REPL:

```
% perl6
To exit type 'exit' or '^D'
>
```

The > is the prompt that waits for you to type something. When you type Return the REPL does its work. Try it by adding two numbers:

```
% perl6
> 2 + 2
4
```

If there's an error it lets you know about it and prompts you again:

```
% perl6
> 2 + Hamadryas
===SORRY!=== Error while compiling:
Undeclared name:
    Hamadryas used at line 1
>
```

You don't know why this failed yet because you're at the beginning of the book. That doesn't really matter as long as you know the REPL catches the error and gives you a new prompt. If you need to correct a mistake you should be able to use the up arrow to go back to the previous line (or further) to edit and rerun something.

Before you move on, you should know a few other tricks that can help you learn the geography of the language.

When I write about methods in this book I generally preface them with the method call dot so you know they're methods, as in `.is-prime`. The dot is not part of the name.

A *method* is a label for predefined behavior of an object. Every object has a *type*, and the `.^name` method tells you that type:

```
% perl6
> 3.^name
Int
```

The literal 3 is an object of type `Int`, for integer. Once you know what type something is you can read its documentation to find out what you can do with it.

Behavior is defined in *classes* (Chapter 12), and these classes can be based on more general classes through *inheritance*. You can use the `.^mro` method to see the inheritance chain (although the documentation also tells you):

```
% perl6
> 3.^mro
((Int) (Cool) (Any) (Mu))
```

An object can do all the behavior of all the classes it inherits from. This shows that 3 is an `Int`, which is a `Cool` (Convenient Object-Oriented Loop), which is an `Any` (a base class for just about everything), which is, finally, a `Mu` (a *thingy* that is not a thingy—think on that for awhile!).

Use `.^methods` to see the list of methods for an object:

```
% perl6
> 3.^methods
(Int Num Rat FatRat abs Bridge chr sqrt base
polymod expmod is-prime floor ceiling round
...)
```

The type is also an object (a *type object*). It's the abstract expression of the thingy without a concrete value. It has methods too:

```
% perl6
> Int.^methods
(Int Num Rat FatRat abs Bridge chr sqrt base
polymod expmod is-prime floor ceiling round
...)
```

You can't call many of those methods on a type object, though. You get an error because there's no value yet:

```
% perl6
> Int.sqrt
```

```
Invocant of method 'sqrt' must be an object instance of
type 'Int', not a type object of type 'Int'.
```

The methods .^name, .^mro, and .^methods come from the language's metaprogramming underpinnings. That's a bit advanced for this book given the number of pages I have, so you won't read more about that here.

Reading the Documentation

Now that you know about the REPL and how to find the type of an object, you probably want to read about those in the documentation. The *p6doc* program can do that:

```
% p6doc Int
... lots of text
```

If you want to know about a method you can add it to the type:

```
% p6doc Int.polymod
      method polymod

Defined as:
    method polymod(Int:D: +@mods)

Usage:
    INTEGER.polymod(LIST)
...
```

Sometimes you don't find the docs where you expect them. When that happens try one of the inherited classes:

```
% p6doc Int.sqrt
No documentation found for method 'sqrt'

% p6doc Cool.sqrt
  routine sqrt

Defined as:
    sub sqrt(Numeric(Cool) $x)
    method sqrt()

  ...
```

I find myself mostly reading the docs online at *https://docs.perl6.org*. Worse than that, I Google something like "perl6 Int" and follow the first result. That site also has a handy search feature to help you find things without using a full text search. You can run the same site locally. Look for those details at the bottom of each page.

Basic Syntax

You often need to read code from the inside out, as you would a math formula, so that's how I approach it here: starting from the very tiny and building up from there.

This is a survey of the things you need to know and will read about in upcoming chapters. Don't worry if you are a bit overwhelmed at this point. You'll get used to these things as you practice.

Terms

At the lowest level a program has *terms*. These are the building blocks that form everything else. Think of these as the nouns of the language. Here are some terms:

```
2
e
π
'Hello'
$x
now
```

These include literal data, such as 2 and 'Hello'; variables, such as $x; and defined symbols, such as π. now is a term that represents the current time as an Instant object.

A variable typically starts with a *sigil*—a special character that denotes something about that variable. The variable $x has the $ sigil. Don't worry about those just yet, although you'll see more later in this chapter.

Operators and Expressions

An *expression* is a combination of terms and operators that produce a new value. If the terms are the nouns, *operators* are the verbs that specify the action. They turn one or more terms into a new value. *Operands* are the values that an operator uses. A *unary operator* does something to a single operand:

```
- 137        # negate 137 to make -137
+ '137'      # convert the string '137' to a number
$x++         # add 1 to the current value in $x
```

That # and the text following it is a comment (which you'll see more about in a moment). It's some text that the program ignores and is a convenient way for you to leave notes about your code. I'll often use comments to reinforce a point or show the output of an expression.

A *binary operator* works on two operands. Normally these operators show up between the operands (*infixed*):

```
2 + 2            # add two numbers
$object.method() # the . method call operator
$x = 137         # assign a value to a variable
```

A *ternary operator*, such as the conditional operator, ?? !!, has three operands:

```
$some_value ?? 'Yes' !! 'No'    # choose one of two values
```

If the first thingy evaluates to True, it selects the second thingy. Otherwise it selects the third thingy. You'll see more of these in Chapter 3.

Before, after, and around

Operators come in several varieties, with names that describe their position and the number of operands they expect. You'll see these terms throughout the book. A *prefix operator* comes before its operand and usually takes only one operand. The increment operator is an example. It adds one to the number in $x:

```
++$x
```

A *postfix operator* comes after its operand. There are increment forms of this type as well:

```
$x++
```

A *circumfix operator* surrounds its operand. Examples include the parentheses and the double quote marks:

```
( 1, 2, 3 )
"Hello"
```

A *postcircumfix operator* surrounds its operand but comes after something else. A single-element access to an Array or a Hash surrounds the index and comes after the variable name. The [] and <> are the operators that come after the name but surround the key:

```
@array[0]
%hash<key>
```

Those terms are in the documentation. There are other ways you can arrange operators that don't have standard terms, so I've fashioned my own that I don't expect to use that much.

A *precircumfix operator* surrounds an operand and comes before other operands. The reduction operator (Chapter 6) surrounds an operator that it places between each of the items that follow it. This adds all the numbers without having to specify a + between every pair:

```
[+] 1, 2, 3
```

A *circumfix infix operator* surrounds an *infix operator*. The hyperoperators <<>> surround an operator and distribute that infix operator along the two lists (Chapter 6):

```
(1, 2, 3) <<+>> (4, 5, 6)
```

There are other arrangements you might encounter in this book, but you can generally tell how they work by picking apart the name.

Operators are actually methods. Their names look a bit complicated because they start with the sort of operator they are and have the symbol in angle brackets:

```
infix:<+>(1, 2)      # 3

my @array = 1, 2, 3
postcircumfix:<[ ]>( @array, 1 )
```

You won't need these forms, but you should know that the operators figure out what to do based on the arguments.

Precedence

You can chain operations one after the other. Try this in the REPL:

```
1 + 2 + 3 + 4
```

The expression is evaluated in order of operator *precedence* and *associativity*. Precedence decides which operators go first and associativity figures out the order among operators of the same precedence (or even two of the same operator).

An operator's precedence is relatively *looser* or *tighter* than other operators. With a chain of terms the tighter operator goes first. Multiplication (*) happens before addition (+), just like in high school algebra:

```
2 + 3 * 4         # 14
```

If you don't like the order you can change it with parentheses. Things inside parentheses are computed before things outside. Another way to say that is that parentheses have the highest precedence. Now the addition happens first:

```
(2 + 3) * 4       # 20
```

If you have two operators of the same precedence then associativity decides the order of evaluation. Operators can be either *left associative* or *right associative*. The exponentiation operator is right associative, so the operation on the right happens first:

```
2 ** 3 ** 4       # 2.4178516392293e+24
```

It's the same order as if you put explicit parentheses around the right two numbers:

```
2 ** (3 ** 4)     # 2.4178516392293e+24
```

Use parentheses to make the left operation happen first:

```
(2 ** 3) ** 4     # 4096
```

Some operators can't be combined and don't have associativity. The range operator is one of the operators you can't combine:

```
0 .. 5       # Range operator, nonassociative
0 .. 3 .. 5 # Illegal
```

Statements

A *statement* is a complete, standalone part of a program. An expression can be a statement but it can also be part of a statement. Here's a statement using put to output a message. It adds a newline for you:

```
put 'Hello Perl 6!'
```

You separate statements with a semicolon. Here are two statements; they are on separate lines but you still need a semicolon between them:

```
put 'Hello Perl 6!';
put 'The time is ', now;
```

You don't need the ; unless another statement follows, but I tend to put a semicolon at the end of every statement because I know I'll forget to add it when I add more code:

```
put 'Hello Perl 6!';
put 'The time is ', now;
```

Most whitespace is insignificant, which means you can use it how you like to format your program. These statements have a differently organized manner:

```
put
     'Hello Perl 6!'

; put 'The time is ',
now                    ;
```

There are a few situations where whitespace matters, but you'll read about that when you need to know about it.

Blocks

A *block* (Chapter 5) combines one or more statements into a single unit by surrounding them with a set of braces. Sometimes the block has a control keyword, such as loop, attached to it. This block continually evaluates its statements until you stop the program with Control-C. This is an *infinite loop*:

```
loop {
    state $count = 0;
    sleep 1;
    print $count, "\r";
    }
```

Each statement is separated by a semicolon and the last statement has a semicolon for good measure.

You don't see a ; after the closing brace for that `loop`, but it's implicitly there. A }
followed by nothing more than whitespace until the end of the line implies a ;. If you
have more stuff on the same line, though, you need a ; after the }:

```
loop { ... }; put "Done";
```

The ... (*yada yada*) operator is the way you signal that there's something there but
you don't care to say what it is at the moment. Use it when you intend to fill in the
details later. I'll use those to hide code to save space in examples. It compiles but gives
you an error when you run it. You'll see this used throughout the book to shorten
examples to fit on the page.

A block creates a *lexical scope*. You can see what this scope is based on the position of
the braces (hence, lexical). Things you define inside a scope only matter inside that
scope and the deeper scopes it defines. This limits the effects of many things to
exactly where you need them. The effects of variables and modules are limited to
their lexical scope.

Comments

Comments are a way to leave ourselves notes that the program doesn't care about. The
compiler mostly ignores these things. You can make a comment with a # when the
compiler is expecting a new token. The compiler skips everything from that # to the
end of the line. Here's a mostly useless comment:

```
put 'Hello Perl 6!'; # output a message
```

A better comment expounds on the purpose, not the effect, of the code. This type of
little program is often used as a first exercise to check that everything is working. The
comment can say that:

```
put 'Hello Perl 6!'; # show that the program ran
```

An alternative is an *embedded comment*. Put your message inside the parentheses in
#`( ) somewhere in your statement (or even between statements):

```
put #`(Marketing asked for this) 'Hello Perl 6!';
```

This is a nice way to have multiline comments:

```
#`(
* show that the program ran
* need to add blockchain email AI feature
)
put  'Hello Perl 6!';
```

Since a closing parenthesis ends the comment, you can't have one in your comment.

Both of those are fine for short comments. Sometimes you want to *comment out* several lines to prevent them from running. If you put the # at the beginning of a line you effectively remove that line from the program:

```
loop {
    state $count = 0;
#    sleep 1;
    print $count, "\r";
    }
```

You might add another comment to remind yourself why that line is still in the code. Often programmers do this as they are debugging so they remember what was there before they started:

```
loop {
    state $count = 0;
# Testing this for ticket 1234 (bug://1234)
# I think that the sleep slows the program down too much
#    sleep 1;
    print $count, "\r";
    }
```

Unspace

In most places Perl 6 doesn't care about whitespace, but there are some parts of the Perl 6 syntax that don't allow spaces. Space between the name of a subroutine and its opening parenthesis for an argument list changes the meaning:

```
my-sub 1, 2, 3;          # three arguments
my-sub( 1, 2, 3 );       # three arguments
my-sub ( 1, 2, 3 );      # one argument (a List)
```

In that last line there's a space between my-sub and the (. That compiles and runs, but instead of three arguments the subroutine gets a single List argument (Chapter 6). You can *unspace* that space with a backslash. Any whitespace following the \ is basically invisible to the compiler:

```
my-sub\ (1, 2, 3 );
```

You might want to do this to format code into columns to make it easier to read:

```
my-sub\             ( 2, 4, 8 );
my-much-longer-name( 1, 3, 7 );
```

Objects and Classes

Perl 6 is a class-based object system. I'll skip most of the theory of object-oriented programming (that could be a whole other book), but you should know that in these systems a *class* (Chapter 12) defines the abstract structure and behavior of an object. The *object* is a particular concrete version of that class.

Most of the data in Perl 6 are objects, and each object knows what class defines it. Classes define methods, which are the behaviors of the object. Classes can *inherit* from another class to include its behavior, but they can also include *roles* that add behavior without inheritance. When you see class names in the digital version of this book the name should link to the online documentation for that class (for example, the Int class).

You create objects by calling a *constructor* method, often called .new (Chapter 12). You pass *arguments* to the method in parentheses after the method name:

```
my $fraction = Rat.new( 5, 4 );
```

There's also a colon syntax for method arguments which relieves you from the burden of typing the closing parenthesis as long as there's nothing more in the statement:

```
my $fraction = Rat.new: 5, 4;
```

Type objects represent the abstract idea of a class but aren't objects. Sometimes they are useful as placeholders when you know what sort of object you want but you don't know its value yet:

```
my $fraction = Rat;
```

With gradual typing you can restrict variables to fit into a type. These are runtime checks, so you don't know that it didn't work until you try it:

```
my Int $n;
```

Since you haven't assigned a value to $n yet, it's an Int type object. When you want to assign a value it must match that type:

```
$n = 137;          # works because it's an integer
$n = 'Hamadryas';  # fails
```

Look through a class's documentation to see what sorts of things its objects can do. In many of the exercises I'll ask you to use a method that I haven't shown you. This trains you to go to the docs, but also lets you learn things about seeing what's out there. This saves some space in the book. Let's try some of those now.

Exercise 1.1

What type of object is 137? Compute its square root. Is it a prime number? You should be able to do each of these with a simple method.

Variables

Perl 6 has *named values*. They can be *immutable*, which means you can't change the values once you set them. They can also be *mutable*, which means you can change the values. The mutable ones are commonly called *variables*, but they are also known as *containers*. A container holds a value and you can replace that value with another. You'll read more about that in the next chapter. Despite the possibility that you can't change the value, I'll still call all of these "variables."

A named value has an *identifier*—a fancy word for "name." Names can include letters, digits, the underscore, the hyphen, and the apostrophe (`'`). You must start your name with a letter or digit. These are valid identifiers:

```
butterfly_name
butterfly-name
butterfly'name
```

The underscore, hyphen, or apostrophe can separate words to make them easier to read. Sometimes the underscore pattern is called *snake case* since the word separators crawl along the ground. The hyphen pattern is called *kebab case* (or sometimes *lisp case*).

Some people might feel more at home capitalizing the first letter of each word instead. This is known as *camel case* since it imitates the humps on a camel's back. In this example there's one hump, which is the best number of humps for a camel:

```
butterflyName
```

There are some rules with - and `'`. You can't have two - or `'` characters in a row, and the character after either must be a letter (not a number). Also, you cannot start an identifier with these characters. None of these are valid:

```
butterfly--name
butterfly''name
'butterfly
butterfly-1
```

A *variable* name combines a sigil with an identifier. The sigil is a character that gives some context to the identifier. A *scalar* is a single thingy. A *scalar variable* holds a single value and has a $ sigil. The $ looks similar to S, for scalar:

```
$butterfly_name
```

As you encounter the different types you'll encounter the other sigils. The @ is for positionals (Chapter 6), the % is for associatives (Chapter 9), and the & is for callables (Chapter 11).

The first time you use a variable you must *declare* it. You do this so the compiler knows you definitely want to use that name and to avoid problems with misspelling variables. The my keyword declares the variable to be private to the current scope:

```
my $number;
```

The next time you use $number in that same scope you don't need to declare it. You probably want to assign it a value. The = is the assignment operator:

```
$number = 137;
```

You *initialize* a variable first time you assign a value to it. You can do this at the same time that you declare it:

```
my $number = 137;
```

Since Perl 6 already knows which variables you intend to use it knows when you misspell one:

```
$numbear = 137;
```

You get an error that's often aware enough to guess what you meant:

```
Variable '$numbear' is not declared. Did you mean '$number'?
```

Simple Output

To see what's in a variable you can use (or "call") the put routine. This outputs the value to standard output and adds a newline to the end:

```
put $number;
```

If you use say it calls the .gist method for you. This often results in the same output, but some complicated objects may summarize or elide data to give you something easier to read. These two do the same thing:

```
say $number;
put $number.gist;
```

If you don't want to add a newline you can use print:

```
print $number;
```

There are also method forms of each of these:

```
$number.put;
$number.say;
$number.print;
```

Lexical Scope

A variable is only visible in its lexical scope. If you define a variable inside braces you can't use it outside the braces:

```
{
my $number = 137;
}

$number = 5; # a compilation error
```

This is caught when you try to compile the program:

```
Variable '$number' is not declared
```

A variable of the same name can exist in the outer scope and isn't disturbed when the same name is reused in a deeper scope:

```
my $number = 5;
put $number;

{
my $number = 137;
put $number;
}

put $number;
```

These are two different variables that happen to use the same name. The compiler can tell them apart based on where you declared them. The inner scope declaration "hides" the outer scope one, so the result is:

```
5
137
5
```

Sometimes a named value doesn't have a sigil. These *sigilless variables* don't create containers, which means that you can't change their values. This makes them handy for values you don't want anyone to accidentally change. Prefix the identifier with a \:

```
my \magic-number = 42;
magic-number.put;
```

These statements actually create terms, but since you declare them like variables it's slightly easier to be a little wrong than pedantically correct.

Predefined Variables

Perl 6 defines several variables for you. These are prefixed with a sigil and then an additional character called a *twigil*. The combination of characters tells you something about the variable. Don't worry about all the sorts of twigils that exist. Know that they do exist and that you can read about them at *https://docs.perl6.org/language/ variables* or with *p6doc*:

```
% p6doc language/variables
```

The ? twigil marks values that the compiler sets as it does its work. These are *compile-time variables*. If you want to know the file the compiler is working on you can look in $?FILE. The $ is the sigil and the ? is the twigil:

```
put $?FILE;
```

The * twigil marks *dynamic variables*. These are looked up through the caller's scope, but that's not the important part for this section. Your program automatically sets these values. Some of them are about the environment of the program:

```
% perl6
To exit type 'exit' or '^D'
> $*EXECUTABLE
"/Applications/Rakudo/bin/perl6".IO
> $*PROGRAM
"interactive".IO
> $*USER
hamadryas
> $*CWD
"/Users/hamadryas".IO
```

Others provide information about your version of Perl 6. This information might be useful if you need to report an issue:

```
> $*PERL
Perl 6 (6.c)
> $*VM
moar (2018.04)
```

There are other dynamic variables for the standard *filehandles*. Each program gets output, input, and error filehandles. The standard output (the default place where output goes) is in `$*OUT` and standard error is in `$*ERR`. These are `IO::Handle` objects and you can call `.put` on them to make output:

```
$*OUT.put: 'Hello Hamadryas!';
$*ERR.put: 'Hello Hamadryas!';
```

Exercise 1.2

What is the `$*CWD` variable? What's its value on your system?

Making and Running a Program

It's time you wrote a program. That's just a plain-text file that contains your source code. You don't need any special software to create these files. They must be plain text though; word processors insert extra stuff and the compiler won't tolerate that.

The first line in the program is typically the *shebang* line. That's a Unix thing that lets a text file pretend to be a program. When you "run" the text file the system sees that the first two characters are `#!`. It uses the rest of that line as the name of the program that will actually run the code. That's the *interpreter*:

```
#!/Applications/Rakudo/bin/perl6
```

Your package (or custom installation) may have installed it somewhere else, in which case you'd use that path:

```
#!/usr/local/bin/perl6
```

Some people use *env* since that looks through your PATH to find the program:

```
#!/bin/env perl6
```

Windows doesn't know about shebangs, but it's a good idea to include the shebang anyway since useful programs tend to escape into the world (life will find a way). For the rest of the book I'll leave off the shebang line just to save space.

The rest of your file is your program. Here's a common one that tests that you've probably done everything right. If you can run this program you've probably installed everything correctly:

```
put 'Hello World!';
```

Ensure your editor is set to encode your file as *UTF-8*. Save the file using any name that you like. *perl6* doesn't care about the name, although the docs suggest a *.p6* or *.pl6* extension.

Run your program from the command line:

```
% perl6 hello-world.p6
```

When you do this *perl6* first compiles the program. It sees all of your program text and parses it. That's the *compile time* part of the process. If it finds no problem it then runs what it has already compiled.

If you want to check your program without running it you can use the -c switch. This is a *syntax check*:

```
% perl6 -c hello-world.p6
```

Most errors at this point are *syntax errors*; you wrote a program that Perl 6 couldn't parse.

Exercise 1.3

Create the "Hello World" program and get it to run. Use any tools you like for that.

Summary

You've seen the basic structure of a program and how you build up a program from smaller elements. You wrote some very small programs. You have some insights into the documentation; you'll get more practice with that throughout your programming career. Now the trick is to make slightly larger programs.

## CHAPTER 2

Number Guessing

You're about to be thrown in the deep end. There are some basic things you need to know to write useful programs, and you'll meet a lot of them in this chapter so you can write a number-guessing program by the end. It's quite a bit to take in all at once but it should make the rest of the chapters more interesting.

Binding and Assignment

You read a little about variables in Chapter 1. To store a value in a variable you *assign* to it. The item assignment operator, =, stores a single thingy for you. $number is a scalar variable; it can store exactly one thingy. This is *item assignment* because there's one thingy. This "sets" the value:

```
my $number = 2;
```

If you decide that you don't want that value you can replace it:

```
$number = 3;
```

Sometimes you want a value that you can't change (more likely a value you don't want another part of your program to change). Instead of the assignment operator you can use the binding operator, :=, to set the value:

```
my $sides-of-a-square := 4;
$sides-of-a-square = 5
```

When you try to change the value you get an error:

```
Cannot assign to an immutable value
```

It's not the binding operator that makes the variable immutable. It merely makes the thingy on the left the same as the one on the right. In this case, $sides-of-square is actually 4 and not just a variable that happens to store 4. You can't assign to 4, so you can't assign to `$sides-of-a-square`.

If you first assign to a scalar variable then *bind* to that variable you end up with two names for the same variable:

```
my $number = 3;
my $sides := $number;
```

You can change `$sides` or `$number`, and the "other" will change. But there is no "other" to change because they are the same thing! You might think of these as aliases, but it's a bit more complicated.

There's an important concept here that you should learn early. A variable assignment with = creates a container, then puts a value in that container. A container is just a box that can store a value. You can add, remove, and replace the value in that box. This is mostly invisible to you because the language handles it for you.

The binding operator skips this containerization. It aliases the thingy on the right side directly. If it's already a container that's what you bind to. You can break down the action of assignment into two steps. First you bind to an anonymous container. That's right: a container can exist without a name. An anonymous container is just the $ sigil:

```
my $number := $;
```

After that you can change the value in the container using =:

```
$number = 3;
```

Sometimes you'll need to know if the thingy you have is a container, and there will be times you'll want to skip the container. Start thinking about this early, before you develop bad habits, and your programming life will be easier.

A MAIN Program

In Chapter 1 you saw some examples of statements. This is a complete program:

```
put 'Hello Perl 6!';
```

If you've programmed in some other languages you may have encountered a subroutine called `main` or something similar. Those languages probably required you to put your program inside that routine; when you ran your program it automatically ran that subroutine for you. Perl 6 is a little different because it assumes that your entire file is already that `main`.

You can still have such a subroutine though. If you define a `MAIN` subroutine (all caps!) your program will call that automatically if you run the program:

```
sub MAIN {
    put 'Hello Perl 6!'
    }
```

You won't read about subroutines until Chapter 11, so trust me for a bit on this one. You'll read more of an explanation of MAIN as you go through the book.

Exercise 2.1

Create both versions of the "Hello Perl 6" program. The one-line version and MAIN version should give you the same output.

Program Arguments

You probably have seen other command-line programs that take *arguments*. The file-names you give to *more* or *type* are arguments that tell those programs which file's contents you want to see:

```
% more hello-world.p6
```

```
C:\ type hello-world.p6
```

Your Perl 6 program can take arguments too. When you try it with your existing program you get a help message instead of the output that you expected:

```
% perl6 hello-world-main.p6 1 2 3
Usage:
    hello-world-main.p6
```

To accept arguments you have to tell MAIN to expect them. Your program had an implicit set of empty parentheses in it. Those parentheses define the *parameters*, which are the templates for the arguments. Arguments are what you get; parameters are what you wanted. In this case you didn't specify any parameters, so your program expects no arguments and complains if you try to give it some:

```
sub MAIN () {
    put 'Hello Perl 6!'
    }
```

You can change this. You can specify a variable in the parameter list. One parameter allows your MAIN subroutine to take exactly one argument. Change your put statement to output the value in $thingy by defining a *signature* after the subroutine name:

```
sub MAIN ( $thingy ) {
    put $thingy;
    }
```

When you run this program with no command-line arguments you get a different help message. You needed one argument and gave it none. Curiously, the help message tells you the name of the variable you used in the parameter:

```
% perl6 main-one-thingy.p6
Usage:
  main-one-thingy.p6 <thingy>

% perl6 main-one-thingy.p6 Hello
Hello
```

Quote the entire value or escape the whitespace (Unix shells only) to preserve whitespace inside a value you want to give to the thingy:

```
% perl6 main-one-thingy.p6 "Hello Perl 6"
Hello Perl 6

% perl6 main-one-thingy.p6 Hello\ Perl\ 6
Hello Perl 6
```

You can specify more than one parameter by separating them with commas. You can also output multiple things in a single put by separating them with commas:

```
sub MAIN ( $thingy1, $thingy2 ) {
    put '1: ', $thingy1;
    put '2: ', $thingy1;
    }
```

Now you have to give your program two arguments. If you don't give it exactly two arguments it doesn't work:

```
% perl6 main-two-thingys.p6 Hamadryas
Usage:
  main-two-thingys.p6 <thingy1> <thingy2>

% perl6 main-two-thingys.p6 Hamadryas perlicus
1: Hamadryas
2: perlicus
```

Hamadryas perlicus is the (un)scientific name I've given to the butterfly on the cover. Sometimes I call him "Hama" for short because it rhymes with "llama."

Sometimes you don't want to specify two arguments even though you need two values. You can specify a default value for some parameters. Use the = to specify the default:

```
sub MAIN ( $thingy1, $thingy2 = 'perlicus' ) {
    put '1: ', $thingy1;
```

```
    put '2: ', $thingy2;
    }
```

When you call it with two arguments it works as before, but when you specify exactly one argument it uses the default for the second:

```
% perl6 main-two-thingys-default.p6 Hamadryas februa
1: Hamadryas
2: februa

% perl6 main-two-thingys-default.p6 Hamadryas
1: Hamadryas
2: perlicus
```

Any parameters with defaults have to show up after those without them. You'll see much more about parameters in Chapter 11.

Exercise 2.2

Create a program that takes three command-line arguments and outputs them on separate, numbered lines. Give two of the parameters default values.

Prompting for Values

The prompt routine outputs a message asking for input. When you type some text followed by Return prompt reads that text and returns it. You can assign that value to a variable:

```
my $answer = prompt 'What is your favorite number? ';
put 'Your answer was [', $answer, ']';
```

When you run the program you see the prompt and start typing right after it on the same line:

```
% perl6 prompt.p6
What is your favorite number? 137
Your answer was [137]
```

The value you get back from prompt does not include the line ending from Return.

Exercise 2.3

Write a program that asks for your name and then outputs a greeting to that name. If your name is Gilligan it should output "Hello Gilligan." Can you use a MAIN subroutine and only prompt if there's no command-line argument?

Literal Numbers

Literal values are those that you type directly into the program. They are fixed and are sometimes called "hardcoded" values because they exist directly in the program instead of coming from input or configuration. These are terms, and you can write them in several ways.

An *integer* is a whole number. These are the numbers of everyday life expressed with the digits from 0 to 9:

```
137
4
-19
0
```

Digital computers are more comfortable with powers of two. Prefix a literal number with 0x to specify a *hexadecimal number*. That's base 16 and uses the digits 0 to 9 and the letters *A* to *F* (in either case) to represent 0 to 15:

```
0x89
0xBEEF
-0x20
```

Octal numbers are base 8 and use the digits 0 to 7. Prefix a literal octal number with 0o:

```
0o211
-0o177
```

Binary numbers are base 2 and use the digits 0 and 1. These are handy when you deal with binary formats. Prefix them with 0b:

```
0b10001001
```

Choose a representation that's easy for you to understand or that's natural for the task. The compiler converts those representations into values that the physical computer can use. It doesn't care which one you use; they are just numbers. These are all the same value:

```
137          # decimal,     base 10
0b10001001   # binary,      base  2
0o211        # octal,       base  8
0x89         # hexadecimal, base 16
```

Exercise 2.4

In the REPL try the different base examples. What decimal value does the REPL echo?

Perhaps you don't like the ASCII digits 0 to 9. You can use any digits that Unicode supports; Perl 6 knows about anything that's a number character. Eastern Arabic numerals work. Notice that the radix prefixes are the same:

```
١٣٧
0b١...١..١
0o٢١١
0x٨٩
```

So do Bengali digits:

```
১৩৭
0b১০০০১০০১
0o২১১
0x৮৯
```

I don't encourage you to represent numbers like this in your program, but Perl 6 understands them. This is useful when you are processing text that contains them. Your program will be able to convert these to a number type.

You can choose other bases up to base 36. You've already seen base 16, which uses 0 to 9 and *A* to *F*. Base 17 would add *G*, and so on up to base 36, which includes *Z*. Use a colon before the base (in decimal), then put the digits inside angle brackets:

```
:7<254>
:19<IG88>
:26<HAL9000>
:36<THX1138>
```

Exercise 2.5

Try the unusual base examples in the REPL. What decimal numbers are they?

Formatting Numbers

Literal numbers are objects. You can call methods on objects. The `.base` method allows you to specify the base that you want to represent:

```
put 0x89.base: 10;    #  137
```

You can choose some other base, up to 36:

```
put 0x89.base:  2;    # 10001001
put 0x89.base:  8;    # 211
put 0x89.base: 16;    # 89
```

Exercise 2.6

Write a program that takes a decimal number as its single command-line argument. Output its binary, octal, decimal, and hexadecimal values. What happens if you give it a hexadecimal number on the command line? What if you specify the decimal number in Eastern Arabic digits?

In the previous exercise you couldn't specify a hexadecimal number as an argument. That's because you weren't actually specifying a number as an argument. It was text made up of digit characters. If you want to use a hexadecimal number you have to tell your program how to convert the number. You can use `.parse-base` for that. You tell it which base you expect and it does the rest:

```
my $number = $thingy.parse-base: 16;
```

Exercise 2.7

Modify your answer from the previous exercise to accept a hexadecimal number command-line argument. Your program will now only handle hexadecimal numbers if you're using only what you've seen so far.

Numeric Operations

Numeric operators transform numbers into new values. The simplest demonstration is to immediately output the result. The + is the addition operator:

```
put 2 + 2;
```

You can also store the result in a variable and then output it. The item assignment is an operation and so is the addition. The + happens first because it has higher precedence:

```
my $sum = 2 + 2;
put $sum;
```

There are operators for subtraction (-), multiplication (*), division (/), and exponentiation (**). You'll see more in the next chapter.

Outputting a single number is easy. If you want to output a series of numbers, you could have multiple lines:

```
my $sum = 0;
put $sum + 1;
put $sum + 1 + 1;
put $sum + 1 + 1 + 1;
```

Each time you add one more to it. That repeats a lot of structure. You can back up a little to make an improvement where the put statement is the same in each case:

```
my $sum = 0;

$sum = $sum + 1;
put $sum;

$sum = $sum + 1;
put $sum;

$sum = $sum + 1;
put $sum;
```

The $sum variable shows up on the left and right of the assignment. That's okay; the compiler's not going to get confused. It evaluates everything on the right side using the current value of $sum. When it's reduced the right side to its value it assigns that to $sum, replacing the value that's already there. You're still doing the same thing over and over again, but now that same thing looks exactly like the other things.

Now it's time to introduce loop. It repeatedly executes the code inside its braces. This code will run until you interrupt the program (probably with Control-C):

```
my $sum = 0;
loop {
    $sum = $sum + 1;
    put $sum;
    }
```

You can combine the two statements inside loop. The result of an assignment is the value that you assigned. Here, you add to $sum then assign that result back to $sum, and use that expression as the value you give to put:

```
my $sum = 0;
loop {
    put $sum = $sum + 1;
    }
```

This sort of structure is so common that it has its own operator: the ++ unary prefix autoincrement operator. It adds one before you use the value:

```
my $sum = 0;
loop {
    put ++$sum;
    }
```

There's also a unary postfix version. It adds one to the value, but after you use it:

```
my $sum = 0;
loop {
    put $sum++;
    }
```

What's the difference in output in the two programs that use the prefix and postfix autoincrement operators? Can you figure it out without running the programs?

So far you've declared variables with my. That limits their definition to the current scope. That's a problem for variables you want in a loop if they should keep their values. This wouldn't work because each time through the loop would get a new variable even though you used the same name:

```
loop {
    my $sum = 0;
    put $sum++;
    }
```

Declare the variable with state instead: this makes the variable private to the block but doesn't reset it each time through it. A state declaration only executes the first time through the block and is ignored after that. The assignment to $sum happens once:

```
loop {
    state $sum = 0;
    put $sum++;
    }
```

This is a bit nicer because everything about $sum is contained inside the block. Always try to give variables the smallest scope they need. If they don't need to be outside the block define them inside it.

Those operators add or subtract one. If you want to increment by a different number you're back to using +:

```
loop {
    state $sum = 0;
    put $sum = $sum + 2;
    }
```

That's still one too many $sums in that code. There's a special form of the assignment operator that lets you shorten this. You can put the infix operator before the =, like this:

```
$sum += 2;
```

This convenient shorthand is *binary assignment*. It's the same as using the variable on both sides of the = but it's easier to type:

```
$sum = $sum + 2;
```

Most binary operators can do this, even if they are multiple characters:

```
$product *= 5;
$quotient /= 2;
$is-divisible %%= 3;
```

Exercise 2.9

Rewrite the looping program to output only multiples of three by adding the appropriate interval to the previous value. Further modify the program to accept the multiple as a command-line argument.

Conditional Execution

This chapter has been working its way to a number-guessing program. You know a little bit about numbers, command-line arguments, prompting, and looping. Next you need to know how to decide between two or more paths in your code. That comes in two parts: comparing things to get an answer and using that answer to select the next thing to do.

Boolean Values

Boolean values are logical values that can be one thing or the other: yes or no, on or off, or True or False. These are of type Bool. You'll use these values to decide between different paths in your program. First, a little Boolean math.

You can combine Boolean values with *logical operators*. The && logical AND operator evaluates to True if both operands are True. The || logical OR operator evaluates to True if one or more operators are True:

```
% perl6
> True && True
True
> True && False
False
> True || True
True
> True || False
True
```

All of these operators have spelled out "word" versions. These are the lowest-precedence operators (aside from the sequence operators). These operations always happen last:

```
% perl6
> True and True
True
> True and False
False
> True or False
True
```

The ! unary prefix operator changes one Bool value to the other one: True becomes False, and the other way around. This is called *negating* the condition. not is the low-precedence version of that:

```
% perl6
> ! True
False
> ! False
True
> not True
False
> not False
True
```

Many objects can collapse themselves to a Bool value when needed, but it's up to each object how it does that. For numbers, 0 is False and everything else is True.

For most objects (not just numbers) you can use a prefix ? to coerce into either True or False. It calls the .Bool method on the object. The builtin types know how to convert their values to Booleans using whatever rule they decide. For numbers, 0 is False and everything else is True:

```
% perl6
> ?1
True
> ?0
False
> ?-1
True
> 1.Bool
True
> 0.Bool
False
> (-1).Bool
True
```

The .so method and so routine do the same thing:

```
> 1.so
True
> 0.so
False
> (-1).so
True
```

```
> so 0
False
> so 1
True
```

Type objects know what they are but they have no concrete value. They are always
`False`:

```
% perl6
> Int.so
False
```

Some things that want Boolean values will implicitly do these coercions for you.

Short-circuit operators

The logical operators don't really evaluate to Boolean values. `&&` and `||` test their
expressions for `True` or `False`, but the entire structure evaluates to the last expression
it evaluated.

`||` needs only one expression to be `True` for the entire thing to be `True`. If it gets back
anything that's `True`, then the entire thing is `True`. All of these are `False`, but you can
see the last expression `||` evaluated:

```
% perl6
> 0 || Nil
Nil
> 0 || False
False
> 0 || Failure
(Failure)
```

These are `True`. When `||` finds any value that would evaluate to `True` as a Boolean it
stops right away. These are sometimes called *short-circuit operators*:

```
% perl6
> True || 0
True
> 137 || True
137
```

It's the same with `&&`. It returns the last expression it evaluated. If that value is `False`
then one of those expressions was `False`:

```
% perl6
> 0 && 137
0
> 42 && 8
8
```

There's a third operator that's similar. The defined-or operator, `//`, tests its left side for
definedness. If the left value is defined that's the result, even if that value is `False`:

```
% perl6
> 0 // 137
0
> Nil // 19
19
```

A type object is never defined:

```
% perl6
> Int // 7
7
```

The defined-or is part of a common technique to set a value if a variable doesn't already have one (or has one that is not defined). You'll see it as a binary assignment:

```
$value //= 137;
```

Comparing Things

A *comparator* evaluates to True or False based on some relative measure. The numeric equality operator, ==, compares two numbers to test if they are exactly the same. If they are the same it evaluates to True; otherwise it evaluates to False:

```
% perl6
> 1 == 1
True
> 1 == 3
False
```

The numeric inequality operator != tests that two numbers are *not* the same:

```
% perl6
> 1 != 1
False
> 1 != 3
True
```

Some operators have two versions. You just saw the "ASCII" version, but there's also a "fancy" Unicode version with ≠:

```
% perl6
> 1 ≠ 3
True
```

Instead of a literal value you can compare a variable. It doesn't matter which side you put the values on:

```
% perl6
> my $number = 37
37
> $number == 38
False
> 39 == $number
False
```

```
> $number == 37
True
```

You can have an expression on either side of the comparator or variables on both sides:

```
% perl6
> 2 + 2 == 4
True
> 5 == 2
False
> my $thing1 = 17
17
> my $thing2 = 13
13
> $thing1 == $thing2
False
> $thing1 != $thing2
True
```

The > tests that the first operand is numerically greater than the second number and the < tests that the first is less than the second:

```
% perl6
> 1 > 3
False
> 1 < 3
True
> 3 < 3
False
```

With an equals sign the test can include the number. >= tests that the first number is numerically equal to or greater than the second, and <= tests that it is less than or equal:

```
% perl6
> 3 < 3
False
> 3 <= 3
True
> 7 > 7
False
> 7 >= 7
True
```

You can also write these with fancier symbols: >= as ≥ and <= as ≤.

Although not a comparator, the %% operator also returns a Boolean. It tests if the number on the left side is evenly divisible by the number on the right side. This is quite handy:

```
% perl6
> 10 %% 2
```

```
True
> 10 %% 3
False
```

Chained comparisons

You can chain comparison operators. You can test that a number is inside or outside of a window (remember the > at the start of the input lines is the REPL prompt) like this:

```
% perl6
> $n  = 10
10
> 7 < $n < 15
True
> 7 <= $n < 15
True
> 7 < $n > 15
False
> 7 > $n < 15
False
```

Without this you'd have to perform additional and separate comparisons:

```
> 7 < $n and $n < 15
True
```

Conditionally running a statement

The if keyword allows you to evaluate a statement only when some *condition* is satisfied. The postfix form is the easiest. The part after the if is the condition; it evaluates to True or False:

```
my $number = 10;
put 'The number is even' if $number %% 2;
```

The condition is *satisfied* when it evaluates to True. "Satisfaction" is getting what you want; the if wants (roughly) its condition to be True before it allows the statement to run. If the condition is False the program skips that statement.

The if condition is a Boolean context; it calls .Bool for you when you don't do it explicitly. All of these are the same, but you'll probably do the last one:

```
put 'Always outputs' if 1.Bool;
put 'Always outputs' if 1.so;
put 'Always outputs' if ?1;
put 'Always outputs' if 1;
```

With this you can improve your looping program. Previously you had no way to stop it. The last keyword immediately leaves the loop:

```
loop {
    state $sum = 0;
    put $sum++;
    last;
    }
```

This outputs one line then finishes the loop. That's what `last` said to do, but that's not very useful. This version evaluates `last` only when `$sum` is 5:

```
loop {
    state $sum = 0;
    put $sum++;
    last if $sum == 5;
    }
```

Exercise 2.10

What is the output of this program? Can you work it out without running the program?

The `next` command is similar to `last`, but it goes on to the next iteration of the loop. You can use a postfix `if` to skip numbers that are divisible by two (when more than one thingy is using a variable in a condition it's probably better to change it in a separate step):

```
loop {
    state $sum = 0;
    $sum += 1;
    next if $sum %% 2;
    put $sum;
    last if $sum > 5;
    }
```

Now you get the odd numbers:

```
1
3
5
7
```

Conditional Branching

You can also write `if` in a block form. The code inside the block runs only when the `if` is satisfied:

```
if $number %% 2 {
    put 'The number is even';
    }
```

You can use parentheses for *grouping* if you like but they can't be immediately next to the if; there must be some whitespace:

```
if ($number %% 2) {
    put 'The number is even';
    }
```

With no space between the if and the (it looks like a subroutine call, which it isn't. This is a syntax error:

```
if($number %% 2) {  # ERROR!
    put 'The number is even';
    }
```

An unless is the opposite sense of if. It executes its block when the condition is False. Another way to think about that is that it skips the block when the condition is True:

```
unless $number %% 2 {
    put 'The number is odd';
    }
```

Some people prefer an if with a negated condition:

```
if ! $number %% 2 {
    put 'The number is odd';
    }
```

An else allows you to provide a default block to run when the if is not satisfied:

```
if $number %% 2 {
    put 'The number is even';
    }
else {
    put 'The number is odd';
    }
```

These different possibilities are *branches* of your code. You go down one or the other branch but not both. This is one example of a *control structure* that decides which code runs.

The entire if structure evaluates to a value when you put a do in front of it. The do allows you to treat a control structure as an expression. The result is the last evaluated expression from inside the structure. This way you can isolate only the parts that are different, then use one statement for output:

```
my $type = do if $number %% 2 { 'even' }
            else            { 'odd'  }

put 'The number is ', $type;
```

You can skip the intermediate variable (although if that's confusing it's okay to do it the longer way):

```
put 'The number is ',
    do if $number %% 2 { 'even' }
       else            { 'odd'  }
```

There's a shortcut for this. The conditional operator has three parts: the condition, the `True` branch, and the `False` branch. Between those parts are `??` and `!!`:

```
CONDITION ?? TRUE BRANCH !! FALSE BRANCH
```

Using this operator you can rewrite the preceding example. The particular formatting isn't important, but this fits nicely on the page and lines up the different parts. You don't use a block, which makes this useful for short bits of code:

```
put 'The number is ',
    $number %% 2 ?? 'even' !! 'odd';
```

An `elsif` specifies another branch with its own condition, so you have three ways this code might run. Some people think zero is neither odd nor even, and they can add another branch for that:

```
if $number == 0 {
    put 'The number is zero';
    }
elsif $number %% 2 {
    put 'The number is even';
    }
else {
    put 'The number is odd';
    }
```

This code works, but it has some repeated structure because each branch has a `put`. A `do` cleans that up nicely. Here's another way to write that:

```
put 'The number is ', do
      if $number == 0 { 'zero' }
   elsif $number %% 2 { 'even' }
   else               { 'odd'  }
```

Exercise 2.11

Create a program that outputs the numbers from 1 to 100. However, if the number is a multiple of three, output "Fizz" instead of the number. If it's a multiple of five, output "Buzz". If it's a multiple of both three and five, output "FizzBuzz".

Putting It All Together

With a few more things you can now write the number-guessing program. The `.rand` method returns a fractional number between 0 and the integer (exclusively):

```
% perl6
> 100.rand
62.549491627582
```

The `.Int` method coerces that to a whole number. It discards the fractional portion; it does not round the number. Put that together with `.rand` and you get a whole number between 0 and the starting number:

```
% perl6
> 100.rand.Int
23
```

Put that together in a complete program. Choose the number, then test what side of another number (sometimes called the "pivot") it's on:

```
my $number = 100.rand.Int;

if $number > 50 {
    put 'The number is greater than 50';
    }
elsif $number < 50 {
    put 'The number is less than 50';
    }
else {
    put 'The number is 50';
    }
```

Run that several times and you should get different output eventually:

```
% perl6 random.p6
The number is less than 50
% perl6 random.p6
The number is less than 50
% perl6 random.p6
The number is greater than 50
```

Exercise 2.12

Wrap the pivot program in a `MAIN` subroutine so you can specify the highest possible number as a command-line argument. Default to `100` if you don't supply an argument. Adjust that so the program can take another command-line argument to specify the pivot number.

In the previous exercise you set the default for the second argument using a hard-coded literal integer:

```
sub MAIN ( $highest = 100, $pivot = 50 ) { ... }
```

If you run the program with one command-line argument that is less than 50 (or whatever you chose as your default) the output will always be the same:

```
% perl6 number-program.p6 37
The number is less than 50
```

You can use parameters you've already specified to compute defaults for other parameters. Use $highest to compute $pivot:

```
sub MAIN ( $highest = 100, $pivot = $highest / 2 ) {
```

Exercise 2.13

Modify your answer to the previous exercise so you can set the pivot to half the highest value. Default to 50 if you don't specify two arguments.

Now you have everything you need to write your number-guessing program. Your program chooses a secret number that you then have to figure out. This early in the book that seems like a complicated program, but you've seen just enough to make it:

- Choose a secret number (.rand).
- Loop repeatedly until the person guesses the number (next and last).
- Get the person's guess (prompt).
- Give the person a hint about their guess. Tell them if they are too high or low (comparators, if).

Exercise 2.14

Implement the number-guessing program. If you supply a command-line argument use that as the maximum number; otherwise use 100. It may help to immediately output the secret number as you get your program working.

Summary

You made it! First chapters are typically the toughest because you're getting your bearings. You've made at least one meaty program that incorporates several things that you haven't seen in depth yet. You can take input from the command line or from a prompt. You can compare values and follow different code branches. Not bad for a first chapter.

## CHAPTER 3

Numbers

This chapter steps back from the breadth of the previous chapter to focus on the idea of numbers and their representation in your programs. Perl 6 supports several types of numbers and works hard to keep them exact as long as it can.

Number Types

Not all numbers are created alike. You've seen whole numbers, how to do basic mathematical operations on them, and how to compare them. But whole numbers are just one of the numeric types. You can see what type a number is by calling .^name on it:

```
% perl6
> 137.^name
Int
```

That's an Int, short for "integer"—whole numbers, positive or negative, and zero. The compiler recognizes it because it has decimal digits; it parses it and creates the object for you. But try it with a negative number:

```
% perl6
> -137.^name
Cannot convert string to number
```

The minus sign isn't actually part of the number. It's an operator (a unary prefix one) that *negates* the positive number. That means that -137 isn't a term; it's an expression. The .^name happens first and evaluates to Int as before. When - tries to negate the type name it realizes it can't do that and complains. You can fix the ordering problem with parentheses—things inside parentheses happen before those outside:

```
% perl6
> (-137).^name
```

There are other types of numbers, some of which are shown in Table 3-1.

Table 3-1. Examples of different number types

Value	Class	Description
137	Int	Positive integer (whole number)
-17	Int	Negative integer (whole number)
3.1415926	Rat	Fractional number
6.026e34	Num	Scientific notation
0+i	Complex	Complex number with real and imaginary parts

Exercise 3.1

Call .^name on some of the other kinds of numbers from Table 3-1. What other sorts of numbers does Perl 6 support? Which ones need parentheses to group them?

Integers

The integers are the whole numbers. You've seen that they can be represented in many ways and in different bases:

```
137
-19
0x89
:7<254>
```

Including underscores between digits can make larger numbers easier to read. They aren't part of the number and can only come between digits (so, not two in a row). You could separate by thousands:

```
123_456_789
```

Two hexadecimal digits represent an *octet*; it's easy to see those when you have underscores between pairs of digits:

```
0x89_AB_CD_EF
```

Type Constraints

When you declare a variable without assigning to it there's still "something" there. It's a type object with the type Any—a generic type that's the basis for most Perl 6 objects:

```
my $number;
put $number.^name;  # Any
```

If you coerce Any to a Boolean value you get False. Any type object is undefined, but this is slightly more undefined because it's a general class.

When you want to assign to a container that holds a type object you have to replace it with a value of the same type or something based on that type. You can replace Any with almost any literal value:

```
my $number;       # starts as Any
$number = 137;
$number = 'Hamadryas';
```

That's the same as explicitly constraining the value to the Any type. Without an assignment the variable gets the type object of its constraint:

```
my Any $number;   # starts as Any
$number = 137;
$number = 'Hamadryas';
```

You can be as specific as you like. If your variable should only store an integer you can use the Int type to constrain it even before you assign to it. Even without a value it knows its type:

```
my Int $number;
put $number2.^name;  # Int
```

Whatever you assign to it must be an Int (or something derived from an Int):

```
my Int $number;
$number = 137;
$number = 'Hamadryas';  # NOPE! Error
```

When you try to assign something that is not the correct type you get an error:

```
Type check failed in assignment to $n; expected Int but got Str
```

This check happens when you assign to the variable. Perl 6 calls this "gradual typing." You don't have to use it until you want it, but you still have to be careful to obey it when you do use it. The compiler can't catch all type errors before you run the program.

You can use types in your MAIN signature too. These types apply to the command-line arguments. If you don't supply appropriate values you'll get an error right away:

```
sub MAIN ( Int $n ) { ... }
```

Exercise 3.2

Create a program that takes two arguments from the command line and outputs their types. Try it with numbers and text in each position. What types do you get?

When you ran your program for the previous exercise you saw the type name IntStr. This is an *allomorph*—a type that's both an Int and a Str at the same time.

All of the command-line arguments are actually text, even though some of them look like numbers. There's a hidden `val` routine that inspects the arguments and turns those that look like some sort of number into the appropriate allomorph. This type has the behavior of both numbers and strings at the same time. You might think that's a little weird at first, but it's one of the things that allows a language such as Perl 6 to easily process text.

Smart Matching

The *smart match operator*, `~~`, stands in for many sorts of comparisons and picks the right one for its operands. With a value or variable on the left side and a type on the right side it returns `True` if the value is that type or derives from that type:

```
% perl6
> 1 ~~ Int
True
> 1.^mro
((Int) (Cool) (Any) (Mu))
> 1 ~~ Cool
True
> 1 ~~ Any
True
```

This works because literals are implicitly created objects and know what they are. Comparing it to any other type returns `False` even if the value could be a valid value for that type:

```
% perl6
> 1 ~~ Complex
False
```

However, you can easily convert between number types with a coercer method named after the type you want (if the type provides one):

```
% perl6
To exit type 'exit' or '^D'
> 1.Complex
1+0i
> 1.Complex ~~ Complex
True
```

Smart matching is easy with `given-when`. Two things happen with this feature. First, `given` binds `$_` to the value of the variable you specify. The `$_` is the *topic*; this allows you to write some code that uses `$_` to process the current thing you care about without knowing what that thing is.

Second, `when` looks at the condition you supply. If there's no explicit comparator it smart matches `$_` against the value you gave it. The first `when` block that is satisfied is the one that wins. A `default` block (no condition!) catches it when no `when` does.

The conditions for these whens are type objects to smart match against $_:

```
given $some-number {
    when Int     { put 'Saw an integer' }
    when Complex { put 'Saw a complex number' }
    when Rat     { put 'Eek! Saw a rat!' }
    default      { put 'Saw something' }
}
```

Making everything explicit, you'd get something like this mess of repeated typing:

```
given $some-number -> $_ {
    when $_ ~~ Int     { put 'Saw an integer' }
    when $_ ~~ Complex { put 'Saw a complex number' }
    when $_ ~~ Rat     { put 'Eek! Saw a rat!' }
    default            { put 'Saw something' }
}
```

You can make this shorter using do in the same way you did with if. The last evaluated expression becomes the value of the entire given structure:

```
put 'Saw ', do given $some-number {
    when Int     { 'an integer' }
    when Complex { 'a complex number' }
    when Rat     { 'a rat! Eek!' }
    default      { 'something' }
}
```

Exercise 3.3

Using given, create a program that reports the type of number you specify on the command line. Try it with arguments such as 17, 17.0, 17i, and Hamadryas.

There's another interesting thing you can do with $_. A method call dot with no object to the left uses $_ as the object:

```
$_.put;
.put;

put $_.roots unless $_.is-prime;
put .roots unless .is-prime;
```

You can use a postfix given to set $_ for a single statement to avoid typing out a variable multiple times. You'll see the implicit topic much more as you go through the book:

```
my $some-number = 19;
put .^name, ' ', .is-prime given $some-number;
```

Rational Numbers

Perl 6 represents nonwhole numbers as fractions using integers. You might literally represent it as a number with a decimal point (sometimes called a *floating-point number*), but the compiler turns that into a fraction. You can see the numerator and denominator for that reduced fraction:

```
% perl6
> 3.1415926
3.1415926
> 3.1415926.^name
Rat
> 3.1415926.numerator
15707963
> 3.1415926.denominator
5000000
```

Exercise 3.4

Create a program that takes a single decimal number command-line argument and shows it to you as a fraction. What are the numerator and denominator?

You can add rational numbers to get another fraction; Perl 6 does the work for you:

```
% perl6
> 1/7 + 1/3
0.476190
```

The `.perl` method shows you how Perl 6 thinks about it. You can see the fraction with the least common multiple in the denominator:

```
% perl6
> (1/7 + 1/3).perl
<10/21>
```

It didn't divide the numbers then try to store the result as a floating-point number; that would lose accuracy. It keeps it as an exact fraction as long as it can. This means that these sums are exactly right.

Try this in your favorite programming language:

```
% perl6
> 0.1 + 0.2
0.3
```

Another way to define a `Rat` is to write it as a literal fraction inside angle brackets, `<>`:

```
% perl6
> <10/21>
0.476190
```

```
> <10/21>.^name
Rat
> <10/21>.perl
<10/21>
```

It's the same in a program:

```
my $seventh = <1/7>;
my $third   = <1/3>;

my $added = $seventh + $third;

put $added.perl;
```

You can't do this with a variable inside the angle brackets. You'll see what's going on in the next chapter, but inside the <> that's not really a variable. The $ is a literal character:

```
% perl6
> <1/$n>
1/$n
```

At some point the fractions will be too large and you'll get an error. Here's a program that adds the reciprocals of the powers of two. It uses loop and uses ++ to make higher powers of two:

```
my $n   = 0;
my $sum = 0;
loop {
    $sum += 1 / 2**$n++;
    put .numerator, '/', .denominator, ' = ' given $sum;
    }
```

You get progressively larger fractions even though this series converges on 2. Eventually it fails because the denominator is limited to a 64-bit integer size:

```
% perl6 converging.p6
1/1 = 1
3/2 = 1.5
7/4 = 1.75
15/8 = 1.875
31/16 = 1.9375
63/32 = 1.96875
...
4611686018427387903/2305843009213693952 = 2
9223372036854775807/4611686018427387904 = 2
18446744073709551615/9223372036854775808 = 2
No such method 'numerator' for invocant of type 'Num'.
```

There's another class that can handle this. A FatRat is a fraction with an arbitrarily large denominator. This is the first time you get to construct an object directly. Call the .new method with the numerator and denominator:

```
my $sum = FatRat.new: 0, 1;
```

If you have an existing Rat you can turn it into a FatRat with a method. You'd do that when you know you are going to need it later when you do math with another FatRat:

```
my $fatrat = <10/21>.FatRat;
```

When you need to add a FatRat to the existing one, you can construct that one in the same way:

```
FatRat.new: 1, 2**$n++
```

Otherwise the program is the same, although this version will run much longer. Notice that all the fractions need to be FatRats to keep it going:

```
my $n   = 0;
my $sum = FatRat.new: 0, 1;
loop {
    $sum += FatRat.new: 1, 2**$n++;
    put $sum.^name;
    put .numerator, '/', .denominator, ' = ', $_ given $sum;
    }
```

Exercise 3.5

Create a program that sums the series of fractions 1, 1/2, 1/3, and so on. This is the harmonic series. Calculate the partial sum up to a denominator of 100. Output the value at each stage of the sum.

Imaginary and Complex Numbers

Imaginary numbers are multiples of the square root of –1. Impossible, you say? I'm not going to explain that in this book but Perl 6 has them. If you're an electrical engineer you've likely run into complex numbers when modeling certain properties.

Perl 6 has a term for the *imaginary unit*; it's i. The number 5i is imaginary; it's five times the imaginary unit. Try it in the REPL:

```
% perl6
> 5i
0+5i
> 5*i
0+5i
> 5\i
0+5i
> 5\ i
0+5i
```

That was four ways to write the same thing. The first way puts two terms, 5 and i, next to each other with no whitespace or separator. That works and is likely to be the way you'll type it most of the time. The second multiplies 5 and i to get the same result. The last two use \ to create unspace. One has no space and the other has some space.

You can't have only whitespace between the digits and the i, or the compiler will think that you have terms in a row (because you do):

```
% perl6
> 5 i
===SORRY!=== Error while compiling:
Two terms in a row
------> 5⏏ i
```

When you tried the imaginary number 5i in the REPL you got back 0 + 5i. That's a real number added to an imaginary number. Taken together they form a *complex number* that has real and imaginary parts.

To get the real or imaginary parts of the number you can use the .re or .im methods, which take their short names from the common math notation:

```
% perl6
> my $z = 137+9i;
137+9i
> $z.^name
Complex
> $z.re
137
> $z.im
9
```

You can add, subtract, and multiply Complex numbers. Multiplication involves cross terms with the real part of one number multiplied by the imaginary part of the other:

```
% perl6
> (5+9i) * (6+3i)
3+69i
> (5+9i) + (6+3i)
11+12i
> (5+9i) - (6+3i)
-1+6i
> (5+9i) / (6+3i)
1.26666666666667+0.866666666666667i
```

You can even multiply i by itself:

```
% perl6
> i*i
-1
```

Numbers Small and Large

Everything that doesn't fit into the specific numeric types is in the general Num type. The number e (the natural base) is one of those numbers:

```
% perl6
> e.^name
Num
> e
2.71828182845905
```

You can also use infinities. Putting all the nuances and uses aside, for this book Inf is just something that's larger than any integer. You'll see it in use later:

```
% perl6
> Inf.^name
Num
> (-Inf).^name
Num
```

You can write numbers in exponential notation. You can specify a power of 10 after an *e* of either case. This is a different sort of *e* than the term you just saw:

```
6.02214e23
6.02214E23
```

These are the same as multiplying the number by a power of 10 that you construct explicitly:

```
6.02214 * 10**23
```

These numbers aren't Ints or Rats, although you might be able to convert them. They are the more general Num type:

```
put 1e3.^name;  # 1000, but still a Num
put 1e3.Int;    # 1000, but now an Int
```

Very small numbers have a negative power of 10:

```
6.626176e-34
```

You can use this on not-so-small numbers too:

```
7.297351e-3
```

Exercise 3.6

What is 7.297351e-3 as a fraction? What's its reciprocal?

The Numeric Hierarchy

Perl 6 thinks about numbers relative to their "width." Int comprises the positive and negative whole numbers and is relatively narrow. The Rat type includes the whole numbers and some of the numbers between them (the ones that can be fractions).

Rat is "wider" not because its endpoints are greater but because there are more numbers between the same endpoints. FatRat is even wider because it pushes the endpoints farther apart to contain even more numbers.

Even wider than the rationals, fat or otherwise, are plain ol' Nums. Those include the rest of the numbers; the ones that you can't represent as fractions. We typically call this wider set the Reals but Perl 6 calls them Nums.

And when you think that you are the widest that you can go, the numbers go sideways into the plane of the Complex numbers.

Sometimes you may want to go narrower or wider. Many Perl 6 objects have coercer methods that can do that for you. Start with an Int and turn it into a Complex number. This goes wider:

```
% perl6
> 6.Complex
6+0i
```

Or start with a Complex number and go narrower. This one can also be an Int:

```
% perl6
> (6+0i).Int
6
```

You can do those coercions because you know something about the numbers. If you want the narrowest type without knowing what it is beforehand, you can use .narrow. If you tried to convert π to an Int you wouldn't get an error, but you wouldn't get π. If you use .narrow you get a Num, the narrowest you can go:

```
% perl6
> (π+0i).Int
3
> (π+0i).Int == π
False
> (π+0i).narrow.^name
Num
> (π+0i).narrow == π
True
```

Sometimes you can't go any narrower:

```
% perl6
> (6+3i).narrow.^name
Complex
```

Exercise 3.7

Modify the number-guessing program from the previous chapter so you have to guess a complex number. You have to decide high and low in two directions this time.

Summary

That's most of the story with numbers. You saw some of the methods you can use, and you'll find even more in the documentation for each type. You also saw a bit about constraining variables to only the type you want, and you'll become more sophisticated with that.

## CHAPTER 4

Strings

Strings represent the text data in your program as `Str` objects. Perl 6's facility with text data and its manipulation is one of its major attractions. This chapter focuses on the many ways that you can create `Str`s; for any job you have there's likely a feature that makes that easy for you. Along with that you'll see a bit about inspecting, extracting, and comparing text in preparation for loftier goals coming up.

Literal Quoting

You can type literal text directly into your program. What you type is what the text is, and the compiler does not interpret it as anything other than exactly what you typed. You can surround literal text with half-width corner brackets, ⌜ and ⌟:

```
⌜Literal string⌟
```

This is your first encounter with a *paired delimiter*. These characters mark the beginning and end of the `Str`. There's an opening character and a closing character that surround your text.

Any character that you use is interpreted as exactly what it is, with no special processing:

```
⌜Literal '" string with \ and {} and /⌟
```

You can't use only one of the delimiter characters in the `Str`. These won't work:

```
⌜ Unpaired ⌜ Delimiters ⌟
⌜ Unpaired ⌟ Delimiters ⌟
```

However, if you pair delimiters in the text the compiler will figure out if they are balanced—the opening delimiter comes first and a closing delimiter pairs with it:

```
⌜ Del⌜i⌟miters ⌟
```

The Perl 6 language is a collection of sublanguages, or *slangs*. Once inside a particular slang the compiler parses your source code by that slang's rules. The quoting language is one of those slangs.

If your literal text has corner brackets in it you can use a *generalized quoting* mechanism. These start with a Q (or q) and can get as limiting or as permissive as you like, as you'll see in this chapter.

After the Q you can select almost any character to be the delimiter. It can't be a character valid in a variable name, because that would make it look like a name instead of a delimiter. The paired characters are common; the opening character has to be on the left and its closing partner has to be on the right. Perhaps you want to use square brackets instead of corner brackets. Now the ⌋ isn't special because it's not a delimiter:

```
Q[Unpaired ⌋ Delimiters]
```

Most of the paired characters act the same:

```
Q{Unpaired ⌋ Delimiters}
Q<Unpaired ⌋ Delimiters>
Q<<Unpaired ⌋ Delimiters>>
Q«Works»
```

There's one exception. You can't have an open parenthesis right after the Q because that makes it look like a subroutine call (but it's not):

```
Q(Does not compile)
```

You don't have to use paired characters. You can use the same character for the opening and closing delimiter:

```
Q/hello/
```

You can store a Str in a variable or output it immediately:

```
my $greeting = Q/Hello World!/;
put Q/Hello World!/;
```

And you can call methods on your Str just like you could do with numbers:

```
Q/Hello World!/.^name;  # Str
Q/Hello World!/.put;
```

Escaped Strings

One step up from literal Strs are *escaped strings*. The single tick acts as the delimiter for these Strs. These are often called *single-quoted strings*:

```
% perl6
> 'Hamadryas perlicus'
Hamadryas perlicus
```

If you want to have the single tick as a character in the Str you can *escape* it with a backslash. That tells the quoting slang that the next character isn't the delimiter but belongs as literal text:

```
% perl6
> 'The escaped \' stays in the string'
The escaped ' stays in the string
```

Since the \ is the *escape character*, you can escape it to get a literal backslash:

```
% perl6
> 'Escape the \\ backslash'
Escape the \ backslash
```

A DOS path can be quite annoying to type, but escaped and literal Strs take care of that:

```
% perl6
> 'C:\\Documents and Settings\\Annoying\\Path'
C:\Documents and Settings\Annoying\Path
> Q/C:\Documents and Settings\Annoying\Path/
C:\Documents and Settings\Annoying\Path
```

If you want to use a different delimiter for an escaped string you use the lowercase q followed by the delimiter that you want (following the same rules as for the literal quoting delimiters):

```
q{Unpaired ' Delimiters}
q<Unpaired ' Delimiters>
q<<Unpaired ' Delimiters>>
q«Works»
```

Adverbs for Quoting

Adverbs modify how something works and are a big part of Perl 6. You'll see more of these in Chapter 9, but you'll get a taste for them in this chapter. Adverbs start with a colon followed by letters or numbers.

All of the quoting methods you'll see in this chapter are modifications of basic literal quoting. You use adverbs to adjust the quoting behavior.

The :q adverb modifies Q to become an escaping quote. There must be some whitespace after the adverb, but it's optional after the Q:

```
% perl6
> Q:q 'This quote \' escapes \\'
This quote ' escapes \
> Q :q 'This quote \' escapes \\'
This quote ' escapes \
```

This form doesn't specifically escape the single tick; it escapes the backslash and the delimiter characters. A backslash that doesn't precede a delimiter or another backslash is interpreted as a literal backslash:

```
% perl6
> Q :q 「This quote \' escapes」
This quote \' escapes
> Q :q 「This quote \「 escapes」
This quote 「 escapes
> Q :q 「This quote \「\」 escapes」
This quote 「 escapes
```

The :single adverb is a longer version of :q and might help you remember what you want:

```
% perl6
> Q :single 'This quote \' escapes'
This quote ' escapes
```

Most of the time you aren't going to work this hard. The common uses of quoting have default delimiters so you don't even see the Q. Even though many Strs would be more correctly represented with strict literal quoting, most people tend to use the single ticks simply because it's easier to type. No matter which quoting method you use you get the same type of object.

String Operators and Methods

Use the *concatenation* operator, ~, to combine Strs. Some people call this "string addition." The output shows the two Strs as one with nothing else between them:

```
my $name = 'Hamadryas' ~ 'perlicus';
put $name;      # Hamadryasperlicus
```

You could add a space yourself by putting it in one of the Strs, but you can also concatenate more than two Strs at a time:

```
put 'Hamadryas ' ~ 'perlicus';
put 'Hamadryas' ~ ' ' ~ 'perlicus';
```

The join routine glues together Strs with the first Str you give it:

```
my $butterfly-name = join ' ', 'Hamadryas', 'perlicus'
```

You can make larger Strs by repeating a Str. The x is the Str replication operator. It repeats the Str the number of times you specify. This is handy for making a text-based divider or ruler for your output:

```
put '-' x 70;
put '.123456789' x 7;
```

The .chars methods tells you how many characters are in the Str:

```
put 'Hamadryas'.chars;   # 9
```

Any Str with at least one character is True as a Boolean, including the Str of the single character 0:

```
put ?'Hamadryas';        # True
put ?'0';                # True
```

The *empty string* has no characters. It consists only of the opening delimiter and the closing delimiter. It's False as a Boolean:

```
put ''.chars;            # 0
put ?'';                 # False
```

Be careful that when you test a Str you test the right thing. A Str type object is also False, but .DEFINITE can tell them apart:

```
put ''.DEFINITE          # True
put Str.DEFINITE         # False
```

This is handy in a conditional expression where you don't care what the Str is (empty, '0', or anything else) as long as it's not a type object:

```
given $string {
    when .DEFINITE {
        put .chars ?? 'Has characters' !! 'Is empty';
        }
    default { put 'Type object' }
    }
```

The .lc method changes all the characters in a Str to lowercase, and .uc changes them to uppercase:

```
put 'HaMAdRyAs'.lc;      # hamadryas
put 'perlicus'.uc;       # PERLICUS
```

The .tclc method uses title case, lowercasing everything then capitalizing the first character of the Str:

```
put 'hamadryas PERLICUS'.tc;    # Hamadryas perlicus
```

Exercise 4.1

Write a program to report the number of characters in the text you enter.

Exercise 4.2

Modify the previous exercise to continually prompt for text and report the number of characters in your answers until you provide an empty answer.

Looking Inside Strings

You can also inspect a Str to find out things about it. The .contains method returns a Boolean value indicating whether it finds one Str—the *substring*—inside the target Str:

```
% perl6
> 'Hamadryas perlicus'.contains( 'perl' )
True
> 'Hamadryas perlicus'.contains( 'Perl' )
False
```

Instead of parentheses you can put a colon followed by the substring to search for:

```
% perl6
> 'Hamadryas perlicus'.contains: 'perl'
True
> 'Hamadryas perlicus'.contains: 'Perl'
False
```

The .starts-with and .ends-with methods do the same thing as .contains but require the substring to appear at a particular location:

```
> 'Hamadryas perlicus'.starts-with: 'Hama'
True
> 'Hamadryas perlicus'.starts-with: 'hama'
False
> 'Hamadryas perlicus'.ends-with: 'us'
True
```

These methods are *case sensitive*. The case of each character in the substring must match the case in the target Str. If it's uppercase in the substring it must be uppercase in the target. If you want *case insensitivity* you can use .fc to make a "caseless" Str. This "case folding" method is especially designed for comparisons:

```
> 'Hamadryas perlicus'.fc.starts-with: 'hama'
False
```

.fc also knows about equivalent characters such as the *ss* and the sharp *ß*. The method doesn't change the text; it evaluates to a new Str based on a long list of rules about equivalence defined by Unicode. You should case fold both the target and substrings if you want to allow these sorts of variations:

```
> 'Reichwaldstrasse'.contains: 'straße'
False
> 'Reichwaldstrasse'.fc.contains: 'straße'
False
> 'Reichwaldstrasse'.contains: 'straße'.fc
True
> 'Reichwaldstrasse'.fc.contains: 'straße'.fc
True
```

.substr extracts a substring by its starting position and length inside the Str. The counting starts with zero at the first character:

```
put 'Hamadryas perlicus'.substr: 10, 4;      # perl
```

The .index method tells you where it finds a substring inside the larger Str (still counting from zero), or returns Nil if it can't find the substring:

```
my $i = 'Hamadryas perlicus'.index: 'p';
put $i ?? 'Found at ' ~ $i !! 'Not in string'; # Found at 10
```

Use both of them together to figure out where to start:

```
my $s = 'Hamadryas perlicus';
put do given $s.index: 'p' {
    when Nil { 'Not found' }
    when Int { $s.substr: $_, 4 }
    }
```

Exercise 4.3

Repeatedly prompt for text and report if it contains the substring "Hamad". Stop prompting if the answer has no characters (an empty answer). Can you make this work regardless of casing?

Normal Form Grapheme

Perl 6 is Unicode all the way down. It works on *graphemes*, which most of us think of as "characters" in the everyday sense. These are the full expression of some idea, such as *e*, *é*, or 🦋. It expects your source code to be UTF-8 encoded and outputs UTF-8 text. All of these work, although they each represent a different language:

```
'кѳпѳлѳк'
'तितली'
'蝴蝶'
'Con bướm'
'tauriņš'
'πεταλούδα'
'ਭੰਬੀਰਾ'
'פרפר'
```

You can use emojis too:

```
my $string = '🦋 🐛 🌼 ';
put $string;
```

One of the Perl 6 "characters" might be made of up two or more entries in the Universal Character Database (*UCD*). Perl 6 refers to entries in the UCD as *codes* and to their composition as a "character." It's not the best terminology. In this book, *character* means grapheme and *code point* refers to an entry in the UCD.

Why does any of that matter? The `.chars` method tells you the length of the `Str` in graphemes. Consider the Hebrew word for "caterpillar." It has 11 graphemes but 14 code points:

```
% perl6
> 'קאַטערפּיללאַר'.chars
11
> 'קאַטערפּיללאַר'.codes
14
```

Why the different counts? There are graphemes such as אַ that are more than one code point (in that case, the two code points are the Hebrew Aleph and patah diacritical mark). Most of the time you won't care about this. If you do, you can get a list of the code points with `.ords`:

```
> 'קאַטערפּיללאַר'.ords
(1511 1488 1463 1496 1506 1512 1508 1468 1497 1500
1500 1488 1463 1512)
```

String Comparisons

`Str` objects know if they are relatively greater than, less than, or the same as another `Str`. Perl 6 uses *lexicographic comparison* to go through the `Str`s character by character.

The numbers comparison operators are symbols, but the `Str`s use operators made up of letters. The `eq` operator tests if the `Str`s are exactly equal. Case matters. Every character at each position in the `Str` must be exactly the same in each `Str`:

```
% perl6
> 'Hamadryas' eq 'hamadryas'
False
> 'Hamadryas' eq 'Hamadryas'
True
```

The `gt` operator evaluates to `True` if the first `Str` is strictly lexicographically greater than the second (`ge` allows it to be greater than or equal to the second `Str`). This is not a dictionary comparison, so case matters. The lowercase letters come after the uppercase ones and so are "greater":

```
% perl6
> 'Hama' gt 'hama'
False
> 'hama' gt 'Hama'
True
```

The uppercase letters come before the lowercase ones, so any `Str` that starts with a lowercase letter is greater than any `Str` that starts with an uppercase letter:

```
% perl6
> 'alpha' gt 'Omega'
```

```
True
> 'a' gt 'Ω'
True
```

You can get some weird results if you compare numbers as Strs. The character 2 is greater than the character 1, so any Str starting with 2 is greater than any Str starting with 1:

```
% perl6
> '2' gt '10'
True
```

The lt operator evaluates to True if the first Str is lexicographically less than the second (le allows it to be less than or equal to the second Str):

```
% perl6
> 'Perl 5' lt 'Perl 6'
True
```

If you don't care about their case you can lowercase both sides with .lc:

```
% perl6
> 'Hamadryas'.lc eq 'hamadryas'.lc
True
```

This wouldn't work for the Reichwaldstrasse example you saw previously. If you wanted to allow for equivalent representations you'd use .fc:

```
% perl6
> 'Reichwaldstrasse'.lc eq 'Reichwaldstraße'.lc
False
> 'Reichwaldstrasse'.fc eq 'Reichwaldstraße'.fc
True
```

As with numbers, you can chain the comparisons:

```
% perl6
> 'aardvark' lt 'butterfly' lt 'zebra'
True
```

Prompting for Input

You've already used prompt for simple things. When you call it your program reads a single line and chops off the newline that you typed. A small modification of the program shows you what sort of type you get back:

```
my $answer = prompt( 'What\'s your favorite animal? ' );
put '$answer is type ', $answer.^name;
put 'You chose ', $answer;
```

When you answer the question you get a Str:

```
% perl6 prompt.p6
What's your favorite animal? Fox
```

```
$answer is type Str
You chose Fox
```

When you don't type anything other than a Return the answer is still a Str, but it's an empty Str:

```
% perl6 prompt.p6
What's your favorite animal?
$answer is type Str
You chose
```

You end input with Control-D, which is the same as not typing anything. In that case it returns an Any type object. Notice that the line showing the type appears on the same line as the prompt text—you never typed a Return. There's also a warning about that Any value, and finally your last line of output:

```
% perl6 prompt.p6
What's your favorite animal? $answer is type Any
Use of uninitialized value $answer of type Any in string context.
You chose
```

To guard against this problem you can test $answer. The Any type object is always False. So is the empty Str:

```
my $answer = prompt( 'What\'s your favorite animal? ' );
put do
    if $answer { 'You chose ' ~ $answer }
    else       { 'You didn\'t choose anything.' }
```

prompt takes whatever you type, including whitespace. If you put some spaces at the beginning and end that's what shows up in the Str:

```
% perl6 prompt.p6
What's your favorite animal?               **Butterfly**
You chose            Butterfly
```

You can see this better if you put in something to surround the answer portion of the output, such as <> in this example:

```
my $answer = prompt( 'What\'s your favorite animal? ' );
put do
    if $answer { 'You chose <', $answer, '>' }
    else       { 'You didn't choose anything' }
```

Now you can easily see the extra space in $answer:

```
% perl6 prompt.p6
What's your favorite animal?               **Butterfly**
You chose <            Butterfly         >
```

The .trim method takes off the surrounding whitespace and gives you back the result:

```
my $answer = prompt( 'What\'s your favorite animal? ' ).trim;
```

If you apply it to $answer by itself it doesn't work:

```
$answer.trim;
```

You need to assign the result to $answer to get the updated value:

```
$answer = $answer.trim;
```

That requires you to type $answer twice. However, you know about binary assignment so you can shorten that to use the variable name once:

```
$answer .= trim;
```

If you don't want to remove the whitespace from both sides you can use either .trim-leading or .trim-trailing for the side that you want.

Number to String Conversions

You can easily convert numbers to Strs with the .Str method. They may not look like what you started with. These look like number values but they are actually Str objects where the digits you see are characters:

```
% perl6
> 4.Str
4
> <4/5>.Str
0.8
> (13+7i).Str
13+7i
```

The unary prefix version of ~ does the same thing:

```
% perl6
> ~4
4
> ~<4/5>
0.8
> ~(13+7i)
13+7i
```

If you use a number in a Str operation it automatically converts it to its Str form:

```
% perl6
> 'Hamadryas ' ~ <4/5>
Hamadryas 0.8
> 'Hamadryas ' ~ 5.5
Hamadryas 5.5
```

String to Number Conversions

Going from Strs to numbers is slightly more complicated. If the Str looks like a number you can convert it to some sort of number with the unary prefix version of +.

It converts the `Str` to the number of the narrowest form, which you can check with `.^name`:

```
% perl6
> +'137'
137
> (+'137').^name
Int
> +'1/2'
0.5
> (+'1/2').^name
Rat
```

This only works for decimal digits. You can have the decimal digits 0 to 9 and a possible decimal point followed by more decimal digits. An underscore is allowed with the same rules as for literal numbers. The conversion ignores surrounding whitespace:

```
% perl6
> +' 1234 '
1234
> +' 1_234 '
1234
> +' 12.34 '
12.34
```

Anything else, such as two decimal points, causes an error:

```
> +'12.34.56'
Cannot convert string to number: trailing characters after number
```

When you perform numerical operations on a `Str` it's automatically converted to a number:

```
% perl6
> '2' + 3
5
> '2' + '4'
6
> '2' ** '8'
256
```

Exercise 4.4

Write a program that prompts for two numbers then outputs their sum, difference, product, and quotient. What happens if you enter something that's not a number? (You don't need to handle any errors.)

In the previous exercise you should have been able to create a conversion error even though you didn't have the tools to handle it. If you want to check if a `Str` can convert to a number you can use the `val` routine. That gives you an object that does the

Numeric role if it can convert the Str. Use the smart match operator to check that it worked:

```
my $some-value = prompt( 'Enter any value: ' );
my $candidate = val( $some-value );

put $candidate, ' ', do
    if $candidate ~~ Numeric { ' is numeric' }
    else                     { ' is not numeric' }
```

This seems complicated now because you haven't read about interpolated Strs yet. It will be much clearer by the end of this chapter.

Exercise 4.5

Update the previous exercise to handle nonnumeric values that would cause a conversion error. If one of the values isn't numeric, output a message saying so.

Sometimes your text is numeric but not decimal. The .parse-base method can convert it for you. It takes a Str that looks like a nondecimal number and turns it into a number:

```
my $octal  = '0755'.parse-base: 8;     # 493
my $number = 'IG88'.parse-base: 36;    # 860840
```

This is the same thing the colon form was doing in Chapter 3:

```
:8<0755>
:36<IG88>
```

Interpolated Strings

You've taken a long path through this chapter to get to the quoting mechanism that you're likely to use the most. An *interpolated string* replaces special sequences within the Str with other characters. These Strs will also make easier some of the code you've already seen.

Interpolated Strs use the double quote, ", as the default delimiter and are sometimes called *double-quoted strings*. You need to escape the " if you want one in the Str, and you can escape the \:

```
% perl6
> "Hamadryas perlicus"
Hamadryas perlicus
> "The escaped \" stays in the string"
The escaped " stays in the string
> "Escape the \\ backslash"
Escape the \ backslash
```

The backslash also starts other special interpolating sequences. A \t represents a tab character. A \n represents a newline:

```
put "First line\nSecond line\nThird line";
```

If you want a character that's not easy to type you can put its code number (a hexadecimal value) after \x or inside \x[ ]. Don't use the 0x prefix; the \x already assumes that:

```
put "The snowman is \x[2603]";
```

Several comma-separated code numbers inside \x[ ] turn into multiple characters:

```
put "\x[1F98B, 2665, 1F33B]";  # 🦋 🖤 🌻
```

If you know the name of the character you can put that inside \c[ ]. You don't quote these names and the names are case insensitive:

```
put "\c[BUTTERFLY, BLACK HEART, TACO]";  # 🦋 🖤 🌮
```

Those are nice, but it's much more handy to interpolate variables. When a double-quoted Str recognizes a sigiled variable name it replaces the variable with its value:

```
my $name = 'Hamadryas perlicus';
put "The best butterfly is $name";
```

The quoting slang looks for the longest possible variable name (and not the longest name actually defined). If the text after the variable name looks like it could be a variable name that's the variable it looks for:

```
my $name = 'Hamadryas perlicus';
put "The best butterfly is $name-just saying!";
```

This is a compile-time error:

```
Variable '$name-just' is not declared
```

If you need to separate the variable name from the rest of the text in the double-quoted Str you can surround the entire variable in braces:

```
my $name = 'Hamadryas perlicus';
put "The best butterfly is {$name}-just saying!";
```

Escape a literal $ where it might look like a sigil that starts a variable name:

```
put "I used the variable \$name";
```

Now here's the powerful part. You can put any code you like inside the braces. The quoting slang will evaluate the code and replace the braces with the last evaluated expression:

```
put "The sum of two and two is { 2 + 2 }";
```

This means that the previous programs in this chapter are much easier to type than they first appear. You can construct the Str inside the delimiters rather than using a series of separate Strs:

```
my $answer = prompt( 'What\'s your favorite animal? ' );
put "\$answer is type {$answer.^name}";
put "You chose $answer";
```

Like with the previous Strs, you can choose a different delimiter for interpolated Strs. Use qq (double q for double quoting) in front of the delimiter:

```
put qq/\$answer is type {$answer.^name}/;
```

The \n is interpolated as a newline and the \t becomes a tab:

```
put qq/\$answer is:\n\t$answer/;
```

This Str has two lines and the second one is indented:

```
answer is:
    Hamadryas perlicus
```

qq// is the same as Q with the :qq or :double adverb:

```
put Q :qq /\$answer is type {$answer.^name}/;
put Q :double /\$answer is type {$answer.^name}/;
```

If you want to interpolate only part of a Str you can use \qq[] for that part:

```
my $genus = 'Hamadryas';
put '$genus is \qq[$genus]';
```

Going the other way, you can turn off interpolation for part of a Str by making that part act like a single-quoted Str with \q[]:

```
put "\q[$genus] is $genus";
```

Table 4-1 shows many other special sequences available inside a double-quoted context.

Table 4-1. Selected backslash-escape sequences

Escape sequence	Description
\a	The ASCII bell character
\b	Backspace
\r	Carriage return
\n	Newline
\t	Tab
\f	Form feed
\c[*NAME*]	Character by name
\q[…]	Single quote the part inside the brackets
\qq[…]	Double quote the part inside the brackets

Escape sequence	Description
\x[*ABCD*]	Character by code number in hex

Exercise 4.6

Modify your character-counting program to show the Str as well as the number of characters it counts. For example, 'Hamadryas' has 10 characters. You should be able to output a single interpolated Str.

Here Docs

For multiline quoting you could use the quoting you've seen so far, but every character between those delimiters matters. This often results in ugly outdenting:

```
my $multi-line = '
    Hamadryas perlicus: 19
    Vanessa atalanta: 17
    Nymphalis antiopa: 0
    ';
```

Interpolating \n doesn't make it any prettier:

```
my $multi-line = "Hamadryas perlicus: 19\n...";
```

A *here doc* is a special way of quoting a multiline text. Specify a delimiter with the :heredoc adverb. The Str ends when the slang finds that same Str on a line by itself:

```
my $multi-line = q :heredoc/END/;
    Hamadryas perlicus: 19
    Vanessa atalanta: 17
    Nymphalis antiopa: 0
    END

put $multi-line;
```

This also strips the same indentation it finds before the closing delimiter. The output ends up with no indention even though it had it in the literal code:

```
Hamadryas perlicus: 19
Vanessa atalanta: 17
Nymphalis antiopa: 0
```

The :to adverb does the same thing as :heredoc:

```
my $multi-line = q :to<HERE>;
    Hamadryas perlicus: 19
    Vanessa atalanta: 17
    Nymphalis antiopa: 0
    HERE
```

This works with the other quoting forms too:

```
put Q :to/END/;
    These are't special: $ \
    END

put qq :to/END/;
    The genus is $genus
    END
```

Shell Strings

Shell strings are the same sort of quoting that you've seen so far, but they don't construct a Str to store in your program. They create an external command to run in the shell. A shell string captures the command's output and gives it to you. Chapter 19 covers this, but here's something to get you started.

qx uses the same rules as escaped Strs. The *hostname* command works on both Unix and Windows systems:

```
my $uname = qx/hostname/;
put "The hostname is $uname";
put "The hostname is { qx/hostname/ }"; # quoting inside quoting
```

In this output there's a blank line between the lines because it includes the newline in the normal command output:

```
The hostname is hamadryas.local

The hostname is hamadryas.local
```

Use .chomp to fix that. If there's a newline on the end of the text it removes it (although put adds its own):

```
my $uname = qx/hostname/.chomp;
put "The hostname is $uname";
put "The hostname is { qx/hostname/.chomp }";
```

print doesn't add a newline for you, so you don't need to remove the one from the command output:

```
print "The hostname is { qx/hostname/ }";
```

qx and qqx are shortcuts for single and double quoting Strs with the :x or :exec adverbs:

```
print Q :q      :x    /hostname/;
print Q :q      :exec /hostname/;
print Q :single :exec /hostname/;
```

Shell Safety

In the previous examples, the shell looks through its PATH environment variable to find the *hostname* command and executes the first one that it finds. Since people can set their PATH (or something can set it for them), you might not get the command you expect. If you use an absolute path you don't have this problem. Literal quoting is handy to avoid inadvertent escaping:

```
put Q :x '/bin/hostname';
put Q :x 'C:\Windows\System32\hostname.exe'
```

 I won't cover secure programming techniques here, but I do write more about these problems in *Mastering Perl*. Although that's a Perl 5 book, the risks to your program are the same.

Although you have not seen hashes yet (Chapter 9), you could change the environment for your program. If you set PATH to the empty Str your program won't be able to search for any programs:

```
%*ENV<PATH> = '';
print Q :x 'hostname';       # does not find this
print Q :x '/bin/hostname';  # this works
```

If that's too restrictive you can set the PATH to exactly the directories that you consider safe:

```
%*ENV<PATH> = '/bin:/sbin';
print Q :x 'hostname';       # does not find this
print Q :x '/bin/hostname';  # this works
```

There's also a double-quoted form of shell Strs:

```
my $new-date-string = '...';
my $output = qqx/date $new-date-string/
```

What's in that $new-date-string? If it descends from user data, external configuration, or something else that you don't control, you might be in for a surprise. That could be malicious or merely accidental, so be careful:

```
my $new-date-string = '; /bin/rm -rf';
my $output = qqx/date $new-date-string/
```

Fancier Quoting

You can combine adverbs in generalized quoting to use just the features that you need. Suppose that you want to interpolate only things in braces but nothing else. You can use the :c adverb:

```
% perl6
> Q :c "The \r and \n stay, but 2 + 2 = { 2 + 2 }"
The \r and \n stay, but 2 + 2 = 4
```

To get only variable interpolation use the :s adverb. No other processing happens:

```
% perl6
> my $name = 'Hamadryas'
Hamadryas
> Q :s "\r \n { 2 + 2 } $name"
\r \n { 2 + 2 } Hamadryas
```

You can combine adverbs to get any mix of features that you like. Cluster the adverbs or space them out. They work the same either way:

```
% perl6
> Q :s:c "\r \n { 2 + 2 } $name"
\r \n 4 Hamadryas
> Q :s:c:b "\r \n { 2 + 2 } $name"

 4 Hamadryas
> Q :s :c :b "\r \n { 2 + 2 } $name"

 4 Hamadryas
```

The :qq adverb is actually the combination of :s :a :h :f :c :b. This interpolates all of the variables, the stuff in braces, and all backslash sequences. If you don't want to interpolate everything, you can turn off an adverb. This might be easier than specifying several just to leave one out. Put a ! in front of the one to disable. :!c turns off brace interpolation:

```
qq :!c /No { 2+2 } interpolation/;
```

Selected quoting forms and adverbs are summarized in Table 4-2 and Table 4-3.

Table 4-2. Selected quoting forms

Short name	Long name	Description
「...」	Literal	Default delimiter, corner brackets
Q '...'	Literal	Generalized quoting with alternate delimiter
Q[...]	Literal	Generalized quoting with paired delimiter
'...'	Escaped	Default delimiter, single quote
q{...}	Escaped	Use alternate paired delimiter
Q:q [...]	Escaped	Generalized quoting with :q adverb
"..."	Interpolated	Default delimiter, double quote
qq[...]	Interpolated	Use alternate paired delimiter
Q:qq '...'	Interpolated	Generalized quoting with :qq adverb
Q:c '...{ }...'	Interpolated	Generalized quoting only interpolating closures
Q:to(HERE)	Literal	Here doc
q:to(HERE)	Escaped	Here doc
qq:to(HERE)	Interpolated	Here doc

Table 4-3. Selected quoting adverbs

Short name	Long name	Description
:x	:exec	Execute shell command and return results
:q	:single	Interpolate \\, \qq[...], and an escaped delimiter
:qq	:double	Interpolate with :s, :a, :h, :f, :c, :b
:s	:scalar	Interpolate $ variables
:a	:array	Interpolate @ variables
:h	:hash	Interpolate % variables
:f	:function	Interpolate & calls
:c	:closure	Interpolate code in {...}
:b	:backslash	Interpolate \n, \t, and others
:to	:heredoc	Parse result as here doc terminator
:v	:val	Convert to allomorph if possible

Summary

The quoting slang offers several ways to represent and combine text, so you can get exactly what you need in an easy fashion. Once you have the text, you have many options for looking inside the Str to find or extract parts of it. This is still early in the book, though. You'll see more features along the way and then really have fun in Chapter 15.

## CHAPTER 5

Building Blocks

Blocks are the thingys that group multiple statements into a single thingy. You've already used some of them, based on the faith I asked you to have in the introduction. Now it's time to look at those more closely. This chapter covers the basics and works up to simple subroutines. You'll see just enough here to get you through the next couple of chapters, then quite a bit more in Chapter 11.

Blocks

A `Block` is a group of statements surrounded by braces. You've already used `loop` to repeat a group of statements. You also used the `if-else` structure, which used a `Block` in each branch and executed only one of them:

```
loop { ... }

if $n %% 2 { put "Even!" }
else       { put "Odd!"  }
```

A *bare block* is one that has nothing around it. It is in *sink context* because you do nothing with its result. It provides a scope and runs once immediately. The result is the last evaluated expression (not necessarily the last lexical expression) in the `Block`. Here's a simple one that does nothing:

```
{ ; }
```

There's a bit of discouraged syntax that's just {}. It constructs an empty hash (Chapter 9). With a statement separator inside the braces the compiler recognizes it as a `Block`.

Here, you can't tell which expression your program will evaluate last until the `Block` knows what time it is. `now` is a term that gives the current time, which you can coerce to an `Int`:

```
{ now.Int %% 2 ?? 'Even' !! 'Odd' }
```

Sometimes you'll get `Even` and sometimes you'll get `Odd`. However, since you do nothing with the result, you'll never find out. You do get warnings:

```
Useless use of constant string "Odd" in sink context
Useless use of constant string "Even" in sink context
```

The compiler knows when it's doing useless work and complains about it. That data goes into the "sink" never to be seen again.

A `do` in front of the `Block` does the same thing it did in front of `if` or `given`. The `Block` becomes its last evaluated expression:

```
my $parity = do { now.Int %% 2 ?? 'Even' !! 'Odd' }
put do { now.Int %% 2 ?? 'Even' !! 'Odd' }
```

The `Block` is actually an expression itself, so you need to use a semicolon to separate a `Block` and a following statement:

```
{ print 'Hamadryas ' }; put 'perlicus';
```

But there's a special rule: if the closing curly brace is the last character on the line (not counting whitespace), you get the statement-separating semicolon for free:

```
{ print 'Hamadryas ' }
put 'perlicus';
```

Lexical Scope

A `Block` defines a scope. The variables that you define in a `Block` aren't available outside of that `Block`. You can use a bare `Block` to limit the visibility or lifetime of your variables:

```
{
my $n = 2;
my $m = 3;
put 'The sum is ';
put $n + $m;
}
```

Your code inside the `Block` won't change variables of the same name outside the `Block`. Here you have a few variables outside the `Block` (the *outer scope*). The bare `Block` reuses the same names:

```
my $n = 2;
my $m = 3;
```

```
{
my $n = 'Hamadryas';
my $m = 'perlicus';
put "$n $m";          # Hamadryas perlicus
}

put "n $n m $m";      # n 2 m 3
```

Scoping liberates you from any requirement to know every variable name in the entire program when choosing the ones you'd like to use in a short piece of code. It allows you to choose the names that make sense for your task without worrying about some other part of the code using the same names.

Control Structures

Bare Blocks don't have a keyword that controls them. You can put loop in front of a Block and call it repeatedly, forever:

```
my $n = 0;
loop {
    put $n++;
    }
```

That loop controls how you execute the Block. Since you haven't been specific, it keeps looping. Forever.

 Some time in your career you'll accidentally make an infinite loop. You'll probably sit there awhile looking at your screen wondering why nothing is happening. In this case, you can interrupt (stop) your program with Control-C.

It's a bit ugly to have the statement that declares $n before the loop. Often you want that variable only inside the loop, but if you declare it with my each time through the Block gets a new version of $n. What you do think this outputs?

```
loop {
    my $n = 0;
    put $n++;
    }
```

The first time through the Block, you define a new lexical variable $n, assign it 0, output its value (0), and finally increment the value. The second time through, you do the same thing: you define a new lexical $n, assign it 0, and so on. You do this until you give up.

You don't want a new variable, though. You'd like the loop to have one variable $n that retains its value. Instead of my, declare your variable with state:

```
loop {
    state $n = 0;
    put $n++;
    }
```

A `state` declaration runs only the first time through a `Block`. It defines a persistent variable that remembers its value between runs of the loop.

There's another trick possible here. You can skip the declaration, and even the name. The anonymous `$` creates a persistent scalar variable that's limited not only to its scope but to the one place that you use it:

```
loop {
    put $++;    # an anonymous scalar
    }
```

Now take care of that incessant looping:

```
loop {
    state $n = 0;
    put $n++;
    last;
    }
```

The `last` immediately breaks out of the loop, so you get a single line of output:

```
0
```

Often you'll combine `last` with a condition to specify when you want to break out of the loop. This loop ends once `$n` is greater than 2:

```
loop {
    state $n = 0;
    put $n++;
    if $n > 2 { last }
    }
```

Here's the same thing in its postfix form, which you'll probably see more often:

```
loop {
    state $n = 0;
    put $n++;
    last if $n > 2
    }
```

Either program makes it through a few iterations of the loop before the `last` breaks out:

```
0
1
2
```

There are other loop controls. A `next` skips the rest of the `Block` and starts a new pass through the `Block`:

```
loop {
    state $n = 0;
    next unless $n %% 2;
    put $n++;
    last unless $n < 3;
    }
```

A redo restarts the current iteration:

```
loop {
    state $n = 0;
    put $n++;
    redo if $n == 3;
    last if $n > 2;
    }
```

Here, when $n is 3 it goes back to the top of the loop and tries again. It calls put again and increments $n to 4. That's why you see 3 in the output even though the last would have stopped it:

```
0
1
2
3
```

Phasers

There are some other interesting Block features that I'll merely introduce here. A *phaser* is a special subroutine that runs at a particular time in the Block lifecycle. The LAST phaser runs at the end of the last Block iteration:

```
loop {
    state $n = 0;
    put $n++;
    last if $n > 2;
    LAST { put "Finishing loop. \$n is $n" }
    }
```

The output shows that the LAST Block knows the ending value for $n:

```
0
1
2
Finishing loop. $n is 3
```

Similarly, FIRST runs before the first loop starts. You can put phasers anywhere in the Block; they don't execute in the order they appear:

```
loop {
    state $n = 0;
    put $n++;
    last if $n > 2;
    FIRST { put "Starting loop. \$n is $n" }
```

```
    LAST { put "Finishing loop. \$n is $n" }
    }
```

This one throws a warning; you haven't initialized $n yet. The FIRST phaser knows
that the scope has an $n, but its value is undefined when that phaser runs because the
state declaration hasn't done its job yet. The starting value for $n is the type object
Any, and all type objects are undefined:

```
Starting loop. $n is
0
1
2
Finishing loop. $n is 3
Use of uninitialized value $n of type Any in string context.
```

The NEXT phaser kicks in for each additional iteration past the first one:

```
loop {
    state $n = 0;
    put $n++;
    last if $n > 2;
    FIRST { put "Starting loop. \$n is $n" }
    NEXT  { put "Next loop. \$n is $n" }
    LAST  { put "Finishing loop. \$n is $n" }
    }
```

The output shows up after the first loop:

```
Starting loop. $n is
0
Next loop. $n is 1
1
Next loop. $n is 2
2
Finishing loop. $n is 3
Use of uninitialized value $n of type Any in string context.
```

There's another form of loop where you can specify the initialization, test, and increment steps. This C-style version does the same thing that you were doing before:

```
loop ( my $n = 0; $n < 3; $n++ ) {
    put $n;
    }
```

This is the same thing, with separate statements for each of the three things in the
parentheses:

```
my $n = 0;
loop {
    put $n;
    last unless $n < 3;
    $n++
    };
```

Notice that $n is defined in a more expansive scope than it needs in that case. This might surprise you. If you already have a variable of the same name, you'll get an error about redeclaration of that name in the scope:

```
my $n = 5;
loop ( my $n = 0; $n < 3; $n++ ) {  # redefinition error!
    put $n;
    }

put "Outside: $n"; # Outside: 3
```

Exercise 5.1

Create a loop that outputs the numbers from 12 to 75 in multiples of 3. On the first run through the loop, output "Starting".

The while structure

A while executes the Block as long as its condition is True. This produces the same output as the loop examples from the previous section. You must define the variable outside the Block so the condition can see it:

```
my $n = 0;
while $n < 3 {
    put $n++;
    }
```

The while evaluates its condition first. If $n starts off greater than 5 this Block does not execute at all:

```
my $n = 6;
while $n < 5 {
    put $n++;
    }
```

The repeat while, however, executes the Block first and then checks the condition:

```
my $n = 6;
repeat while $n < 3 {
    put $n++;
    }
```

Even though $n is not less than 3 the Block executes and produces a single line of output before while checks the condition and finds that it is False:

```
6
```

You can put the Block between the repeat and the while. You might like this better because it's in the order that everything happens:

```
my $n = 6;
repeat {
    put $n++;
    } while $n < 3;
```

Exercise 5.2

Modify your answer from the previous exercise to use while instead of loop. Also
output a message on the last time through the Block.

Storing Blocks

You can store a Block in a variable without executing it immediately. now is a builtin
term that gives you an Instant. Binding with := makes the right side the same thing
as the left side. This means that $block is the same as the Block:

```
my $block := { now };
```

You won't be able to assign to $block, though, because there's no container involved.

You don't have to bind a Block. Assignment works too, and you can change the value
later:

```
my $block = { now };
$block = 'Hamadryas';
```

This isn't that interesting, because you could simply use now anywhere you would use
this. But how about a Block that evaluates to a time that's a minute later? Add 60 seconds to now:

```
my $minute-later := { now + 60 };
```

When you execute the Block its result is the last evaluated expression. Execute the
Block with the () operator:

```
put $minute-later();  # some Instant
sleep 2;
put $minute-later();  # some Instant 62 seconds later
```

Since $block is an object you could call the () like a method:

```
put $minute-later.();  # some Instant
sleep 2;
put $minute-later.();  # some Instant 62 seconds later
```

Instead of a scalar variable you can use a *callable* variable; those use the & sigil:

```
my &hour-later := { now + 3_600 };

put &hour-later();  # some Instant
```

```
sleep 2;
put &hour-later();  # some some Instant an hour later
```

With the &block form you can call it without the & and even without the parentheses:

```
my &hour-ago := { now - 3_600 };

put &hour-ago();  # some Instant
sleep 2;
put hour-ago();   # some Instant two seconds later

put hour-ago;     # some Instant immediately
```

Either way, a Block isn't quite a subroutine (coming up), so you can't use return (more on that later). It doesn't know how to pass a result to the code that called it. This will compile even though it isn't going to work:

```
my $block := -> { return now };
```

You'll get a runtime error, which you'll read more about in Chapter 11:

```
Attempt to return outside of any Routine
```

Blocks with Parameters

A signature defines the parameters for a Block. This includes the number (*arity*), type, and restrictions on the arguments you give to the Block.

If a Block has no signature it expects zero arguments. However, if you use $_ inside the Block it creates a signature with a single optional parameter:

```
my $one-arg := { put "The argument was $_" };

$one-arg();             # The argument was  (with warning!)
$one-arg(5);            # The argument was 5
$one-arg('Hamadryas');  # The argument was Hamadryas
```

If you change that $_ you change the original value (if it's mutable) because the implicit signature makes the argument writable:

```
my $one-arg := {
        put "The argument is $_";
        $_ = 5;
        };

my $var = 'Hamadryas';
say "\$var starts as $var";
$one-arg($var);
say "\$var is now $var";
```

The output shows that the Block changed the variable's value:

```
$var starts as Hamadryas
The argument is Hamadryas
$var is now 5
```

If you use @_ in the Block you can pass zero or more parameters:

```
my $many-args := {
    put "The arguments are @_[]";
    }

$many-args( 'Hamadryas', 'perlicus' );
```

That @_ is an Array, but you'll have to wait until the next chapter to see what those
can do.

Exercise 5.3

Create a Block that trims the whitespace and lowercases its argument. The original
value should change. This is the sort of thing you'd want to use when you normalize
data.

Implicit parameters

The Blocks get fancier. You can use *placeholder variables* (or *implicit parameters*)
inside them to specify how many parameters you want:

```
my $adding-block := { $^a + $^b }
```

The ^ denotes a placeholder variable, which tells the compiler to construct an implicit
signature for the Block. Your Block has exactly the same number of parameters as
there are placeholder values and you must provide one argument per parameter:

```
my $adding-block := { $^a + $^b }

$adding-block();          # Nope - too few parameters
$adding-block( 1 );       # Nope - too few still
$adding-block( 1, 37 );   # Just right!
$adding-block( 1, 2, 3 ); # Nope - too many parameters
```

The arguments are assigned to the placeholder variables in the lexicographical order
of their names and not the order you use them. Each of these Blocks divides two
numbers; the difference is the order in which they use the placeholder variables:

```
my $forward-division  := { $^a / $^b };
my $backward-division := { $^b / $^a };
```

You can call them with the same arguments in the same order. Even though you use
the same placeholder variable names and pass the same arguments, you get different
answers:

```
put $forward-division( 2, 3 );    # 0.66667
put $backward-division( 2, 3 );   # 1.5
```

You can reuse the same placeholder variable without it creating an additional parameter. This is still one parameter and multiplies the single argument by itself:

```
my $square := { $^a * $^a }
```

Calling .signature gives you the Signature object for that Block. Outputting it with say gives you a .gist representation:

```
my $square := { $^a * $^a }
say $square.signature;  # ($a)
```

Exercise 5.4

Create a Block that uses three placeholder variables and evaluates to the maximum number. The max routine can help. Run the Block with different arguments.

Explicit signatures

The pointy arrow (->) is the start of a signature in which you can specify your parameters. With nothing between the -> and the {, your signature has zero parameters:

```
my $block := -> { put "You called this block"; };
```

When you call the Block you have to specify one argument per parameter:

```
put $block();     # No argument, so it works
put $block( 2 );  # Error - too many parameters
```

You define parameters between the -> and the {:

```
my $block := -> $a { put "You called this block with $a"; };
```

The order of parameters in a signature defines the order in which the arguments will fill them. If $b is the first parameter, it gets the first argument. Their lexicographical order doesn't matter:

```
my $block := -> $b, $a { $a / $b };
put $block( 2, 3 );  # 1.5
put $block( 3, 2 );  # 0.666667
```

These sorts of parameters are *positional parameters*. There's another sort where you can specify which argument goes with which parameter. These are *named parameters*:

```
my $block := -> :$b, :$a { $a / $b };
put $block( b => 3, a => 2 );  # 0.666667
put $block( a => 3, b => 2 );  # 1.5
```

You'll see more about signatures in Chapter 11, but this is enough to get you started.

Type constraints

The parameter variables can constrain the types they allow. This `Block` numerically divides two values but it doesn't force you to give it numbers:

```
my $block := -> $b, $a { $a / $b };

$block( 1, 2 );
$block( 'Hamadryas', 'perlicus' );
```

The second call fails:

```
Cannot convert string to number: base-10 number must
begin with valid digits ...
```

That fails inside the `Block`. It should have never reached that code. If you are doing numeric operations you should only allow numbers:

```
my $block := -> Numeric $b, Numeric $a { $a / $b };

put $block( 1, 2 );
put $block( 'Hamadryas', 'perlicus' );
```

The first call works but the second call tries to use `Str`s and fails:

```
2
Type check failed in binding to parameter '$b';
expected Numeric but got Str ("Hamadryas")
```

Choose another type if the `Numeric` type is too wide for you:

```
my $block := -> Int $b, Int $a { $a / $b };
```

This still has a problem, though. The `Int` constraint allows anything that smart matches as an `Int`. An `Int` type object satisfies that:

```
$block( Int, 3 ); # call still works
```

That makes it past the parameter gatekeeper and fails in the division. Add a `:D` after the type to constrain it to a defined value. Type objects are always undefined:

```
my $block := -> Int:D $b, Int:D $a { $a / $b };
```

You'll see more of this in Chapter 11.

Simple Subroutines

A *subroutine* is a `Block` of code with some additional features. Instead of the pointy arrow you use `sub`:

```
my $subroutine := sub { put "Called subroutine!" };
```

You execute it in the same way:

```
$subroutine();
```

A subroutine can *return* a value (a Block can't). Calling a Sub computes some value and makes it available to you in the calling scope.

Previously the Blocks handled the output. It's generally poor form to handle that from a subroutine since that's giving it the double job of computing the value and then outputting. It's less flexible because it decides what to do with the value. Returning the value lets you decide later:

```
my $subroutine := sub { return "Called subroutine!" };
put $subroutine();
```

Instead of outputting it you could save the result:

```
my $result = $subroutine();
```

A return exits the innermost Routine (a superclass of Sub) that it finds itself in. You can have a return in a Block if that Block is inside some sort of Routine. In this subroutine you declare a Block that includes a return statement and you execute it immediately. This ends the subroutine right away:

```
my $subroutine := sub {
    -> { # not a sub!
        return "Called subroutine!"
        }.();    # execute immediately
    put 'This is unreachable and will never run';
    };

put $subroutine();    # Called subroutine!
```

You're more likely to use this with something that uses a Block, such as an if construct. Both of these Blocks can use return because they are inside of a Routine, which knows how to handle it:

```
my $subroutine := sub {
    if now.Int %% 2 { return 'Even' }
    else            { return 'Odd'  }
    };

put $subroutine();
```

The do if only needs one return:

```
my $subroutine := sub {
    return do if now.Int %% 2 { 'Even' }
            else              { 'Odd'  }
    };

put $subroutine();
```

Named Subroutines

A subroutine can have a name. Specify it after the `sub`. You can then execute the subroutine through its name as well as through its variable. They both do the same thing because they actually are the same thing:

```
my $subroutine := sub show-me { return "Called subroutine!" };
put $subroutine.(); # Called subroutine!
put show-me();      # Called subroutine!
```

More often you'll probably skip the variable altogether:

```
sub show-me { return "Called subroutine!" };
put show-me();      # Called subroutine!
```

To define its signature, put it in parentheses after the subroutine name (that's slightly different than with a `Block`):

```
sub divide ( Int:D $a, Int:D $b ) { $a / $b }
put divide( 5, 7 ); # 0.714286
```

If it won't confuse the parser, you can omit the parentheses. This is the same thing:

```
put divide 5, 7;     # 0.714286
```

The subroutine definition is an expression just like a `Block`. If you have something other than trailing space after the closing brace, you need the semicolon:

```
sub divide ( Int:D $a, Int:D $b ) { $a / $b }; put divide( 5, 6 );
```

Subroutines are lexically scoped by default. If you define one in a `Block` it exists only inside that `Block`. The outer scope doesn't know that `divide` exists, so this is an error:

```
{
    sub divide ( Int:D $a, Int:D $b ) { $a / $b }
    put divide( 3, 2 );
}

put divide( 3, 2 );  # Error!
```

This has the same advantage as lexical variable names: you don't have to know all the other subroutines to define your own. This also means that if you have a subroutine you would like to temporarily replace, you can create your own version in the scope that you need:

```
sub divide ( Int:D $a, Int:D $b ) { $a / $b }

put divide 1, 137;

{ # a scope for the fixed version of divide
sub divide ( Numeric $b, Numeric $a ) {
    put "Calling my private divide!";
    $a / $b
    }
```

```
put divide 1.1, 137.003;
}
```

Whatever Code

The intent of this chapter was to get to this interesting feature that you'll use throughout the language. You'll need this for the next few chapters.

The Whatever, *, is a stand-in for something that you will fill in later. The thing that fills in that value decides what it should be. Here's what it looks like in an expression where you add two to something:

```
my $sum = * + 2;
```

You know that's not the * for multiplication because that would need two operands. So what happens? The compiler recognizes the * and creates a WhateverCode (also called a *thunk*). It's a bit of code that doesn't define its own scope but isn't executed immediately. It's almost like a Block with one argument:

```
my $sum := { $^a + 2 }
```

Call the WhateverCode with an argument to get the final value:

```
$sum = * + 2;
put $sum( 135 );    # 137
```

Perhaps you want to have two arguments. You can use two *s and your WhateverCode will take two arguments:

```
my $sum = * + *;
put $sum( 135, 2 );    # 137
```

The Whatever * shows up in many other interesting constructs; that's the reason you're reading about subroutines so early in this book. There are two interesting uses right away.

Subsets

WhateverCodes allow you to insert code into statements. You can use them to create more interesting types with subset and where. First define a new type with no constraint. You tell subset which existing type you want to start with. This creates something that's the same as Int:

```
subset PositiveInt of Int;
my PositiveInt $x = -5;
put $x;
```

This checks the assignment at runtime. The type you put in $x must be a PositiveInt, but that's the same as an Int (so far). -5 is an Int, so this works.

Now constrain the valid values of `Int` by specifying a `where` clause with a `Block` of code:

```
subset PositiveInt of Int where { $^a > 0 };
my PositiveInt $x = -5;
put $x;
```

When you try to assign to `$x` you trigger the runtime type checking. The variable `$x` knows it needs to be a `PositiveInt`. It takes a value that might fit into `PositiveInt` and gives it to the `Block` in the `where` clause. If that code evaluates to `True`, the variable accepts that value. If it is `False` you get an error:

```
Type check failed in assignment to $x;
expected PositiveInt but got Int (-5)
```

The `Whatever` allows you to omit some of the typing. The * will do most of that work for you. It stands in for the thingy you want to test. These aren't full types but act like they are:

```
subset PositiveInt of Int where * > 0;
my PositiveInt $x = -5;
put $x;
```

Once you have a subset you can use it in a signature. If an argument is not a positive integer you get a runtime error:

```
subset PositiveInt of Int where * > 0;

sub add-numbers ( PositiveInt $n, PositiveInt $m ) {
    $n + $m
    }

put add-numbers 5, 11;     # 16
put add-numbers -5, 11;    # Error
```

You don't need to define an explicit subset, though. You can use `where` inside the signature. This is handy when you only need the constraint once:

```
sub add-numbers ( $n where * > 0, $m where * > 0 ) {
    $n + $m
    }
```

You'll see more subsets as you go along; they are handy ways to limit values without a lot of code. You haven't read about modules yet, but `Subset::Common` has several examples you might find handy.

Exercise 5.5

Use `subset` to create a `divide` subroutine that doesn't allow the denominator to be zero.

Summary

This chapter provided a brief introduction to subroutines and code-like things. There are simple `Blocks` that group code and define a scope, and there are more sophisticated subroutines that know how to pass a value back to their caller. Each of these have sophisticated ways to handle arguments. This chapter gave you enough detail so you can use them in the next couple of chapters. You'll see more powerful subroutine features in Chapter 11.

CHAPTER 6

Positionals

Your programming career is likely to be, at its heart, about moving and transforming ordered lists of some kind. Those might be to-do lists, shopping lists, lists of web pages, or just about anything else.

The broad term for such as list is `Positional`. Not everything in this chapter is strictly one of those; it's okay to pretend that they are, though. The language easily interchanges among many of the types you'll see in this chapter, and it's sometimes important to keep them straight. Mind their differences and their different uses to get exactly the behavior you want.

This is the first chapter where you'll experience the laziness of the language. Instead of computing things immediately as you specify them in your code, your program will remember it needs to do something. It then only does it if you later use it. This feature allows you to have infinite lists and sequences without actually creating them.

Constructing a List

A `List` is an immutable series of zero or more items. The simplest `List` is the *empty list*. You can construct one with no arguments. The `List` as a whole is one thingy and you can store it in a scalar:

```
my $empty-list = List.new;
put 'Elements: ', $empty-list.elems;  # Elements: 0
```

The `.elems` method returns the number of elements, which is 0 for the empty `List`. This might seem like a trivial result, but imagine those cases where you want to return no results: an empty `List` can be just as meaningful as a nonempty one.

Instead of the call to `.new`, you can use empty parentheses to do the same thing. Normally parentheses simply group items, but this is special syntax:

```
my $empty-list = (); # Also the empty List
```

There's also a special object for that. `Empty` clearly shows your intent:

```
my $empty-list = Empty;
```

You can specify elements in `.new` by separating the elements with commas. Both the colon and parentheses forms work:

```
my $butterfly-genus = List.new:
    'Hamadryas', 'Sostrata', 'Junonia';

my $butterfly-genus = List.new(
    'Hamadryas', 'Sostrata', 'Junonia'
    );
```

 You cannot make an empty `List` with `$()`: that's just `Nil`.

The `$(...)` with a list inside also constructs a `List`. The `$` indicates that it is an item. This one happens to be a `List` object. You can check the number of elements in it with `.elems`:

```
my $butterfly-genus = $('Hamadryas', 'Sostrata', 'Junonia');
put $butterfly-genus.elems;     # 3
```

Or you can leave off the `$` in front of the parentheses. You still need the grouping parentheses because item assignment is higher precedence than the comma:

```
my $butterfly-genus = ('Hamadryas', 'Sostrata', 'Junonia');
put $butterfly-genus.elems;     # 3
```

A container can be an element in a `List`. When you change the value in the container it looks like the `List` changes, but it doesn't actually change because the container is the `List` item and that container itself was still the `List` item:

```
my $name = 'Hamadryas perlicus';
my $butterflies = ( $name, 'Sostrata', 'Junonia' );
put $butterflies; # (Hamadryas perlicus Sostrata Junonia)

$name = 'Hamadryas';
put $butterflies; # (Hamadryas Sostrata Junonia)
```

You don't need the named variable, though. You can use an anonymous scalar container as a placeholder that you'll fill in later. Since it has no value (or even a type), it's an Any type object:

```
my $butterflies = ( $, 'Sostrata', 'Junonia' );
put $butterflies; # ((Any) Sostrata Junonia)
```

All of this quoting and comma separating is a bit tedious, but there's a shortcut. You can quote a list with qw. It creates items by breaking the text apart by whitespace. This makes a three-element List:

```
my $butterfly-genus = qw<Hamadryas Sostrata Junonia>;
put 'Elements: ', $butterfly-genus.elems;  # Elements: 3
```

qw is another form of the generalized quoting you saw in Chapter 4. It uses the :w adverb and returns a List. You won't see this form much, but it's what you're doing here:

```
my $butterfly-genus = Q :w/Hamadryas Sostrata Junonia/
```

That's still too much work. You can enclose the Strs in angle brackets and leave out the item quoting and the separating commas. This acts the same as qw:

```
my $butterfly-genus = <Hamadryas Sostrata Junonia>;
```

The <> only works if you don't have whitespace inside your Strs. This gives you four elements because the space between 'Hamadryas and perlicus' separates them:

```
my $butterflies = < 'Hamadryas perlicus' Sostrata Junonia >;
put 'Elements: ', $butterflies.elems; # Elements: 4
```

Perl 6 has thought of that too and provides a List quoting mechanism with quote protection. The <<>> keeps the thingy in quotes as one item even though it has whitespace in it:

```
my $butterflies = << 'Hamadryas perlicus' Sostrata Junonia >>;
put 'Elements: ', $butterflies.elems; # Elements: 3
```

With the <<>> you can interpolate a variable. After that the value of the variable is an item but isn't linked to the original variable:

```
my $name = 'Hamadryas perlicus';
my $butterflies = << $name Sostrata Junonia >>;
say $butterflies;
```

Instead of <<>>, you can use the fancier quoting with the single-character «» version (double angle quotes). These are sometimes called *French quotes*:

```
my $butterflies = « $name Sostrata Junonia »;
```

Both of these quote-protecting forms are the same as the :ww adverb for Q:

```
my $butterflies = Q :ww/ 'Hamadryas perlicus' Sostrata Junonia /;
put 'Elements: ', $butterflies.elems; # Elements: 3
```

Sometimes you want a List where all the elements are the same. The xx list replication operator does that for you:

```
my $counts = 0 xx 5; # ( 0, 0, 0, 0, 0 )
```

A List interpolates into a Str like any other scalar variable:

```
my $butterflies = << 'Hamadryas perlicus' Sostrata Junonia >>;
put "Butterflies are: $butterflies";
```

The `List` stringifies by putting spaces between its elements. You can't tell where one element stops and the next starts:

```
Butterflies are: Hamadryas perlicus Sostrata Junonia
```

The `.join` method allows you to choose what goes between the elements:

```
my $butterflies = << 'Hamadryas perlicus' Sostrata Junonia >>;
put "Butterflies are: ", $butterflies.join: ', ';
```

Now the output has commas between the elements:

```
Butterflies are: Hamadryas perlicus, Sostrata, Junonia
```

You can combine both of these, which makes it easier to also surround the `List` items with characters to set them off from the rest of the `Str`:

```
my $butterflies = << 'Hamadryas perlicus' Sostrata Junonia >>;
put "Butterflies are: /{$butterflies.join: ', '}/";
```

If you needed to parse this `Str` in some other program you'd know to grab the elements between the slashes:

```
Butterflies are: /Hamadryas perlicus, Sostrata, Junonia/
```

Exercise 6.1

Write a program that takes two arguments. The first is a `Str` and the second is the number of times to repeat it. Use xx and `.join` to output the text that number of times on separate lines.

Iterating All the Elements

Iteration is the repetition of a set of operations for each element of a collection. The for control structure iterates through each element of a `List` and runs its `Block` once for each element as the topic. You can use the `.List` method to treat the one thing in your scalar variable (your `List`) as its individual elements:

```
for $butterfly-genus.List {
    put "Found genus $_";
    }
```

You get one line per element:

```
Found genus Hamadryas
Found genus Sostrata
Found genus Junonia
```

Although I tend to call these things `Positionals` there is actually a separate role for `Iterables` that does the magic to make `for` work. The `Positionals` I present in this book also do the `Iterable` role, so I don't distinguish them even though I'm strictly wrong.

Calling `.List` is a bit annoying though, so there's a shortcut for it. Prefix the variable with @ to do the same thing:

```
for @$butterfly-genus {
    put "Found genus $_";
    }
```

Skip the $ sigil altogether and use the @ sigil to store a `List` in a variable:

```
my @butterfly-genus = ('Hamadryas', 'Sostrata', 'Junonia');

for @butterfly-genus {
    put "Found genus $_";
    }
```

This is actually different from the item assignment you've seen before. It's a list assignment where the = operator has a lower precedence:

```
my @butterfly-genus = 'Hamadryas', 'Sostrata', 'Junonia';
```

Why would you choose $ or @? Assigning to `$butterfly-genus` gives you a `List` and all the restrictions of that type. You can't add or remove elements. You can change the values inside a container but not the container itself. What do you get when you assign this way?

```
my @butterfly-genus = 'Hamadryas', 'Sostrata', 'Junonia';
put @butterfly-genus.^name;  # Array
```

You get an `Array`, which you'll see more of later in this chapter. An `Array` relaxes all those restrictions. It allows you to add and remove elements and change values. Choose the type that does what you want. If you want the data to stay the same, choose the one that can't change.

This looks a little better with interpolation, which means you're less likely to forget explicit whitespace around words:

```
for @butterfly-genus {
    put "$_ has {.chars} characters";
    }
```

You'll often want to give your variable a meaningful name. You can use a pointy `Block` to name your parameter instead of using the topic variable, $_:

```
for @butterfly-genus -> $genus {
    put "$genus has {$genus.chars} characters";
    }
```

That looks a lot like the definition of a subroutine with `-> { ... }`, because that's what it is. That parameter is lexical to that `Block` just as it would be in a subroutine.

If your `Block` has more than one parameter, then the `for` takes as many elements as it needs to fill in all of them. This goes through the `List` by twos:

```
my @list = <1 2 3 4 5 6 7 8>;

for @list -> $a, $b {
    put "Got $a and $b";
    }
```

Each iteration of the `Block` takes two elements:

```
Got 1 and 2
Got 3 and 4
Got 5 and 6
Got 7 and 8
```

Ensure that you have enough elements to fill all of the parameters or you'll get an error. Try that bit of code with one less element to see what happens!

You can use placeholder variables in your `Block`, but in that case you don't want to use a pointy `Block`, which would already create a signature for you. Using placeholder variables also works:

```
my @list = <1 2 3 4 5 6 7 8>;

for @list {
    put "Got $^a and $^b";
    }
```

Reading lines of input

The `lines` routine reads lines of input from the files you specify on the command line, or from standard input if you don't specify any. You'll read more about this in Chapter 8 but it's immediately useful with `for`:

```
for lines() {
    put "Got line $_";
    }
```

Your programs reads and reoutputs all of the lines from all of the files. The line ending was *autochomped*; it was automatically stripped from the value because that's probably what you wanted. The put adds a line ending for you:

```
% perl6 your-program.p6 file1.txt file2.txt
Got line ...
Got line ...
...
```

You need those parentheses even without an argument. The `lines` routine can take an argument that tells it how many lines to grab:

```
for lines(17) {
    put "Got line $_";
    }
```

You can break the lines into "words." This takes a `Str` (or something that can turn into a `Str`) and gives you back the nonwhitespace chunks as separate elements:

```
say "Hamadryas perlicus sixus".words; # (Hamadryas perlicus sixus)
put "Hamadryas perlicus sixus".words.elems; # 3
```

Combine this with `lines` to iterate one word at a time:

```
for lines.words { ... }
```

The `.comb` method takes it one step further by breaking it into characters:

```
for lines.comb { ... }
```

You'll see more about `.comb` in Chapter 16, where you'll learn how to tell it to divide up the `Str`.

With those three things you can implement your own *wc* program:

```
for lines() {
    state $lines = 0;
    state $words = 0;
    state $chars = 0;
    $lines++;
    $words += .words;
    $chars += .comb;
    LAST {
        put "lines: $lines\nwords: $words\nchars: $chars";
        }
    }
```

The character count with this version doesn't count all of the characters because the line ending was automatically removed.

Exercise 6.2

Read the lines from the files you specify on the command line. Output each line prefixed by the line number. At the end of each line show the number of "words" in the line.

Ranges

A `Range` specifies the inclusive bounds of possible values without creating all of the items that would be in that `List`. A `Range` can be infinite because it doesn't create all the elements; a `List` would take up all your memory.

Create a `Range` with `..` and your bounds on either side:

```
my $digit-range =   0 .. 10;
my $alpha-range = 'a' .. 'f';
```

If the lefthand value is larger than the righthand value you still get a `Range`, but it will have no elements and you won't get a warning:

```
my $digit-range = 10 .. 0;
put $digit.elems; # 0
```

You can exclude one or both endpoints with ^ on the appropriate side of the `..` operator. Some people call these the *cat ears*:

```
my $digit-range = 0 ^..  10; # exclude  0        ( 1..10 )
my $digit-range = 0  ..^ 10; # exclude 10        ( 0..9  )
my $digit-range = 0 ^..^ 10; # exclude  0 and 10 ( 1..9  )
```

As a shortcut for a numeric range starting from 0, use the ^ and the upper (exclusive) bound. This is very common Perl 6 code:

```
my $digit-range = ^10; # Same as 0 ..^ 10
```

This gives you the values 0 to 9, which is 10 values altogether even though 10 is not part of the range.

A `Range` knows its bounds. To see all of the values it would produce you can use `.List` to turn it into a list. Be aware that if your `Range` is very large you might suddenly hog most of the memory on your system, so this isn't something you'd normally want to do. It's nice for debugging though:

```
% perl6
> my $range = 'a' .. 'f';
"a".."f"
> $range.elems
6
> $range.List
(a b c d e f)
```

Exercise 6.5

Show all of the spreadsheet cell addresses from B5 to F9.

A smart match against a Range checks if a value is between the Range's bounds:

```
% perl6
> 7 ~~ 0..10
True
> 11 ~~ ^10
False
```

A Range isn't a List, though. Any value between the bounds is part of the Range, even if it's not a value that you would get if you listified the Range:

```
% perl6
> 1.37 ~~ 0..10
True
> 9.999 ~~ 0..10
True
> -137 ~~ -Inf..Inf # infinite range!
True
```

Excluding the endpoint doesn't mean that the last element is the next-lowest integer. Here, it's the exact value 10 that's excluded; everything positive and less than 10 is still in the Range:

```
% perl6
> 9.999 ~~ ^10
True
```

This is quite different from the listified version!

The @ Coercer

A Range isn't a List. In some situations it acts like separate elements instead of merely bounds but in others it maintains its rangeness. Usually that works because something implicitly coerces it for you.

Start with a `Range`. Output it using `put` and `say`. These show you different representations because their text representations of the object are different: `put` uses `.Str` and `say` uses `.gist`:

```
my $range = 0..3;
put $range.^name; # Range
say $range;      # 0..3
put $range;      # 0 1 2 3
```

This distinction in the representation of the object is important. When you see `say` in this book it's because I want to show you `.gist` because that's closer to a summary of the object.

You can make that a `List` by coercing it with the `.List` method:

```
my $list = $range.List;
put $list.^name; # List
say $list;      # (0 1 2 3)
```

Which one of these you have matters. A `List` works differently in a smart match because the element must be part of the `List`:

```
put "In range? ", 2.5 ~~ $range;  # True
put "In list? ", 2.5  ~~ $list;   # False
```

Instead of typing `.List` everywhere that you want something treated as such, you can use the prefix list context operator, `@`, just like you've seen with the context operators `+` and `~`:

```
my $range = 0..3;

put "In range? ",  2.5 ~~ $range;       # True (Range object)
put "In .List? ",  2.5 ~~ $range.List;  # False (List object)
put "In @?     ",  2.5 ~~ @$range;      # False (List object)
```

Later you'll use the `@` sigil for `Array` variables. For now it's a convenient way to treat something like a `List`.

Sequences

A sequence, `Seq`, knows how to make a future `List`. It's similar to a `List` but it's *lazy*. It knows where its values will come from and defers producing them until you actually need them.

 A `Seq` isn't really a `Positional` but it has a way to fake it. Rather than explain that I'm going to fake it too.

You call `.reverse` on a `List` to flip the list around. When you call `List` methods it just works:

```
my $countdown = <1 2 3 4 5>.reverse;
put $countdown.^name; # Seq
put $countdown.elems; # 5
```

The result isn't actually a `Seq`, but in most common cases that isn't important. The things that try to use it as a `List` will get what they expect, and there's no immediate need to create another `List` when the `Seq` knows the values from the original one.

However, calling `.eager` converts the `Seq` to a `List`:

```
my $countdown = <1 2 3 4 5>.reverse.eager;
put $countdown.^name; # Seq
put $countdown.elems; # 5
```

If you assign the `Seq` to a variable with the `@` sigil the `Seq` also turns into a `List`. This is an *eager assignment* to an `Array` (coming up soon):

```
my @countdown = <1 2 3 4 5>.reverse;
put @countdown.^name; # Array
put @countdown.elems; # 5
```

The `.pick` method chooses a random element from a `List`:

```
my $range = 0 .. 5;
my $sequence = $range.reverse;
say $sequence.^name; # Seq;

put $sequence.pick;  # 5 (or maybe something else)
```

By default you can only iterate through a `Seq` once. You use an item, then move on to the next one. This means that a `Seq` needs to know how to make the next element, and once it uses it it can discard it—it doesn't remember past values. If you try to use the `Seq` after it's gone through all of its elements you get an error:

```
put $sequence.pick;  # 3 (or maybe something else)
put $sequence;       # Error
```

The error tells you what to do:

```
This Seq has already been iterated, and its values consumed
(you might solve this by adding .cache on usages of the Seq, or
by assigning the Seq into an array)
```

Adding `.cache` remembers the elements of the `Seq` so you can reuse them. After the `.pick` there's no error:

```
my $range = 0 .. 5;
my $sequence = $range.reverse.cache;
say $sequence.^name; # Seq;
```

```
put $sequence.pick;  # 5 (or maybe something else)
put $sequence;       # 5 4 3 2 1 0
```

This isn't something you want to do carelessly, though. Part of the benefit of the Seq is the memory saving it provides by not duplicating data unless it needs to.

Infinite Lazy Lists

The Seq has to make all of the elements to .pick one of them. Once it does that it forgets them and doesn't have a way to make more elements. Perl 6 does this to support infinite lazy lists. You make these with the triple-dot sequence operator, ... By binding to the Seq you give it a name without immediately reducing it to its values:

```
my $number-sequence := 1 ... 5;
```

That's the integers from 1 to 5. The Seq looks at the start and figures out how to get to the end. That sequence is easy; it adds a whole number.

You can make an exclusive endpoint (but not an exclusive startpoint). This Seq is the integers from 1 to 4:

```
my $exclusive-sequence := 1 ...^ 5;
```

A Range can't count down, but a Seq can. This one subtracts whole numbers:

```
my $countdown-sequence := 5 ... 1;
```

The same thing works for letters:

```
my $alphabet-sequence := 'a' ... 'z';
```

You can tell the Seq how to determine the next element. You can specify more than one item for the start to give it the pattern:

```
my $s := 0, 1, 2 ... 256; # 257 numbers, 0 .. 256
```

This is the series of whole numbers from 0 to 256. That's the easiest pattern there. But add a 4 after the 2 and it's a different series. Now it's the powers of 2:

```
my $s := 0, 1, 2, 4 ... 256; # powers of 2
say $s; # (0 1 2 4 8 16 32 64 128 256)
```

The ... can figure out arithmetic or geometric series. But it gets better. If you have a more complicated series you can give it a rule to make the next item. That rule can be a Block that grabs the previous argument and transforms it. Here it adds 0.1 to the previous element until it gets to 1.8. You couldn't do this with a Range:

```
my $s := 1, { $^a + 0.1 } ... 1.8;
say $s; # (1 1.1 1.2 1.3 1.4 1.5 1.6 1.7 1.8)
```

If you have more than one positional parameter in your Block it looks farther back in the series. Here are the Fibonacci numbers up to 21:

```
```

```
my $s := 1, 1, { $^a + $^b } ... 21;
say $s; # (1 1 2 3 5 8 13 21)
```

The Seq only ends when it creates an item that is exactly equal to the endpoint. If you change that to 20 you get an infinite series and your program hangs while it creates every element so it can count them:

```
my $s := 1, 1, { $^a + $^b } ... 20;
say $s.elems;  # never gets an answer but keeps trying
```

Instead of a literal endpoint you can give it a Block. The Seq stops when the Block evaluates to True (but keeps the element that makes it True):

```
my $s := 1, 1, { $^a + $^b } ... { $^a > 20 };
say $s.elems; # (1 1 2 3 5 8 13 21)
```

Those Blocks are unwieldy, but you know that you can shorten them with Whatevers. Do the endpoint first:

```
my $s := 1, 1, { $^a + $^b } ... * > 20;
```

You can reduce the first Block with two Whatevers. That WhateverCode sees two *s and knows it needs two elements:

```
my $s := 1, 1, * + * ... * > 20;
```

That stops the Fibonacci numbers at 21. What if you wanted all of the Fibonacci numbers? The Whatever by itself can be the endpoint and in that context it is never True; this series never ends:

```
my $s := 1, 1, * + * ... *;
```

This is one of the reasons .gist exists. It gives a summary of the object. It knows that this is an infinite Seq so it doesn't try to represent it:

```
put $s.gist; # (...)
say $s;      # (...), .gist implicitly
```

That's it. That's the heart of Seq. It can produce an infinite number of values but it doesn't do it immediately. It knows the pattern to get to the next one.

Recall that a Seq doesn't remember all the values. Once it goes through them it doesn't store them or regenerate them. In this example it reverses the list and exhausts the series. That's all in the first put. There's nothing left for the second put:

```
my $s := 1 ... 5;

put $s.reverse; # (5 4 3 2 1)
put $s;         # Error
```

You get this error:

```
This Seq has already been iterated, and its values consumed
(you might solve this by adding .cache on usages of the Seq, or
by assigning the Seq into an array)
```

The error tells you what to do. You can call `.cache` on a `Seq` to force it to remember the values, even if this will eat up all of your memory:

```
my $s := 1 ... 5;
put $s.cache.reverse; # 5 4 3 2 1
put $s;               # 1 2 3 4 5
```

Should you need to treat a `Seq` as a `List`, coerce it with `@`. This generates all of its values:

```
my $s = ( 1 ... 5 );
put $s.^name; # Seq

my $list-from-s = @$s;
put $list-from-s.^name; #List
```

Most of the time a `Seq` will act like a `List`, but sometimes you need to give some hints.

Gathering Values

The previous `Seqs` could easily compute their next values based on the ones that came before. That's not always the case. A `gather` with a `Block` returns a `Seq`. When you want the next value the `gather` runs the code. A `take` produces a value. Here's the same thing as 1 ... 5 using `gather`:

```
my $seq := gather {
    state $previous = 0;

    while $previous++ < 5 { take $previous }
    }

say $seq;
```

Each time the code encounters a `take` it produces a value, then waits until the next time something asks for a value. The `Seq` stops when the code gets to the end of the `gather` `Block`. In this example, the `while` `Block` runs once for each access to the `Seq`.

You don't need the braces for the `Block` if the statement fits on one line. This is an infinite `Seq`:

```
my $seq := gather take $++ while 1;
```

Those are easily done with the tools you already had. What about a random `Seq` of random values? This `gather` keeps choosing one value from `@array`, forever:

```
my @array = <red green blue purple orange>;
my $seq := gather take @array.pick(1) while 1;
```

Here's a `gather` that provides only the lines of input with `eq` in them. It doesn't have to wait for all of the input to start producing values. And since the `Seq` controls access to the lines, you don't need to use or store them right away:

```
my $seq := gather for lines() { next unless /eq/; take $_ };

for $seq -> $item {
    put "Got: $item";
    }
```

You can store these in a `Positional` without being eager:

```
my @seq = lazy gather for lines() { next unless /eq/; take $_ };

for @seq -> $item {
    put "Got: $item";
    }
```

It doesn't matter how you create the `Seq`. Once you have it you can use it and pass it around like any other sequence.

Exercise 6.6

Use `gather` and `take` to produce an infinite cycle of alternating values from an `Array` of color names. When you get to the end of the array, go back to the beginning and start again.

Single-Element Access

You can extract a particular element by its position in the object, whether that's a `List`, `Range`, `Seq`, or other type of `Positional` thingy. Each position has an `index` that's a positive integer (including 0). To get the element, append [*POSITION*] to your thingy:

```
my $butterfly-genus = <Hamadryas Sostrata Junonia>;
my $first-butterfly = $butterfly-genus[0];
put "The first element is $first-butterfly";
```

[*POSITION*]is a *postcircumfix* operator. Operators are actually methods (Chapter 12), so you can use the method dot between the object and the [*POSITION*] (although you mostly won't):

```
my $first-butterfly = $butterfly-genus.[0];
```

You can interpolate either form in double-quoted `Str`s:

```
put "The first butterfly is $butterfly-genus[0]";
put "The first butterfly is $butterfly-genus.[0]";
```

Since the index counts from zero the last position is one less than the number of elements. The .end method knows that position:

```
my $end = $butterfly-genus.end;              # 2
my $last-butterfly = $butterfly-genus[$end];  # Junonia
```

If the thingy happens to be a lazy list you'll get an error trying to find its end element; you can check if it is with .is-lazy and perhaps do something different in that case:

```
my $butterfly-genus = <Hamadryas Sostrata Junonia>;
$butterfly-genus = (1 ... * );
put do if $butterfly-genus.is-lazy { 'Lazy list!' }
    else {
        my $end = $butterfly-genus.end;
        $butterfly-genus[$end]
        }
```

If you specify a position less than 0 you get an error. If you try to do it with a literal value the error message tells you that you've carried a habit over from a different language:

```
$butterfly-genus[-1];  # fine in Perl 5, but error in Perl 6!
```

The error message tells you to use *-1 instead, which you'll read more about in just a moment:

```
Unsupported use of a negative -1 subscript to index from the end;
in Perl 6 please use a function such as *-1
```

But if you've put that index in a variable, perhaps as the result of poor math, you get a different error:

```
my $end = -1;
$butterfly-genus[$i];
```

This time it tells you that you are out of bounds:

```
Index out of range. Is: -1, should be in 0..^Inf
```

This doesn't work the same way on the other side. If you try to access an element beyond the last one, you get back Nil with no error message:

```
my $end = $butterfly-genus.end;
$butterfly-genus[$end + 1];  # Nil!
```

Curiously, though, you can't use Nil to tell if you specified a wrong position because Nil can be an element of a List:

```
my $has-nil = ( 'Hamadryas', Nil, 'Junonia', Nil );
my $butterfly = $has-nil.[3]; # works, but still Nil!
```

You can also put almost any code you like inside the square brackets. It should evaluate to an Int, but if it doesn't the operator will try to convert it to one. You can skip the $end variable you've used so far and use .end directly:

```
my $last-butterfly = $butterfly-genus[$butterfly-genus.end];
```

If you wanted the next-to-last element, you could subtract one:

```
my $next-to-last = $butterfly-genus[$butterfly-genus.end - 1];
```

This way of counting from the end is quite tedious though, so there's a shorter way to do it. A Whatever *star* inside the [ ] is the number of elements in the list (not the last index!). That * is one greater than the last position. Subtract 1 from * to get the index for the last element:

```
my $last-butterfly = $butterfly-genus[*-1];
```

To get the next-to-last element, subtract one more:

```
my $next-to-last = $butterfly-genus[*-2];
```

If you subtract more than the number of elements, you'll get Nil (rather than an out-of-index error like you would without the *).

If you have a Seq it will create whatever items it needs to get to the one that you ask for. The triangle numbers add the index of the element to the previous number to get the next number in the series. If you want the fifth one ask for that index:

```
my $triangle := 0, { ++$ + $^a } ... *;
say $triangle[4];
```

Exercise 6.7

The squares of numbers is the sequence where you add *2n–1* to the previous value. *n* is the position in the sequence. Use the sequence operator ... to compute the square of 25.

Changing a Single Element

If your List element is a container you can change its value. Previously you used an anonymous scalar container as a placeholder in one of your lists:

```
my $butterflies = ( $, 'Sostrata', 'Junonia' );
say $butterflies; # ((Any) perlicus Sostrata Junonia)
```

You can't change the container, but you can change the value that's in the container:

```
$butterflies.[0] = 'Hamadryas';
say $butterflies; # (Hamadryas Sostrata Junonia)
```

If you try to change an item that is not a container you get an error:

```
$butterflies.[1] = 'Ixias';
```

The error tells you that the element there is something that you cannot change:

```
Cannot modify an immutable Str (...)
```

Multiple-Element Access

You can access multiple elements at the same time. A *slice* specifies more than one index in the brackets:

```
my $butterfly-genus = <Hamadryas Sostrata Junonia>;
my ( $first, $last ) = $butterfly-genus[0, *-1];
put "First: $first Last: $last";
```

Notice that you can declare multiple variables at the same time by putting them in parentheses after the my. Since that's not a subroutine call you still need a space after my. The output shows the first and last elements:

```
First: Hamadryas Last: Junonia
```

The indices can come from a Positional. If you've stored that in a scalar variable you have to coerce or *flatten* it:

```
put $butterfly-genus[ 1 .. *-1 ];     # Sostrata Junonia

my $indices = ( 0, 2 );
put $butterfly-genus[ @$indices ]; # Hamadryas Junonia
put $butterfly-genus[ |$indices ]; # Hamadryas Junonia

my @positions = 1, 2;
put $butterfly-genus[ @positions ]; # Sostrata Junonia
```

Assigning to multiple elements works the same way inside the brackets. However, the elements must be mutable. If they aren't containers you won't be able to change them:

```
my $butterfly-genus = ( $, $, $ );
$butterfly-genus[ 1 ] = 'Hamadryas';
$butterfly-genus[ 0, *-1 ] = <Gargina Trina>;
put $butterfly-genus;
```

You can fix that by using an Array, which you're about to read more about. The Array automatically containerizes its elements:

```
my @butterfly-genus = <Hamadryas Sostrata Junonia>;
@butterfly-genus[ 0, *-1 ] = <Gargina Trina>;
put @butterfly-genus;
```

Arrays

You can't change a List. Once constructed it is what it is and keeps the same number of elements. You can't add or remove any elements. Unless the item is a container, each List item's value is fixed.

Arrays are different. They containerize every item so that you can change any of them, and the `Array` itself is a container. You could start with the `Array` class to make an object:

```
my $butterfly-genus = Array.new: 'Hamadryas', 'Sostrata', 'Junonia';
```

You'll probably never see that, though. Instead, you can use square brackets to make an `Array`. Each item in the `Array` becomes a container even if it didn't start as one:

```
my $butterfly-genus = ['Hamadryas', 'Sostrata', 'Junonia'];
```

Since every item is a container you can change any value by assigning to it through a single-element access:

```
$butterfly-genus.[1] = 'Paruparo';
say $butterflies; # [Hamadryas Paruparo Junonia]
```

This new behavior gets its own sigil, the @ (which looks a bit like an *a* for *Array*). When you assign a listy thing to an @ variable you get an `Array`:

```
my @butterfly-genus = <Hamadryas Sostrata Junonia>;
put @butterfly-genus.^name;  # Array
```

The = here is the list assignment operator you met earlier. Since you have an `Array` on the left side of the operator the = knows it's the list variety. That one is lower precedence than the comma, so you can leave off the grouping parentheses you've been using so far:

```
my @butterfly-genus = 1, 2, 3;
```

Exercise 6.8

You've already used an `Array` that you haven't seen. @*ARGS is the collection of `Str`s that you've specified on the command line. Output each element on its own line.

Constructing an Array

There's a hidden list assignment here that makes this possible. In its expanded form there are a couple of steps. Greatly simplified, the `Array` sets up a scalar container for the number of items it will hold and binds to that:

```
my @butterfly-genus := ( $, $, $ ); # binding
```

Then it assigns the items in the incoming list to the containers in the `Array`:

```
@butterfly-genus = <Hamadryas Sostrata Junonia>;
```

You don't need to do any of this yourself because it happens automatically when you assign to an `Array` (the @ variable). `Array` items are always containers, and the `Array` itself is a container.

The square brackets construct an `Array` (and it's the square brackets that index Arrays). You can assign to a scalar or `Array` variable:

```
my $array = [ <Hamadryas Sostrata Junonia> ];
put $array.^name;        # Array
put $array.elems;        # 3
put $array.join: '|';    # Hamadryas|Sostrata|Junonia

my @array = [ <Hamadryas Sostrata Junonia> ];
put @array.^name;        # Array
put @array.elems;        # 3
put @array.join: '|';    # Hamadryas|Sostrata|Junonia
```

If you are going to assign to `@array` you don't need the brackets, though. This is the same thing:

```
my @array = <Hamadryas Sostrata Junonia>;
put @array.^name;        # Array
put @array.elems;        # 3
```

The brackets are handier when you want to skip the variable. You would do this for temporary data structures or subroutine arguments. You'll see more of those as you go on.

Interpolating Arrays

A double-quoted `Str` can interpolate single or multiple elements of a `Positional` or even all the elements. Use the brackets to select the elements that you want:

```
my $butterflies = <Hamadryas Sostrata Junonia>;
put "The first butterfly is $butterflies[0]";
put "The last butterfly is $butterflies[*-1]";
put "Both of those are $butterflies[0,*-1]";
put "All the butterflies are $butterflies[]";
```

When it interpolates multiple elements it inserts a space between the elements:

```
The first butterfly is Hamadryas
The last butterfly is Junonia
Both of those are Hamadryas Junonia
All the butterflies are Hamadryas Sostrata Junonia
```

You can interpolate Ranges too:

```
my $range = 7 .. 13;
put "The first is $range[0]";     # The first is 7
put "The last is $range[*-1]";    # The last is 13
put "All are $range";             # All are 7 8 9 10 11 12 13
```

The other `Positional`s behave similarly based on how they generate their elements.

Array Operations

Since the `Array` is a container you can change it. Unlike with a `List`, you can add and remove items. The `.shift` method removes the first item from the `Array` and gives it back to you. That item is no longer in the `Array`:

```
my @butterfly-genus = <Hamadryas Sostrata Junonia>;
my $first-item = @butterfly-genus.shift;
say @butterfly-genus;  # [Sostrata Junonia]
say $first-item;       # Hamadryas
```

If the `Array` is empty you get a `Failure`, but you won't learn about those until Chapter 7. You don't get an immediate error; the error shows up when you try to use it later:

```
my @array = Empty;
my $element = @array.shift;
put $element.^name;  # Failure (soft exception)
```

That error is `False` but won't complain when it's in a conditional:

```
while my $element = @array.shift { put $element }
```

The `.pop` method removes the last item:

```
my @butterfly-genus = <Hamadryas Sostrata Junonia>;
my $first-item = @butterfly-genus.pop;
say @butterfly-genus;  # [Hamadryas Sostrata]
say $first-item;       # Junonia
```

To add one or more items to the front of the list, use `.unshift`. One top-level item becomes one element in the `Array`:

```
my @butterfly-genus = Empty;
@butterfly-genus.unshift: <Hamadryas Sostrata>;
say @butterfly-genus;  # [Hamadryas Sostrata]
```

`.push` adds a list of items to the end of the list:

```
@butterfly-genus.push: <Junonia>;
say @butterfly-genus;  # [Hamadryas Sostrata Junonia]
```

With `.splice` you can add elements to or remove them from anywhere in the `Array`. It takes a starting index, a length, and the items to remove from the list. It gives you the elements it removed:

```
my @butterfly-genus = 1 .. 10;
my @removed = @butterfly-genus.splice: 3, 4;
say @removed;          # [4 5 6 7]
say @butterfly-genus;  # [1 2 3 8 9 10]
```

You can give `.splice` items to replace those that you removed:

```
my @butterfly-genus = 1 .. 10;
my @removed = @butterfly-genus.splice: 5, 2, <a b c>;
say @removed;        # [6 7]
say @butterfly-genus; # [1 2 3 4 5 a b c 8 9 10]
```

If the length is 0 you don't remove anything, but you can still insert items. You get an empty Array back:

```
my @butterfly-genus = 'a' .. 'f';
my @removed = @butterfly-genus.splice: 5, 0, <X Y Z>;
say @removed;        # []
say @butterfly-genus; # [a b c d e X Y Z f]
```

Each of these Array methods have routine versions:

```
my $first = shift @butterfly-genus;
my $last  = pop @butterfly-genus;

unshift @butterfly-genus, <Hamadryas Sostrata>;
push @butterfly-genus, <Junonia>;

splice @butterfly-genus, $start-pos, $length, @elements;
```

Exercise 6.9

Start with an Array that holds the letters from *a* to *f*. Use the Array operators to move those elements to a new Array that will have the same elements in reverse order.

Exercise 6.10

Start with the Array that holds the letters from *a* to *f*. Use only .splice to make these changes: remove the first element, remove the last element, add a capital *A* to the front of the list, and add a capital *F* to the end of the list.

Lists of Lists

A List can be an element of another List (or Seq). Depending on your previous language experience your reaction to this idea will be either "Of course!" or "This is so wrong!"

The .permutations method produces a Seq of sublists where each one represents a unique ordering of all the elements of the original:

```
my $list = ( 1, 2, 3 );
say $list.permutations;
put "There are {$list.permutations.elems} elements";
```

The output shows a List of Lists where each element is another List:

```
((1 2 3) (1 3 2) (2 1 3) (2 3 1) (3 1 2) (3 2 1))
There are 6 elements
```

You can make these directly. This List has two elements, both of which are Lists:

```
my $list = ( <a b>, <1 2> );
put $list.elems;              # 2
say $list;                    # ((a b) (1 2))
```

You can explicitly create the sublists with parentheses:

```
my $list = ( 1, 2, ('a', 'b') );
put $list.elems;  # 3
say $list;        # (1 2 (a b))
```

You can separate sublists with semicolons. Elements between ; end up in the same sublist, although sublists of a single element are just that element:

```
my $list = ( 1; 'Hamadryas'; 'a', 'b' );
put $list.elems;     # 3
say $list;           # (1 2 (a b))
put $list.[0].^name;  # Int
put $list.[1].^name;  # Str
put $list.[*-1].^name; # List
```

Flattening Lists

You may be more comfortable with flat Lists, if you want a bunch of elements with no structure. .flat extracts all the elements of the sublist and makes it a single-level *simple list*. The flat List created here has four elements instead of three:

```
my $list = ( 1, 2, ('a', 'b') );
put $list.elems;  # 3

my $flat = $list.flat;
put $flat.elems;  # 4
say $flat;        # (1 2 a b)
```

This works all the way down into sublists of sublists (of sublists…). Here, the last element is a sublist that has a sublist. The flat List ends up with six elements:

```
my $list = ( 1, 2, ('a', 'b', ('X', 'Z') ) );
put $list.elems;  # 3

my $flat = $list.flat;
put $flat.elems;  # 6
say $flat;        # (1 2 a b X Z)
```

Sometimes you don't want a sublist to flatten. In that case you can *itemize* it by putting a $ in front of the parentheses. An itemized element resists flattening:

```
my $list = ( 1, 2, ('a', 'b', $('X', 'Z') ) );
put $list.elems;  # 3
```

```
my $flat = $list.flat;
put $flat.elems;  # 5
say $flat;        # (1 2 a b (X Z))
```

A List held in a scalar variable is already itemized and does not flatten:

```
my $butterfly-genus = ('Hamadryas', 'Sostrata', 'Junonia');

my $list = ( 1, 2, ('a', 'b', $butterfly-genus ) );
my $flat = $list.flat;
say $flat;        # (1 2 a b (Hamadryas Sostrata Junonia))
```

Then what do you do to un-itemize something? You can use the prefix | to flatten it. This *decontainerizes* the thingy:

```
my $butterfly-genus = ('Hamadryas', 'Sostrata', 'Junonia');

my $list = ( 1, 2, ('a', 'b', |$butterfly-genus ) );
my $flat = $list.flat;
put $flat.elems;  # 7
say $flat;        # (1 2 a b Hamadryas Sostrata Junonia)
```

The | takes certain types (Capture, Pair, List, Map, and Hash) and flattens them. You'll see more of this in Chapter 11. It actually creates a Slip, which is a type of List that automatically flattens into an outer list. You could coerce your List with .Slip to get the same thing:

```
my $list = ( 1, 2, ('a', 'b', $butterfly-genus.Slip ) );
```

Now the elements in $butterfly-genus are at the same level as the other elements in its sublist:

```
(1 2 (a b Hamadryas Sostrata Junonia))
```

The slip routine does the same thing:

```
my $list = ( 1, 2, ('a', 'b', slip $butterfly-genus ) );
```

These Slips will be handy later in this chapter.

Interesting Sublists

Here's something quite useful. The .rotor method breaks up a flat List into a List of Lists where each sublist has the number of elements you specify. You can get five sublists of length 2:

```
my $list = 1 .. 10;
my $sublists = $list.rotor: 2;
say $sublists;       # ((1 2) (3 4) (5 6) (7 8) (9 10))
```

This is especially nice to iterate over multiple items at the same time. It grabs the number of items that you specify and supplies them as a single List:

```
my $list = 1 .. 10;
for $list.rotor: 3 {
    .say
    }
```

By default it only grabs exactly the number you specify. If there aren't enough elements it doesn't give you a partial List. This output is missing 10:

```
(1 2 3)
(4 5 6)
(7 8 9)
```

If you want a short sublist at the end, the :partial adverb will do that:

```
my $list = 1 .. 10;
for $list.rotor: 3, :partial {
    .say
    }
```

Now there's a short list in the last iteration:

```
(1 2 3)
(4 5 6)
(7 8 9)
(10)
```

Exercise 6.11

Use lines and .rotor to read chunks of three lines from input. Output the middle line in each chunk.

Combining Lists

Making and manipulating Positionals is only the first level of your programming skill. Perl 6 has several facilities to manage, combine, and process multiple Positional things together.

The Zip Operator, Z

The Z operator takes elements from the same positions in the lists you provide and creates sublists from them:

```
say <1 2 3> Z <a b c>;  # ((1 a) (2 b) (3 c))
```

When it reaches the end of the shortest list, it stops. It doesn't matter which list is shorter:

```
say <1 2 3> Z <a b>;  # ((1 a) (2 b))

say <1 2> Z <a b c>;  # ((1 a) (2 b))
```

The zip routine does the same thing:

```
say zip( <1 2 3>, <a b> );  # ((1 a) (2 b))
```

This one gives the same output because `$letters` doesn't have enough elements to make more sublists:

```
my $numbers = ( 1 .. 10 );
my $letters = ( 'a' .. 'c' );

say @$numbers Z @$letters; # ((1 a) (2 b) (3 c))
```

You can do it with more than two lists:

```
my $numbers = ( 1 .. 3 );
my $letters = ( 'a' .. 'c' );
my $animals = < 🐱 🐰 🐭 >; # cat rabbit rat
say @$numbers Z @$letters Z @$animals;
```

Each sublist has three elements:

```
((1 a 🐱)(2 b 🐰)(3 🐭))
```

zip does the same thing as Z:

```
say zip @$numbers, @$letters, @$animals;
```

You can use it with for:

```
for zip @$numbers, @$letters, @$animals {
    .say;
    }
```

```
(1 a 🐱)
(2 b 🐰)
(3 c 🐭)
```

Exercise 6.12

Use the Z operator to make an Array of Lists that pair each letter with its position in the alphabet.

The Cross Operator, X

The X cross operator combines every element of one Positional with every element of another:

```
my @letters = <A B C>;
my @digits  = 1, 2, 3;
```

```
my @crossed = @letters X @digits;
say @crossed;
```

The output shows that every letter was paired with every number:

```
[(A 1) (A 2) (A 3) (B 1) (B 2) (B 3) (C 1) (C 2) (C 3)]
```

Exercise 6.13

A deck of 52 playing cards has four suits, ♣ ♡ ♠ ◇, each with 13 cards, 2 to 10, jack, queen, king, and ace. Use the cross operator to make a List of Lists that represents each card. Output the list of cards so all the cards of one suit show up on the same line.

The Hyperoperators

Instead of combining Positionals, you can operate on pairs of them to create a List of the results. The *hyperoperators* can do that. Surround the + operator with <<>>. This numerically adds the first element of @right to the first element of @left. The result of that addition becomes the first element of the result. This happens for the second elements, then the third, and so on:

```
my @right = 1, 2, 3;
my @left  = 5, 9, 4;

say @left <<+>> @right;  # [6 11 7]
```

Pick a different operator and follow the same process. The concatenation operator joins the Str versions of each element:

```
my @right = 1, 2, 3;
my @left  = 5, 9, 4;

say @left <<~>> @right;  # [51 92 43]
```

If one of the sides has fewer elements the <<>> hyper recycles elements from the shorter one. It doesn't matter which side the shorter list is on. Here, @left has fewer elements. When it's time to operate on the third elements the hyper starts at the beginning of @left again to reuse 11:

```
my @right =  3,  5, 8;
my @left  = 11, 13;

say @left <<+>> @right;  # [14 18 19]
say @right <<+>> @left;  # [14 18 19]
```

Point the angle brackets toward the inside to insist that both sides have the same number of elements. You'll get an error when the sizes don't match:

```
```

```
say @left >>+<< @right;  # Error!
```

Another option is to allow one side to be smaller than the other but to not recycle elements. If both sets of angle brackets point away from the shorter side then the hyper does not reuse elements from the shorter side:

```
my @long  =  3,  5, 8;
my @short = 11, 13;

say @short >>+>> @long;    # [14 18]    no recycling
say @long  >>+>> @short;   # [14 18 19]

say @short <<+<< @long;    # [14 18 19]
say @long  <<+<< @short;   # [14 18]    no recycling
```

Instead of the double angle brackets you can use the fancier »« versions:

```
my @long  =  3,  5, 8;
my @short = 11, 13;

say @short  «+» @long;    # [14 18 19]
say @short  »+« @long;    # Error

say @short  »+» @long;    # [14 18]  no recycling
say @long   »+» @short;   # [14 18 19]

say @short  «+« @long;    # [14 18 19]
say @long   «+« @short;   # [14 18]  no recycling
```

The Reduction Operator

The reduction operator is a bit different from Z, X, or the hyperoperators. It turns a Positional into a single value by operating on two elements at a time to turn them into one element.

The prefix [] is the reduction operator. On the inside you put a binary operator. It applies that operator to the first two elements of its Positional to get a single value. It replaces those two values with the result; this makes the input one element shorter. It keeps doing this until there's one element left. That's the final value.

Here's a quick way to sum some numbers:

```
my $sum = [+] 1 .. 10;  # 55
```

This is the same as this expression if you write out the steps:

```
((((((((((1 + 2) + 3) + 4) + 5) + 6) + 7) + 8) + 9) + 10)
```

And to do a factorial:

```
my $factorial = [*] 1 .. 10;  # 3628800
```

Are all the values True? Apply the && to the first two elements and replace them with the result until there's one element left. At the end use the ? (or .so) to coerce the result to a Boolean:

```
my $condition = ?( [&&] 1 .. 10 );  # True
my $condition = ?( [&&] ^10 );      # False
```

There's a binary max operator too:

```
my $max = 1 max 137; # 137;
```

You can put that inside the brackets. This makes one pass through the elements to discover the largest numeric value:

```
my $max = [max] @numbers
```

If you want to use your own subroutine, use an extra set of braces and the & sigil to make it look like an operator:

```
sub longest {
    $^a.chars > $^b.chars ?? $^a !! $^b;
    }

my $longest =
    [[&longest]] <Hamadryas Rhamma Asterocampa Tanaecia>;

put "Longest is $longest"; # Longest is Asterocampa
```

That trick works to convert a subroutine to a binary operator:

```
$first [&longest] $second
```

Filtering Lists

The .grep method filters a Positional to get the elements that satisfy your condition. Any element that satisfies the condition becomes part of the new Seq:

```
my $evens = (0..10).grep: * %% 2;  # (0 2 4 6 8 10)
```

A Block works too. The current element shows up in $_:

```
my $evens = (0..10).grep: { $_ %% 2 };  # (0 2 4 6 8 10)
```

If your condition is only a type .grep smart matches the current element against that type:

```
my $allomorphs = <137 2i 3/4 a b>;
my $int-strs = $allomorphs.grep: IntStr;     # (137)
my $rat-strs = $allomorphs.grep: RatStr;     # (3/4)
my $img-strs = $allomorphs.grep: ComplexStr; # (2i)
my $strs     = $allomorphs.grep:  Str;       # (a b)
```

Remember that a smart match against a type includes matching anything that type is based on. Trying to get all the Strs finds everything since the <> creates allomorphs and every element matches Str:

```
my $everything = $allomorphs.grep: Str; # (1 2i 3/4 a b)
```

The .does method checks if the element has a role. Here, you want the elements that *don't* do that role—if it can be a number, you don't want it:

```
my $just-str = $allomorphs.grep: { ! .does(Numeric) };  # (a b)
```

You can specify some adverbs with .grep. The :v adverb (for "values") gives the same list you get without it:

```
my $int-strs = $allomorphs.grep: IntStr, :v;  # same thing
```

The :k adverb (for key) gives the positions of the matching elements. This returns 1 because that's the index of the matching element:

```
my $int-strs = $allomorphs.grep: ComplexStr, :k;  # (1)
```

You can get both the key and the value with :kv. You get a flat List in key-value order:

```
my $int-strs = $allomorphs.grep: RatStr, :kv;  # (2 3/4)
```

If multiple elements match you get a longer Seq. The even positions are still keys:

```
$allomorphs.grep: { ! .does(Numeric) }, :kv;  # (3 a 4 b)
```

There's also a routine form of grep. The Positional comes after the matcher:

```
my $matched = grep IntStr, @$allomorphs;
```

Transforming a List

.map creates a new Seq based on an existing one by creating zero or more elements from each input element. Here's an example that returns a Seq of squares. .map can take a Block or WhateverCode (although that's a lot of *s):

```
my $squares = (1..5).map: { $_ ** 2 }; # (0 1 4 9 16 25)
my $squares = (1..5).map: * ** 2;
```

There's a routine version of map that does the same :

```
my $even-squares = map { $_ ** 2 }, @(1..5);
```

Perhaps you want to lowercase everything:

```
my $lowered = $words.map: *.lc;
```

You might return no output elements, but you can't merely return the empty List because it will show up as an element in the new Seq. In this example the |() indicates an empty List slipped into the bigger List:

```
my $even-squares = (0..9).map: { $_ %% 2 ?? $_**2 !! |() }; # (0 4 16 36 64)
```

You can use these methods together. This selects the even numbers then squares them:

```
my $squares = $allomorphs
    .grep( { ! .does(Numeric) } )
    .map( { $_ %% 2 ?? $_**2 !! |() } );
```

Sorting Lists

Often you want a list in some order. Perhaps that's increasing numerical or alphabetic order, by the length of the Strs, or anything else that makes sense for you. You can do this with .sort:

```
my $sorted = ( 7, 5, 9, 3, 2 ).sort;    # (2 3 5 7 9)

my $sorted = <p e r l 6>.sort;          # (6 e l p r)
```

By default, .sort compares each pair of elements with cmp. If the two elements are numbers, it compares them as numbers. If it thinks they are Strs, it compares them as such. Here's a Str comparison that may surprise you the first time you see it (and annoy you hereafter):

```
my $sorted = qw/1 11 10 101/.sort;     # (1 10 101 11)
```

What happened? Since you constructed the list with qw, you got a list of Str objects. These compare character by character, so the text 101 is "less than" the text 11. This isn't dictionary sorting, though. Try it with upper- and lowercase letters:

```
my $sorted = qw/a A b B c C/.sort;
```

Did you get what you expected? Some of you probably guessed incorrectly. The lowercase code points come after the uppercase ones, for they are greater:

```
(A B C a b c)
```

cmp sorts by the code number in the Universal Character Set (UCS). If you are used to ASCII, the code number is the same thing. Above ASCII, you may not get what you expect.

 There is a .collate method that can handle Unicode collation for language-specific sorting, but it's experimental.

You can tell .sort how to compare the elements. For dictionary order (so case does not matter), you have to do a bit more work. The .sort method can take a routine that decides how to sort. Start with the default .sort fully written out with its comparison:

```
my $sorted = qw/a A b B c C/.sort: { $^a cmp $^b }
```

You can also write that with two Whatevers so you don't have to type the braces. This is the same thing:

```
my $sorted = qw/a A b B c C/.sort: * cmp *
```

If you want to compare them case insensitively, you can call the .fc method to do a proper case folding:

```
my $sorted = qw/a A b B c C/.sort: *.fc cmp *.fc
```

Now you get the order that ignores case:

```
(A a B b C c)
```

However, if you want to make the same transformation on both elements, you don't need to write it twice; .sort will figure it out. It saves the result and reuses it for all comparisons. This means that Perl 6 has a builtin Schwartzian transform (a Perl 5 idiom for a cached-key sort)!

```
my $sorted = qw/a A b B c C/.sort: *.fc;
```

There's a problem with cmp, though. The order of elements you get depends on the type and order of elements in your input:

```
for ^5 {
    my @numbers = (1, 2, 11, '21', 111, 213, '7', 77).pick: *;
    say @numbers.sort;
    }
```

The .pick method randomly chooses from the List the number of elements you specify. The * translates to the number of elements in the List. The effect is a shuffled List of the same elements. Some of these are Ints and some are Strs. Depending on which element shows up where, they sort differently:

```
(1 2 11 111 21 77 213 7)
(1 2 11 111 21 213 7 77)
(1 2 11 21 77 111 213 7)
(1 2 11 111 21 7 77 213)
(1 2 11 21 77 111 213 7)
```

Use leg (*less-equal-greater*) if you want to order these by their Str values every time:

```
say @numbers.sort: * leg *;
```

If you want numbers, use <=>:

```
say @numbers.sort: * <=> *;
```

Alternatively, you can coerce the input to the type you want:

```
say @numbers.sort: +*;   # numbers

say @numbers.sort: ~*;   # strings
```

Finally, there's a routine version of .sort. It has a single-argument form that takes a List and a two-argument form that takes a sort routine and a List:

```
my $sorted = sort $list;
my $sorted = sort *.fc, $list;
```

Exercise 6.14

Represent a deck of cards as a List of Lists. Create five poker hands of five cards from that. Output the cards in ascending order of their ranks.

Sorting on Multiple Comparisons

You can use a Block to create more complicated comparisons, comparing two things that are the same in one regard in another way. When two people's lasts names are the same, you can sort by the first name. If you sort these with the default .sort you probably won't get what you want:

```
my @butterflies = (
    <John Smith>,
    <Jane Smith>,
    <John Doe>,
    <Jon Smithers>,
    <Jim Schmidt>,
    );

my @sorted = @butterflies.sort;

put @sorted.join: "\n";
```

This comes out in alphabetical order, if you consider the Str to be the combination of the sublist elements as a single Str:

```
Jane Smith
Jim Schmidt
John Doe
John Smith
Jon Smithers
```

Change the sort to work only on the second element of each sublist:

```
my @sorted = @butterflies.sort: *.[1];

put @sorted.join: "\n";
```

The last names sort in alphabetical order now, but the first names show up out of order (though that may depend on the ordering of your input):

```
John Doe
Jim Schmidt
John Smith
Jane Smith
Jon Smithers
```

A more complex comparison can fix that. In each sublist, compare the last names to each other. If they are the same, add another comparison with the logical or:

```
my @sorted = @butterflies.sort: {
    $^a.[1] leg $^b.[1]  # last name
        or
    $^a.[0] leg $^b.[0]  # first name
    };
```

When it compares the sublists for (John Smith) and (Jane Smith) it tries the last names and finds that they are the same. It then sorts on the first names and produces the result that you probably want:

```
John Doe
Jim Schmidt
Jane Smith
John Smith
Jon Smithers
```

Exercise 6.15

Create a deck of cards and create five hands of five cards each. In each hand sort the cards by their rank. If the ranks are the same sort them by their suits.

Summary

The List, Range, and Array types are Positionals, and the Seq type can fake it when it needs to. This allows some amazing lazy features where you don't have to do anything until you actually need it. Not only that, but with a little practice you won't even need to think about it.

Once you have your data structures, you have some powerful ways to combine them to make much more complex data structures. Some of these may be daunting at first. Don't ignore them. You'll find that your programming career will be easier with judiciously chosen structures that are easy to manipulate.

## CHAPTER 7

When Things Go Wrong

Perl 6 doesn't always immediately give up when something goes wrong. It can fail softly. If the result of that problem doesn't affect anything else in the program there's no need to complain about it. However, the moment it becomes a problem that passive failure demands your attention.

This chapter shows you the error mechanisms and how to deal with them. You'll see how to handle the problems that your program notices on your behalf as well as detect and report problems on your own.

Exceptions

Here's a bit of code that tries to convert nonnumeric text into a number. Maybe something else didn't put the right value in the variable:

```
my $m = 'Hello';
my $value = +$m;
put 'Hello there!';  # no error, so, works?
```

Your program doesn't complain because you don't do anything with the problematic result. Change the program to output the result of what you think was a numeric conversion:

```
my $m = 'Hello';
my $value = +$m;
put $value;
```

Now you get some error output instead:

```
Cannot convert string to number: base-10 number must
begin with valid digits or '.' in '⏏Hello' (indicated by ⏏)
    in block <unit> at ... line 2
```

```
Actually thrown at:
    in block <unit> at ... line 3
```

Look at that error message. It reports two line numbers. The error occurred on line 2, but it wasn't until line 3 (the one with `put`) that it became a problem. That's the *soft failure*. What's actually in `$result`? It's a `Failure` object:

```
my $m = 'Hello';
my $value = +$m;
put "type is {$value.^name}";  # type is Failure
```

These soft failures can be quite handy in cases where you don't care if something didn't work. If you can't log a message because the logger is broken what are you going to do about it? Log the failure? Similarly, sometimes you don't care if something fails because that might be a common case. It's up to you to make those decisions, though.

The `Failure` is really a wrapper around an `Exception`, so you need to know about exceptions first.

Catching Exceptions

Something that wants to report an exception *throws* it. You'd say "the subroutine threw an exception." Some people might say it "raised an exception." It's the same thing. If you don't handle an exception it stops your program.

A `try` wraps some code and can *catch* an `Exception`. If it catches an `Exception` it puts it into the `$!` special variable:

```
try {
    my $m = 'Hello';
    my $value = +$m;
    put "value is {$value.^name}";
    }
put "ERROR: $!" if $!;

put 'Got to the end.';
```

You catch the `Exception` and your program continues:

```
ERROR: Cannot convert string to number
Got to the end.
```

With a single line you don't need the braces:

```
my $m = 'Hello';
try my $value = +$m;
```

If the code succeeds `try` gives back the value. You can move the `try` to the other side of the assignment:

```
my $m = 'Hello';
my $value = try +$m;
```

Most `Exception` types are under X and inherit from `Exception`—in this example it's `X::Str::Numeric`:

```
put "Exception type is {$!.^name}";
```

If there was no `Exception`, the thingy in $! is Any. This is a bit annoying because `Exception` inherits from Any too. The $! in a condition is defined if there was a problem. Use it with `given` and smart match against the types you want to handle. A `default` Block handles anything you don't:

```
put 'Problem was ', do given $! {
    when X::Str::Numeric { ... }
    default { ... }
    };
```

`Exception` types use different methods to give you more information. Each type defines a method that makes sense for its error. Look at each type to see which information it captures for you. The `X::Str::Numeric` Exception type knows at which position in the `Str` it discovered the problem:

```
put 'Problem was ', do given $! {
    when X::Str::Numeric  { "Char at {.pos} is not numeric" }
    when X::Numeric::Real { "Trying to convert to {.target}" }
    default { ... }
    };
```

The $! and `given` happen outside of the `try`. A CATCH Block inside the try can do the same thing. The `X::Str::Numeric` Exception shows up in $_:

```
try {
    CATCH {
        when X::Str::Numeric { put "ERROR: {.reason}" }
        default { put "Caught {.^name}" }
        }
    my $m = 'Hello';
    my $value = +$m;
    put "value is {$value.^name}";
    }

put 'Got to the end.';
```

The `X::Str::Numeric` Exception is thrown at the line `my $value = +$m;`, then it skips the rest of the Block. Handle this by outputting an error and continuing with the program:

```
ERROR: base-10 number must begin with valid digits or '.'
Got to the end.
```

Most of these objects inherit from `Exception` and have a `.message` method that provides more information. Catch those with `default` where you can output the name of the type:

```
try {
    CATCH {
        default { put "Caught {.^name} with ⌈{.message}⌋" }
        }
    my $m = 'Hello';
    my $value = +$m;
    put "value is {$value.^name}";
    }

put "Got to the end.";
```

Now the output has the same message that the unhandled error showed you:

```
Caught X::Str::Numeric with ⌈Cannot convert string to number:
base-10 number must begin with valid digits or '.' in '⏚Hello'
(indicated by ⏚)⌋
Got to the end.
```

Exercise 7.1

Divide a number by zero. What `Exception` type do you get?

Backtraces

The `Exception` contains a `Backtrace` object that documents the path of the error. This example has three levels of subroutine calls with some code at the end that throws an `Exception`:

```
sub top    { middle()   }
sub middle { bottom()   }
sub bottom { 5 + "Hello" }

top();
```

You don't handle the `Exception` in `middle`, you don't handle it in `top`, and finally, you don't handle it at the top level. The `Exception` complains and shows you its path through the code:

```
Cannot convert string to number: base-10 number must
begin with valid digits or '.' in '⏚Hello' (indicated by ⏚)
  in sub bottom at backtrace.p6 line 3
  in sub middle at backtrace.p6 line 2
  in sub top at backtrace.p6 line 1
  in block <unit> at backtrace.p6 line 5

Actually thrown at:
```

```
in sub bottom at backtrace.p6 line 3
in sub middle at backtrace.p6 line 2
in sub top at backtrace.p6 line 1
in block <unit> at backtrace.p6 line 5
```

Don't fret when you see long messages like this. Find the first level of the error and think about that. Work your way through the chain one level at a time. Often a simple fix makes it all go away.

You can handle the Exception anywhere in that chain. The simplest option might be to wrap the call to bottom in a try. With a single-line expression you can omit the Block around the code. In middle, you don't specify a CATCH so there's a default handler that discards the Exception:

```
sub top    { middle()    }
sub middle { try bottom() }
sub bottom { 137 + 'Hello' }

put top();
```

That program doesn't produce an error (or any output). That's probably not what you want. The middle layer can handle the case where you can't convert a Str to a number by returning the special number NaN (for "not a number"):

```
sub top    { middle() }
sub middle {
    try {
        CATCH { when X::Str::Numeric { return NaN } }
        bottom()
        }
    }

sub bottom { 137 + 'Hello' }

put top();
```

Change the code to make a different error that the CATCH in middle doesn't handle. Try to divide by zero and convert the result to a Str:

```
sub top    { middle() }
sub middle {
    try {
        CATCH { when X::Str::Numeric { return NaN } }
        bottom()
        }
    }

sub bottom { ( 137 / 0 ).Str  }

put top();
```

The CATCH in middle doesn't handle this new type of error, so the Exception interrupts the program at the call to top:

```
Attempt to divide 137 by zero using div
  in sub bottom at nan.p6 line 12
  in sub middle at nan.p6 line 8
  in sub top at nan.p6 line 4
  in block <unit> at nan.p6 line 14
```

Catch this one inside top. The Exception passes through middle, which has nothing to handle it. Since nothing handles that error it continues up the chain and ends up in top, which handles it by returning the special value Inf (for infinity):

```
sub top {
    try {
        CATCH {
            when X::Numeric::DivideByZero { return Inf }
            }
        middle()
        }
    }
sub middle {
    try {
        CATCH {
            when X::Str::Numeric { return NaN }
            }
        bottom()
        }
    }

sub bottom { ( 137 / 0 ).Str  }

put top();
```

Extend this process as far up the chain as you like. The next example changes the error by trying to call an undefined method on 137:

```
sub top {
    try {
        CATCH {
            when X::Numeric::DivideByZero { return Inf }
            }
        middle()
        }
    }

sub middle {
    try {
        CATCH {
            when X::Str::Numeric { return NaN }
            }
        bottom()
```

```
            }
        }

    sub bottom { 137.unknown-method }

    try {
        CATCH {
            default { put "Uncaught exception {.^name}" }
            }
        top();
        }
```

That's a new sort of error that you don't handle so far:

```
Uncaught exception X::Method::NotFound
```

Sometimes you don't care about unfound methods. If it's there you call it and if not you want to ignore it. There's special syntax for this. If you place a ? after the method call dot, you don't get an Exception if the method is not found:

```
    sub bottom { 137.?unknown-method }
```

Rethrowing Errors

It gets better. You can catch an exception but not handle it. Modify the CATCH in middle to intercept X::Method::NotFound and output a message, then .rethrow it:

```
    sub top     {
        try {
            CATCH {
                when X::Numeric::DivideByZero { return Inf }
                }
            middle()
            }
        }

    sub middle {
        try {
            CATCH {
                when X::Str::Numeric      { return NaN }
                when X::Method::NotFound {
                    put "What happened?";
                    .rethrow
                    }
                }
            bottom()
            }
        }

    sub bottom { 137.unknown-method  }

    try {
        CATCH {
```

```
            default { put "Uncaught exception {.^name}" }
        }
    top();
    }
```

You can see that middle was able to do its work but the Exception was ultimately handled by top:

```
What happened?
Uncaught exception X::Method::NotFound
```

Exercise 7.2

Implement a subroutine whose only code is . . . . That denotes code that you intend to fill in later. Call that from another subroutine and catch the Exception. What's the type you get? Can you output your own Backtrace?

Throwing Your Own Exceptions

Up to now you've seen exceptions that come from problems in the source code. Those are easy to see without complicating the examples. You can also throw your own Exceptions. The easiest way is to use die with a Str argument:

```
die 'Something went wrong!';
```

The die subroutine takes the Str as the message for an Exception of type X::AdHoc. That's a catch-all type for anything that doesn't have a more appropriate type.

Dying with a Str is the same as constructing an X::AdHoc. You can die with a particular Exception type by constructing it yourself:

```
die X::AdHoc.new( payload => "Something went wrong!" );
```

 You're actually creating a Pair here, but you won't see the => until Chapter 9 or named parameters until Chapter 11, so take this on faith.

The die is important. Merely constructing the Exception does not throw it:

```
# nothing happens
X::AdHoc.new( payload => "Something went wrong!" );
```

You can .throw it yourself if you like, though. This is the same as die:

```
X::AdHoc
    .new( payload => "Something went wrong!" )
    .throw;
```

You can also create Exceptions of other predefined types. The X::NYI type is for features not yet implemented:

```
X::NYI.new: features => 'Something I haven't done yet';
```

Exercise 7.3

Modify the previous exercise to die with a Str argument. What type do you catch? Further modify that to die with an X::StubCode object that you construct yourself.

Defining Your Own Exception Types

It's a bit early to create subclasses—you'll see how to do that in Chapter 12—but with a little faith you can do this right away. Base your class on Exception without doing anything else:

```
class X::MyException is Exception {}

sub my-own-error {
    die X::MyException.new: payload => 'I did this';
    }

my-own-error();
```

When you run the my-own-error subroutine it dies with the new error type that you've defined:

```
Died with X::MyException
```

Now that your new type exists you can use it in a CATCH (or smart match). Even without any sort of customization its name is enough to tell you what happened:

```
try {
CATCH {
    when X::MyException { put 'Caught a custom error' }
    }

my-own-error();
}
```

Chapter 12 will cover class creation and show you more about what you can do inside a class and how to reuse existing classes.

Failures

Failures are wrappers around unthrown Exceptions. They're passive until you try to use them later—hence "soft" exceptions. They don't interrupt your program until something tries to use them as a normal value. It's then that they throw their Exceptions.

As a Boolean a `Failure` is always `False`. You can "disarm" the `Failure` by checking it. That might be with an `if`, with a logical test, or by Booleanizing it with `.so` or `?`. All of those mark the `Failure` as handled and prevent it from implicitly throwing its Exception:

```
my $result = do-something();
if $result { ... }
my $did-it-work = ?$results;
```

A `Failure` is always undefined; maybe you want to set a default value if you encounter one:

```
my $other-result = $result // 0;
```

You can handle a `Failure` yourself without the `try`. The `.exception` method extracts that object so you can inspect it:

```
unless $result {
    given $result.exception {
        when    X::AdHoc { ... }
        default          { ... }
        }
    }
```

Create your own `Failures` by substituting `die` with `fail`:

```
fail "This ends up as an X::AdHoc";

fail My::X::SomeException.new(
    :payload( 'Something wonderful' ) );
```

When you use `fail` in a subroutine the `Failure` object becomes the return value. Instead of `die`-ing you should probably use `fail` so that the programmers who use your code can decide for themselves how to handle the problem.

Exercise 7.4

Create a subroutine that takes two arguments and returns their sum. If either argument is not a number return a `Failure` object saying so. How would you handle the `Failure`?

Warnings

Instead of `die`-ing you can use `warn` to give the same message without stopping the program or forcing the program to catch the Exception:

```
warn 'Something funny is going on!';
```

Warnings are a type of Exception and you can catch them. They aren't the same type of exception so they don't show up in a CATCH Block. They are control exceptions that you catch in a CONTROL Block:

```
try {
    CONTROL {
        put "Caught an exception, in the try";
        put .^name;
        }
    do-that-thing-you-do();
    }

sub do-that-thing-you-do {
    CONTROL {
        put "Caught an exception, in the sub";
        put .^name;
        }
    warn "This is a warning";
    }
```

If you don't care about the warnings (they are annoying after all) you can wrap the annoying code in a quietly Block:

```
quietly {
    do-that-thing-you-do();
    }
```

Exercise 7.5

Modify the previous exercise to warn for each argument that cannot be converted to a number. Once you've seen those warnings, further modify the program to ignore the warnings.

The Wisdom of Exceptions

Exceptions can be a contentious subject. Some people love them and some hate them. Since they are a feature, you need to know about them. I want to leave you with some words of caution before you get yourself in too much trouble. Your love/hate relationship with Exceptions will most likely fluctuate over your career.

Exceptions are a way of communicating information. By design this feature expects you to recognize the type of error and handle it appropriately. This implies that you can actually handle the error. If you encounter a situation that your program cannot correct, an Exception might not be the appropriate feature to use.

Even if your program could correct the error, many people don't expect most programmers to handle errors. Your Exception may be a nuisance that they catch and ignore. Think about that before you spend too much time crafting fine-grained Exception types that cover all situations.

As part of program flow Exceptions are really a fancy break mechanism. You're in one bit of code, then suddenly in another. Those cases should truly be exceptional and rare. Anything else that you expect to happen you should handle with normal program flow.

That's all I'll say about that. Perhaps you have a different opinion. That's fine. Read more about this on your own and judge your particular situation.

Summary

Exceptions are a feature of Perl 6, but it doesn't hit you over the head with them. They can be soft failures until they would actually cause a problem.

Don't become overwhelmed by the different types of Exceptions your program may report. You'll continue to see these throughout the rest of the book. Use them appropriately (whatever definition you choose) and effectively to note problems in your program. Try to detect those as early as you can.

## CHAPTER 8

Files and Directories, Input and Output

Reading and writing text are the bread and butter of many of the programs you'll want to write. You'll store data in files and retrieve that data later. This chapter is all about the features you need to do that. Along the way you'll see how to deal with file paths, move files around, and work with directories. Most of this is done with the same syntax that you've already seen, but now with different types of objects.

Many of the tasks in this chapter can fail for reasons that exist outside of your program. If you expected to work in a different directory or a certain file to exist, you might not want to continue if those conditions aren't true. That's just the reality of a program that deals with external resources.

File Paths

An `IO::Path` object represents a file path. It knows how to put together and take apart paths based on your filesystem's rules. It doesn't matter if that path is to a file that actually exists, as long as the form of the path obeys those rules. You'll see how to deal with missing files in a moment. For now, call `.IO` on any `Str` to turn it into an `IO::Path` object:

```
my $unix-path = '/home'.IO;
my $windows-path = 'C:/Users'.IO;
```

To build a deeper path, use `.add`. You can more than one level at a time. `.add` doesn't change the original object; it gives you a new object:

```
my $home-directory = $unix-path.add: 'hamadryas';
my $file = $unix-path.add: 'hamadryas/file.txt';
```

Assign back to your original object if you want to build the path there:

```
$unix-path = $unix-path.add: 'hamadryas/file.txt';
```

The binary assignment form may be more useful:

```
$unix-path .= add: 'hamadryas/file.txt';
```

`.basename` and `.parent` methods break apart the path:

```
my $home = '/home'.IO;
my $user = 'hamadryas';     # Str or IO::File will work
my $file = 'file.txt'.IO;

my $path = $home.add( $user ).add( $file );

put 'Basename: ', $path.basename;  # Basename: file.txt
put 'Dirname: ',  $path.parent;    # Dirname: /home/hamadryas
```

.basename returns a Str, not another IO::Path. You can use .IO again if you need that.

With `.parent` you decide how many levels you want to go up:

```
my $home = '/home'.IO;
my $user = 'hamadryas';
my $file = 'file.txt'.IO;

my $path = $home.add( $user ).add( $file );

put $path;                      # /home/hamadryas/file.txt
put 'One up:', $path.parent;    # One up: /home/hamadryas
put 'Two up: ', $path.parent(2); # Two up: /home
```

You can ask questions to find out if you have an absolute or relative path:

```
my $home = '/home'.IO;
my $user = 'hamadryas';
my $file = 'file.txt'.IO;

for $home, $file {
    put "$_ is ", .is-absolute ?? 'absolute' !! 'relative';
    # put "$_ is ", .is-relative ?? 'relative' !! 'absolute';
    }
```

Make a relative path an absolute one. With no argument `.absolute` uses the current working directory when you created the IO::Path object. Give it an argument if you want some other base directory. Either way you get a Str instead of another IO::Path object. The `.absolute` method doesn't care if that path actually exists:

```
my $file = 'file.txt'.IO;
put $file.absolute;             # /home/hamadryas/file.txt
put $file.absolute( '/etc' );  # /etc/file.txt
put $file.absolute( '/etc/../etc' ); # /etc/../etc/file.txt
```

Calling `.resolve` checks the filesystem. It figures out `.` and `..` and translates symbolic links to their targets. Notice that */etc/..* is replaced with */private* since */etc* is a symbolic link to */private/etc* on macOS:

```
my $file = 'file.txt'.IO;
put $file.absolute( '/etc/..' ); # /etc/../file.txt
put $file.absolute( '/etc/..' ).IO.resolve; # /private/file.txt
```

You can insist that the file exist with the `:completely` adverb. If any part (other than the last part) of the path does not exist or can't resolve you get an error:

```
my $file = 'file.txt'.IO;

{
CATCH {
    default { put "Caught {.^name}" }   # Caught X::IO::Resolve
    }
put $file.absolute( '/homer/..' ).IO.resolve: :completely; # fails
}
```

File Test Operators

A file test operator answers a question about a file path. Most of them return `True` or `False`. Start with a `Str` and call the `.IO` method to create the `IO::Path` object. Use `.e` to check if the file exists (Table 8-1 shows other file tests):

```
my $file = '/some/path';

unless $file.IO.e {
    put "The file <$file> does not exist!";
    }
```

Why `.e`? It comes from the Unix *test* program that used command-line switches (such as `-e`) to answer a question about a path. Those same letters become the names of methods. Table 8-1 shows the file tests. Most of these are the same as in similar languages, although a few multiletter ones combine several tests into one.

Table 8-1. File test methods

Method	The question it answers
e	Exists
d	Is a directory
f	Is a plain file
s	Size in bytes
l	Is a symbolic link
r	Is readable by the current user
w	Is writable by the current user
rw	Is readable and writable by the current user

Method	The question it answers
x	Is executable by the current user
rwx	Is readable, writable, and executable by the current user
z	Exists with zero size

Almost all of the file tests return a Boolean value. The one odd test is .s, which asks for the file size in bytes. That's not a Boolean, so how would it note a problem such as a missing file? It might return 0 in that case, because a file can have nothing in it (hence the .z method to ask if it exists with zero size). .s returns a Failure instead of False if there's a problem:

```
my $file = 'not-there';
given $file.IO {
    CATCH {
        # $_ in here is the exception
        when X::IO::NotAFile
            { put "$file is not a plain file" }
        when X::IO::DoesNotExist
            { put "$file does not exist"      }
    }
    put "Size is { .s }";
}
```

You might check that the file exists and is a plain file before you try to get its size (although .f implies .e), but this way is probably less safe since the file might disappear between the time you enter the Block and when you try to get the file size:

```
my $file = 'not-there';
given $file.IO {
    when .e && .f { put "Size is { .s }"  }
    when .e       { put "Not a plain file" }
    default       { put "Does not exist"   }
}
```

This isn't the only syntax for file tests, though. There are also the adverbial versions. You can smart match against the tests that you want. This example uses a Junction to combine tests, even though you won't see those until Chapter 14:

```
if $file.IO ~~ :e & :f {  # Junction!
    put "Size is { .s }"
}
```

Exercise 8.1

Create a program that takes a list of files from the command-line arguments and reports if they are readable, writable, or executable by the current user. What would you do if a file doesn't exist?

File Metadata

Files record more than just their contents. They retain extra information about themselves; this is the *metadata*. The `.mode` method returns the POSIX permissions for a file (if your filesystem supports such a thing). This is a single integer that represents the settings for the user, group, and everyone else:

```
my $file = '/etc/hosts';
my $mode = $file.IO.mode;
put $mode.fmt: '%04o';   # 0644
```

 Some POSIX- or Unix-specific ideas won't work on Windows. As I write, this there aren't Windows-specific modules to fill in those gaps.

Each set of permissions takes three bits: one for each read, write, and execute. You use bit operators (you haven't seen those yet) to extract the individual permissions from the single number.

The bitwise AND operator, +&, isolates the set using a bitmask (such as 0o700 in the following example). The bitwise right shift operator, +>, extracts the right numbers:

```
my $file = '/etc/hosts';
my $mode = $file.IO.mode;
put $mode.fmt: '%04o';   # 0644

my $user  = ( $mode +& 0o700 ) +> 6;
my $group = ( $mode +& 0o070 ) +> 3;
my $all   = ( $mode +& 0o007 );
```

Inside each permission set you can use another mask to isolate the bit you want. In this part you'll end up with `True` or `False`:

```
put qq:to/END/;
mode: { $mode.fmt: '%04o' }
  user: $user
    read:    { ($user +& 0b100).so }
    write:   { ($user +& 0b010).so }
    execute: { ($user +& 0b001).so }
  group: { $group }
  all:   { $all }
END
```

You can change these permissions with the `chmod` subroutine. Give it the same number. It's probably easiest to represent it as a decimal number:

```
chmod $file.IO.chmod: 0o755;
```

File times

The `.modified`, `.accessed`, and `.changed` methods return `Instant` objects representing the modification, access, and inode change times of the file (if your system supports those). You can use the `.DateTime` method to turn the `Instant` into a human-readable date:

```
my $file = '/home/hamadryas/.bash_profile';

given $file.IO {
    if .e {
        put qq:to/HERE/
        Name:     $_
            Modified: { .modified.DateTime }
            Accessed: { .accessed.DateTime }
            Changed:  { .changed.DateTime  }
            Mode:     { .mode          }
        HERE
    }
}
```

This gives something like this:

```
Name:     /home/hamadryas/.bash_profile
    Modified: 2018-08-15T01:19:09Z
    Accessed: 2018-08-16T10:07:00Z
    Changed:  2018-08-15T01:19:09Z
    Mode:     0664
```

Linking and Unlinking Files

A filename is a label for some data that you've stored somewhere. It's important to remember that the name is not the data. Likewise, the metaphor of a directory or folder is just that. It doesn't really "contain" files. It knows the list of filenames it should remember. Keeping that in mind should make the next parts easier to grasp.

The name is a *link* to data, and the same data can have multiple links to it. As long as there are links you can get to that data. This doesn't mean that the data disappears when it has no links. Those parts of storage are merely available for something else. This is why you can sometimes recover data. Your particular filesystem might do things differently, but that's the basic idea.

Typically your ability to remove the link depends on the directory permissions and not the file permissions. You are really removing the file from the list of files the directory comprises.

To get rid of a file, you use `.unlink` to remove the link to it. You aren't removing the data; that's why it's not called `.delete` or something similar. Other links to the same data may still be there. If `.unlink` could remove the file it returns `True`. It fails with `X::IO::Unlink`:

```
my $file = '/etc/hosts'.IO;

try {
CATCH {
    when X::IO::Unlink { put .message }
    }
$file.unlink;
}
```

You can get rid of several files at the same time with the subroutine form. It returns the names of the files that you'll have to restore from backups (also known as the files successfully unlinked):

```
my @unlinked-files = unlink @files;
```

A `Set` difference is useful here, although you won't see `Set`s until Chapter 14. Note that you are able to unlink files that don't exist, and they won't show up in `@error-files`:

```
my @error-files = @files.Set (-) @unlinked-files.Set;
```

You can get rid of the original filename but the data will still be there. The data behind the file sticks around until all the links are gone. None of this works to remove directories, but you'll see how to do that in a moment.

Create a new label for some data with `.link`. The path must be on the same disk or partition as the data. If that doesn't work it fails with `X::IO::Link`:

```
my $file = '/Users/hamadryas/test.txt'.IO;

{
CATCH {
    when X::IO::Unlink { ... }
    when X::IO::Link { ... }
    }

$file.link: '/Users/hamadryas/test2.txt';
$file.unlink;
}
```

There's another sort of link, called a *symbolic link* ("symlink" for short). It's not an actual link; it's a file that points to another filename (the "target"). When the filesystem encounters a symlink it uses the target path instead.

The target is the final filename. The symlink you create points to that. Call `.symlink` on the target to create the file that points to it:

```
    {
CATCH {
    when X::IO::Symlink { ... }
    }

$target.symlink: '/opt/different/disk/test.txt';
}
```

Renaming and Copying Files

To change the name of a file, use .rename. Like .link, this only works on the same disk or partition. It changes the label without moving data around. If it can't do that it fails with X::IO::Rename:

```
my $file = '/Users/hamadryas/test.txt'.IO;

{
CATCH {
    when X::IO::Rename { put .message }
    }
$file.rename: '/home/hamadryas/other-dir/new-name.txt';
}
```

You can .copy the data to a different device or partition. This physically puts the data in a new place on the disk. The original data and its links stay there and the copied data has its own link. After that the two are not connected and you have two separate copies of the data. If it doesn't work it fails with X::IO::Copy:

```
my $file = '/Users/hamadryas/test.txt'.IO;

{
CATCH {
    when X::IO::Copy { put .message }
    }
$file.copy: '/opt/new-name.txt';
}
```

Using .move first copies the data then removes the original. The .copy will replace the new file if it already exists (and it has the right permissions):

```
my $file = '/Users/hamadryas/test.txt'.IO;

{
CATCH {
    when X::IO::Move { put .message }
    }
$file.copy: '/opt/new-name.txt';
}
```

Use the :create-only adverb to prevent that:

```
$file.copy: '/opt/new-name.txt', :create-only;
```

The .move method combines a .copy and an .unlink:

```
$file.move: '/opt/new-name.txt';
```

After copying the file .move might not be able to remove the original. You might want to check that permission before you start, but there's no guarantee that the permissions won't change.

Manipulating Directories

When your program starts it has some notion of its *current working directory*. That's stored in the special variable $*CWD. When you deal with relative file paths your program looks in the current directory to find them:

```
put "Current working directory is $*CWD";
```

To change that directory, use chdir. Give it an absolute path to change to exactly that directory:

```
chdir( '/some/other/path' );
```

Give it a relative path to change into a subdirectory of the current working directory:

```
chdir( 'a/relative/path' );
```

If this fails it returns a Failure with an X::IO::Chdir Exception:

```
unless my $dir = chdir $subdir {
    ... # handle the error
    }
```

chdir with no argument gives you an error. You may have expected that to go to your home directory. If you want that, use $*HOME as the argument. That's the special variable that stores your home directory:

```
chdir( $*HOME );
```

How $*HOME is set depends on your particular system. On something Unix-like, that's probably the HOME environment variable. On Windows, it's probably HOMEPATH.

Exercise 8.2

Output your home directory path. Create a new path to an existing subdirectory and change into that directory. Output the value of the current working directory. What happens if the subdirectory doesn't exist?

Sometimes you only need to change the directory for a short part of your program and after that you'd like to be back where you started. The indir subroutine takes a directory and a code block and runs that code as if that were the current working directory. It doesn't actually mess with $*CWD:

```
my $result = indir $dir, { ... };
unless $result {
    ... # handle the error
    }
```

If everything works out `indir` returns the result of the block, although that might be a `False` value or even a `Failure`. If `indir` can't change to the directory it returns a `Failure`. Be careful which situation you are handling!

Directory Listings

`dir` gets a `Seq` of the files in a directory as `IO::Path` objects. It includes hidden files (but not the . and .. virtual files). With no argument it uses the current directory:

```
my @files = dir();
my $files = dir();
```

With an argument it gets a `Seq` of the files in the specified directory:

```
my @files = dir( '/etc' );

for dir( '/etc' ) -> $file {
    put $file;
    }
```

The elements in the `Seq` have that path component included. A relative directory argument returns relative paths. Those paths probably won't be valid if you change the working directory after you create the `Seq`:

```
say dir( '/etc' ); # ("/etc/emond.d".IO ...)
say dir( 'lib' ); # ("lib/perl6".IO ...)
```

`dir` returns a `Failure` if it runs into a problem, such as a directory that does not exist.

There's another nice feature of `dir`: it knows what entries to skip. There's an optional second parameter that can test the entries to decide if they should be part of the result. By default the test is a `Junction` (Chapter 14) that excludes the . and .. virtual directories:

```
say dir( 'lib', test => none( <. ..> ) );
```

Exercise 8.3

Output a list of all the files in another directory. Show them one per line and number each line. Can you sort the file list? If you don't have a directory you'd like to explore, try */etc* on Unix-like systems or *C:\rakudo* on Windows.

Exercise 8.4

Create a program that takes a directory name and lists all the files in it. Descend into subdirectories and list their files. You'll be able to use this program later, in Chapter 19.

Creating Directories

You can create your own directories with `mkdir`. It can create multiple levels of subdirectories for you at once if that's what you ask for. If `mkdir` can't create the directory it throws an `X::IO::Mkdir` Exception:

```
try {
    CATCH {
        when X::IO::Mkdir { put "Exception is {.message}" }
        }
    my $subdir = 'Butterflies'.IO.add: 'Hamadryas';
    mkdir $subdir;
    }
```

The optional second argument is the Unix-style octal mode (Windows ignores this argument). Unix permissions are easiest to read as octal numbers:

```
mkdir $subdir, 0o755;
```

You can also start with a `Str` and turn it into an `IO::Path` object with `.IO`, then call `.mkdir` on all that. You can leave off the mode or not:

```
$subdir.IO.mkdir;
$subdir.IO.mkdir: 0o755;
```

Exercise 8.5

Write a program to create a subdirectory that you specify on the command line. What happens when you specify a full path as the argument? What if the directory already exists?

Removing Directories

There are two ways to remove a directory, but you'll probably only want to use one of them. Before you start playing with these you might consider working in a snapshot of a virtual machine or in a special account where you can't delete anything important. Be careful!

The first, `rmdir`, removes one or more directories as long as they are empty (no files or subdirectories):

```
my @directories-removed = rmdir @dirs;
```

With the method form you can remove one at a time. If it fails it throws an
X::IO::Rmdir Exception:

```
try {
    CATCH {
        when X::IO::Rmdir { ... }
        }
    $directory.IO.rmdir;
    }
```

That's a bit inconvenient. Often you want to remove a directory and everything that it
contains. The rmtree subroutine from File::Directory::Tree is useful for that:

```
use File::Directory::Tree;
my $result = try rmtree $directory;
```

Formatted Output

You can format values before you output them or interpolate them into Strs. The
options follow what you may have already seen in other languages so you only get a
taste of them here.

Give the template Str to .fmt to describe how the value should appear. The template
uses *directives*; these start with % and have characters to describe the format. Here is
the same number formatted in hexadecimal (%x), octal (%o), and binary (%b):

```
$_ = 108;

put .fmt: '%x';    # 6c
put .fmt: '%X';    # 6C (uppercase!)
put .fmt: '%o';    # 154
put .fmt: '%b';    # 1101100
```

Some directives have additional options that show up as characters between the % and
the letter. A number specifies the minimum width of the column (it may overflow
though). A leading zero pads unused columns with zeros. You can see this when you
interpolate the Str; the characters around the formatted output make it clear
what .fmt created:

```
put "$_ is ={.fmt: '%b'}=";     # 108 is =1101100=
put "$_ is ={.fmt: '%8b'}=";    # 108 is = 1101100=
put "$_ is ={.fmt: '%08b'}=";   # 108 is =01101100=
```

The template text can have other characters. If those aren't part of a directive they are
literal characters. This turns the previous example inside out so all the characters are
in the template:

```
put .fmt: "$_ is =%08b=";  # 108 is =01101100=
```

If you want a literal % sign escape it with another %. The `%f` directive formats a floating-point number and is handy for percentages. You can specify a total width (including the decimal point) and the number of decimal places:

```
my $n = 1;
my $d = 7;
put (100*$n/$d).fmt: "$n/$d is %5.2f%%";  # 1/7 is 14.29%
```

Leaving off the total width still works and allows you to specify just the number of decimal places. This rounds the final displayed decimal digit:

```
put (100*$n/$d).fmt: "$n/$d is %.2f%%";  # 1/7 is 14.29%
```

Calling `.fmt` on a `Positional` formats each element according to the template, joins them with a space, and gives you a single `Str`:

```
put ( 222, 173, 190, 239 ).fmt: '%02x';  # de ad be ef
```

A second argument to `.fmt` changes the separator:

```
put ( 222, 173, 190, 239 ).fmt: '%02x', '';  # deadbeef
```

`sprintf` can do the same job with a bit more control. It's a routine that takes the same template as its first argument, then a list of values. Each value fills in one directive in order. You don't have to output the result:

```
my $string = sprintf( '%2d %s', $line-number, $line );
```

`printf` does the same thing and directly outputs the result to standard output (without adding a newline):

```
printf '%2d %s', $line-number, $line;
```

Table 8-2 lists some of the available `sprintf` directives.

Table 8-2. Selected sprintf directives

Directive	Description
%d	A signed integer in decimal
%u	An unsigned integer in decimal
%o	An unsigned integer in octal
%x	An unsigned integer in hexadecimal (lowercase)
%X	An unsigned integer in hexadecimal (uppercase)
%b	An unsigned integer in binary
%f	A floating-point number
%s	A text value

Common Formatting Tasks

Round numbers with `%f`. Specify the width of the entire template and the number of decimal places. The decimal point and following digits count as part of the width:

```
put (2/3).fmt: '%4.2f';  # 0.67;
```

The total width doesn't limit the columns, though. It will be at least that number of columns but could be more:

```
put (2/3).fmt: '%4.5f';  # 0.66667;
```

If you don't care about the width you can leave it off. This merely rounds the value to the number of decimal places you specified:

```
put (2/3).fmt: '%.3f';  # 0.667;
```

A # after the % adds the number system prefix, but not the one that Perl 6 uses. It's the prefix that the rest of the universe uses; the octal number gets a leading zero:

```
put 108.fmt: '%#x'; # 0x6c
put 108.fmt: '%#o'; # 0154
```

`%s` formats a text value. With a width it pushes the value to the right and pads it with spaces if necessary. A - in front of the width pushes it to the left:

```
put 'Hamadryas'.fmt: '|%s|';     # |Hamadryas|
put 'Hamadryas'.fmt: '|%15s|';   # |      Hamadryas|
put 'Hamadryas'.fmt: '|%-15s|'; # |Hamadryas      |
```

Use `sprintf` to create columnar output. The width makes everything line up:

```
my $line = sprintf '%02d %-20s %5d %5d %5d', @values;
```

The Standard Filehandles

A *filehandle* is a connection between your program and a file. You get three of these for free. Two are for output and one is for input. Standard output is the one you've been using since the very beginning of this book. It's the default filehandle for your output. You've also used standard error, because that's the filehandle for warnings and errors. Standard input connects your program to the data someone is trying to give it.

You may find it useful to review the basic filehandles before you move on to the general process of reading and writing arbitrary files. If you already know about these things don't feel bad about skipping this section.

Standard Output

Standard output is the default filehandle for most output methods. When you use any of these in their routine form you are using standard output:

```
put $up-the-dishes;
say $some-stuff;
print $some-stuff;
printf $template, $thing1, $thing2;
```

Calling methods on `$*OUT` makes that explicit. That's the special variable that holds the default filehandle:

```
$*OUT.put: $up-the-dishes;
$*OUT.say: $some-stuff;
$*OUT.print: $some-stuff;
$*OUT.printf: $template, $thing1, $thing2;
```

You've probably used redirection on the command line at some point. A > sends the standard output of your program to a file (or somewhere else):

```
% perl6 program.p6 > output.txt
```

If you want to run your program but don't care to see the output you can send it to the null device. The output goes nowhere and disappears. That's slightly different for Unix systems and Windows:

```
% perl6 program.p6 > /dev/null
C:\ perl6 program.p6 > NUL
```

Exercise 8.9

Create a program that writes something to standard output. Run the program and redirect the output to a file. Run it again and redirect the output to the null device.

Standard Error

Standard error is another avenue for output. Programs typically use standard error for warnings and other messages when they don't want to infect normal output. You can get the warning without messing up your nicely formatted output.

`warn` outputs its message to standard error and your program continues. As its name suggests, it's designed for warnings when you run into a situation that you can anticipate and you think someone should know about:

```
warn 'You need to use a number between 0 and 255';
```

`fail` and `die` are similar. They send their messages to standard error, but they can also stop your program unless you catch or handle them.

`note` is like `say`; it calls `.gist` on its argument and outputs the result to standard error. This could be useful for debugging output:

```
note $some-object;
```

Often this sort of output is enabled by some command-line switch or other setting:

```
note $some-object if $debugging > 0;
```

The output methods work on `$*ERR`—that holds the default error filehandle:

```
$*ERR.put: 'This is a warning message';
```

When you work in a terminal you normally see both standard output and standard error together (or "merged"). Redirect the error output with 2>; that takes file descriptor number 2 (standard error) and sends it to somewhere that is not the terminal. If you don't understand any of that just follow the example:

```
% perl6 program.p6 2> error_output.txt
C:\ perl6 program.p6 2> error_output.txt

% perl6 program.p6 2> /dev/null
C:\ perl6 program.p6 2> NUL
```

Redirect file descriptor 2 to file descriptor 1 to merge standard output and error. Again, you can follow the example without delving into the plumbing:

```
% perl6 program.p6 2>&1 /dev/null
```

Exercise 8.10

Create a program that outputs something to standard output and to standard error. Run it and redirect standard output to a file. Run it again but redirect standard error to the null device.

Standard Input

When you use `lines()` without command-line arguments it reads from standard input. The data flows through into your program:

```
for lines() {
    put ++$, ': ', $_;
    }
```

Your program waits for you to type something and outputs it back to you:

```
% perl6 no-args.p6
Hello Perl 6
0: Hello Perl 6
this is the second line
1: this is the second line
```

If you only want standard input you can explicitly use `$*IN`. Call `.lines` as follows:

```
for $*IN.lines() {
    put ++$, ': ', $_;
    }
```

Standard input can also come from another program. You can pipe the output of one program into the input of another one:

```
% perl6 out-err.p6 | perl6 no-args.p6
```

Exercise 8.11

Create two programs. The first one should output all the lines from the command-line files that contain the first argument. Pipe that output to the second program, which reads its input and outputs it as all uppercase. Pipe the output from the first program into the second.

Reading Input

You've already seen a few ways to get data into your program. The `prompt` routine outputs a message and waits for a single line of input:

```
my $answer = prompt( 'Enter some stuff> ' );
```

Read an entire file in one shot with `slurp`. It works as a method or a routine:

```
my $entire-file = $filename.IO.slurp;
my $entire-file = slurp $filename;
```

If you can't read the file you'll get a `Failure`. Always check that you were able to do what you wanted:

```
unless my $entire-file = slurp $filename.IO.slurp {
    ... # handle error
    }
```

Reading Lines

In Chapter 6 you saw how to use lines() to read from the filenames you specify on the command line. Do this yourself by going through @*ARGS and calling lines on the individual files. You can filter out the files that don't exist or have other problems (something lines() doesn't do):

```
for @*ARGS {
    put '=' x 20, ' ', $_;

    # maybe more error checking here
    unless .IO.e { put 'Does not exist'; next }

    for .IO.lines() {
        put "$_:", ++$, ' ', $_;
        }
    }
```

That's a bit too much work. lines() reads from the $*ARGFILES filehandle. That's the same as using it explicitly:

```
for $*ARGFILES.lines() {
    put ++$, ': ', $_;
    }
```

Extract the current filename with $*ARGFILES.path:

```
for $*ARGFILES.lines() {
    put "{$*ARGFILES.path}:", ++$, ' ', $_;
    }
```

This doesn't handle starting the line numbering a fresh for each file, but there's a trick for that: $*ARGFILES knows when it's switching files and lets you run some code when that happens. Give .on-switch a block of code to run when the file changes. Use that to reset a persistent counter:

```
for lines() {
    state $lines = 1;
    FIRST { $*ARGFILES.on-switch = { $lines = 1 } }

    put "{$*ARGFILES.path}:{$lines++} $_";
    }
```

As I write this, if lines encounters a file it can't read it throws an Exception that you can't resume. I'll ignore that here because I expect the situation to change soon.

Exercise 8.12

Create a program to output all the lines of the files you specify on the command line. Output a file banner showing its name before you output each file's lines. What happens after you finish the last file?

Reading a File

Both `slurp` and `lines` handle the details implicitly. `open` lets you do it in whatever manner you like. It returns a filehandle that you use to get the data from the file. If there's a problem `open` returns a `Failure`:

```
my $fh = open 'not-there';
unless $fh {
    put "Error: { $fh.exception }";
    exit;
    }

for $fh.lines() { .put }
```

You might like the method form instead:

```
my $fh = $filename.IO.open;
```

You can change the encoding, line ending processing, and the particular line ending. The `:enc` adverb sets the input encoding:

```
my $fh = open 'not-there', :enc('latin1');
```

To keep the line endings instead of autochomping them, use `:chomp`:

```
my $fh = open 'not-there', :chomp(False);
```

The line ending is set with `:nl-in` and can be multiple `Str`s where any will work:

```
my $fh = open 'not-there', :nl-in( "\f" );
my $fh = open 'not-there', :nl-in( [ "\f", "\v" ] );
```

If you want no line ending (like with `slurp`), an empty `Str` or `False` works:

```
my $fh = open 'not-there', :nl-in( '' );
my $fh = open 'not-there', :nl-in( False );
```

You can read a single line. Tell `.lines` how many you want:

```
my $next-line = $fh.lines: 1;
```

`.lines` is lazy. That didn't actually read a line. It's not until you try to use `$next-line` that it will do that. If you want to make it happen right away you can make it eager:

```
my $next-line = $fh.lines(1).eager;
```

If you want all of the lines you can still `.slurp` from the filehandle:

```
my $rest-of-data = $fh.slurp;
```

Close the filehandle when you are done with it. The program will do this for you automatically at some point, but you don't want these things to hang around potentially to the end of the program:

```
$fh.close;
```

Exercise 8.13

Open each file you specify on the command line. Output its first line and last line. Between those two report the number of lines that you left out.

Writing Output

The easiest way to write a file is with `spurt`. Give it a filename and some data and it does the rest for you:

```
spurt $path, $data;
```

If the file already exists it overwrites anything that is already there. To add to what's already there use the `:append` adverb:

```
spurt $path, $data, :append;
```

You can output the data only when the file doesn't yet exist by specifying `:exclusive`. If the file is already there this will fail:

```
spurt $path, $data, :exclusive;
```

When `spurt` works it returns `True`. If there's a problem it returns a `Failure`:

```
unless spurt $path, $data {
    ... # handle error
    }
```

Opening a File for Writing

Using `spurt` might be convenient, but every time you use it you're really opening a file, writing to it, and closing it. If you want to keep adding to the file you can open the file yourself and keep it open until you are done:

```
unless my $fh = open $path, :w {
    ...;
    }

$fh.print: $data;
$fh.print: $more-data;
```

Any of the output methods work on the filehandle:

```
$fh.put: $data;
$fh.say: $data;
```

Call `.close` when you are done with the file. This ensures that any data the lower levels may have been buffering makes it into the file:

```
$fh.close;
```

If you don't like the default line separator you can specify your own. The form feed, \f, is handy as a "line" separator when you have items that have multiple lines that you want to keep together as a single record:

```
unless my $fh = open $path, :w, :nl-out("\f") {
    ...;  # handle the error
    }

$fh.print: ...;
```

Using `try` might be cleaner here:

```
my $fh = try open $path, :w, :exclusive, :enc('latin1'), :nl-out("\f");
if $! {
    ... # handle the error
    }
```

Exercise 8.14

Create a program that writes to a file all the prime numbers between the two numbers you specify on the command line. What should you do if the file already exists?

Binary Files

Binary files aren't character based. Images, movies, and so on are examples. You don't want your file reader to decode these into Perl's internal character format; you want the raw data just as it is. Use the `:bin` adverb with `slurp` for this. Instead of returning a `Str` it returns a `Buf`. You can process that `Buf` like any other `Positional`:

```
my $buffer = slurp $filename, :bin;  # Buf object
for @$buffer { ... }
```

Open a file with the same `:bin` adverb to get its raw contents:

```
unless my $fh = open $path, :bin {
    ... # handle the error
    }
```

Moving Around

Tell .read how many octets you want to read and it returns a Buf where each element is a whole number between 0 and 255 (the unsigned 8-bit range):

```
my Buf $buffer = $fh->read( $count );
```

A Buf is a sort of Positional. Each octet is one element of the buffer and you can get an octet by its position:

```
my $third_byte = $buffer[2];
```

The next time you call .read you get the octets starting where you left off in the file. Move to a different position with .seek. Specifying SeekFromCurrent moves from the position where you left off:

```
my $relative_position = 137;
$fh.seek( $relative_position, SeekFromCurrent );
```

Move backward with a negative value:

```
my $negative_position = -137;
$fh.seek( $negative_position, SeekFromCurrent );
```

If you specify SeekFromBeginning it counts from the beginning of the file and moves to the absolute position you specify:

```
my $absolute_position = 1370;
$fh.seek( $absolute_position, SeekFromBeginning );
```

Exercise 8.15

Write a little hex dump program. Read a raw file 16 octets at a time. Print the hexadecimal values for each of those octets, with spaces between them and a newline at the end. Each line should have a form like this:

```
20 50 65 72 6c 20 36 2c 20 4d 6f 61 72 56 4d 20
```

Writing Binary Files

Going the other way, you can write octets to a file. Open the file for writing with the same :bin adverb:

```
unless my $fh = open $path, :w, :bin {
    ...;
    }
```

Use .write and give it a Buf object. Each element must be a whole number between 0 and 255:

```
my $buf = Buf.new: 82, 97, 107, 117, 100, 111, 10;
$fh.write: $buf;
```

It might be easier to note them in hexadecimal:

```
my $buf = Buf.new: <52 61 6b 75 64 6f 0a>.map: *.parse-base: 16;
```

Exercise 8.16

Implement the program to write that Buf to the file. What ends up in the file?

Summary

The features you saw in this chapter are likely to be the heart of many useful programs you write. You can put data in files and retrieve that data later. You can create directories, move files into those directories, or get rid of them all. Most of the operations are simple and straightforward; you'll easily find the method you need once you know the right object. However, most of these thingys interact with the outside world and complain forcefully when things don't work out. Don't ignore those complaints!

## CHAPTER 9

Associatives

An `Associative` indexes to a value with an arbitrary name called the *key*. `Associatives` are unordered because the keys have no relative order. Other languages have similar data types they call associative arrays, dictionaries, hashes, maps, or something similar that do the same thing. There are several types of specialized associative data structures, and you've already been using some of them.

Pairs

A `Pair` has a single key and a value. You've already used these in their adverbial form, although you didn't know they were `Pairs`. Create a `Pair` through general object construction with the name and value as arguments:

```
my $pair = Pair.new: 'Genus', 'Hamadryas';
```

The => is the `Pair` constructor. You don't have to quote the lefthand side because the => does that for you as long as it looks like a term:

```
my $pair = Genus => 'Hamadryas';  # this works
my $nope = 🐛  => 'Hamadryas';  # this doesn't
```

Any value can be a `Pair` value. Here's a value that's a `List`:

```
my $pair = Pair.new: 'Colors', <blue black grey>;
```

Combining `.new` and => probably doesn't do what you want. Passing it a single `Pair` means that you are missing its value. The `.new` method thinks that the `Pair` is the key and you forgot the value:

```
my $pair = Pair.new: 'Genus' => 'Hamadryas';  # WRONG!
```

Adverbs

A more common syntax is the adverbial form that you have already seen with Q quoting. Start with a colon, add the unquoted name, and specify the value inside <> for allomorphic quoting or inside () where you quote the value yourself:

```
my $pair = :Genus<Hamadryas>;
my $pair = :Genus('Hamadryas');

my $genus = 'Hamadryas';
my $pair  = :Genus($genus);
```

Without an explicit value an adverb has the value True:

```
my $pair = :name;  #  name => True
```

Using an adverb with Q with no value means you turn on that feature (everything else is False by default):

```
Q :double /The name is $butterfly/;
```

If you'd like it to be False instead, put a ! in front of the key name:

```
my $pair = :!name; #  name => False
```

You can create a Pair from a scalar variable. The identifier becomes the key and the value is the variable's value. You'll see more of this coming up:

```
my $Genus = 'Hamadryas';
my $pair = :$Genus;    # same as 'Genus' => 'Hamadryas';
```

There's also a tricky syntax that reverses a numeric value and alpha-headed text key. This is a bit prettier for adverbs representing positions, such as 1st, 2nd, 3rd, and so on:

```
my $pair = :2nd; # same as nd => 2
```

The .key and .value methods extract those parts of the Pair:

```
put "{$p.key} => {$pair.value}\n";
```

The .kv method returns both as a Seq:

```
put join ' => ', $pair.kv;
```

Exercise 9.1

Develop a subroutine that creates Pairs for the numbers from 0 to 10. Given the argument 1, it returns the Pair :1st. Given 2, it returns :2nd. Given 3, it returns :3rd. For all other numbers, it uses th as the suffix.

Modifying a Pair

You can't change the key of a Pair. You'd have to make a new Pair to get a different key:

```
my $pair = 'Genus' => 'Hamadryas';
$pair.key = 'Species';  # Nope!
```

If the Pair value is a container you can change the value inside the container, but if you constructed it with a literal Str there's no container and you can't change the value:

```
my $pair = 'Genus' => 'Hamadryas';
$pair.value = 'Papillo'; # Nope!
```

You can assign to it if that value came from a variable storing a container:

```
my $name = 'Hamadryas';
my $pair = 'Genus' => $name;
$pair.value = 'Papillo';
```

Remember that not all variables are mutable. You may have bound to a value:

```
my $name := 'Hamadryas';  # bound directly to value, no container
my $pair = 'Genus' => $name;
$pair.value = 'Papillo';  # Nope! Still a fixed value
```

To ensure that you get a container, assign the value to an anonymous scalar. You don't create a new named variable and you end up with a container:

```
my $pair = 'Genus' => $ = $name;
$pair.value = 'Papillo';  # Works!
```

.freeze the Pair to make the value immutable no matter how it came to you:

```
my $name = 'Hamadryas';
my $pair = 'Genus' => $name;
$pair.freeze;
$pair.value = 'Papillo';  # Nope!
```

There's one last thing about Pairs. You can line up the colon forms head-to-foot and it will create a list even though you don't use commas:

```
my $pairs = ( :1st:2nd:3rd:4th );
```

That's the same as the form with commas:

```
my $pairs = ( :1st, :2nd, :3rd, :4th );
```

You've already seen this with Q: you can turn on several features by lining up adverbs. The :q:a:c here are three separate adverbs:

```
Q :q:a:c /Single quoting @array[] interpolation {$name}/;
```

Maps

A `Map` is an immutable mapping of zero or more keys to values. You can look up the value if you know the key. Here's a translation of color names to their RGB values. The `.new` method takes a list of `Str`s and their values:

```
my $color-name-to-rgb = Map.new:
    'red',    'FF0000',
    'green',  '00FF00',
    'blue',   '0000FF',
    ;
```

You can use the *fat arrow* to make a list of `Pair`s:

```
my $color-name-to-rgb = Map.new:
    'red'    => 'FF0000',
    'green'  => '00FF00',
    'blue'   => '0000FF',
    ;
```

Using the fat arrow notation with autoquoting won't work; the method thinks these are named arguments instead of `Pair`s for the `Map` and they are treated as options to the method instead of keys and values. This gives you a `Map` with no keys or values:

```
# don't do this!
my $color-name-to-rgb = Map.new:
    red    => 'FF0000',
    green  => '00FF00',
    blue   => '0000FF',
    ;
```

A `Map` is fixed; you can't change it once you've created it. This may be exactly what you want since it can keep something else from accidentally modifying it:

```
$color-name-to-rgb<green> = '22DD22'; # Error!
```

To look up one of the color codes you subscript the object. This is similar to `Positionals` but uses different postcircumfix characters. Use the autoquoting <> or quote it yourself with {}:

```
put $color-name-to-rgb<green>;     # quoted key with allomorph
put $color-name-to-rgb{'green'};   # quoted key
put $color-name-to-rgb{$color};    # quoted key with interpolation
```

If you want to look up more than one key at a time, you can use a slice to get a `List` of values:

```
my @rgb = $color-name-to-rgb<red green>
```

Checking Keys

To check that a key exists before you try to use it, add the `:exists` adverb after the single-element access. This won't create the key. You'll get `True` if the key is in the `Map` and `False` otherwise:

```
if $color-name-to-rgb{$color}:exists {
    $color-name-to-rgb{$color} = '22DD22';
    }
```

The `.keys` method returns a `Seq` of keys:

```
for $color-name-to-rgb.keys {
    put "$^key => {$color-name-to-rgb{$^key}}";
    }
```

You do something similar to get only the values:

```
my @rgb-values = $color-name-to-rgb.values;
```

The `.kv` method returns a key and its value at the same time. This saves you some complexity inside the `Block`:

```
for $color-name-to-rgb.kv -> $name, $rgb {
    put "$name => $rgb";
    }
```

Placeholder values inside the `Block` (but not a pointy `Block`) can do most of the work for you:

```
for $color-name-to-rgb.kv {
    put "$^k => $^v";
    }
```

Creating from a Positional

You can create a `Map` from a `Positional` using `.map`. That returns a `Seq` that you can use as arguments to `.new`. These create new values based on the original ones:

```
my $plus-one-seq =  (1..3).map: * + 1;
my $double       = (^3).map: { $^a + $^a }
```

 Although the `Map` type and the `.map` method have the same name and do a similar job, one is an immutable object that provides the translation whereas the other is a method that transforms a `Positional` into a `Seq`.

Your `Block` or thunk can take more than one parameter. Use two parameters to construct `Pairs`:

```
my $pairs = (^3).map: { $^a => 1 }; # (0 => 1 1 => 1 2 => 1)
my $pairs = (^3).map: * => 1;        # same thing
```

There's also a routine form of `map` where the code comes first and the values come after it. There's a required comma between them in either form:

```
my $pairs = map { $^a => 1 }, ^3;
my $pairs = map * => 1, ^3;
```

The result of the `.map` can go right into the arguments for `.new`:

```
my $map-thingy = Map.new: (^3).map: { $^a => 1 }
```

These examples work because you want to produce `Pairs`. If you want to simply create multiple items for a larger list you need to create a `Slip` so you don't end up with a `List` of `Lists`:

```
my $list = map { $^a, $^a * 2 }, 1..3; # ((1 2) (2 4) (3 6))
put $list.elems;  # 3
```

You can fix that with `slip`. This creates a `Slip` object that automatically flattens into the structure that contains it:

```
my $list = map { slip $^a, $^a * 2 }, 1..3; # (1 2 2 4 3 6)
put $list.elems;  # 6
```

Exercise 9.2

Rewrite the subroutine from the previous section using a `Map` to decide which `Pair` you should return. If a number is not in the `Map`, use th. Add a new rule that numbers ending in 5 (but not 15) should get the suffix ty (like, 5ty).

Checking Allowed Values

A common use for a `Map` is to look up permissible values. Perhaps you only allow certain inputs in your subroutines. You can make those the keys of a `Map`. If they are in the `Map` they are valid. If they aren't, well, they aren't.

Go through the list of colors and return the color names, which you'll use as the keys, and some value (1 is serviceable). You really want just the keys, so you can look them up later:

```
my @permissable_colors = <red green blue>;
my $permissable_colors =
    Map.new: @permissable_colors.map: * => 1;

loop {
    my $color = prompt 'Enter a color: ';
    last unless $color;
```

```
    if $permissable_colors{$color}:exists {
        put "$color is a valid color";
        }
    else {
        put "$color is an invalid color";
        }
    }
```

This sort of data structure makes the lookup time the same no matter how many keys you have. Consider what you'd have to do with just the List. This scan-array subroutine checks each element of the array until it finds a match:

```
sub scan-array ( $list, $item ) {
    for @$list {
        return True if $^element eq $item;
        }
    return False;
    }
```

You might shorten your search by using .first to stop when it finds an appropriate element. At worst this checks every element every time:

```
sub first-array ( Array $array, $item ) {
    $array.first( * eq $item ).Bool;
    }
```

Exercise 9.3

Use the .map technique to construct a Map from numbers between 1 and 10 (inclusively) to their squares. Create a loop to prompt for a number. If the number is in the Map, print its square.

Hashes

The Hash is like a Map but mutable. You can add or delete keys and update values. This is the Associative type you'll probably use the most. Create a Hash through its object constructor:

```
my $color-name-to-rgb = Hash.new:
    'red',      'FF0000',
    'green',    '00FF00',
    'blue',     '0000FF',
    ;
```

That's a bit tedious. You can enclose the key-value list in %() instead:

```
my $color-name-to-rgb = %(  # Still makes a Hash
    'red',      'FF0000',
    'green',    '00FF00',
```

```
    'blue',   '0000FF',
    );
```

Curly braces also work, but this is a discouraged form. With the fat arrow there are
Pairs inside the braces so the parser thinks this is a Hash:

```
my $color-name-to-rgb = {  # Still makes a Hash
    'red'   => 'FF0000',
    'green' => '00FF00',
    'blue'  => '0000FF',
    };
```

If the parser doesn't get enough hints about the contents of the braces, you might end
up with a Block instead of a Hash:

```
my $color-name-to-rgb = {  # This is a Block!
    'red',   'FF0000',
    'green', '00FF00',
    'blue',  '0000FF',
    };
```

There's a special sigil for Associative. If you use the % sigil you can assign a List to
create your Hash:

```
my %color-name-to-rgb =
    'red',   'FF0000',
    'green', '00FF00',
    'blue',  '0000FF'
    ;
```

Perhaps you don't like your definition of blue. You can assign a new value to it. Notice
that the sigil does not change for the single-element access:

```
%color<blue> = '0000AA';  # a bit darker
```

You can remove a key with the :delete adverb. It returns the value of the just-deleted
key:

```
my $rgb = %color<blue>:delete
```

You can add new colors by assigning to the key that you want:

```
%color<mauve> = 'E0B0FF';
```

Exercise 9.4

Update your ordinal suffix program to use a Hash. That's the easy part. Once you've
got that working, use your Hash to cache values so you don't have to compute their
result again.

Accumulating with a Hash

Counting is another common use for a `Hash`. The key is the thing you want to count and its value is the number of times you've encountered it. First, you need something to count. Here's a program that simulates rolling some dice:

```
sub MAIN ( $die-count = 2, $sides = 6, $rolls = 137 ) {
    my $die_sides = 6;

    for ^$rolls {
        my $roll = (1..$sides).roll($die-count).List;
        my $sum = [+] $roll;
        put "($roll) is $sum";
        }
    }
```

The `.roll` method picks an element from your `List` the number of times you specify. Each time it picks an element is independent of other times, so it might repeat some values. This produces output that shows the individual die values and the sum of the values:

```
(3 4) is 7
(4 1) is 5
(6 4) is 10
(2 6) is 8
(6 6) is 12
(1 4) is 5
(5 6) is 11
```

Now you have several things to count. Start by counting the sums. Inside that `for`, use the sum as the `Hash` key and the number of times you encounter it as the value:

```
sub MAIN ( $die-count = 2, $sides = 6, $rolls = 137 ) {
    my $die_sides = 6;

    my %sums;
    for ^$rolls {
        my $roll = (1..$sides).roll($die-count).List;
        my $sum = [+] $roll;
        %sums{$sum}++;
        }

    # sort the hash by its value
    my $seq = %sums.keys.sort( { %sums{$^a} } ).reverse;

    for @$seq {
        put "$^a: %sums{$^a}"
        }
    }
```

Now you get a dice sum frequency report:

```
 7: 27
 8: 25
 5: 19
 4: 13
 9: 12
 6: 11
11: 9
10: 8
 3: 7
 2: 3
12: 3
```

If you are motivated enough, you can compare those values to the probabilities for perfect dice. But there's another interesting thing you can count—the rolls themselves. If you use $roll as the key it stringifies it. You can then count the unique stringifications. Sort the results so equivalent rolls such as (1 6) and (6 1) become the same key:

```
sub MAIN ( $die-count = 2, $sides = 6, $rolls = 137 ) {
    my $die_sides = 6;

    my %sums;
    for ^$rolls {
        my $roll = (1..$sides).roll($die-count).sort.List;
        %sums{$roll}++;
        }


    my $seq = %sums.keys.sort( { %sums{$^a} } ).reverse;

    for @$seq {
        put "$^a: %sums{$^a}"
        }
    }
```

Now you get a sorted list of your dice rolls:

```
3 4: 15
1 4: 11
1 2: 10
2 5: 9
3 5: 9
3 6: 9
2 3: 8
```

Exercise 9.5

Exercise 9.5

Create a program to count the occurrences of words in a file and output the words sorted by their count. Store each lowercased word as the key in a hash and increment its value every time you see it. Don't worry about punctuation or other characters; you'll learn how to deal with those later. What happens if two words have the same count?

Multilevel Hashes

Hash values can be almost anything, including another `Hash` or `Array`. Here's an example with a couple of `Hashes` that count the number of butterflies in the *Hamadryas* and *Danaus* genera:

```
my %Hamadryas = map { slip $_, 0 }, <
    februa
    honorina
    velutina
    >;

my %Danaus = map { slip $_, 0 }, <
    gilippus
    melanippus
    >;
```

But you want to contain all of that in one big `Hash`, so you construct that. The `Hash` value is another `Hash`:

```
my %butterflies = (
    'Hamadryas' => %Hamadryas,
    'Danaus'    => %Danaus,
    );

say %butterflies;
```

The `%butterflies` data structure looks like this (using the discouraged braces form):

```
{Danaus => {gilippus => 0, melanippus => 0},
 Hamadryas => {februa => 0, honorina => 0, velutina => 0}}
```

Suppose you want to see the count for *Danaus melanippus*. You have to look in the top-level `Hash` to get the value for `Danaus`, then take that value and look at its `melanippus` keys:

```
my $genus = %butterflies<Danaus>;
my $count = $genus<melanippus>;
```

That's too much work. Line up the subscripts in one expression:

```
put "Count is  %butterflies<Danaus><melanippus>";
```

When you want to count a particular butterfly, you can do that:

```
%butterflies<Danaus><melanippus>++;
```

Exercise 9.6

Read the lines from the butterfly census file (from *https://www.learningperl6.com/downloads/*) and break each line into a genus and species. Count each combination of genus and species. Report your results.

Exercise 9.7

Modify the previous exercise to write the genus and species counts to a file. Each line of the file should have the genus, species, and count separated by a tab. You'll need this file for an exercise in Chapter 15.

Summary

Associatives let you quickly get from a Str to another value. There are several types that facilitate this. At the lowest level is the Pair of one key and one value. A Map fixes those once created (much like a List), while a Hash is more flexible (much like an Array). These will probably be some of the most useful and hard-working data structures that you'll encounter.

## CHAPTER 10

Using Modules

Modules allow you to compartmentalize, distribute, and reuse code. Someone creates a general solution to something, then packages it so you can reuse it in your programs. Sometimes people make these modules available to everyone. You can find some Perl 6 modules at *https://modules.perl6.org* or by looking for them on GitHub (*https://www.github.com*).

You don't have to understand the code inside a module to benefit from its features. You can usually follow the examples in its documentation even if it uses syntax that you haven't already seen.

Installing Modules

zef is one of the Perl 6 module managers. It can install, update, and uninstall modules. It comes with Rakudo Star but you can install it yourself:

```
% git clone https://github.com/ugexe/zef.git
% cd zef
% perl6 -Ilib bin/zef install .
```

Once you have *zef* you can install modules. The `Task::Popular` module installs those most used by other modules:

```
% zef install Task::Popular
```

You can install a module by name if the author has registered it in the module ecosystem:

```
% zef install HTTP::Tiny
```

You can also tell it to install the code directly from a Git repository:

```
% zef install https://github.com/sergot/http-useragent.git
```

```
% zef install git://github.com/sergot/http-useragent.git
```

Ensure that you are using the clone URL and not the project page URL.

You can install from a local directory if the module infrastructure is there and there's a *META6.json* file. You have to make the argument to *zef* not look like a module name. This one looks for a module directory in the current directory:

```
% zef install ./json-tiny
```

You can install the modules from the current directory by using the . as the current working directory:

```
% zef install .
```

 You may find references to *panda*, an early module installation tool. It's the old, unsupported tool. *zef* is the new hotness. Double-check the documentation (*https://docs.perl6.org/language/modules*), though, since the favored tool may change by the time you read this book.

Exercise 10.1

Install the `Inline::Perl5` module by its name. You'll use that module later in this chapter. Install the `Grammar::Debugger` module by its repository URL. You'll use that module in Chapter 17. Find and clone the `Grammar::Tracer` module repository, change into its local directory, and install it from that directory.

Loading Modules

You load a module into your program with need. This searches through the module *repository* looking for a match. If you've installed modules with *zef* they should be in the repository (in the next section I show you how to tell your program to look in other places too):

```
need Number::Bytes::Human;
my $human = Number::Bytes::Human.new;

put $human.format(123435653); # '118M'
put $human.parse('3GB');      # 3221225472
```

Loading a module with use does the same thing but also automatically *imports* anything the module has set to *export*. This allows modules to define thingys in your current scope as if you'd defined the code there yourself:

```
use Number::Bytes::Human;
```

This is the same as doing a need and then an import:

```
need Number::Bytes::Human;
import Number::Bytes::Human;
```

Some modules import things automatically and others wait until you ask for them. You can specify a list after the module name that asks for specific imports. The `Number::Bytes::Human` module uses an adverb for that:

```
use Number::Bytes::Human :functions;

put format-bytes(123435653); # '118M'
put parse-bytes('3GB');     # 3221225472
```

No matter which way you load it, follow the examples in the documentation (or maybe look in the module tests).

Finding the Module

When you install a module with *zef* the module's filename becomes a digest of that file and is saved in one of the module repositories—this allows several versions and sources of the file to be simultaneously installed. You can see this path with the command `zef locate`:

```
% zef locate Number::Bytes::Human
===> From Distribution: Number::Bytes::Human:ver<0.0.3>:auth<>:api<>
Number::Bytes::Human => /opt/perl6/site/sources/A5EA...
```

As you can see in the output, the module shows up in a cryptically named file. Perl 6 uses several methods to store and retrieve *compunits* in repositories. This is very flexible but also much more than I have space to explain here. For the most part you don't need to worry about that.

 The repository system is complicated because it can manage the same module name with different versions or authors. This means it's possible to store or load old and new module versions simultaneously.

The lib pragma

No matter where the module is, you need to tell your program where to find it. *zef* uses the repositories that *perl6* has configured by default. The `lib` pragma can add a directory as a repository. You can store plain files in there (that is, unmanaged by Perl 6). The module name is translated to a path by replacing `::` with a `/` and adding a *.pm* or *.pm6* extension:

```
use lib </path/to/module/directory>;
use Number::Bytes::Human
```

This looks for *Number/Bytes/Human.pm* or *Number/Bytes/Human.pm6* in */path/to/
module/directory*.

You can specify multiple directories:

```
use lib </path/to/module/directory /other/path>;
```

Or specify `lib` multiple times:

```
use lib '/path/to/module/directory';
use lib '/other/path';
```

Relative paths resolve themselves according to the current working directory:

```
use lib <module/directory>;  # looks for module/ in current dir
```

The `.` works as the current working directory. People tend to do this if the module file
and the program are in the same directory:

```
use lib <.>:
```

You should carefully consider using the current working directory in your library
search path. Since it's a relative location you're never quite sure where it's looking.
Running your program from a different directory (with a command like the following) means your program looks in a different directory and probably won't find the
module:

```
% perl6 bin/my-program
```

It takes a bit more work to figure out the relative directory. Your program's path is in
the special variable $*PROGRAM. You can turn that into an IO::Path object with .IO
and use .parent to get its directory. You can use that to add a *lib* directory at the
same level as your program:

```
# random-between.p6
use lib $*PROGRAM.IO.parent;
use lib $*PROGRAM.IO.parent.add: 'lib';
```

There's also the $?FILE *compile-time variable*:

```
use lib $?FILE.IO.parent;
use lib $?FILE.IO.parent.add: 'lib';
```

For this to work you must add the paths to search before you try to load the library. It
does no good to tell it where to look after it has already looked!

The environment

The PERL6LIB environment variable applies to every program you run in the current session. Separate the directories with commas (no matter which system you are using). Here it is in *bash* syntax:

```
% export PERL6LIB=/path/to/module/directory,/other/path
```

And in Windows syntax:

```
C:\ set PERL6LIB=C:/module/directory,C:/other/path
```

The -I switch

The `-I` switch to *perl6* works for a single run of a program. This is handy inside a project repository (a different sort of repository!) that you haven't installed. You can use the development version of the module from the project repository instead of a previous one you might have installed:

```
% perl6 -Ilib bin/my_program.p6
```

Specify more than one extra directory with multiple `-I` switches or by separating them with commas:

```
% perl6 -Ilib -I../lib bin/my_program.p6
% perl6 -Ilib,../lib bin/my_program.p6
```

You can see the `-I` at work if you want to use *prove* to run Perl 6 module tests. The argument to `-e` is the interpreter to use (with Perl 5 being the default). You want a *perl6* that looks for the development modules in the current repository:

```
% prove -e "perl6 -Ilib"
```

The `$*REPO` variable can tell you where Perl 6 will look for modules. These aren't just directories. The repositories could be almost anything—including other code:

```
for $*REPO.repo-chain -> $item {
    say $item;
    }
```

Exercise 10.2

Create a program to show the repository chain. Run it in several situations using PERL6LIB, `-I`, and `use lib`.

Lexical Effect

Loading a module only affects the current scope. If you load a module in a Block it's only available in that Block, and anything it imports is only available in that Block. Outside of the Block the program doesn't know about the module:

```
{
use Number::Bytes::Human;

my $human = Number::Bytes::Human.new; # works in here

put $human.format(123435653); # '118M'
}

my $human = Number::Bytes::Human.new; # ERROR: not defined here
```

You'll get an odd error where your program is looking for a subroutine that has a name that's the same as the last part of the module name:

```
Could not find symbol '&Human'
```

You can limit module imports to just where you need them. If you only need it in a subroutine you can load it there:

```
sub translate-it ( Int $bytes ) {
    use Number::Bytes::Human;
    state $human = Number::Bytes::Human.new;
    $human.format( $bytes );
    }
```

This means that you could load different versions of the same module for different parts of your program. The lib declaration is lexically scoped as well:

```
sub stable-version {
    use Number::Bytes::Human;
    ...
    }

sub experimental-version {
    use lib </home/hamadryas/dev-module/lib>;
    use Number::Bytes::Human;
    ...
    }
```

This sort of thing is often handy to convert data formats when they change between module versions:

```
sub translate-to-new-format ( Str $file ) {
    my $data = do {
        use lib </path/to/legacy/lib>;
        use Module::Format;
        Module::Format.new.load: $file;
        };

    use Module::Format; # new version
    Module::Format.new.save: $data, $file;
    }
```

Loading a Module at Runtime

need and use load a module as the program compiles. Sometimes you don't know which module you want until you want to use it, or you know that you might use one of several modules but only want to load the one you'll actually use. You can wait until runtime to load it with require. If the module isn't there the require throws an exception:

```
try require Data::Dump::Tree;
if $! { die "Could not load module!" }
```

 Even if the module fails to load, the require still creates the type. You can't rely on the type being defined as a signal of successful loading.

Perhaps you want to check that a module is installed before you try to load it. The $*REPO object has a .resolve method that can find a module from its dependency specification:

```
my $dependency-spec =
    CompUnit::DependencySpecification.new: :short-name($module);

if $*REPO.resolve: $dependency-spec {
    put "Found $module";
    }
```

Exercise 10.3

Write a program that reports whether a module is installed. Try this with Number::Bytes::Human (assuming you installed it so it is present) and Does::Not::Exist (or any other name that isn't a module).

Interpolating module names

You can interpolate a Str where you'd normally have a literal class name by putting the Str inside ::():

```
require ::($module);
```

Anywhere you'd use the literal class name you can use that ::($module). When you want to create an object but you don't know the literal module name, you interpolate it just as you did in the require:

```
my $new-object = ::($module).new;
```

Not only that, but you can use a method name from a `Str` by putting it in double quotes. You must use the parentheses for the argument list when you do this:

```
$new-object."$method-name"( @args );
```

You can use the return value of `require`. If it was able to load the module that value is the type:

```
my $class-i-loaded = (require ::($module));
my $object = $class-i-loaded.new;
```

This might work better with a literal name that you don't want to repeatedly type:

```
my $class-i-loaded = (require Digest::MD5);
my $object = $class-i-loaded.new;
```

Checking this is a bit tricky. You can't simply check for the type because that will be defined no matter which way it goes. Check that it's not a `Failure`:

```
my $module = 'Hamadryas';

try require ::($module);
put ::($module).^name; # Failure
say ::($module).^mro;  # ((Failure) Nil (Cool) (Any) (Mu))
if ::($module) ~~ Failure {
    put "Couldn't load $module!"; # Couldn't load Hamadryas!
    }
```

These aren't tricks to use frequently, but they are there as a last resort should you need them. Here's a program that lets you choose which dumper class to use. It uses a `Hash` to translate the class name to the method name it uses. At the end it merely dumps the only `Hash` defined in the program:

```
sub MAIN ( Str $class = 'PrettyDump' ) {
    my %dumper-adapters = %(
        'Data::Dump::Tree' => 'ddt',
        'PrettyDump'       => 'dump',
        'Pretty::Printer'  => 'pp',
        );

    CATCH {
        when X::CompUnit::UnsatisfiedDependency {
            note "Could not find $class";
            exit 1;
            }
        default {
            note "Some other problem with $class: {.message}";
            exit 2;
            }
        }
    require ::($class);

    my $method = %dumper-adapters{$class};
```

```
unless $method {
    note "Do not know how to dump with $class";
    exit 2;
    }

put ::($class).new."$method"( %dumper-adapters );
}
```

Exercise 10.4

Modify the dumping program. Create another subroutine that takes a list of modules and returns the ones that are installed. Use that subroutine to provide the default for MAIN.

Fetching Data from the Web

HTTP::UserAgent is a handy module to fetch data from the web. Install it with *zef* and follow the example:

```
use HTTP::UserAgent;
my $ua = HTTP::UserAgent.new;
$ua.timeout = 10;

my $url = ...;
my $response = $ua.get( $url );
my $data = do with $response {
    .is-success ?? .content !! die .status-line
    }
```

Once you have the data you can do whatever you like, including reading some lines from it:

```
for $data.lines(5) -> $line {
    put ++$, ': ', $line;
    }
```

Exercise 10.5

Write a program that fetches the URL you provide on the command line, then outputs its contents to standard output.

Running Perl 5 in Perl 6

One of Perl 6's original goals was Perl 5 interoperability. Larry Wall said that if the new Perl 6 could run "with 95-percent accuracy 95 percent of the [Perl 5] scripts, and 100-percent accuracy 80 percent of the [Perl 5] scripts, then that's getting into the ballpark." This meant, as a goal, that a lot of the current Perl 5 contents of the Comprehensive Perl Archive Network (CPAN) would be available in Perl 6.

The `Inline::Perl5` module allows you to load Perl 5 modules or evaluate Perl 5 snippets from a Perl 6 program. Add the source `:from<Perl5>` after the module you want to load, then translate the syntax to Perl 6 (so, `.` for a method call and so on). You don't have to load `Inline::Perl5` explicitly in this case:

```
use Business::ISBN:from<Perl5>;
my $isbn = Business::ISBN.new( '9781491977682' );
say $isbn.as_isbn10.as_string;
```

You can have Perl 5 code in your program and call it when you need it, dropping in and out of it as you like. Create an object that will handle the Perl 5 code for you:

```
use Inline::Perl5;
my $p5 = Inline::Perl5.new;

$p5.run: q:to/END/;
    sub p5_test { return 'Hello from Perl 5!' }
END

put 'Hello from Perl 6!';

$p5.run: 'print p5_test()';
```

Exercise 10.6

Compare the results of the Perl 5 and 6 versions of `Digest::MD5` by loading them into the same program. Get the digest of the program itself. You can use `slurp` to read the entire contents of a file.

Summary

You've learned how to find and install modules with *zef*. You can often simply follow the example in the module's documentation to get what you want. Before you set out to program something, see if someone else has already done it.

You're not limited to modules from Perl 6 either. The `Inline` modules allow you to use code from other languages. If you have a favorite module you might not have to give it up.

## CHAPTER 11

Subroutines

Now it's time for more sophisticated subroutines. You were introduced to them in Chapter 5 but you only saw enough to support the upcoming chapters. Now that you've seen Arrays and Hashes, there's much more you can do with subroutine signatures.

A Basic Subroutine

When you run a subroutine you get some sort of result: the last evaluated expression. That's the *return value*. This sets basic routines apart from the simpler Blocks you saw in Chapter 5. A Routine knows how to send a value back to the code that called it. This subroutine returns a different Str if the argument is odd or even:

```
sub odd-or-even {
    if ( @_[0] %% 2 ) { 'Even' }
    else              { 'Odd'  }
    }

odd-or-even( 2 );    # Even
odd-or-even( 137 );  # Odd
```

Without a signature the arguments show up in @_. Each subroutine has its own version of that variable so it doesn't conflict with any other subroutine's @_. This code calls one subroutine that calls another. top-call shows its @_ before and after show-args:

```
top-call( <Hamadryas perlicus> );

sub show-args { say @_ }
sub top-call {
    put "Top: @_[]";
    show-args( <a b c> );
```

```
    put "Top: @_[]";
    }
```

Even though both use @_ they are separate. The @_ in top-call isn't disturbed by show-args:

```
Top: Hamadryas perlicus
[a b c]
Top: Hamadryas perlicus
```

The subroutine definition is lexically scoped. If you need it for only part of the code you can hide it in a Block. Outside the Block that subroutine is not visible:

```
{
put odd-or-even( 137 );
sub odd-or-even { ... } # only defined in this block
}

put odd-or-even( 37 );  # undeclared routine!
```

Extra Arguments

What does odd-or-even accept, though? The parameter is an Array but you only use the first element. These calls still work without warnings or errors:

```
put odd-or-even( 2, 47       );  # Even
put odd-or-even( 137, 'Hello' );  # Odd
```

This isn't necessarily wrong. It depends on what you are trying to do. Maybe you specifically want as many arguments as the caller decides to send:

```
sub plus-minus {
    [-]
    @_
        .rotor(2, :partial)
        .map: { $^a[0] + ($^a[1] // 0) }
    }

put plus-minus( 9,1,2,3 );
```

With the signatures you'll see later in the chapter you'll be able to control this to get the situation that you want.

Explicit Returns

You can explicitly return from anywhere in a subroutine with return. This distinguishes a subroutine from the Blocks you used in Chapter 5. This version is the same thing but with an explicit return:

```
sub odd-or-even ( $n ) {
    if ( $n %% 2 ) { return 'Even' }
    else           { return 'Odd'  }
    }
```

Call this with extra arguments and you get an error:

```
put odd-or-even( 2, 47 );  # Error
```

The message tells you the argument list does not match the signature:

```
Calling odd-or-even(Int, Int) will never work with declared signature ($n)
```

You could write this differently. do converts the entire if structure into something that evaluates to its last evaluated expression. Return the value of the do instead of repeating the return:

```
sub odd-or-even ( $n ) {
    return do {
        if ( $n %% 2 ) { 'Even' }
        else           { 'Odd'  }
        }
    }
```

The conditional operator is the same thing expressed differently:

```
sub odd-or-even ( $n ) {
    return $n %% 2 ?? 'Even' !! 'Odd'
    }
```

Another way to do the same thing is to have a default return value but return sooner for other situations:

```
sub odd-or-even ( $n ) {
    return 'Even' if $n %% 2;
    'Odd';
    }
```

Or back to where you started with an implicit return:

```
sub odd-or-even ( $n ) { $n %% 2 ?? 'Even' !! 'Odd' }
```

These techniques are more appealing in more complex situations that I'm not going to show here. No matter which of these serves your situation, they all do the same thing: they send a value back to the code that called it.

Exercise 11.1

Create a subroutine that returns the least common multiple of two integers. Use that in a program that takes two integers from the command line. The particulars of this exercise are very simple but it's the structure of the subroutine definitions that matter.

Recursing

Subroutines can call themselves; this is called *recursion*. The classic example is Fibonacci numbers, where the next number in the series is the sum of the preceding two given that the first two numbers are 0 and 1:

```
sub fibonacci ( $n ) {
    return 0 if $n == 0;  # special case of n = 0
    return 1 if $n == 1;
    return fibonacci( $n - 1 ) + fibonacci( $n - 2 );
    }

say fibonacci( 10 );  # 55
```

When you call this subroutine with the value of 10 it calls itself twice to get the values for 9 and 8. When it calls itself for 9, it creates two more calls for 8 and 7. It keeps creating more and more calls to itself until the arguments are 0 or 1. It can then return a value one level up, working its way back to where it started.

A Perl 6 subroutine knows what it is inside its own `Block`. The variable `&?ROUTINE` is the same subroutine object. You don't have to know the current subroutine's name. This is the same thing:

```
sub fibonacci ( $n ) {
    return 0 if $n == 0;
    return 1 if $n == 1;
    return &?ROUTINE( $n - 1 ) + &?ROUTINE( $n - 2 );
    }
```

This is only slightly better. You'll read more about this later when you encounter `multi` subroutines.

Exercise 11.2

Another favorite example of recursion is the factorial function. Start with a positive whole number and multiply it by all the strictly positive numbers that come before it. The factorial of 6 would be 6*5*4*3*2*1. Implement this as a recursive function. Once you've done that, implement it in the amazingly simple Perl 6 fashion. How big a number can you get your program to produce?

Iterating Instead of Recursing

You can turn many recursive solutions into iterative ones. Instead of repeatedly calling subroutines with all the overhead they entail (each call sets up a new scope, defines new variables, and so on), rearrange things so you don't need a subroutine.

The factorial case is easy. The reduction operator does that for you:

```
my $factorial = [*] 1 .. $n;
```

 The operators are actually methods, so you don't actually avoid calling something.

The Fibonacci case is easy too when you use a `Seq`:

```
my $fibonacci := 1, 1, * + * ... *;
put "Fib(5) is ", $fibonacci[5];
```

You can make a queue of things to work on. With a queue you can add items anywhere you like. Instead of processing the next thingy immediately you can put it at the end of the queue. When it's time to process the next thingy you can take it from the beginning, end, or middle. You can add as many elements as you want:

```
my @queue = ( ... );
while @queue {
    my $thingy = @queue.shift; # or .pop
    ... # generate more items to process
    @queue.append: @additional-items; # or .push or .unshift
    }
```

Storing Subroutines in Libraries

Start with a simple subroutine to choose a random integer between two integers (including the endpoints). Use `.rand` and coerce the result with `.Int`, then shift the result into the right range:

```
sub random-between ( $i, $j ) {
    ( $j - $i ).rand.Int + $i;
    }

say random-between( -10, -3 );
```

You might need to convince yourself that works. Your program gets its job done, so you don't think about it again. Then you write a different program doing something similar and you want to use that subroutine again. You do what many people don't want to admit to: you cut and paste the subroutine into a different program. Again, it works. Or does it?

Did you really get a number between `$i` and `$j` inclusively?

Once you've done that exercise you know that random-between didn't ever select the
second endpoint as one of the random values. If you had copied it into other programs it would have been wrong in several places. There's a way to fix that.

To use the same subroutine in several programs you can define it once in a *library*.
That's a separate file that you can import into your program.

Move random-between to a new file that has the *.pm* or *.pm6* extension:

```
# MyRandLibrary.pm6
sub random-between ( $i, $j ) {
    ( $j - $i ).rand.Int + $i;
    }
```

In your original program import your library with use. Set lib as you saw in Chapter 10:

```
# random-between.p6
use lib <.>
use MyRandLibrary;
say random-between( -10, -3 );
```

Your program finds your library but now you get a different error:

```
% perl6 random-between.p6
===SORRY!=== Error while compiling ...
Undeclared routine:
    random-between used at line ...
```

Exporting Subroutines

Subroutines are lexically scoped by default, so they can't be seen outside their files. If
you want another file to use them you need to export those subroutines. The is
export trait does that and comes right after the signature:

```
# MyRandLibrary.pm6
sub random-between ( $i, $j ) is export {
    ( $j - $i ).rand.Int + $i;
    }
```

Your program now finds the library, imports the subroutine, and produces a number
between your endpoints:

```
% perl6 random-between.p6
11
```

Exercise 11.4

Create the library that exports the `random-between` subroutine and use it in a program to get a random number between the two command-line arguments. What happens when the first argument is greater than the second? What happens if one of the arguments is not a number?

Positional Parameters

There are two types of parameters. The first are the positional parameters that you've seen already in Chapter 5. These parameters handle the arguments by their order in the argument list. We'll look at them in a bit more detail here. You'll see the other sort, named parameters, later in this chapter.

With no explicit signature the arguments show up in the array `@_`. Each subroutine gets its own `@_` so it doesn't conflict with that for any other subroutine. So, if you write this:

```
sub show-the-arguments {
    put "The arguments are: ", @_.gist;
    }

show-the-arguments( 1, 3, 7 );
```

You get:

```
The arguments are: [1 3 7]
```

Using `@_` inside the subroutine automatically adds the implicit signature. But it's not as simple as an explicit `@_` parameter by itself. This signature expects a single Positional argument:

```
sub show-the-arguments ( @_ ) { # Single Positional argument
    put "The arguments are: ", @_.gist;
    }
```

Calling it with multiple arguments is a compile-time error:

```
show-the-arguments( 1, 3, 7 );   # Won't compile
```

The (`@_`) signature wants a single argument that's some sort of `Positional` (not necessarily an `Array`):

```
show-the-arguments( [ 1, 3, 7 ] );   # Single argument
```

Slurpy Parameters

A *slurpy parameter* gets all of the remaining arguments into a single Array. Prefix the array parameter with a *. This is the same as the version with no explicit signature:

```
sub show-the-arguments ( *@_ ) {  # slurpy
    put "The arguments are: ", @_.gist;
    }

show-the-arguments( 1, 3, 7 );
```

The output shows the three numbers:

```
The arguments are: [1 3 7]
```

There's not much special about @_. You can use your own variable name instead:

```
sub show-the-arguments ( *@args ) {  # slurpy
    put "The arguments are: ", @args.gist;
    }
```

Try it with something slightly different now. Include a List as one of the arguments:

```
sub show-the-arguments ( *@args ) {  # slurpy
    put "The arguments are: ", @args.gist;
    }

show-the-arguments( 1, 3, ( 7, 6, 5 ) );
```

Did you expect this output? It's a flat List with no structure:

```
The arguments are: [1 3 7 6 5]
```

This isn't a problem with formatting the data; the slurpy parameter flattens the data. Try it again with another level:

```
show-the-arguments( 1, 3, ( 7, (6, 5) ) );
```

You get the same output with no structure:

```
The arguments are: [1 3 7 6 5]
```

The slurpy parameter only flattens objects that you can iterate. If you itemize one of the Lists that item is no longer iterable. Items resist flattening:

```
show-the-arguments( 1, 3, ( 7, $(6, 5) ) );
```

The output is a bit different:

```
The arguments are: [1, 3, 7, (6, 5)]
```

How about this one?

```
show-the-arguments( [ 1, 3, ( 7, $(6, 5) ) ] );
```

Instead of a List you have an Array. Remember that an Array already itemizes each of its elements. The (7, $(6, 5)) is itemized because it's an element of an Array:

```
The arguments are: [1, 3, (7, $(6, 5))]
```

Use a `**` in front of the parameter if you don't want this automatic flattening:

```
sub show-nonflat-arguments ( **@args ) {  # nonflattening slurpy
    put "The nonflat arguments are: ", @args.gist;
    }

show-nonflat-arguments( [ 1, 3, ( 7, $(6, 5) ) ] );
```

This output has a double set of square brackets around the data. The single argument is the inner `Array` and the entire argument list is the outer one:

```
The nonflat arguments are: [[1 3 (7 (6 5))]]
```

Exercise 11.5

Create a subroutine that outputs its argument count and shows each argument on a separate line. Try it with these argument lists:

```
1, 3, 7
1, 3, ( 7, 6, 5 )
1, 3, ( 7, $(6, 5) )
[ 1, 3, ( 7, $(6, 5) ) ]
```

Have It Both Ways

What if you want both flattening and nonflattening at the same time? If there's one argument, you want to flatten that. If there's more than one argument you want to leave that `List` alone. Use a `+` in front of a parameter to use the *single argument rule*:

```
sub show-plus-arguments ( +@args ) {  # single argument rule
    put "There are {@args.elems} arguments";
    put "The nonflat arguments are: ", @args.gist;
    }
```

If you pass one argument that argument is flattened into `@args`. With more than one argument you don't get flattening:

```
my @a = (1,3,7);

show-plus-arguments( @a );    # flattened
show-plus-arguments( @a, 5 ); # not flattened
```

The output shows the difference. In your first call to `show-plus-arguments` it looks like you have single `Array` argument. By the time it gets inside the subroutine that `Array` has been flattened into three `Int` arguments:

```
There are 3 arguments
The nonflat arguments are: [1 3 7]
```

```
There are 2 arguments
The nonflat arguments are: [[1 3 7] 5]
```

Your second call has the `Array` along with 5. With more than one argument you don't get flattening and the argument list has an `Array` argument and an `Int` argument.

Combining Slurpies

You can have only one slurpy `Array` parameter, since it will take up the rest of the positional arguments. However, you can have positional parameters before a slurpy parameter:

```
sub show-the-arguments ( $i, $j, *@args ) { # slurpy
    put "The arguments are i: $i j: $j and @args[]";
    }
```

```
show-the-arguments( 1, 3, 7, 5 );
```

The first two arguments fill in `$i` and `$j` and anything left over goes into `@args`:

```
The arguments are i: 1 j: 3 and 7 5
```

What if you put all but one of the arguments into an `Array`?

```
my @a = ( 3, 7, 5 );
show-the-arguments( 1, @a );
```

Now the output shows that `$j` has an `Array` value and `@args` has nothing:

```
The arguments are i: 1 j: 3 7 5 and
```

Exercise 11.6

Create a library that provides a `head` and a `tail` function that each take a `List` parameter. Make your `head` function return the first item in the `List` and your `tail` function return everything else. Do not change the original `List`. If you're used to Lisp you might call these `car` and `cdr`:

```
use lib <.>;
use HeadsTails;

my @a = <1 3 5 7 11 13>;

say head( @a ); # 1
say tail( @a ); # [ 3 5 7 11 13 ]
```

Optional and Default Arguments

By default all positional parameters require arguments. A question mark, ?, after a parameter marks it as optional so that you don't need to supply an argument. This subroutine takes one or two arguments:

```
sub one-or-two ( $a, $b? ) {
    put $b.defined ?? "Got $a and $b" !! "Got $a";
    }

one-or-two( 'Hamadryas' );
one-or-two( 'Hamadryas', 'perlicus' );
```

If you have an optional argument you probably want a default value. Assign to a parameter to give it a default value. That assignment occurs only when you don't supply an argument:

```
sub one-or-two ( $a, $b = 137 ) {
    put $b.defined ?? "Got $a and $b" !! "Got $a";
    }

one-or-two( 19 );                      # one number
one-or-two( 'Hamadryas', 'perlicus' ); # two strings
one-or-two( <Hamadryas perlicus> );    # one array
one-or-two( |<Hamadryas perlicus> );   # flattened array
```

The output shows that the arguments fill in the parameters differently each time:

```
Got 19 and 137
Got Hamadryas and perlicus
Got Hamadryas perlicus and 137
Got Hamadryas and perlicus
```

You can't have required positional parameters after an optional one:

```
sub one-or-two ( $a?, $b ) {
    put $b.defined ?? "Got $a and $b" !! "Got $a";
    }
```

That's a compile-time error:

```
Error while compiling
Cannot put required parameter $b after optional parameters
```

Parameter Traits

The parameter variables are filled in with read-only aliases to the original data. You see the same values but you can't change them. This subroutine tries to add one to its value:

```
sub increment ( $a ) { $a++ }

my $a = 137;
put increment( $a );
```

This doesn't work because you can't change the parameter variable:

```
Cannot resolve caller postfix:<++>(Int); the following candidates
match the type but require mutable arguments:
```

The read-only alias is the default. You can change that by applying traits to the parameters. Apply the is copy trait to get a mutable value that's separate from the original argument. You can change it without changing the original value:

```
sub mutable-copy ( $a is copy ) { $a++; put "Inside: $a" }

my $a = 137;

put "Before: $a";
mutable-copy( $a );
put "After: $a";
```

The output shows that the original variable's value did not change:

```
Before: 137
Inside: 138
After: 137
```

Use the is rw trait to change the original value. If the argument is a writable container you can change the value. If the value is not some sort of container you'll get an error:

```
sub read-write ( $a is rw ) { $a++ }

my $a  = 137;
my $b := 37;
my \c  = 7;

read-write( $a );  # writable so okay
read-write( $b );  # literal,  not mutable - ERROR!
read-write( c );   # constant, not mutable - ERROR!
read-write( 5 );   # literal,  not mutable - ERROR!
```

Parameter Constraints

You can constrain a parameter to a particular type. You already saw some of this in Chapter 5:

```
sub do-something ( Int:D $n ) { ... }
```

The sigils impose their own constraints. An @ accepts something that is a Positional, the % accepts something that does Associative, and the & accepts something that does Callable:

```
sub wants-pos    ( @array )  { put "Got a positional: @array[]" }
sub wants-assoc  ( %hash )   { put "Got an associative: {%hash.gist}" }
sub wants-code   ( &code )   { put "Got code" }

wants-pos( <a b c> );
wants-assoc( Map.new: 'a' => 1 );
wants-code( { put "Mini code" } );
```

These won't work because they don't supply the right types of arguments:

```
wants-pos( %hash );
wants-assoc( <x y z> );
wants-code( 1 );
```

Additionally, something that accepts a code block can specify its own signature that must match the argument's signature. Put the desired signature after the parameter variable:

```
sub one-arg  ( &code:( $a ), $A )          { &code.($A) }
sub two-args ( &code:( $a, $b ), $A, $B ) { &code.($A, $B) }

one-arg( { put "Got $^a" }, 'Hamadryas' );

two-args( { put "Got $^a and $^b" }, 'Hamadryas', 'perlicus' );
```

Same Name, Different Signature

You can define the same subroutine name twice by giving it different signatures. Each of these is a *candidate*. A dispatcher decides which candidate to call based on your arguments. There are several things the dispatcher considers, in this order:

1. Literal value

2. Number of arguments (arity)

3. Types of arguments

4. Other constraints

To define candidates, declare the subroutine with `multi`. And since `multi` works on a subroutine by default (you'll see methods in Chapter 12), you can leave off the `sub`:

```
multi sub some-subroutine { ... }
multi some-subroutine { ... }
```

Literal Value Parameters

You can also make a signature that has a literal value. These `multi`s are selected when the argument value is the same as the literal parameter:

```
multi something (  1 ) { put "Got a one" }
multi something (  0 ) { put "Got a zero" }
```

```
multi something ( $a ) { put "Got something else" }

something(   1 );
something(   0 );
something( 137 );
```

The literal value parameters decide the appropriate subroutine for the first two cases:

```
Got a one
Got a zero
Got something else
```

What if you wanted a Rat as one of the literal values? Put the value inside <> so the compiler doesn't think the / is the start of a regex (Chapter 15):

```
multi something ( 1 )        { put "Got a one" }
multi something ( 0 )        { put "Got a zero" }
multi something ( <1/137> ) { put "Got something fine" }
multi something ( $b )       { put "Got something else" }

something( 1 );
something( 0 );
something( 1/137 );
something( 'Hello' );
```

Think about the previous Fibonacci example:

```
sub fibonacci ( $n ) {
    return 0 if $n == 0;
    return 1 if $n == 1;
    return &?ROUTINE( $n - 1 ) + &?ROUTINE( $n - 2 );
    }
```

That implementation has two special cases for 0 and 1. You have to provide special code to handle those. You can move those special cases away from the main idea by giving each case its own multi:

```
multi fibonacci ( 0 ) { 0 }
multi fibonacci ( 1 ) { 1 }

multi fibonacci ( $n ) {
    return fibonacci( $n - 1 ) + fibonacci( $n - 2 );
    }

put fibonacci(0);
put fibonacci(1);
put fibonacci(5);
```

Notice that you can't use &?ROUTINE because $n-1 might not be handled by the same subroutine.

Number of Arguments

Declare the sub with `multi`. One candidate takes a single positional argument and the other candidate takes two positional arguments:

```
multi subsomething ( $a     ) { put "One argument"; }
multi subsomething ( $a, $b ) { put "Two arguments"; }

something( 1 );
something( 1, 3 );
# something();
```

The output shows that you called two different subroutines:

```
One argument
Two arguments
```

Uncomment the call with no arguments, and you'll get a compile-time error. The compiler knows no signatures can match:

```
Calling something() will never work with any of these multi signatures:
    ($a)
    ($a, $b)
```

You can shorten the `multi sub` to simply `multi` since that implies sub:

```
multi something ( $a     ) { put "One argument";  }
multi something ( $a, $b ) { put "Two arguments"; }
```

This sort of dispatch depends on *arity*—the number of arguments that you supply. This means that the compiler also knows when you try to define subroutines with the same arity, like this:

```
multi something ( $a ) { put "One argument"; }
multi something ( $b ) { put "Also one arguments"; } # Error
```

This is also a runtime error because the dispatcher can't choose one candidate over the other (and it won't run all of them):

```
Ambiguous call to 'something'; these signatures all match:
:($a)
:($b)
```

Parameter Types

You can also choose amongst `multis` by parameter type. These each take the same number of arguments but distinguish them by type:

```
multi something ( Int:D $a ) { put "Int argument";  }
multi something ( Str:D $a ) { put "Str arguments"; }

something( 137 );
something( 'Hamadryas' );
```

These call different subroutines because the argument types are different:

```
Int argument
Str arguments
```

You might have the different subroutines take the same type. In those cases you can select the right one by a custom constraint. The dispatcher chooses the most specific one:

```
multi something ( Int:D $a ) { put "Odd arguments"; }
multi something ( Int:D $a where * %% 2 ) { put "Even argument" }

something( 137 );
something( 538 );
```

Notice that this works regardless of the order in which you define the subroutines:

```
Odd arguments
Even arguments
```

In the next example the first subroutine constrains its parameter to numbers that are odd. The second subroutine constrains its parameter to numbers greater than 5. These both have one parameter and they both have a `where` clause, so the dispatcher chooses the first one it encounters:

```
multi sub something ( Int:D $a where * % 2 ) { put "Odd number" }
multi sub something ( Int:D $a where * > 5 ) { put "Greater than 5" }

something( 137 );
```

The argument satisfies either signature. The output shows that the first subroutine ran:

```
Odd number
```

Reverse the order of definition:

```
multi sub something ( Int:D $a where * > 5 ) { put "Greater than 5" }
multi sub something ( Int:D $a where * % 2 ) { put "Odd number" }

something( 137 );
```

The first defined subroutine still runs even though it's a different definition:

```
Greater than 5
```

What if you do *not* want multiple definitions with the same name? Declare one of the subroutines without `multi`:

```
sub something ( Int $a ) { put "Odd arguments" }

multi something ( Int $a where * %% 2 ) { # redefinition!
    put "Even argument";
    }
```

You get a compile-time error asking if you meant that to be a `multi sub`:

```
===SORRY!=== Error while compiling
Redeclaration of routine 'something' (did you mean to declare a multi-sub?)
```

Named Parameters

Named parameters do not depend on their position in the parameter or argument lists. By default they are optional. You can specify them anywhere in the arguments and in any order. These are often used to set options for a routine or method.

Specify named parameters with a colon before the parameter variable. In the signature, use the unquoted parameter variable name, the fat arrow, and the value that you want to supply. The order of the names or values does not matter:

```
sub add ( Int:D :$a, Int:D :$b ) {
    $a + $b;
    }

put add( a => 1,  b => 36 );  # 37
put add( b => 36, a => 1  );  # Same thing
```

For this to work you cannot quote the keys or use variables as the keys. This call is actually two `Pair` objects treated as positional parameters:

```
put add( 'a' => 1,  'b' => 36 );    # Will not work!
put add( $keya => 1, $keyb => 36 );  # Will not work!
```

More often you'll use the adverb syntax. With values that are positive integers you can specify the value first and the name after it:

```
put add( :a(1), :b(36) );  # 37
put add( :36b, :1a );      # 37
```

Default values and other constraints work the same as they do with positional parameters:

```
sub add ( Int:D :$a = 0, Int:D :$b = 0 ) {
    $a + $b;
    }

put add();        # 0
put add( :36b ); # 36
```

You don't have to use the same names for the arguments and the parameter variables. In complicated code in `power-of` you might not want to retype `$base` or `$power` every time. The subroutine still uses the long names for the interface but the implementation can use the short names:

```
sub power-of ( Int:D :power($n) = 0, Int:D :base($a) ) {
    $a ** $n
    }
```

```
put power-of( base => 2, power => 5 ); # 32
```

So far these named parameters have all taken values. Without any other constraints and no argument value, a named parameter is a Boolean. The adverb form with no value (and no constraint) gets `True` (because that's what `Pairs` do):

```
sub any-args ( :$state ) { say $state  }
any-args( :state );  #  True
```

A ! in front of the adverb name makes it a `False` value:

```
any-args( :!state );  #  False
```

Required Named Parameters

A positional parameter is required simply because it exists, and you have to mark it as optional to make it such. That's reversed with named parameters, which are optional unless you say otherwise. The parameters get their default values if you don't specify them:

```
sub not-required ( :$option ) { say $option; }

not-required();            # (Any)
not-required( :option );   # True
not-required( :!option );  # False
not-required( :5option );  # 5
```

To make `option` mandatory put a ! after it in the signature (this is not the same as ! before an argument):

```
sub not-required ( :$option! ) { say $option; }

not-required();              # Error!
```

The error tells you that you forgot an argument:

```
Required named parameter 'option' not passed
```

Named Parameters for Free

Rather than define every named parameter, you can accept all of them. Don't specify any in your parameters and they all show up in %_. This is the equivalent of @_ but for named parameters. Each routine gets its own version of this variable:

```
sub any-args { say %_ }
any-args( genus => 'Hamadryas' );
any-args( genus => 'Hamadryas', species => 'perlicus' );
```

You didn't define either :genus or :species but they show up in %_:

```
{genus => Hamadryas}
{genus => Hamadryas, species => perlicus}
```

A slurpy Hash does the same thing:

```
sub any-args ( *%args ) { say %args }
any-args( genus => 'Hamadryas' );
any-args( genus => 'Hamadryas', species => 'perlicus' );
```

That's how that implicit %_ worked. When you use it in a subroutine you automatically get a slurpy for it in the signature:

```
sub any-args { say %_ }
sub any-args ( *%_ ) { say %_ }
```

Mixed Parameters

You can mix positional and named parameters. If you use @_ and %_ in the code they are both in the implicit signature:

```
sub any-args {
    put '@_ => ', @_.gist;
    put '%_ => ', %_.gist;
    }

any-args( 'Hamadryas', 137, :status, :color('Purple') );

@_ => [Hamadryas 137]
%_ => {color => Purple, status => True}
```

You can mix in the named parameters in any order that you like. The positional parameters have to be in the right order but named parameters can come between them:

```
any-args( :color('Purple'), 'Hamadryas', :status, 137 );
```

It's the same if you name the parameters yourself:

```
sub any-args ( *@args, *%named ) {
    put '@args => ', @args.gist;
    put '%named => ', %named.gist;
    }

any-args( :color('Purple'), 'Hamadryas', :status, 137 );
```

Return Types

You can constrain the return values of subroutines. If you try to return a value that doesn't fit the restriction you get a runtime Exception. Specify the type after the signature with a -->. You want this subroutine to return a defined Int:

```
sub returns-an-int ( Int:D $a, Int:D $b --> Int:D ) { $a + $b }

put returns-an-int( 1, 3 );
```

That works:

```
4
```

But what if you make a mistake where you return a Str?

```
sub returns-an-int ( Int:D $a, Int:D $b --> Int:D ) { ($a + $b).Str }

put returns-an-int( 1, 3 );
```

At runtime you get an error because the types do not match:

```
Type check failed for return value; expected Int but got Str ("4")
```

An alternate way is to note it with `returns` (with an s at the end) outside of the signature's parentheses:

```
sub returns-an-int ( Int $a, Int $b ) returns Int { $a + $b }
```

You might also see these forms that do the same thing:

```
sub returns-an-int ( Int $a, Int $b ) of Int { $a + $b }

my Int sub returns-an-int ( Int $a, Int $b ) { $a + $b }
```

No matter which way you define the return type you can always return either `Nil` or a `Failure` object (usually to signal that something went wrong). All of these calls "succeed" even though some of them don't return a `Str`:

```
sub does-not-work ( Int:D $a --> Str ) {
    return Nil if $a == 37;
    fail 'Is not a fine number' unless $a == 137;
    return 'Worked!'
    }

put does-not-work(  37 ).^name;   # Nil
put does-not-work( 137 ).^name;   # Str
put does-not-work( 538 ).^name;   # Failure
```

You can't make complex checks in the constraint, but you can define a subset that does these. Here's one that returns either a `Rat` or, if you try to divide by zero, an `Inf`:

```
subset RatInf where Rat:D | Inf;

sub divide ( Int:D $a, Int:D $b --> RatInf ) {
    return Inf if $b == 0;
    $a / $b;
    }

put divide( 1, 3 );  # <1/3>
put divide( 1, 0 );  # Inf
```

That `Rat:D | Inf` is a `Junction`. You'll see those in Chapter 14.

Summary

Much of the work of ensuring your program does the right things can be done with the judicious use of constraints on the inputs and outputs of subroutines. With a little planning these features will catch the cases that you did not expect and that shouldn't show up in your program. Once they've been found you can work your way through the code to find them even sooner—and the sooner you find them, the easier your debugging life should be.

## CHAPTER 12

Classes

A class is the blueprint for an object and manages an object and its behavior. It declares *attributes* to define what an object will store and *methods* to define how an object can behave. Classes model the world in a way that makes it easier for your program to do its job.

I'm mostly going to ignore object-oriented analysis and design. This chapter is about the mechanism of classes and objects. The examples show you how things work and do not endorse a particular way. Use what works for your task and stop using that when it doesn't.

Your First Class

Declare a class by giving it a name and a `Block` of code:

```
class Butterfly {}
```

That's it! It looks like this class is empty, but it's not. You get much of its basic behavior for free even though you don't see it explicitly. Try calling some methods on it. You can see that it derives from `Any` and `Mu` and that you can create new objects:

```
% perl6
> class Butterfly {}
(Butterfly)
> Butterfly.^mro
((Butterfly) (Any) (Mu))
> my $object = Butterfly.new
Butterfly.new
> $object.^name
Butterfly
> $object.defined
True
```

You can have as many of these class declarations as you like in one file:

```
class Butterfly {}
class Moth {}
class Lobster {}
```

These types are available to your program as soon as they are defined in the code, but not before. If you try to use one before you define it you get a compilation error:

```
my $butterfly = Butterfly.new;  # Too soon!

class Butterfly {};  # Error: Illegally post-declared type
```

Instead of defining all of your classes at the beginning of the file (and having to scroll past all of them to get to the good stuff), you're more likely to want one class per file so you can easily find the class definition again. In that case you can use unit to declare that the entire file is your class definition. You don't use a Block:

```
unit class Butterfly;
```

Put your class in *Butterfly.pm6* (or *Butterfly.pm*) and load it from your program:

```
use Butterfly;
```

Exercise 12.1

Create a single-file program that has the Butterfly, Moth, and Lobster empty class definitions. Create a new object for each, even though the objects don't do anything interesting yet.

Exercise 12.2

Define the Butterfly, Moth, and Lobster classes in separate files named after the classes they contain. The class files should be in the same directory as the program that loads them. Load those files in your program and create new objects for each.

Defining Methods

Methods are like subroutines but know who called them and can be inherited; instead of sub you define these with method. This example uses it to output the type name:

```
class Butterfly {
    method who-am-i () { put "I am a " ~ self.^name }
    }

Butterfly.who-am-i;
```

That `self` term is the *invocant* of the method. That's the object that called the method. It doesn't need to be in the signature. It also doesn't need to be in the method. Calling a method on $ does the same thing (you'll see why later):

```
class Butterfly {
    method who-am-i () { put "I am a " ~ $.^name }
    }

Butterfly.who-am-i;  # I am a Butterfly
```

Give the invocant a different name by putting it before a colon in the signature. C++ people might like `$this`:

```
method who-am-i ( $this : ) { put "I am a " ~ $this.^name }
```

A backslash makes the invocant name a term so you don't need a sigil:

```
method who-am-i ( \this : ) { put "I am a " ~ this.^name; }
```

The default topic can be the invocant, which means that it's implicit inside the `Block`:

```
method who-am-i ( $_ : ) { put "I am a " ~ .^name; }
```

If you want to change the invocant name, choose something that describes what it represents:

```
method who-am-i ( $butterfly : ) { ... }
```

Private Methods

A *private method* is available only inside the class where it's defined. You use these to compartmentalize code that you don't want code outside the class to know about.

Previously `who-am-i` directly called `.^name`. That's a very specific way to figure out the "type." You might want to change that later or use other methods to figure it out, and other methods in your class may need the same thing. Hide it in a method, `what's-the-name`:

```
class Butterfly {
    method who-am-i () { put "I am a " ~ self.what's-the-name }

    method what's-the-name () { self.^name }
    }

Butterfly.who-am-i;              # I am a Butterfly
put Butterfly.what's-the-name;   # Butterfly
```

That works, but it's now available as a method that you didn't intend anyone to use outside of the class. Prefix the method name with a ! to hide it from code outside the class. Replace the method call dot with a ! too:

```
class Butterfly {
    method who-am-i () { put "I am a " ~ self!what's-the-name }
```

```
    method !what's-the-name () { self.^name }
    }

Butterfly.who-am-i;  # I am a Butterfly
put Butterfly.what's-the-name;  # Butterfly
```

Now you get an error if you try to use it outside the class:

```
No such method 'what's-the-name' for invocant of type 'Butterfly'.
```

Defining Subroutines

A class can contain subroutines. Since subroutines are lexically scoped they are also invisible outside the class. A subroutine can do the same job as a private method. To make this work you need to pass the object as a subroutine argument:

```
class Butterfly {
    method who-am-i () { put "I am a " ~ what's-the-name( self ) }

    sub what's-the-name ($self) { $self.^name }
    }

Butterfly.who-am-i;  # I am a Butterfly
```

Objects

Objects are particular *instances* of a class; sometimes those terms are used interchangeably. Each object has its own variables and data, separate from all the others. Each object, however, still shares the behavior of the class.

Start with the simplest class, as before. To create an object you need a constructor method. Any method that creates an object is a constructor. By default that is .new:

```
class Butterfly {}

my $butterfly = Butterfly.new;
```

The object is a defined instance of the class (the type object is the undefined one). The .DEFINITE method tells you which one you have:

```
put $butterfly.DEFINITE
    ?? 'I have an object' !! 'I have a type';
```

 Every object also has a .defined method, but each class can change what that means. Any object of the Failure class is undefined, so it's always False as a conditional. Use .DEFINITE to avoid that gotcha.

Private Attributes

Attributes are per-object data. You declare these with `has`. The attribute variables use a twigil to denote their access. Before you see the easy way you should see the hard way so you appreciate it more. The `$!` twigil defines a private attribute:

```
class Butterfly {
    has $!common-name;
    }
```

By itself this `has` definition doesn't effectively add anything to your class. Nothing can see the attribute, so you have no way to change its value.

The special `.BUILD` method is automatically called after `.new` with the same arguments. You can define your own `.BUILD` to bind or assign a value to your private attribute (or do any other work that you want):

```
class Butterfly {
    has $!common-name;

    method BUILD ( :$common-name ) {
        $!common-name = $common-name;
        }
    }
```

```
my $butterfly = Butterfly.new: :common-name('Perly Cracker');
```

Be careful here. This `.BUILD` accepts all named parameters without warning. It doesn't know which ones you intend to use or what they mean to your class. It's a default way that almost everything uses to set up objects—but if you misspell a name, you won't get a warning:

```
my $butterfly = Butterfly.new: :commen-name('Perly Cracker');
```

You also don't get a warning for leaving something out. Maybe you don't want to require every setting any time you build an object. You might not want this to fail:

```
my $butterfly = Butterfly.new;
```

But if you want to require a named parameter you know how to do that. Put a `!` after it:

```
class Butterfly {
    has $!common-name;

    method BUILD ( :$common-name! ) { # required now
        $!common-name = $common-name;
        }
    }
```

For the rest of this example that's not what you want. You're going to set default values and provide other ways to change the name.

You can add an *accessor method* to allow you to see the name that you've stored in the private attribute:

```
class Butterfly {
    has $!common-name;

    method BUILD ( :$common-name ) {
        $!common-name = $common-name;
        }

    method common-name { $!common-name }
    }

my $butterfly = Butterfly.new: :common-name('Perly Cracker');
put $butterfly.common-name;  # Perly Cracker
```

This is a problem if you don't supply a :common-name. There's nothing in $!common-name and you didn't give .BUILD anything to work with. When you try to output it you get a warning about the empty value:

```
my $butterfly = Butterfly.new;
put $butterfly.common-name;  # Warning!
```

A default value in the common-name method could solve this. If the attribute is not defined you could return an empty Str (or fail or warn):

```
method common-name { $!common-name // '' }
```

The attribute can have a default value:

```
class Butterfly {
    has $!common-name = '';
    ...
    }
```

Instead of the empty Str you can make the default something a little more interesting:

```
class Butterfly {
    has $!common-name = 'Unnamed Butterfly';
    ...
    }

my $butterfly = Butterfly.new;
put $butterfly.common-name;  # Unnamed Butterfly!
```

To change the value for $!common-name you can mark .common-name with the rw trait to make it read-write. If you assign to the method you change the value of the last thingy in the Block (if you can modify it, that is). The last thingy in this Block is a container for $!common-name:

```
class Butterfly {
    has $!common-name = 'Unnamed butterfly';

    method BUILD ( :$common-name ) {
        $!common-name = $common-name;
        }

    method common-name is rw { $!common-name }
    }

my $butterfly = Butterfly.new;
$butterfly.common-name = 'Perly Cracker';

put $butterfly.common-name;  # Perly Cracker!
```

The attributes can be typed like other variables. Constraining the type to Str means you can assign only that type to .common-name:

```
class Butterfly {
    has Str $!common-name = 'Unnamed butterfly';
    ...
    }
```

Exercise 12.3

Implement the Butterfly class with the $!common-name private attribute. Add a $!color private attribute. Create a new Butterfly object, set its name and color, then output those values.

Public Attributes

But enough of the hard way. *Public attributes* do a lot of that work for you. Use $.common-name with a dot instead of a bang (!). The accessor method is automatically defined for you and the default .BUILD handles the setup by filling in the attributes from the named parameters in your call to .new:

```
class Butterfly {
    has $.common-name = 'Unnamed Butterfly'
    }

my $butterfly = Butterfly.new: :common-name('Perly Cracker');
put $butterfly.common-name;  # Perly Cracker
```

Make it read-write with the rw trait immediately after the attribute name but before the default value. After you create the object you can assign to the .common-name method:

```
class Butterfly {
    has $.common-name is rw = 'An unknown butterfly';
    }

my $butterfly = Butterfly.new;
put $butterfly.common-name; # An unknown butterfly

$butterfly.common-name = 'Hamadryas perlicus';
put $butterfly.common-name; # Hamadryas perlicus
```

The attributes can have types just like other variables. Try to assign the wrong type and you get an exception:

```
class Butterfly {
    has Str $.common-name is rw = 'Unnamed butterfly';
    }

my $butterfly = Butterfly.new;
$butterfly.common-name = 137;  # Error!
```

To have a mixture of private and public attributes you have to do some work. You probably don't want to define your own `.BUILD` since you'd have to handle everything that the default one does for you. Instead, you can define a private attribute and assign to it later through a method. An `rw` trait on the method either returns or assigns to the value of the last thingy in the `Block`:

```
class Butterfly {
    has Str $.common-name is rw = 'Unnamed butterfly';
    has Str $!color;

    method color is rw { $!color }
    }
my $butterfly = Butterfly.new;
$butterfly.common-name = 'Perly Cracker';
$butterfly.color = 'Vermillion';

put "{.common-name} is {.color}" with $butterfly;
```

multi Methods

Read-write methods are one way to handle private attributes, but you can also create `multi` methods for each case. Although this example looks simple, your validation and conversion requirements can be arbitrarily complex inside the `Block`s:

```
class Butterfly {
    has $!common-name = 'Unnamed butterfly';
    has $!color       = 'White';

    multi method common-name ()        { $!common-name }
    multi method common-name ( Str $s ) { $!common-name = $s }
```

```
    multi method color ()          { $!color }
    multi method color ( Str $s ) { $!color = $s }
    }

my $butterfly = Butterfly.new;
$butterfly.common-name: 'Perly Cracker';
$butterfly.color: 'Vermillion';

    put $butterfly.common-name;  # Perly Cracker!
```

This gets annoying when you have many attributes. There's another way that you could do this. Return the object in every method that sets a value. This allows you to chain methods to set many attributes in one statement where you don't repeat the object each time:

```
class Butterfly {
    has $!common-name = 'Unnamed butterfly';
    has $!color       = 'White';

    multi method common-name ()         { $!common-name; }
    multi method common-name ( Str $s ) {
        $!common-name = $s; self
        }

    multi method color ()          { $!color; }
    multi method color ( Str $s ) { $!color = $s; self }
    }

my $butterfly = Butterfly
    .new
    .common-name( 'Perly Cracker' )
    .color( 'Vermillion' );

    put "{.common-name} is {.color}" with $butterfly;
```

That looks similar to using do given to *topicalize* the object and call methods on it:

```
my $butterfly = do given Butterfly.new {
    .common-name( 'Perly Cracker' );
    .color( 'Vermillion' );
    };

    put "{.common-name} is {.color}" with $butterfly;
```

Which technique you use depends on your task and personal preferences. You haven't seen this with error handling or complex code, either. Those impact your choice too.

Inheriting Types

An existing type might already do most of what you want. Instead of redefining everything that class already does, you can *extend* it, also known as inheriting from it. Declare the class with `is` and the type you want to extend:

```
class Butterfly is Insect {};
```

You can do this inside the class definition with `also`:

```
class Butterfly {
    also is Insect
    };
```

Here, `Insect` is a *parent class* (or super class or base class). `Butterfly` is the *child class* (or derived type). The terminology isn't particularly important; the base type is the more general one and the derived type is the more specific one.

Everything you've seen in the `Butterfly` class so far (a name and a color) applies to any insect. The name and color attributes are general things that describe any insect, so should be in the more general class. The `Butterfly` class now has nothing in it (a "null subclass"), but it should still work the same as it did before:

```
class Insect {
    has $.common-name is rw = 'Unnamed insect';
    has $.color       is rw = 'Brown';
    }

class Butterfly is Insect {}

my $butterfly = Butterfly.new;
$butterfly.common-name = 'Perly Cracker';
$butterfly.color = 'Vermillion';

put "{.common-name} is {.color}" with $butterfly;
```

`Butterfly` can have its own `$.color` that overrides the one from `Insect`. Declaring the attribute in `Butterfly` effectively hides the one in its parent class:

```
class Insect {
    has $.common-name is rw = 'Unnamed insect';
    has $.color       is rw = 'Brown';
    }

class Butterfly is Insect {
    has $.color       is rw = 'Mauve';
    }

my $butterfly = Butterfly.new;
$butterfly.common-name = 'Perly Cracker';
```

```
# Perly Cracker is Mauve
put "{.common-name} is {.color}" with $butterfly;
```

Sometimes that's not the right thing to do. The parent class might need to run some code in its version of the method to make everything else work. Instead of hiding the parent method you want to *wrap* it (or extend it).

The `callsame` routine can do this for you. It redispatches the call with the same arguments. You run the parent method in your child method:

```
class Insect {
    has $.common-name is rw = 'Unnamed insect';
    has $!color = 'Brown';

    method color is rw {
        put "In Insect.color!";
        $!color
        }
    }

class Butterfly is Insect {
    has $!color = 'Mauve';

    method color is rw {
        put "In Butterfly.color!";
        my $insect-color = callsame;
        put "Insect color was {$insect-color}!";
        $!color
        }
    }

my $butterfly = Butterfly.new;
$butterfly.common-name = 'Perly Cracker';

put "{.common-name} is {.color}" with $butterfly;
```

Inheritance isn't the only way to add features to your class. You should save inheritance for specific cases where your class is a more specific type of the same thingy.

Exercise 12.4

Create classes for the kingdom, phylum, class, order, family, and genus of a *Hamadryas* butterfly. The phylum inherits from kindgom, the class inherits from phylum, and so on. Each class notes its place in the hierarchy:

```
class Nymphalidae is Lepidoptera { }
```

Define a `.full-name` method in `Hamadryas` to join all the levels together.

The genus *Hamadryas* is classified in *Animalia, Arthropodia, Insecta, Lepidoptera,* and *Nymphalidae.*

Checking Inheritance

You've already seen `.^mro` to get a `List` of classes. The `.isa` method returns `True` or `False` if the type you specify is in that `List`. You can test a type or an object with a type object as the argument (a `Str`):

```
put Int.isa: 'Cool';       # True
put Int.isa: Cool;         # True

put Butterfly.isa: Insect; # True;
put Butterfly.isa: Int     # False;

my $butterfly-object = Butterfly.new;
put $butterfly.isa: Insect; # True
```

Smart matching does the same job. That's what `when` is checking if you give it only a type:

```
if Butterfly ~~ Insect {
    put "Butterfly is an Insect";
    }

if $butterfly ~~ Insect {
    put "Butterfly is an Insect";
    }

put do given $butterfly {
    when Int    { "It's a integer" }
    when Insect { "It's an insect" }
    }
```

You may have been wondering about the name of the `.^mro` method. That's for *method resolution order* in cases where you inherit from multiple classes:

```
class Butterfly is Insect is Flier {...}
```

I'm not going to tell you more about *multiple inheritance* in the hopes that you never do it. It's possible, but you'll likely solve your problem with the roles you'll see in Chapter 13.

Stub Methods

A parent class can define a method but not implement it—this is known as an *abstract method* (or *stub method*). Use `!!!` inside the `Block` to denote that something later will implement a method with that name:

```
class Insect {
    has $.color is rw = 'Brown';

    method common-name { !!! }
    }

class Butterfly is Insect {
    has $.color is rw = 'Mauve';
    }

my $butterfly = Butterfly.new;
$butterfly.common-name = 'Perly Cracker';

put "{.common-name} is {.color}" with $butterfly;
```

When you run this the ! ! ! throws an exception:

```
Stub code executed
```

Instead of the ! ! ! you can use . . . . The triple dot calls `fail` instead of `die`. Either way something else needs to implement that method. A public attribute would do that for you:

```
class Butterfly is Insect {
    has $.common-name is rw;
    has $.color       is rw = 'Mauve';
    }
```

Controlling Object Creation

Sometimes you want more control over your object creation. When you call `.new` there are several steps and you're able to hook into each of them. You don't need all the gory details at the programmer level so I'll spare you.

When you call `.new` you're reaching into the root of the object system, `Mu`. `.new` calls `.bless`, which actually creates your object. Now you have an empty object. It's not quite ready for use yet.

`.bless` does some more work by calling `.BUILDALL` on your empty object, passing it all the same arguments that you passed to `.new`. `.BUILDALL` visits each class in your inheritance chain, starting with `Mu`. You typically don't want to mess with `.BUILDALL` since it's driving the process rather than affecting your objects.

`.BUILDALL` calls the `.BUILD` method in your class if you've defined one. `.BUILD` gets the same arguments as `.new`. This is how your attributes get their values from your arguments. If no class defined a `.BUILD` you get the default one that fills in your attributes from the named parameters.

The default object creation mechanism wants to work with named parameters. You could rework everything for positional parameters but that would be a lot of work.

After .BUILD is done you have a completely built object that's ready for use (but not the final object yet). The .TWEAK method gives you a chance to adjust that object before you move on to the next class to go through the process again.

You should declare both .BUILD and .TWEAK with submethod. This is a hybrid of sub and method; it acts just like a method but a subclass doesn't inherit it (just like you don't inherit subroutines):

```
# $?CLASS is a compile-time variable for the current class
# &?ROUTINE is a compile-time variable for the current routine
class Insect {
    submethod BUILD { put "In {$?CLASS.^name}.{&?ROUTINE.name}" }
    submethod TWEAK { put "In {$?CLASS.^name}.{&?ROUTINE.name}" }
    }

class Butterfly is Insect {
    submethod BUILD { put "In {$?CLASS.^name}.{&?ROUTINE.name}" }
    submethod TWEAK { put "In {$?CLASS.^name}.{&?ROUTINE.name}" }
    }

my $b = Butterfly.new;
```

The .TWEAK method is called before .BUILDALL moves on to the next class:

```
In Insect.BUILD
In Insect.TWEAK
In Butterfly.BUILD
In Butterfly.TWEAK
```

Now that you've seen the order in which things happen, let's look at each step a little more closely.

Building Objects

.BUILD lets you decide how to treat your newly created object. Start with a submethod that does nothing:

```
class Butterfly {
    has $.color;
    has $.common-name;

    submethod BUILD {} # does nothing
    }

my $butterfly = Butterfly.new: :color('Magenta');
```

```
put "The butterfly is the color {$butterfly.color}";
```

The color isn't set and you get a warning about an uninitialized value:

```
The butterfly is the color
Use of uninitialized value of type Any in string context.
```

`.BUILDALL` found your `.BUILD` so it used your version to set up the object. The color value in your call to `.new` isn't assigned to the `$!color` attribute because your empty `.BUILD` didn't handle that. You need to do that yourself. By default all the named parameters are in `%_` and `.BUILD` gets all of the same arguments as `.new`:

```
class Butterfly {
    has $.color;
    has $.common-name;

    submethod BUILD {
        $!color = %_<color>;
        }
    }
```

Use the argument list for `.BUILD` to automatically define some named parameters to variables:

```
class Butterfly {
has $.color;
has $.common-name;

submethod BUILD ( :$color ) {
    $!color = $color;
    }
}
```

If you don't specify a `color` named argument you get another warning because the value in `$color` is uninitialized. In some cases you might want that named parameter to be required, so you put a ! after it:

```
class Butterfly {
    has $.color;
    has $.common-name;

    submethod BUILD ( :$color! ) {
        $!color = $color;
        }
    }
```

Other times you might want to set a default value. Another attribute won't work because the object build process hasn't set its default value yet:

```
class Butterfly {
    has $!default-color = 'Wine'; # Won't work
    has $.color;
```

```
    has $.common-name;

    submethod BUILD ( :$color! ) {
        $!color = $color // $!default-color; # No setup yet!
        }
    }
```

A private method could work; a private method can only be seen from code inside the class and cannot be inherited. A submethod isn't inheritable either but is still a public method:

```
class Butterfly {
    method default-color { 'Wine' }
    has $.color;
    has $.common-name;

    submethod BUILD ( :$color ) {
        $!color = $color // self.default-color;
        }
    }
```

Class variables can do the same job. A lexical variable defined in the class Block is only visible to the code in the same Block and the Blocks inside it:

```
class Butterfly {
    my $default-color = 'Wine';
    has $.color;
    has $.common-name;

    submethod BUILD ( :$color ) {
        $!color = $color // $default-color;
        }
    }
```

What's more interesting to .BUILD is the extra setup you don't want to be part of the interface. Perhaps you want to track when you used the default value so you can distinguish it from the case where the specified color happened to be the same:

```
class Butterfly {
    my $default-color = 'Wine';
    has $.used-default-color;
    has $.color;

    submethod BUILD ( :$color ) {
        if $color {
            $!color = $color;
            $!used-default-color = False;
            }
        else {
            $!color = $default-color;
            $!used-default-color = True;
            }
        }
```

```
    }

my $without = Butterfly.new;
put "Used the default color: {$without.used-default-color}";

my $with = Butterfly.new: :color('Wine');
put "Used the default color: {$with.used-default-color}";
```

Even though those two butterflies are the same color, you know which one specified a color and which one didn't:

```
Used the default color: True
Used the default color: False
```

Tweaking Objects

When you create an object you can use .TWEAK to set either the color you supplied as a named argument or the default color:

```
class Insect {
    has $!default-color = 'Brown';
    has $.common-name is rw = 'Unnamed insect';
    has $.color      is rw;

    submethod TWEAK ( :$color ) {
        self.color = $color // $!default-color;
        }
    }

class Butterfly is Insect {}

my $butterfly = Butterfly.new;
$butterfly.common-name = 'Perly Cracker';

put "{.common-name} is {.color}" with $butterfly;
```

The output shows that you got the default from Insect. .TWEAK ran inside Insect and set an attribute inside Insect. The .color method is defined in Insect so it works out:

```
Perly Cracker is Brown
```

If you specify a color, that color is actually set:

```
my $butterfly = Butterfly.new: :color('Purple');
```

You can modify Butterfly to have its own default color and .TWEAK. The .TWEAK method is the same but you wouldn't want to inherit it. It depends on the presence of an attribute that it can't know the child class has:

```
class Butterfly is Insect {
    has $.default-color = 'Vermillion';
```

```
submethod TWEAK ( :$color ) {
    self.color = $color // $!default-color;
    }
}
```

Private Classes

You can declare classes with my to make them private to the current scope. At the file level that class is only available in that file. If you load the file that contains it you won't be able to see it:

```
# PublicClass.pm6
my class PrivateClass { # Hidden from outside the file
    method hello { put "Hello from {self.^name}" }
    }

class PublicClass {
    method hello { PrivateClass.hello }
    }
```

In your program you can load PublicClass and call a method on the PublicClass type. PublicClass can see PrivateClass because it's in the same file. From your program you can't call PrivateClass directly, though. That scope doesn't know about that type:

```
use PublicClass;
PublicClass.hello;  # Hello from PrivateClass
PrivateClass.hello; # Error: Undeclared name: PrivateClass
```

If you need a class only inside another class (and not the rest of the file), you can declare it inside the class. This can be handy to compartmentalize and organize behavior inside a class:

```
class Butterfly {
    my class PrivateHelper {}
    }
```

Private classes are a great tool when you want to compartmentalize some behavior that you need but don't want to expose to normal users. You can use them for intermediate objects that the main program never need know exist.

Exercise 12.5

Create a Butterfly class that contains a private class that tracks when the object was created and updated. Use it to count the number of updates to the class. A method in Butterfly should access the private class to output a summary.

Summary

Classes will likely be your main way of organizing information in your programs, though you don't see it so much in this book because you need to see mostly syntactic topics rather than application design advice. I didn't have the space for good coverage of object-oriented design or analysis, but you should definitely research those on your own. The right design will make your life so much easier.

## CHAPTER 13

Roles

Roles are *mixins* that augment your class as if their contents were defined in it. Once defined their source is effectively forgotten (unlike a parent class). You can use roles to change classes, make a new class from an existing one, and enhance single objects. They are a more flexible and often a better solution than inheritance. These are for code reuse whereas classes are for managing objects.

Adding Behavior to Classes

Construct an empty `Butterfly` class. You can give arguments to `.new` even though no attribute receives their value:

```
class Butterfly {}
my $butterfly = Butterfly.new: :common-name('Perly Cracker');
```

Now give your butterfly a name. Should that be part of the `Butterfly` class? A name isn't the object. *Hamadryas guatemalena* is the name of a butterfly. So are Guatemalan Cracker, Calicó, and Soñadora común. Those are all names for the same butterfly.

Ultimately the code you write has to operate within the framework of the language. The syntax sometimes lets you cognitively separate things.

A name is not a more specific version of something the class already does and it's not limited to butterflies or butterfly-like things. Many dissimilar things can have a common name—animals, cars, food. Not only that, but different people, cultures, or even sections of your office may choose different names. This fact does not define your thingy or its behavior. It's not something that makes a butterfly what it is.

Create a role that contains everything you need for a common name. Everything about a name (and nothing else!) can show up in that role. The role doesn't care what sort of thingy uses it, whether that's a butterfly, a car, or a pizza. Declare it with `role` just as you would a class:

```
role CommonName {
    has $.common-name is rw = 'An unnamed thing';
    }
```

In fact, a role can act just like a class. You can make an object from a role. This *puns* the role into a class:

```
role CommonName {
    has $.common-name is rw = 'An unnamed thing';
    }

my $name = CommonName.new: :common-name('Perly Cracker');
put $name.common-name; # Perly Cracker
```

Apply a role to a class with `does` after the class name in the same way you used `is` for inheritance:

```
class Butterfly does CommonName {};
```

Every `Butterfly` object now has a `$.common-name` attribute and `.new` now sets the `:common-name` using either the default or the name you provide:

```
my $unnamed-butterfly = Butterfly.new;
put $unnamed-butterfly.common-name;   # An unnamed thing

my $butterfly = Butterfly.new: :common-name('Perly Cracker');
put $butterfly.common-name;   # Perly Cracker
```

You can use the same role for something completely different. An SSL certificate has a common name, although its semantic meaning is different:

```
class SSLCertificate does CommonName {}
```

Butterflies and SSL certificates are completely different things and it wouldn't make sense for them to inherit from the same thing. However, they can use the same role.

Exercise 13.1

Create a `ScientificName` role that adds an attribute to store a `Str` for the scientific name. Apply that role to `Butterfly`, create an object, and output the scientific name.

Applying Multiple Roles

You can give a butterfly a scientific name as well as a common name by creating a different role for that. This one has several attributes:

```
role ScientificName {
    has $.kingdom is rw;
    has $.phylum is rw;
    has $.class is rw;
    has $.order is rw;
    has $.family is rw;
    has $.genus is rw;
    has $.species is rw;
    }
```

You can replace the `CommonName` role with `ScientificName` and things work as before:

```
class Butterfly does ScientificName {};
my $butterfly = Butterfly.new: :genus('Hamadryas');
put $butterfly.genus;  # Hamadryas;
```

Multiple `does` expressions apply multiple roles:

```
class Butterfly does ScientificName does CommonName {};
my $butterfly = Butterfly.new:
    :genus('Hamadryas'),
    :common-name('Perly Cracker')
    ;
put $butterfly.genus;
put $butterfly.common-name;
```

Each role inserts its code into `Butterfly` so it can respond to methods from either source:

```
Hamadryas
Perly Cracker
```

Exercise 13.2

Create a role `Lepidoptera` to represent butterflies. Fill in everything from kingdom *Animalia*, phylum *Athropoda*, class *Insecta*, and order *Lepidoptera*. Allow the role to change the family, genus, and species. Use that role in your own `Butterfly` class. After you get that working add the `CommonName` role.

Methods in Roles

You can define methods in roles too. Give the `ScientificName` role a `.gist` method to create your own human-readable text version of the object:

```
role ScientificName {
    ...; # all the attributes specified earlier

    method gist {
        join ' > ', $.kingdom, $.genus;
        }
```

```
        }

    role CommonName {
        has $.common-name is rw;
        }

    class Butterfly does ScientificName does CommonName {};

    my $butterfly = Butterfly.new:
        :genus('Hamadryas'),
        :common-name('Perly Cracker')
        ;
    put $butterfly.genus;
    put $butterfly.common-name;
    put $butterfly.gist;
```

Exercise 13.3

Update your `Lepidoptera` role to have a `binomial-name` method that returns a `Str` that combines the genus and species of the butterfly (in biospeak that's the "binomial name").

To reuse these roles you want to make them available for any code to find and load. You can store roles by themselves in files just as you can with classes. Load them with `use` and they are available in that scope.

Exercise 13.4

Separate the `Lepidoptera` and `CommonName` roles and the `Butterfly` class into their own files. Load those files into your program where you create your `Butterfly` object. Make this program work:

```
    use Butterfly;

    my $butterfly = Butterfly.new:
        :family(  'Nymphalidae' ),
        :genus(   'Hamadryas' ),
        :species( 'perlicus' ),
        ;

    put $butterfly.binomial-name;
```

De-Conflicting Roles

If two roles try to insert the same names you may have to do extra work. Suppose that both `ScientificName` and `CommonName` had a `.gist` method:

```
role ScientificName {
    ...; # all the attributes specified earlier

    method gist {
        join ' > ', $.kingdom, $.genus;
        }
    }

role CommonName {
    has $.common-name is rw;

    method gist { "Common name: $.common-name" }
    }

class Butterfly does ScientificName does CommonName {};
```

The `.gist` method has an explicit signature and isn't marked with `multi`. When you try to compile this you get an error telling you that two roles tried to insert the same method:

```
Method 'gist' must be resolved by class Butterfly because
it exists in multiple roles (CommonName, ScientificName)
```

You can add a `.gist` method to `Butterfly`. Neither role replaces a method already in the class:

```
role ScientificName {
    ...; # all the attributes specified earlier

    method gist {
        join ' > ', $.kingdom, $.genus;
        }
    }

role CommonName {
    has $.common-name is rw;

    method gist { "Common name: $.common-name" }
    }

class Butterfly does ScientificName does CommonName {
    method gist {
        join "\n",
            join( ' > ', $.kingdom, $.genus ),
            "Common name: $.common-name";
        }
    };
```

Or if you want both methods from the roles you can distinguish them with different signatures (and use `multi`). Their role names as a type might do:

```
role ScientificName {
    ...; # all the attributes specified earlier
```

```
    multi method gist ( ScientificName ) {
        "$.genus $.species";
        }
    }

role CommonName {
    has $.common-name is rw;

    multi method gist ( CommonName ) {
        "Common name: $.common-name";
        }
    }

class Butterfly does ScientificName does CommonName {};

my $butterfly = Butterfly.new:
    :genus('Hamadryas' ),
    :species('perlicus'),
    :common-name( 'Perly Cracker' ),
    ;

put '1. ', $butterfly.gist( CommonName );
put '2. ', $butterfly.gist( ScientificName );
```

This way you get both methods:

```
1. Common name: Perly Cracker
2. Hamadryas perlicus
```

You can have the same method in the Butterfly class as long as you declare it with multi and give it a unique signature:

```
class Butterfly does ScientificName does CommonName {
    multi method gist {
        join "\n", map { self.gist: $_ },
            ( ScientificName, CommonName );
        }
    };
my $butterfly = Butterfly.new:
    :genus('Hamadryas'),
    :species('perlicus'),
    :common-name('Perly Cracker')
    ;

put '1. ', $butterfly.gist( CommonName );
put '2. ', $butterfly.gist( ScientificName );
put '3. ', $butterfly.gist;
```

Your output shows all three and you can pick whichever you like:

```
1. Common name: Perly Cracker
2. Hamadryas perlicus
```

```
3. Hamadryas perlicus
Common name: Perly Cracker
```

Anonymous Roles

Not every role needs a name. If you want a role that you don't expect to use again you can add it directly with but. You can apply that directly to a class name. This actually creates a new class with the role applied to it. The new class inherits from the original:

```
class Butterfly {};
my $class-role = Butterfly but role { has $.common-name };

put $class-role.^name; # Butterfly+{<anon|140470326869504>}
say $class-role.^mro; # ((...) (Butterfly) (Any) (Mu))

my $butterfly = $class-role.new:
    :common-name( 'Perly Cracker' );

put $butterfly.common-name;
```

You can do the same thing with less work by removing the variables that stored the classes:

```
my $butterfly2 = ( Butterfly but role { has $.common-name } ).new:
    :common-name('Perlicus Cracker');
put $butterfly2.^name;
put $butterfly2.common-name;
```

That's still messy. You can apply it to the object directly:

```
my $butterfly = Butterfly.new;
my $butterfly2 = $butterfly
    but role { has $.common-name is rw };
$butterfly2.common-name = 'Perlicus Cracker';
put $butterfly2.^name;
put $butterfly2.common-name;
```

You can even skip the variable to store the first object. Without the variable to store the initial object you get something a little shorter:

```
my $butterfly = Butterfly.new
    but role { has $.common-name is rw };
$butterfly.common-name = 'Perlicus Cracker';
put $butterfly.^name;
put $butterfly.common-name;
```

This has the drawback that the original object doesn't know about the roles, so you can't set the common name in the constructor. Your role has to allow the object to change the value to set a value.

Adding a role to an object is handy when you have an object that you may not have created; perhaps it was an argument to your method or the return value from a method you don't control. In this example you take an argument (and make it is copy so you can add the role). You call show-common-name once with a plain Butterfly. The subroutine sees that the object doesn't know about common-name, so it adds it. In your second call to show-common-name your argument already has the common-name attribute so it doesn't need show-common-name to add it:

```
sub show-common-name ( $butterfly is copy ) {
    unless $butterfly.can: 'common-name' {
        put "Adding role!";
        $butterfly = $butterfly
            but role { has $.common-name is rw };
        $butterfly.common-name = 'Perlicus Cracker';
        }

    put $butterfly.common-name;
    }

# an object without the role
my $butterfly = Butterfly.new;
show-common-name( Butterfly.new );

# an object that already has the role
my $class-role = Butterfly but role { has $.common-name };
show-common-name( $class-role.new: :common-name( 'Camelia' ) );
```

The output shows that you added the role in your first call but not the second:

```
Adding role!
Perlicus Cracker
Camelia
```

When should you apply your role? Whenever it makes sense for your problem.

Exercise 13.5

Take your Lepidoptera role to its logical conclusion. Start with a new Animalia role to represent only the kingdom. Create an Arthropoda role to include the Animalia role and represent the phylum. Do this all the way down to the *Hamadryas* genus. From there, create a Hamadryas class that inherits from Butterfly but does all the taxonomic roles down to the genus. From the Hamadryas class you should be able to set a species. Make this program work:

```
use lib <.>;
use Hamadryas;

my $cracker = Hamadryas.new:
    :species( 'perlicus' ),
    :common-name( 'Perly Cracker' ),
    ;
```

```
    put $cracker.binomial-name;
    put $cracker.common-name;
```

Summary

You can define common code in a role and reuse it with disparate things. Since it doesn't create an inheritance relationship it's perfectly suited for features that don't define the basic idea of the type.

## CHAPTER 14

Junctions and Sets

Junctions

A `Junction` is a combination of values that is mostly indistinguishable from a single value. They have their roots in the math of quantum mechanics. You may have heard of Schrödinger's cat, who is both dead and alive at the same time—an analogy that physicist used to show how ridiculous this all is. Well, the joke was on him.

any

The first `Junction` is the any. This "any" is lowercase and is not related to the type `Any`. It creates a value that can act like, well, any of the ones you gave it:

```
my $first-junction = any( 1, 3, 7 );
```

You can make a `Junction` from an `Array` or any other `Positional`:

```
my $junction = any( @array   );   # Array
my $junction = any( 1 ..  10 );   # Range
my $junction = any( 1 ... 10 );   # Sequence
```

Now you have a `Junction` of three values. It will only ever have three values. You can't take one away or add one. There's no interface to extract them or count them. You're not supposed to know—or even care—which values are in there. In fact, `Junction` is the only builtin type that does not inherit from Any:

```
% perl6
To exit type 'exit' or '^D'
> my $first-junction = any( 1, 3, 7 );
any(1, 3, 7)
> $first-junction.^name
Junction
```

```
> $first-junction.^mro
((Junction) (Mu))
```

These are quite handy in complex conditions. Consider the annoying code you've had to write to test if a value is one of three possible numbers:

```
my $n = any( 1, 3, 7 );

if $n == 1 || $n == 3 || $n == 7 {
    put "n is one of those values";
    }
```

Being clever with a Hash doesn't actually feel that much more clever:

```
my Int %hash = map { $_ => True }, (1, 3, 7);
if %hash{$n}:exists {
    put "n is one of those values";
    }
```

Not only does the Junction equal any of those values, but it also equals all of them. This looks like a Block that would never execute, but it does:

```
if $n == 1 && $n == 3 && $n == 7 {
    put "n is all of those values";
    }
```

A Junction is much closer to how you'd probably describe this in speech:

```
if $n == any( 1, 3, 7 ) {
    put "n is one of those values";
    }
```

When you operate on a Junction your code may distribute (*autothread*) that operation over all of its values to produce a Junction of intermediate results. The first step might look like this:

```
if any( 1 == $n, 3 == $n, 7 == $n ) {
    put "n is one of those values";
    }
```

These evaluate to their Boolean values. If $n is 3 one of the comparisons is True:

```
my $n = 3;
if any( False, True, False ) {
    put "n is one of those values";
    }
```

Any True makes the entire junctive expression True:

```
my $n = 3;
if True {
    put "n is one of those values";
    }
```

You don't have to define the `Junction` in the condition. It might already be in a variable and ready for use:

```
my $any = any( 1, 3, 7 );
if $n == $any {
    put "n is one of those values";
    }
```

Here's the beauty of `Junctions`—you don't have to know that you are using one. Here's an `Array` that has some "normal" values and one that is a `Junction`:

```
my @array = 5, any( 1, 7 ), 8, 9;
for @array -> $item {
    put "$item was odd" unless $item %% 2;
    }
```

The loop works with single "normal" values as well as `Junctions`. Notice that the `Junction` creates two lines of output. The stringification happened for each value:

```
5 was odd
1 was odd
7 was odd
9 was odd
```

That multiple stringification could change in the future; it wasn't this way when I started the book and it might change again. The `.gist` on `$item` prevents that:

```
my @array = 5, any( 1, 7 ), 8, 9;
for @array -> $item {
    put "{$item.gist} was odd" unless $item %% 2;
    }

5 was odd
any(1, 7) was odd
9 was odd
```

Exercise 14.1

Make an any `Junction` of the prime numbers between 1 and 10 (so, 2, 3, 5, and 7). Use that `Junction` to note which numbers from 1 to 10 are prime.

There's a symbolic notation for any. The | between values creates a `Junction`. It looks similar to the || for the logical OR operator but is not related:

```
my $n = 3;
my $any = 1 | 3 | 7;
if $n == $any {
    put "n is one of those values";
    }
```

Perl 6 uses |, &, and ^ to create `Junctions`. You might be used to these as numeric bit operators in other languages. You'll find those now are called +|, +^, and +&. That leading + denotes the numeric flavor.

You can change `Junctions` by affecting their values. Numerically adding to a `Junction` adds to every value in it:

```
my $junction = any( 1, 3, 7 );
$junction += 1;
if $junction %% 2 {
    put "{$junction.gist} is even";
    }
```

The output shows that you were able to add one to each of the values:

```
any(2, 4, 8) is even
```

This generally applies to all of the operations, and you can get quite creative with that. What if you add two `any` `Junctions`? Think about this for a minute before you read ahead to the output:

```
my $any-any = any( 6, 7 ) + any( 9, 11 )
put "Result is $any-any";
```

Now figure out what this means:

```
Result is any(any(15, 17), any(16, 18))
```

That's an `any` of anys! Suppose you wanted to check if that value was less than 17. This virtual series of steps finds the answer:

```
$any-any < 17

any( any(15, 17), any(16, 18) ) < 17

any( any(15, 17) < 17, any(16, 18) < 17 )

any( any(15 < 17, 17 < 17), any(16 < 17, 18 < 17) )

any( any(True,False), any(True, False) )

any( True, True )

True
```

This has the same effect as `any( 15, 16, 17, 18 )` but with more steps involved. That's a warning. If you aren't careful you could have an explosion of `Junctions` in there.

all

An `all` Junction requires that each of its values satisfy the condition or method you apply:

```
my $all-of-u = all( <Danaus Bicyclus Amauris> );
if $all-of-u.contains: 'u' {
    put "Everyone has a u";
    }
```

Perhaps you want to check that all of the values are a particular type. In this example there's a `Str` in `@mixed-types`:

```
my @mixed-types = <1 2/3 4+8i Hello>;
if all(@mixed-types) ~~ Numeric {
    put "Every value is a numeric thingy";
    }
else {
    put "One of these things is not like the others";
    }
```

The `Hello` cannot become a number, so a smart match against `Numeric` fails. The entire `Junction` evaluates to `False` because one of its values does.

The `all` is much easier to read than almost anything else that might accomplish the task. Comparing the result of a `.grep` to the original number of elements in the source is too much typing:

```
if @mixed-types.grep( * !~~ Numeric ) == +@mixed-types {
    put "One of these things is not a number";
    }
```

You can create an `all` Junction with the &:

```
my $all-of-u = 'Danaus' & 'Bicyclus' & 'Amauris';
if $all-of-u.contains: 'u' {
    put "Everyone has a u";
    }
```

Exercise 14.2

Using `all`, test if all the numbers you specify on the command line are prime.

---

one

The `one` Junction allows only one of its values to satisfy its condition. If more than one would make the condition `True` the `Junction` fails:

```
put one( 1, 2, 3 ) %% 2 ??      # True
    "Exactly one is even"
```

```
    !!
    "More (or less) than one is even";
```

If more than one thing in the `one` is `True`, then the entire `Junction` is `False`:

```
one( True, True, False ).so     # False;
```

You can create a `one` `Junction` with the `^`:

```
put ( 1 ^ 2 ^ 3 ) %% 2 ??       # True
    "Exactly one is even"
    !!
    "More (or less) than one is even";
```

none

The `none` `Junction` requires that all of the values cause its condition to be `False`. That means that everything should evaluate to `False`. There's no symbolic operator version for this type:

```
put none( 1, 2, 3 ) %% 5 ??     True
    "Exactly one is even"
    !!
    "More (or less) than one is even";
```

Exercise 14.3

Use `none` to test if no numbers you specify on the command line are prime. Once you've done that, use `none` to test that some numbers in an `Array` are prime.

Some Junctive Tricks

`Junctions` aren't designed for introspection and you aren't supposed to care if the value is in a `Junction`. This isn't too hard to work around, though.

You can apply an operation to each value with a hyperoperator (Chapter 6). This one adds one to each element:

```
my $junction = any( 1, -3, 7 );
say $junction »+« 1;
```

The new `Junction` has new values. You still aren't supposed to know what these new values are, but something must know what they are to add one to them:

```
any(2, -2, 8)
```

The `»+«` surrounds the `+` because that's an infix operator and expects arguments on either side of it. You can call a method (a postfix thing) on each item:

```
$junction>>.is-prime; # any((True), (False), (False))
```

That method could be .take, which adds the value to the list that gather makes. This means that the values can escape the Junction:

```
my $junction = any( 1, -3, 7 );
my @values = gather $junction».take;
put "Values are @values[]";
```

Don't make a habit of this because it's slightly naughty. You aren't supposed to know how to do this.

A Junction is handy to allow a combination of types in a type constraint. Use the subset of the Junction of both types as the constraint:

```
subset IntInf where Int | Inf;
sub add ( IntInf $a, IntInf $b ) { $a + $b }

put add( 1, 3 );   # 4
put add( 1, Inf ); # Inf
```

Exercise 14.4

Rewrite the number-guessing game from Chapter 2 to have three secret numbers. This time the hints are a bit trickier. If any of the secret numbers are smaller than the guess, tell the person that one or some of them are smaller. Do the same with larger numbers. For a single guess, some numbers may be larger and others smaller. When the person has guessed all of the secret numbers, end the game. Is it easier to use given-when or if? Using all of the Junction types may make this easier.

Table 14-1 provides a summary of Junctions.

Table 14-1. Summary of Junctions

Junction	Operator	Description
any	|	Any of the values will work.
all	&	All of the values must work.
one	^	Exactly one of the values will work.
none		None of the values can work.

Sets

Sets are another way to combine values. They aren't like Junctions, where several values can act like one value; they combine zero or more values as its own thingy that you can inspect. Each value can be in the Set only once (although there are weighted Sets I won't write about), and once created the Set is fixed.

A `Set` is a type of `Associative`, so many of the things you already know about those work on `Set`s.

You can create a `Set` with a routine or a coercer. Each thingy in the `List` is a *member* of the `Set`. These are the same:

```
set( 1, 2, 3 )
(1, 2, 3).Set
```

You can store any combination or mixture of thingys, including type objects:

```
set( <♠ ♣ ♥ ♦> )
set( Int, 3, Inf, 'Hamadryas', $(1,2,3) )
```

A `Set` stores a thingy only once. It's either in the `Set` or it isn't, so it doesn't need duplicates:

```
put set( 1, 2, 3 ).elems;          # 3
put set( 1, 2, 2, 3, 3, 3 ).elems; # 3
```

You can check that a value is in the `Set` with the (`elem`) operator:

```
my $set = <♠ ♣ ♥ ♦>.Set;
put 'Number is in the set' if '♥' (elem) $set;
```

There's also the fancy Unicode ∈ operator that tests if the thingy is in the set (or is a "member" of the set):

```
put 'Number is in the set' if '♥' ∈ $set;
```

These operators know that they need `Set`s, so they coerce what you give them:

```
put 'Number is in the set' if '♥' ∈ <♠ ♣ ♥ ♦>;
```

With that operator the `Set` is the second operand. The order of operands is reversed for the (`cont`) and ∋ operators. Now you test that a `Set` contains an element:

```
put 'Number is in the set' if $set (cont) '♥';
put 'Number is in the set' if $set ∋ '♥';
```

You can test that a thingy is not a member of a `Set` by either prefacing the ASCII operator with a ! or using the Unicode version with the line through it:

```
put 'Number is not in the set' if '♥' !(elem) $set;
put 'Number is not in the set' if '♥' ∉ $set;
put 'Number is not in the set' if $set !(cont) '♥';
put 'Number is not in the set' if $set ∌ '♥';
```

You can compare `Set`s to other `Set`s. Another `Set` that contains only some of the members is a *subset*. A "strict" or "proper" subset is one that is smaller than the `Set` and only contains elements of the `Set`. Another way to say that is a proper subset is always smaller. The (<) (or ⊂) operator does that with the opening of the angle toward the larger Set. The order of elements does not matter:

```
set( 1, 3 )    (<) set( 1, 3, 7 ); # True
set( 3, 1, 7 ) (<) set( 1, 3 );    # False (not smaller)
set( 5, 7 )     ⊂  set( 1, 3, 7 ); # False (5 not in set)
```

A ! in front of the ASCII operator or a line through the Unicode operator negates the condition:

```
set( 1, 3 )    !(<) set( 1, 3, 7 ); # False
set( 3, 1, 7 ) !(<) set( 1, 3 );    # True
set( 5, 7 )     ⊄   set( 1, 3, 7 ); # True
```

Use the (>=) or ⊆ operators if you want to allow the Sets to be the same size:

```
set( 1, 3 )    (<=) set( 1, 3, 7 ); # True
set( 1, 3, 7 ) (<=) set( 1, 3, 7 ); # True
set( 3, 1, 7 ) ⊆    set( 1, 3 );     # False (subset has 7)
```

Negate those in the same way:

```
set( 1, 3 )    !(<=) set( 1, 3, 7 ); # False
set( 1, 3, 7 ) !(<=) set( 1, 3, 7 ); # False
set( 3, 1, 7 )  ⊈    set( 1, 3 );     # True
```

You can also have *supersets*. That's just a matter of which one you allow to be the larger Set. So far you've seen examples where you expected the larger Set to be to the right of the operator. Flip those operators around so you expect the larger Set to be on the left:

```
set( 3, 1, 7 ) (>) set( 1, 3 );    # False (not smaller)
set( 3, 1, 7 ) ⊃   set( 1, 3 );    # False (not smaller)

set( 3, 1, 7 ) !(>) set( 1, 3 );    # True
set( 3, 1, 7 )  ⊅   set( 1, 3 );    # True
```

Table 14-2 shows the rest of the Set operations.

Table 14-2. Set comparators

Operation	Operator	Code number	Description
$a (elem) $set	∈	U+2208	$a is a member of $set
$a !(elem) $set	∉	U+2209	$a is not a member of $set
$set (cont) $a	∋	U+220B	$set contains $a
$set !(cont) $a	∌	U+220C	$set does not contain $a
$set-a (<) $set-b	⊂	U+2282	$set-a is a proper subset of $set-b
$set-a !(<) $set-b!	⊄	U+2284	$set-a is not a proper subset of $set-b
$set-a (<=) $set-b!	⊆	U+2286	$set-a is the same or is a subset of $set-b
$set-a !(<=) $set-b!	⊈	U+2288	$set-a is not the same and isn't a subset of $set-b
$set-a (>) $set-b!	⊃	U+2283	$set-a is a proper superset of $set-b

Operation	Operator	Code number	Description
$set-a !(>) $set-b!	⊅	U+2285	$set-a is not a proper superset of $set-b
$set-a (>=) $set-b!	⊇	U+2287	$set-a is the same or is a superset of $set-b
$set-a !(>=) $set-b!	⊉	U+2289	$set-a is not the same and isn't a superset of $set-b

---

Exercise 14.5

In Chapter 9 you used a `Map` to check allowed values. Do the same thing with a `List`. Prompt for some starting colors (perhaps all on one line that you break up into elements). Continue to prompt for colors and report if the color was one of the initial colors. Can you do this ignoring case?

Set Operations

You can operate on two `Set`s to create new `Set`s. A *union* is a combination of two `Set`s. Each element still shows up only once:

```
set(1,2) (|) set(3,7);  # set(1 2 3 7)
set(1,2)  ∪  set(3,7);  # set(1 2 3 7)
```

The *intersection* makes the `Set` of the elements they have in common:

```
set(1,3) (&) set(3,7);  # set(3)
set(1,2)  ∩  set(3,7);  # set()
```

The *set difference* creates a `Set` made up of the elements from the first `Set` that aren't in the second. The \ isn't the ASCII backslash; it's (U+2216 SET MINUS):

```
set( <a b> ) (-) set( <b c> );  # set(a)
set( <A b> )  \  set( <x y> );  # set(A b)
```

The *symmetric set difference* does a similar thing in both directions. It creates a `Set` containing all the elements of either `Set` that don't show up in the other:

```
set( <a b> ) (^) set( <b c> );  # set(a c)
set( <A b> )  ⊖  set( <x y> );  # set(A b x y)
```

These operations are summarized in Table 14-3.

Table 14-3. Set creators

Operation	Operator	Code number	Description
(|)	∪	U+222A	Union (combination)
(&)	∩	U+2229	Intersection (overlap)
(-)	\	U+2216	Set difference
(^)	⊖	U+2296	Symmetric set difference

> ### Exercise 14.6
>
> Create two `Set`s of 10 numbers between 1 and 50. Find their intersection and union.

Summary

Junctions make several values pretend to be a single value, in such a way that you can't tell which value it is or how many values there are. You create the `Junction` in a way that makes the values all work together or separately. A `Set` also combines values but lets you look inside to see what those values are. You can combine `Set`s in various ways to create new ones. This is handy to tell what's in, out, or common.

## CHAPTER 15

Regular Expressions

Regular expressions (or *regexes*) are patterns that describe a possible set of matching texts. They are a little language of their own, and many characters have a special meaning inside patterns. They may look cryptic at first, but after you learn them you have quite a bit of power.

Forget what you've seen about patterns in other languages. The Perl 6 pattern syntax started over. It's less compact but also more powerful. In some cases it acts a bit differently.

This chapter shows simple patterns that match particular characters or sets of characters. It's just the start. In Chapter 16 you'll see fancier patterns and the side effects of matching. In Chapter 17 you'll take it all to the next level.

The Match Operator

A pattern describes a set of text values. The simple pattern abc describes all the values that have an a next to a b next to a c. The trick then is to decide if a particular value is in the set of matching values. There are no half or partial matches; it matches or it doesn't.

A pattern inside m/.../ immediately applies itself to the value in $_. If the pattern is in the Str the match operator returns something that evaluates to True in a condition:

```
$_ = 'Hamadryas';
if m/Hama/ { put 'It matched!'; }
else       { put 'It missed!';  }
```

That's a bit verbose. The conditional operator takes care of that:

```
put m/Hama/ ?? 'It matched!' !! 'It missed!';
```

You don't have to match against $_. You can use the smart match to apply it to a different value. That's the target:

```
my $genus = 'Hamadryas';
put $genus ~~ m/Hama/ ?? 'It matched!' !! 'It missed!';
```

That target could be anything, including an Array or Hash. These match a single item:

```
$genus                ~~ m/Hama/;
@animals[0]           ~~ m/Hama/;
%butterfly<Hamadryas> ~~ m/perlicus/;
```

But you can also match against multiple items. The object on the left side of the smart match decides how the pattern applies to the object. This matches if any of the elements in @animals matches:

```
if @animals ~~ m/Hama/ {
    put "Matches at least one animal";
    }
```

This is the same as matching against a Junction:

```
if any(@animals) ~~ m/Hama/ {
    put "Matches at least one animal";
    }
```

The match operator is commonly used in the condition inside a .grep:

```
my @hama-animals = @animals.grep: /Hama/;
```

Match Operator Syntax

The match operator can use alternate delimiters, similar to the quoting mechanism:

```
m{Hama}
m!Hama!
```

Whitespace inside the match operator doesn't matter. It's not part of the pattern (until you say so, as you'll see later). All of these are the same, including the last example with vertical whitespace:

```
m/ Hama /
m{ Hama }
m! Hama !
m/
      Hama
/
```

You can put spaces between alphabetic characters, but you'll probably get a warning because Perl 6 wants you to put those together:

```
m/ Ha ma /
```

If you want a literal space inside the match operator you can escape it (along with other things you'll see later):

```
m/ Ha\ ma /
```

Quoting whitespace makes it literal too (the space around the quoted whitespace is still insignificant), or you can quote it all together:

```
m/ Ha ' ' ma /
m/ 'Ha ma' /
```

You need to quote or escape any character that's not alphabetic or a number, even if those characters aren't "special." The other unquoted characters may be *metacharacters* that have special meaning in the pattern language.

Successful Matches

If the match operator succeeds it returns a `Match` object, which is always a `True` value. If you `put` that object it shows you the part of the `Str` that matched. The `say` calls `.gist` and the output is a bit different:

```
$_ = 'Hamadryas';
my $match = m/Hama/;
put $match; # Hama
say $match; # ?Hama?
```

The output of `say` gets interesting as the patterns get more complicated. That makes it useful for the regex chapters, and you'll see more of that here compared to the rest of the book.

If the match does not succeed it returns `Nil`, which is always `False`:

```
$_ = 'Hamadryas';
my $match = m/Hama/;
put $match.^name;      # Nil
```

It's usually a good idea to check the result before you do anything with it:

```
if my $match = m/Hama/ { # matched
    say $match;
    }
```

You don't need the `$match` variable though. The result of the last match shows up in the special variable $/, which you'll see more of later:

```
if m/Hama/ { # matched
    say $/;
    }
```

Defining a Pattern

Useful patterns can get quite long and unwieldy. Use `rx//` to define a pattern (a Regex) for later use. This pattern is not immediately applied to any target. This allows you to define a pattern somewhere that doesn't distract from what you are doing:

```
my $genus = 'Hamadryas';
my $pattern = rx/ Hama /; # something much more complicated
$genus ~~ $pattern;
```

and reuse the pattern wherever you need it:

```
for lines() -> $line {
    put $line if $line ~~ $pattern;
    }
```

It's possible to combine saved patterns into a larger one. This allows you to decompose complicated patterns into smaller, more tractable ones that you can reuse later (which you'll do extensively in Chapter 17):

```
my $genus = 'Hamadryas';

my $hama  = rx/Hama/;
my $dryas = rx/dryas/;
my $match = $genus ~~ m/$hama$dryas/;

say $match;
```

Rather than storing a variable in an object, declare a lexical pattern with `regex`. This looks like a subroutine because it has a `Block` but it's not code inside; it's a pattern and uses that slang:

```
my regex hama { Hama }
```

Use this in a pattern by surrounding it with angle brackets:

```
my $genus = 'Hamadryas';
put $genus ~~ m/<hama>/ ?? 'It matched!' !! 'It missed!';
```

You can define multiple named regexes and use them together:

```
my regex hama  { Hama }
my regex dryas { dryas }

$_ = 'Hamadryas';
say m/<hama><dryas>/;
```

Each named regex becomes a submatch. You can see the structure when you output it with `say`. It shows the overall result and the results of the subpatterns too:

```
｢Hamadryas｣
 hama => ｢Hama｣
 dryas => ｢dryas｣
```

Treat the `Match` object like a `Hash` (although it isn't) to get the parts that matched the named regexes. The name of the regex is the "key":

```
$_ = 'Hamadryas';
my $result =  m/<hama><dryas>/;

if $result {
    put "First: $result<hama>";
    put "Second: $result<dryas>";
    }
```

Predefined Patterns

Table 15-1 shows several of the predefined patterns that are ready for you to use. You can define your patterns in a library and export them just like you could with subroutines:

```
# Patterns.pm6
my regex hama is export { Hama }
```

Load the module and those named regexes are available to your patterns:

```
use lib <.>;
use Hama;

$_ = 'Hamadryas';
say m/ <hama> /;
```

Table 15-1. Named character classes

Predefined pattern	What it matches
`<alnum>`	Alphabetic and digit characters
`<alpha>`	Alphabetic characters
`<ascii>`	Any ASCII character
`<blank>`	Horizontal whitespace
`<cntrl>`	Control characters
`<digit>`	Decimal digits
`<graph>`	`<alnum>` + `<punct>`
`<ident>`	A valid identifier character
`<lower>`	Lowercase characters
`<print>`	`<graph>` + `<space>`, but without `<cntrl>`
`<punct>`	Punctuation and symbols beyond ASCII
`<space>`	Whitespace
`<upper>`	Uppercase characters
`<|wb>`	Word boundary (an assertion rather than a character)
`<word>`	`<alnum>` + Unicode marks + connectors, like '_' (extra)
`<ws>`	Whitespace (required between word characters, optional otherwise)

Predefined pattern	What it matches
<ww>	Within a word (an assertion rather than a character)
<xdigit>	Hexadecimal digits [0-9A-Fa-f]

Exercise 15.1

Create a program that uses a regular expression to output all of the matching lines from the files you specify on the command line.

Matching Nonliteral Characters

You don't have to literally type a character to match it. You might have an easier time specifying its code point or name. You can use the same \x[*CODEPOINT*] or \c[*NAME*] that you saw in double-quoted Strs in Chapter 4.

If you specify a name it must be all uppercase.

You could match the initial capital *H* by name, even though you have to type a literal H in the name:

```
my $pattern = rx/
    \c[LATIN CAPITAL LETTER H] ama
    /;
$_ = "Hamadryas";

put $pattern ?? 'Matched!' !! 'Missed!';
```

You can do the same thing with the code point. If you specify a code point use the hexadecimal number (with either case):

```
my $pattern = rx/
    \x[48] ama
    /;
$_ = "Hamadryas";

put $pattern ?? 'Matched!' !! 'Missed!';
```

This makes more sense if you want to match a character that's either hard to type or hard to read. If the Str has the 🐱 character (U+1F431 CAT FACE), you might not be able to distinguish that from 😸 (U+1F638 GRINNING CAT FACE WITH SMILING EYES) without looking very closely. Instead of letting another programmer mistake your intent, you can use the name to save some eyestrain:

```
my $pattern = rx/
    \c[CAT FACE]  # or \x[1F431]
    /;
$_ = "This is a catface: 🐱";
put $pattern ?? 'Matched!' !! 'Missed!';
```

Matching Any Character

Patterns have *metacharacters* that match something other than their literal selves. Some of these are listed in Table 15-2 (and most you won't see in this chapter). The . matches any character (*including* a newline). This pattern matches any target that has at least one character:

```
m/ . /
```

To match a Str with an *a* and a *c* separated by a character, put the dot between them in the pattern. This skips the lines that don't match that pattern:

```
for lines() {
    next unless m/a.c/;
    .put
    }
```

Escaping characters

Some characters have special meaning in patterns. The colon introduces an adverb and the # starts a comment. To match those as literal characters you need to escape them. A backslash will do:

```
my $pattern = rx/ \# \: Hama \. /
```

This means to match a literal backslash, you need to escape that too:

```
my $pattern = rx/ \# \: Hama \\ /
```

You can do the same thing with the other pattern metacharacters. To match a literal dot, escape it:

```
my $pattern = rx/ \. /
```

The backslash only escapes the character that comes immediately after it. You can't escape a literal space character, and you can't escape a character that isn't special. Table 15-2 shows what you need to escape, even though I haven't shown you most of those features yet.

Table 15-2. Escapable pattern characters

Metacharacter	Why it's special
#	Starts a comment
\	Escapes the next character or a shortcut
.	Matches any character
:	Starts an adverb, or prevents backtracking
(and)	Starts a capture
< and >	Used to create higher-level thingys
[,], and '	Used for grouping
+, |, &, -, and ^	Set operations

Metacharacter	Why it's special
?, *, +, and %	Quantifiers
|	Alternation
^ and $	Anchors
$	Starts a variable or named capture
=	Assigns to named captures

Characters inside quotes are always their literal selves:

```
my $pattern = rx/ '#:Hama' \\ /
```

You can't use the single quotes to escape the backslash since a single backslash will still try to escape the character that comes after it.

Matching literal spaces

You have a tougher time if you want to match literal spaces. You can't escape a space with \ because unspace isn't allowed in a pattern. Instead, put quotes around the literal space:

```
my $pattern = rx/ Hamadryas ' ' laodamia /;
```

Or put the entire sequence in quotes:

```
my $pattern = rx/ 'Hamadryas laodamia' /;
```

Those single quotes can quickly obscure what belongs where; it can be helpful to spread the pattern across lines and note what you are trying to do:

```
my $pattern = rx/
    Hamadryas    # genus
    ' '              # literal space
    laodamia     # species
    /;
```

You can make whitespace significant with the :s adverb:

```
my $pattern = rx:s/ Hamadryas laodamia /;
```

```
my $pattern = rx/ :s Hamadryas laodamia /;
```

The :s is the short form of :sigspace:

```
my $pattern = rx:sigspace/ Hamadryas laodamia /;
```

```
my $pattern = rx/ :sigspace Hamadryas laodamia /;
```

Notice that this will match Hamadryas laodamia, even though the pattern has whitespace at the beginning and end. The :s turns the whitespace in the pattern into a subrule <.ws>:

```
$_ = 'Hamadryas laodamia';
my $pattern = rx/ Hamadryas <.ws> laodamia /;
if m/$pattern/ {
    say $/;  # ?Hamadryas laodamia?
    }
```

You can combine adverbs, but they each get their own colon. Order does not matter. This pattern has significant whitespace and is case insensitive:

```
my $pattern = rx:s:i/ Hamadryas Laodamia /;
```

Matching Types of Characters

So far, you've matched literal characters. You typed out the characters you wanted, and escaped them in some cases. There are some sets of characters that are so common they get shortcuts. These start with a backslash followed by a letter that connotes the set of characters. Table 15-3 shows the list of shortcuts.

If you want to match any digit, you can use \d. This matches anything that is a digit, not just the Arabic digits:

```
/ \d /
```

Each of these shortcuts comes with a complement. \D matches any nondigit.

Table 15-3. Character class shortcuts

Shortcut	Characters that match
\d	Digits (Unicode property N)
\D	Anything that isn't a digit
\w	Word characters: letters, digits, or underscores
\W	Anything that isn't a word character
\s	Any kind of whitespace
\S	Anything that isn't whitespace
\h	Horizontal whitespace
\H	Anything that isn't horizontal whitespace
\v	Vertical whitespace
\V	Anything that isn't vertical whitespace
\t	A tab character (specifically, only U+0009)
\T	Anything that isn't a tab character
\n	A newline or carriage return/newline pair
\N	Anything that isn't a newline

Exercise 15.2

Write a program that outputs only those lines of input that contain three decimal digits in a row. You wrote most of this program in the previous exercise.

Unicode properties

The Unicode Character Database (UCD) defines the code points and their names and assigns them one or more properties. Each character knows many things about itself, and you can use some of that information to match them. Place the name of the Unicode property in <:...>. That colon must come right after the opening angle bracket. If you wanted to match something that is a letter, you could use the property `Letter`:

```
/ <:Letter> /
```

Instead of matching a property, you can match characters that don't have that particular property. Put a ! in front of the property name to negate it. This matches characters that aren't the title-case letters:

```
/ <:!TitlecaseLetter> /
```

Each property has a long form, like `Letter`, and a short form, in this case `L`. There are other properties, such as `Uppercase_Letter` and `Lu`, or `Number` and `N`:

```
/ <:L> /
/ <:N> /
```

You can match the characters that belong to certain Unicode blocks or scripts:

```
<:Block('Basic Latin')>
<:Script<Latin>>
```

Even though you can abbreviate these property names I'll use the longer names in this book. See the documentation for the other properties.

Combining properties

One property might not be enough to describe what you want to match. To build fancier ones, combine them with character class set operators. These aren't the same operators you saw in Chapter 14; they're special to character classes.

The + creates the union of the two properties. Any character that has either property will match:

```
/ <:Letter + :Number> /
/ <:Open_Punctuation + :Close_Punctuation> /
```

Subtract one property from another with -. Any character with the first property that doesn't have the second property will match this. The following example matches all the identifier characters (in the UCD sense, not the Perl 6 sense). There are the characters that can start an identifier and those that can be in the other positions:

```
/ <:ID_Continue - :Number> /
```

You can shorten this to not match a character without a particular property. It looks like you leave off the first part of the subtraction; the - comes right after the opening angle bracket. That implies you're subtracting from all characters. This matches all the characters that don't have the Letter property:

```
/ <-:Letter> /
```

Exercise 15.3

Write a program to count all of the characters that match either the Letter or Number properties. What percentage of the code points between 1 and 0xFFFD are either letters or numbers? The .chr method may be handy here.

User-Defined Character Classes

You can define your own character classes. Put the characters that you want to match inside <[...]>. These aren't the same square brackets that you saw earlier for grouping; these are inside the angle brackets. This character class matches either a, b, or 3:

```
/ <[ab3]> /
```

As with everything else so far, this matches one character and that one character can be any of the characters in the character class. This character class matches either case at a single position:

```
/ <[Hh]> ama /    # also / [ :i h ] ama /
```

You could specify the hexadecimal value of the code point. The whitespace is insignificant:

```
/ <[ \x[48] \x[68] ]> ama /
```

The character name versions work too:

```
/ <[
    \c[LATIN CAPITAL LETTER H]
    \c[LATIN SMALL LETTER H]
    ]>
/
```

You can make a long list of characters:

```
/ <[abcdefghijklmnopqrstuvwxyz]> / # from a to z
```

Inside the character class the # is just a #. If you try to put a comment in there all of the characters in your message become part of the character class:

```
/ <[
    \x[48] # uppercase
    \x[68] # lowercase
  ]>
/
```

You'll probably get warnings about repeated characters if you try to do that.

Character class ranges

But that's too much work. You can use .. to specify a range of characters. The literal characters work as well as the hexadecimal values and the names. Notice you don't quote the literal characters in these ranges:

```
/ <[a..z]> /
/ <[ \x[61] .. \x[7a] ]> /
/ <[ \c[LATIN SMALL LETTER A] .. \c[LATIN SMALL LETTER Z] ]> /
```

The range doesn't have to be the only thing in the square brackets:

```
/ <[a..z 123456789]> /
```

You could have two ranges:

```
/ <[a..z 1..9]> /
```

Negated character classes

Sometimes it's easier to specify the characters that can't match. You can create a negated character class by adding a - between the opening angle bracket and the opening square bracket. This example matches any character that is *not* a, b, or 3:

```
/ <-[ab3]> /
```

Space inside a character class is also insignificant:

```
/ <-[ a b 3 ]> /
```

You can use a negated character class of one character. Quotes inside the character class are literal characters because Perl 6 knows you aren't quoting:

```
/ <-[ ' ]> /    # not a quote character
```

This one matches any character that is not a newline:

```
/ <-[ \n ]> /   # not a newline
```

The predefined character class shortcuts can be part of your character class:

```
/ <-[ \d \s ]> /   # digits or whitespace
```

Like the Unicode properties, you can combine sets of characters:

```
/ <[abc] + [xyz]> /     # but, also <[abcxyz]>

/ <[a..z] - [ijk]> /    # easier than two ranges
```

Exercise 15.4

Create a program to output all the input lines. Skip any line that contains a letter
unless it's a vowel. Also skip any lines that are blank (that is, only have whitespace).

Matching Adverbs

You can change how the match operator works by applying adverbs, just like you
changed how Q worked in Chapter 4. There are several, but you'll only see the most
commonly used here.

Matching Either Case

So far a character in your pattern matches exactly the same character in the target. An
H only matches an uppercase *H* and not any other sort of *H*:

```
my $pattern = rx/ Hama /;
put 'Hamadryas' ~~ $pattern;  # Matches
```

Change your pattern by one character. Instead of an uppercase H, use a lowercase one:

```
my $pattern = rx/ hama /;
put 'Hamadryas' ~~ $pattern;  # Misses because h is not H
```

The pattern is case sensitive, so this doesn't match. But you can make it case insensitive with an adverb. The :i adverb makes the literal alphabetic characters match
either case. You can put the adverb right after the rx or the m:

```
my $pattern = rx:i/ hama /;
put 'Hamadryas' ~~ $pattern;  # Matches, :i outside
```

This is the reason you can't use the colon as the delimiter!

When you use an adverb on the outside of the pattern, that adverb applies to the
entire pattern. You can also put the adverb on the inside of the pattern:

```
my $pattern = rx/ :i hama /;
put 'Hamadryas' ~~ $pattern;  # Matches, :i inside
```

Isn't that interesting? Now you start to see why whitespace isn't counted as part of the
pattern. There's much more going on besides literal matching of characters.

The adverb applies from the point of its insertion to the end of the pattern. In this
case it applies to the entire pattern because the :i is at the beginning. Put that adverb
later in the pattern, and it applies from there to the rest of the pattern. Here the ha

only match lowercase because the adverb shows up later. The rest of the pattern after the :i is case insensitive:

```
my $pattern = rx/ ha :i ma /; # final ma case insensitive
```

You can *group* parts of patterns with square brackets. This example groups the am but doesn't do much else because there's nothing else special going on:

```
my $pattern = rx/ h [ am ] a /;
```

An adverb inside a group applies only to that group:

```
my $pattern = rx/ h [ :i am ] a /;
```

The rules are the same: the adverb applies from the point of its insertion to the end of the group:

```
my $pattern = rx/ h [ a :i m ] a /; # matches haMa or hama
```

At this point, you're probably going to start mixing up what's going on. There's another reason whitespace doesn't matter—you can add comments to your pattern:

```
my $pattern = rx/
    h
    [           # group this next part
        a
        :i      # case insensitive to end of group
        m
    ]           # end of group
    a
    /;
```

Everything from the # character to the end of the line is a comment. You can use embedded comments too:

```
my $pattern = rx/
    :i #`( case insensitive ) Hama
    /;
```

These aren't particularly good comments because you're annotating what the syntax already denotes. As a matter of good practice, you should comment what you are trying to match rather than what the syntax does. However, the world isn't going to end if you leave a reminder for yourself of what a new concept does.

Exercise 15.5

Write a program that outputs only the lines of input that contain the text ei. You'll probably want to save this program to build on in later exercises.

Ignoring Marks

The :ignoremark adverb changes the pattern so that accents and other marks don't matter. The marks can be there or not. It works if the marks are in the target or the pattern:

```
$_ = 'húdié';   # ??
put m/ hudie /              ?? 'Matched' !! 'Missed';  # Missed
put m:ignoremark/ hudie / ?? 'Matched' !! 'Missed';  # Matched

$_ = 'hudie';
put m:ignoremark/ húdié / ?? 'Matched' !! 'Missed';  # Matched
```

It even works if both the target and the pattern have different marks in the same positions:

```
$_ = 'hüdiê';
put m:ignoremark/ húdié / ?? 'Matched' !! 'Missed';  # Matched
```

Some adverbs can show up inside the pattern. They apply to the parts of the pattern that come after them:

```
$_ = 'hüdiê';
put m/ :ignoremark hudie / ?? 'Matched' !! 'Unmatched';  # Matched
```

Global Matches

A pattern might be able to match several times in the same text. The :global adverb gets all of the nonoverlapping Matches. It returns a List:

```
$_ = 'Hamadryas perlicus';
my $matches = m:global/ . s /;
say $matches;   # (?as? ?us?)
```

No matches gets you an empty List:

```
$_ = 'Hamadryas perlicus';
my $matches = m:global/ six /;
say $matches;   # ()
```

The match operator can find overlapping matches too. Use :overlap to return a potentially longer list. The ?uta? and ?ani? here both match the same *a*:

```
$_ = 'Bhutanitis thaidina';

my $global = m:global/ <[aeiou]> <-[aeiou]> <[aeiou]> /;
say $global;   # (?uta? ?iti? ?idi?)

my $overlap = m:overlap/ <[aeiou]> <-[aeiou]> <[aeiou]> /;
say $overlap; # (?uta? ?ani? ?iti? ?idi? ?ina?)
```

Things That Use Patterns

There are many features that you haven't been able to use so far because you hadn't seen regexes yet. Now you've seen regexes, so you can see these things. There are a couple of `Str` methods that work with a pattern to transform values. This section is a taste of the features you'll use most often.

The `.words` and `.comb` methods break up text. The `.split` method is the general case of that. It takes a pattern to decide how to break up the text. Whatever it matches are the parts that disappear. You could break up a line on tabs, for instance:

```
my @words = $line.split: / \t /;
```

`.grep` can use the match operator to select things. If the match operator succeeds it returns something that's `True`, and that element is part of the result:

```
my @words-with-e = @word.grep: /:i e/;
```

Or, to put it all together:

```
my @words-with-e = $line.split( / \t / ).grep( /:i e/ );
```

`.split` can specify multiple possible separators. Not all of them need be matches. This breaks up a line on a literal comma or whitespace:

```
my @words-with-e = $line
    .split( [ ',', / \s / ] )
    .grep( /:i e/ );
```

`.comb` does a job similar to `.split`, but it breaks up the text by keeping the parts that matched. This keeps all the nonoverlapping groups of three digits and discards everything else:

```
my @digits = $line.comb: /\d\d\d/;
```

With no argument `.comb` uses the pattern of the single `.` to match any character. This breaks up a `Str` into its characters without discarding anything:

```
my @characters = $line.comb: /./;
```

Substitutions

The `.subst` method works with a pattern to substitute the matched text with other text:

```
my $line = "This is PERL 6";
put $line.subst: /PERL/, 'Perl';  # This is Perl 6
```

This one makes the substitution for the first match:

```
my $line = "PERL PERL PERL";
put $line.subst: /PERL/, 'Perl';  # Perl PERL PERL
```

Use the `:g` adverb to make all possible substitutions:

```
my $line = "PERL PERL PERL";
put $line.subst: /PERL/, 'Perl';  # Perl Perl Perl
```

Each of these returns the modified `Str` and leaves the original alone. Use `.subst-mutate` to change the original value:

```
my $line = "PERL PERL PERL";
$line.subst-mutate: /PERL/, 'Perl', :g;
put $line;  # Perl Perl Perl
```

These will be much more useful with the regex features you'll see in the next chapter.

Exercise 15.6

Using `.split`, output the third column of a tab-delimited file. The butterfly census file you made at the end of Chapter 9 would do nicely here.

Summary

You haven't seen the full power of regexes in this chapter since it was mostly about the mechanism of applying the patterns to text. That's not a big deal—the patterns can be much more sophisticated, but the mechanisms are the same. In the next chapter you'll see most of the fancier features you'll regularly use.

## CHAPTER 16

Fancier Regular Expressions

You won't see all the rest of the regular expression syntax in this chapter, but you'll see the syntax you'll use the most. There's much more to patterns, but this should get you most of the way through common problems. With grammars (Chapter 17), the power of even simple patterns will become apparent.

Quantifiers

Quantifiers allow you to repeat a part of a pattern. Perhaps you want to match several of the same letter in a row—an *a* followed by one or more *b*'s then another *a*. You don't care how many *b*'s there are as long as there's at least one of them. The + quantifier matches the immediately preceding part of the pattern one or more times:

```
my @strings = < Aa Aba Abba Abbba Ababa >;
for @strings {
    put $_, ' ', m/ :i ab+ a / ?? 'Matched!' !! 'Missed!';
    }
```

The first `Str` here doesn't match because there isn't at least one *b*. All of the others have an *a* followed by one or more *b*s and another *a*:

```
Aa Missed!
Aba Matched!
Abba Matched!
Abbba Matched!
Ababa Matched!
```

A quantifier only applies to the part of the pattern immediately in front of it—that's the b, not the ab. Group the ab and apply the quantifier to the group (which counts as one thingy):

```
my @strings = < Aa Aba Abba Abbba Ababa >;
for @strings {
```

```
    put $_, ' ', m/ :i [ab]+ a / ?? 'Matched!' !! 'Missed!';
    }
```

Now different Strs match. The ones with repeated *b*'s don't match because the quantifier applies to the [ab] group. Only two of the Strs have repeated *ab*'s:

```
Aa Missed!
Aba Matched!
Abba Missed!
Abbba Missed!
Ababa Matched!
```

Exercise 16.1

Using *butterfly_census.txt* (the file you made at the end of Chapter 9), use a regex to count the number of distinct butterfly species whose names have two or more consecutive *i*'s. Use the + quantifier in your pattern.

Zero or More

The * quantifier is like + but matches *zero* or more times. This makes that part of the pattern optional. If it matches it can repeat as many times as it likes. Perhaps you want to allow the letter *a* between *b*'s. The *a*'s can be there or not be there:

```
my @strings = < Aba Abba Abbba Ababa >;
for @strings {
    put $_, ' ', m/ :i ba*b / ?? 'Matched!' !! 'Missed!';
    }
```

The Strs with consecutive *b*'s match because they have zero *a*'s between the *b*'s, but the Str with *bab* also matches because it has zero or more *a*'s between them:

```
Aba Missed!
Abba Matched!
Abbba Matched!
Ababa Matched!
```

Exercise 16.2

Adapt your solution from the previous exercise to find the butterfly species names that have consecutive *a*'s that may be separated by either *n* or *s*.

Greediness

The + and * quantifiers are *greedy*; they match as much of the text as they can. Sometimes that's too much. Change the earlier example to match another *b* after the quantifier. Now there must be at least two *b*'s in a row:

```
my @strings = < Aba Abba Abbba Ababa >;
for @strings {
    put $_, ' ', m/ :i ab+ ba / ?? 'Matched!' !! 'Missed!';
    }
```

The first `Str` doesn't match because it doesn't have one or more *b*'s followed by another *b*. It's the same for the last `Str`. The middle two `Str`s have enough *b*'s to satisfy both parts of the pattern:

```
Aba Missed!
Abba Matched!
Abbba Matched!
Ababa Missed!
```

But think about how this works inside the matcher. When it sees the b+ it matches as many *b*'s as it can. In `Abbba`, the b+ starts by matching bbb. The b+ part of the pattern is satisfied. The matcher moves on to the next part of the pattern, which is another b. The text doesn't have any leftover *b*'s to satisfy that part because the greedy quantifier matched them all.

The match doesn't fail because of another tactic the matcher can use: it can *backtrack* on the quantifier that just matched to force it to give up some of the text. The b+ needs one or more *b*'s. Whether it matched two or three doesn't matter, because either satisfies that. Backing up one position in the text leaves a *b* for the next part to match. Once it backs up it tries the next part of the pattern.

Zero or One

The ? quantifier matches zero or once only; it makes the preceding part of the pattern optional. In this pattern you can have one or two *b*'s because you used ? to make one of them optional:

```
my @strings = < Aba Abba Abbba Ababa >;
for @strings {
    put $_, ' ', m/ :i ab? ba / ?? 'Matched!' !! 'Missed!';
    }
```

Now the first `Str` can match because the first *b* can match zero times. The third `Str` can't match because there is more than one *b* and the ? can't match more than one of them:

```
Aba Matched!
Abba Matched!
```

```
Abbba Missed!
Ababa Matched!
```

Minimal and Maximal

If you want to match an exact number of times use **. With a single number after it the ** matches exactly that number of times. This matches exactly three *b*'s:

```
my @strings = < Aba Abba Abbba Ababa >;
for @strings {
    put $_, ' ', m/ :i ab**3 a / ?? 'Matched!' !! 'Missed!';
    }
```

There's only one Str that matches:

```
Aba Missed!
Abba Missed!
Abbba Matched!
Ababa Missed!
```

You can use a range after the **. The quantified part must match at least the range minimum and will only match as many repetitions as the range maximum:

```
my @strings = < Aba Abba Abbba Ababa Abbbba >;
for @strings {
    put $_, ' ', m/ :i a b**2..3 a / ?? 'Matched!' !! 'Missed!';
    }
```

Two Strs match—the ones with two or three consecutive *b*'s:

```
Aba Missed!
Abba Matched!
Abbba Matched!
Ababa Missed!
Abbbba Missed!
```

An exclusive range works too. Match two or three times by excluding the 1 and 4 endpoints to get the same output:

```
my @strings = < Aba Abba Abbba Ababa >;
for @strings {
    put $_, ' ', m/ :i ab**1^..^4 a / ?? 'Matched!' !! 'Missed!';
    }
```

Exercise 16.3

Output all the lines from the butterfly census file that have four vowels in a row.

Controlling Quantifiers

Adding a ? after any quantifier makes it match as little as possible—the greedy quantifiers become nongreedy. The modified quantifier stops matching when the next part of the pattern can match.

These two patterns look for an *H*, some stuff, and then an *s*. The first one is greedy and matches all the way to the final *s*. The second one is nongreedy and stops at the first *s* it encounters. The greedy case matches the entire text but the nongreedy case matches only the first word:

```
$_ = 'Hamadryas perlicus';

say "Greedy: ",    m/ H .*  s /;  # Greedy: ⌜Hamadryas perlicus⌟
say "Nongreedy: ", m/ H .*? s /;  # Nongreedy: ⌜Hamadryas⌟
```

You'll probably find that you often want to make the quantifiers nongreedy.

Turning Off Backtracking

The : modifier lets you turn off backtracking by preventing a quantifier from unmatching what it has already matched. In both of these patterns the .+ can match everything to the end of the Str. The first one has to unmatch some of that to allow the rest of the pattern to match. The second one uses .+:, which means it can't give back any of the text to allow the first *s* to match, so that match fails:

```
$_ = 'Hamadryas perlicus';
say "Backtracking: ",
    m/ H .+  s \s perlicus/;  # Backtracking: ⌜Hamadryas perlicus⌟
say "Nonbacktracking: ",
    m/ H .+: s \s perlicus/;  # Nonbacktracking: Nil
```

The : can go immediately after the **. Each tries to match groups of three characters with a *def* at the end. The first one matches the entire Str because it's greedy, but then backs up enough to allow *def* to match. The second one uses **:, so it refuses to unmatch the *def* and the pattern fails:

```
$_ = 'abcabcabcdef';
say "Backtracking: ",
    m/ [ ... ] ** 3..4 def /;  # ⌜abcabcabcdef⌟
say "Nonbacktracking: ",
    m/ [ ... ] **: 3..4 def /;  # Nil
```

Table 16-1 summarizes the behavior of the different types of quantifiers.

Table 16-1. Summary of regex quantifiers

Quantifier	Example	Meaning
?	b?	Zero or one *b*
*	b*	Zero or more *b*'s
+	b+	One or more *b*'s
** N	b ** 4	Exactly four *b*'s
** M..N	b ** 2..4	Between two and four *b*'s
** M^..^N	b ** 1^..^5	Between two and four *b*'s with an exclusive range
??	b??	Zero *b*'s (a trivial case)
*?	b*?	Zero or more *b*'s nongreedily
+?	b+?	One or more *b*'s nongreedily
?:	b?:	Zero or more *b*'s without backtracking
*:	b*?	Zero or more *b*'s greedily without backtracking
+:	b+?	One or more *b*'s greedily without backtracking
**: M..N	b ** 2..4	Between two and four *b*'s greedily without backtracking

Captures

When you group with parentheses instead of square brackets you *capture* parts of the text:

```
say 'Hamadryas perlicus' ~~ / (\w+) \s+ (\w+) /;
```

In the .gist output you see the captures labeled with whole numbers starting from zero. The captures are numbered by their position in their subpattern from left to right:

```
⌜Hamadryas perlicus⌟
 0 => ⌜Hamadryas⌟
 1 => ⌜perlicus⌟
```

You can access the captures with postcircumfix indices (but only if the match succeeds). This looks like a Positional but isn't, but that's a distinction you don't need to worry about here. The output shows the same captures you saw before:

```
my $match = 'Hamadryas perlicus' ~~ / (\w+) \s+ (\w+) /;

if $match {
    put "Genus: $match[0]";   # Genus: Hamadryas
    put "Species: $match[1]"; # Species: perlicus
    }
```

The special variable $/ already stores the result of the last successful match. You can access elements in it directly:

```
$_ = 'Hamadryas perlicus';
if / (\w+) \s+ (\w+) / {
    put "Genus: $/[0]";    # Genus: Hamadryas
    put "Species: $/[1]";  # Species: perlicus
    };
```

It gets better. There's a shorthand to access the captures in $/. The number variables $0 and $1 are actually $/[0] and $/[1] (and this is true for as many captures as you create):

```
$_ = 'Hamadryas perlicus';
if / (\w+) \s+ (\w+) / {
    put "Genus: $0";   # Genus: Hamadryas
    put "Species: $1"; # Species: perlicus
    };
```

If a previous match fails then $/ is empty and you don't see the values from the previous successful match. An unsuccessful match resets to $/ to nothing:

```
my $string = 'Hamadryas perlicus';

my $first-match = $string ~~ m/(perl)(.*)/;
put "0: $0 | 1: $1";  # 0: perl | 1: icus

my $second-match = $string ~~ m/(ruby)(.*)/;
put "0: $0 | 1: $1";  # 0:      | 1: -- nothing in these variables
```

Named Captures

Instead of relying on the numbered captures, you can give them names. These become keys in a Hash in the Match object. Label a capture with a $<LABEL>= in front of the capturing parentheses:

```
$_ = 'Hamadryas perlicus';
if / $<genus>=(\w+) \s+ $<species>=(\w+) / {
    put "Genus: $/<genus>";      # Genus: Hamadryas
    put "Species: $/<species>";  # Species: perlicus
    };
```

The output is often much easier to understand when you label the captures. It's also easier to modify the pattern without disrupting later code, since the positions of labels don't matter.

As before, you can leave off the slash in $/ but only if you use the angle brackets. This looks like Associative indexing even though the Match isn't an Associative type:

```
$_ = 'Hamadryas perlicus';
if / $<genus>=(\w+) \s+ $<species>=(\w+) / {
    put "Genus: $<genus>";      # Genus: Hamadryas
    put "Species: $<species>";  # Species: perlicus
    };
```

A label name in a variable works, but in that case you can't leave off the /:

```
$_ = 'Hamadryas perlicus';
my $genus-key = 'genus';
my $species-key = 'species';
if / $<genus>=(\w+) \s+ $<species>=(\w+) / {
    put "Genus: $/{$genus-key}";        # Genus: Hamadryas
    put "Species: $/{$species-key}";    # Species: perlicus
    };
```

If you save the result the names are in your Match in the same way they show up in $/:

```
my $string = 'Hamadryas perlicus';
my $match = $string ~~ m/ $<genus>=(\w+) \s+ $<species>=(\w+) /;

if $match {
    put "Genus: $match<genus>";      # Genus: Hamadryas
    put "Species: $match<species>";  # Species: perlicus
    };
```

You don't even need to know the names because you can get those from the Match. Calling .pairs returns all the names:

```
my $string = 'Hamadryas perlicus';
my $match = $string ~~ m/ $<genus>=(\w+) \s+ $<species>=(\w+) /;

put "Keys are:\n\t",
    $match
        .pairs
        .map( { "{.key}: {.value}" } )
        .join( "\n\t" );
```

The put shows everything without knowing the names in advance:

```
Keys are:
    species: perlicus
    genus: Hamadryas
```

When patterns get too complex (say, something that you have to spread over multiple lines) the numbered Match variables will probably proliferate beyond your ability to track them. Names do a much better job of reminding you which capture contains what.

A Capture Tree

Inside capture parentheses you can have additional capture parentheses. Each group gets its own numbering inside the group that contains it:

```
my $string = 'Hamadryas perlicus';
say $string ~~ m/(perl (<[a..z]>+))/;
```

The output shows that there are two $0s and one of them is subordinate to the other. The captures are nested so the results are nested:

```
「perlicus」
 0 => 「perlicus」
  0 => 「icus」
```

To access the top-level match, use $/[0] or $0. To get the nested matches you access the next level with the appropriate subscript:

```
my $string = 'Hamadryas perlicus';
$string ~~ m/(perl (<[a..z]>+))/;

# explicit $/
say "Top match: $/[0]";        # Top match: perlicus
say "Inner match: $/[0][0]";  # Inner match: icus

# or skip the $/
say "Top match: $0";           # Top match: perlicus
say "Inner match: $0[0]";      # Inner match: icus
```

This works for named captures in the same way. The outer captures include the inner text as well as the inner captures:

```
my $string = 'Hamadryas perlicus';
$string ~~ m/
    $<top> = (perl
        $<inner> = (<[a..z]>+)
        )
    /;

# explicit $/
say "Top match: $/<top>";          # Top match: perlicus
say "Inner match: $/<top><inner>";  # Inner match: icus

# or skip the $/
say "Top match: $<top>";           # Top match: perlicus
say "Inner match: $<top><inner>";   # Inner match: icus
```

It's not one or the other. You can mix number variables and labels if that makes sense:

```
my $string = 'Hamadryas perlicus';
$string ~~ m/
    ( perl $<inner> = (<[a..z]>+) )
    /;
```

```
# explicit $/
say "Top match: $/[0]";          # Top match: perlicus
say "Inner match: $/[0]<inner>"; # Inner match: icus

# or skip the $/
say "Top match: $0";             # Top match: perlicus
say "Inner match: $0<inner>";    # Inner match: icus
```

This nesting makes it very easy to construct your pattern. The numbering is localized to the level you are in. If you add other captures to the pattern they only disturb their level.

Exercise 16.6

Extract from the *Butterflies_and_Moths.txt* file all the scientific names between underscores (such as _Crocallis elinguaria_). Capture the genus and species separately. Which genus has the most species?

Backreferences

The result of a capture is available inside your patterns. You can use that to match something else in the same pattern. Use the `Match` variables to refer to the part that you want:

```
my $line = 'abba';
say $line ~~ / a (.) $0 a  /;
```

The output shows the entire match and the capture:

```
「abba」
 0 => 「b」
```

Refer to captures at the same level with the number variables. The `$0` and `$1` are *backreferences* to parts of the pattern that have already matched:

```
my $line = 'abccba';
say $line ~~ / a (.)(.) $1 $0 a  /;
```

There are only two captures in the output:

```
「abccba」
 0 => 「b」
 1 => 「c」
```

If the capture is nested you have to do a bit more work. You might think you can subscript the capture variable, but can you see why it fails silently?

```
my $line = 'abcca';
say $line ~~ / a (.(.)) $0[0] a  /;  # does not match!
```

Those square brackets are pattern metacharacters and not postcircumfix indexers! You think that you have an element in $0, but it's really $0 stringified followed by a group that is the literal text 0.

To get around this parsing problem surround the subscript access in $() so the pattern sees it as one thing. There's one more trick to make it work out. Backreferences are only valid at a sequence point where the match operator has filled in all the details. An empty code block can force that:

```
my $line = 'abcca';
say  $line ~~ / a (.(.)) {} $($0[0]) a  /;  # matches
```

Now the $0[0] can match the c:

```
⌜abcca⌟
 0 => ⌜bc⌟
   0 => ⌜c⌟
```

Surrounders and Separators

To match something that has prefix and suffix characters, you could type out the pattern in the order it appears in the Str. Here's an example that matches a word in literal parentheses:

```
my $line = 'outside (pupa) outside';
say $line ~~ / '(' \w+ ')'  /;          # ⌜(pupa)⌟
```

That's not the best way to communicate that you want to match something in parentheses, though. The start and end characters aren't next to each other in the pattern; you have to read ahead then surmise that the parentheses are circumfix parts of the same idea.

Instead, connect the beginning and end patterns with ~, then put the interior pattern after that. This describes something surrounded by parentheses subordinate to the structure:

```
my $line = 'outside (pupa) outside';
say $line ~~ / '(' ~ ')' \w+ /;
```

This is automatically nongreedy; it does not grab everything until the last closing parenthesis:

```
my $line = 'outside (pupa) space (pupa) outside';
say $line ~~ m/ '(' ~ ')' \w+ /; # ⌜(pupa)⌟
```

A global match will still find all the instances:

```
my $line = 'outside (pupa) space (pupa) outside';
say $line ~~ m:global/ '(' ~ ')' \w+ /; # (⌜(pupa)⌟ ⌜(pupa)⌟)
```

Going the other way, suppose that you want to match a series of things that are separated by other characters. A line of comma-separated values is such a thing:

```
my $line = 'Hamadryas,Leptophobia,Vanessa,Gargina';
```

To match the letters separated by commas, you could match the first group of letters then every subsequent occurrence of a comma and another group of letters:

```
say $line ~~ / (\w+) [ ',' (\w+) ]+ /;
```

That works, but it's annoying because you have to use \w+ twice even though it's describing the same thing. The % modifies a quantifier so that the pattern on the right comes between each group:

```
say $line ~~ / (\w+)+ % ',' /;
```

The output shows that you matched each group of letters:

```
「Hamadryas,Leptophobia,Vanessa,Gargina」
 0 => 「Hamadryas」
 0 => 「Leptophobia」
 0 => 「Vanessa」
 0 => 「Gargina」
```

A double percent allows a trailing separator in the overall match:

```
my $line = 'Hamadryas,Leptophobia,Vanessa,';
say $line ~~ / (\w+)+ %% ',' /;
```

Notice that it matches that comma that follows *Vanessa* but does not create an empty capture after it:

```
「Hamadryas,Leptophobia,Vanessa,」
 0 => 「Hamadryas」
 0 => 「Leptophobia」
 0 => 「Vanessa」
```

 Although you'd think that CSV files should be simple, they aren't. In the wild all sorts of weird things happen. The Text::CSV (*https://modules.perl6.org/dist/Text::CSV:cpan:HMBRAND*) module handles all of those tricky bits. Use that instead of doing it yourself.

Assertions

Assertions don't match text; they require that a certain condition be true at the current position in the text. They match a context instead of characters. Specify these in your pattern to allow the matcher to fail faster. You don't need to scan the entire text if the pattern should only work at the beginning of the text.

Anchors

An anchor prevents the pattern from floating over the text to find a place where it can start matching. It requires that a pattern match at a particular position. If the pattern doesn't match at that position the match can immediately fail and save itself the work of scanning the text.

The ^ forces your pattern to match at the absolute beginning of the text. This matches because the *Hama* comes at the beginning of the text:

```
say 'Hamadryas perlicus' ~~ / ^ Hama /;  # 「Hama」
```

Trying to match *perl* after ^ fails because that pattern is not at the beginning of the text:

```
say 'Hamadryas perlicus' ~~ / ^ perl /;  # Nil (fails)
```

Without the anchor the match would drift over the text looking at each position to check for *perl*. That's extra work (and probably incorrect) if you know that you want to match at the beginning. Once the match fails at the beginning it's immediately done.

The $ is the end-of-string anchor and does something similar at the end of the text:

```
say 'Hamadryas perlicus' ~~ / icus $ /;  # 「icus」
```

This one doesn't match because there's more text after *icus*:

```
say 'Hamadryas perlicus navitas' ~~ / icus $ /;  # Nil (fails)
```

There are anchors for the beginning and end of a line; that could be different from the beginning and end of the text. A line ends with a newline and that newline might be in the middle of your multiline text, like in this one (remember that the here doc strips the indention):

```
$_ = chomp q:to/END/;    # chomp removes last newline
    Chorinea amazon
    Hamadryas perlicus
    Melanis electron
    END
```

The beginning-of-line anchor, ^^, matches after the absolute beginning of the text or immediately after any newline. These both work because *Chorinea* is at the start of the text and the start of the first line:

```
say m/ ^ Chorinea /;  # 「Chorinea」
say m/ ^^ Chorinea /;  # 「Chorinea」
```

Likewise, the end-of-line anchor, $$, matches before any newline or at the absolute end of the text. These also both work because *electron* is at the end of the text and the end of the last line:

```
say m/ electron $  /;  # ⌜electron⌟
say m/ electron $$ /;  # ⌜electron⌟
```

Hamadryas can't match at the absolute beginning of the text but it can match at the beginning of a line:

```
say m/ ^  Hamadryas /; # Nil
say m/ ^^ Hamadryas /; # ⌜Hamadryas⌟
```

Similarly, *perlicus* can't match at the absolute end of the text but it can match at the end of a line:

```
say m/ perlicus $  /;  # Nil
say m/ perlicus $$ /;  # ⌜perlicus⌟
```

Conditions

Word boundaries exist when a non-"word" character is next to a "word" character (in either order). Those terms are a bit fuzzy, since you likely think of word characters as the alphabetic characters. They are, however, the ones that match \w, which includes numbers and other things. The beginning and the end of the Str count as nonword characters.

Exercise 16.7

Output all the "word" characters that are not alphabetic characters. How many of them are there? The Range 0 .. 0xFFFF and the .chr method should be helpful.

Assert a word boundary with <|w>. Suppose that you want to match the name *Hamad*. Without a word boundary that would match in *Hamadryas*, but that's not what you want. The word boundary keeps it from showing up in the middle of another word:

```
$_ = 'Hamadryas';
say m/ Hamad /;          # ⌜Hamad⌟
say m/ Hamad <|w> /;  # Nil
```

That second pattern can't match because *Hamadryas* has a word character (a letter) following *Hamad*. The next example matches because a space follows *Hamad*:

```
my $name = 'Ali Hamad bin Perliana';
say $name ~~ / Hamad <|w> /;  # ⌜Hamad⌟
```

Word boundaries on each side isolate a word. These matches look for dry as its own word because it has word boundaries on each side. The first one fails because it's in the middle of a bigger word:

```
$_ = 'Hamadryas';
say m/ <|w> dry <|w> /;  # Nil
```

```
$_ = 'The flower is dry';
say m/ <|w> dry <|w> /;  # ⌈dry⌋
```

Instead of <|w> you can use the << or >> to point to where the nonword characters should be:

```
$_ = 'The flower is dry';
say m/ << dry >> /;  # ⌈dry⌋
```

The arrows can point either way, but always toward the nonword characters:

```
$_ = 'a!bang';
say m/ << .+ >> /;   # ⌈a!bang⌋   - greedy
say m/ << .+? >> /;  # ⌈a⌋        - nongreedy
say m/ >> .+ >> /;   # ⌈!bang⌋
say m/ >> .+ << /;   # ⌈!⌋
```

The opposite of a word boundary assertion is <!|w>. That means that both sides of the assertion must be the same type of character—either both word characters or both nonword characters. Now the results are flipped:

```
$_ = 'Hamadryas';
say m/ <!|w> dry <!|w> /;  # ⌈dry⌋

$_ = 'The flower is dry';
say m/ <!|w> dry <!|w> /;  # Nil
```

Code Assertions

Code assertions are perhaps the most amazing and powerful part of regular expressions. You can inspect what's happened so far and use arbitrarily complex code to decide if you accept that. If your code evaluates to True you satisfy the assertion and the pattern can keep matching. Otherwise, your pattern fails.

Your code for the assertion shows up in <?{}>. You can put almost anything you like in there:

```
'Hamadryas' ~~ m/ <?{ put 'Hello!' }> /;   # Hello!
```

This matches no characters in *Hamadryas* but is also not the null pattern (which is not valid). From inside the assertion you get Hello! as output:

```
put
    'Hamadryas' ~~ m/ <?{ put 'Hello!' }> /
        ?? 'Worked' !! 'Failed';
```

This first outputs from inside the assertion:

```
Hello!
Worked!
```

Change the assertion so that False is the last expression:
```
```

```
put
    'Hamadryas' ~~ m/ <?{ put 'Hello!'; False }> /
        ?? 'Worked' !! 'Failed';
```

You get much more output. As the code assertion fails the match cursor moves along the text and tries again. Each time the code assertion returns False it tries again. It keeps doing that until it gets to the end of the Str:

```
Hello!
Hello!
Hello!
Hello!
Hello!
Hello!
Hello!
Hello!
Hello!
Hello!
Failed
```

Here's something more complex. Suppose you want to match even numbers only. You could create a pattern that looks for an even digit at an end of a Str:

```
say '538' ~~ m/ ^ \d* <[24680]> $ /;    # ⌜538⌟
```

With a code assertion you don't care which digits you match as long as they are even. This makes the pattern a bit simpler by showing the complexity as code. Your intent may be clearer this way:

```
say '538' ~~ m/ ^ (\d+) <?{ $0 %% 2 }> /;
```

There's a capture and that text also is divisible by two, so that match succeeds:

```
⌜538⌟
 0 => ⌜538⌟
```

It stills works if the characters aren't the ASCII decimal digits:

```
say '١٣٨' ~~ m/ ^ (\d+) <?{ $0 %% 2 }> /;
```

Or even:

```
say '١٣٨' ~~ m/ ^ (\d+) <?{ $0 %% ٢ }> /;
```

Matching an IPv4 address

Consider a pattern to match a dotted-decimal IP address. There are four decimal numbers from 0 to 255, such as 127.0.0.1 (the loopback address). You could write a pattern without an assertion, but you have to figure out how to restrict the range of the number:

```
my $dotted-decimal = rx/ ^
    [
    || [ <[ 0 1 ]> <[ 0 .. 9 ]> ** 0..2 ]    # 0 to 199
```

```
|| [
    2
    [
    || <[ 0 .. 4 ]> <[ 0 .. 9 ]>       # 200 to 499
    || 5 <[ 0 .. 5 ]>                  # 250 to 255
    ]
    ]
] ** 4 % '.'
$
/;
```

```
say '127.0.0.1' ~~ $dotted-decimal;  # ⌜127.0.0.1⌟
```

Matching on text to suss out numerical values means careful handling of each character position. That's a lot of work and uses a feature you haven't seen yet (alternations are coming up). You could reduce that to almost nothing with a code assertion that looks at the text you just matched and tells the pattern if you want to accept it:

```
my $easier = rx/
    ^
    ( <[0..9]>+: <?{ 0 <= $/ <= 255 }> ) ** 4 % '.'
    $
    /;
```

The assertion is <?{ 0 <= $/ <= 255 }>. That $/ is the Match for only that level of parentheses. This allows you to be sloppy in the pattern for matching digits. You don't care if you match 4, 5, or 20 digits because the code assertion will check that.

If that code assertion fails after matching digits, you don't want to give back some of the digits to try again. You know the next thing must be the . between groups of digits. To prevent any backtracking you use the : on that + quantifier. You don't need this to get the right match but it creates less work to ultimately fail.

The % modifies the ** 4 quantifier so a literal . shows up between each of the four groups of digits.

Alternations

Sometimes there are several distinct patterns that might match at the same position. An *alternation* is a way to specify that. There are two ways to do this: it can match the first alternative that succeeds or it can match the longest one.

First Match

If you've used regexes in other languages you're probably used to alternations where the leftmost alternative that can match is the one that wins. Set up this type of alternation with a || between the possibilities:

```
my $pattern = rx/ abc || xyz || 1234 /;
```

Either abc, xyz, or 1234 can match:

```
my @strings = < 1234 xyz abc 789 >;
for @strings {
    put "$_ matches" if $_ ~~ $pattern;
    }
```

The first three Strs match because they have at least one of the alternatives:

```
1234 matches
xyz matches
abc matches
```

The alternation has an interesting feature: you can start it with a || with nothing before it. This is the same pattern and does not create an empty alternative at the beginning:

```
my $pattern = rx/ || abc || xyz || 1234 /;
```

This looks better spread out so each alternation gets its own line. The reformatted pattern starts with || and has a more pleasing parallel structure that allows you to remove lines without disturbing the other alternatives:

```
my $pattern = rx/
    || abc
    || xyz
    || 1234
    /;
```

Instead of placing a || between each alternative, you can put it before a bunch of alternatives. Do that with an Array directly in your pattern:

```
my $pattern = rx/ || @(<abc xyz 1234>) /;
```

An existing variable after the || does the same thing:

```
my @variable = <abc xyz 1234>;
my $pattern = rx/ || @variable /;
```

You aren't interpolating that Array. The pattern uses the current value of the Array when it matches. In this example the Array has 1234 as the last element when you define the pattern. Before you use the pattern you change that last element:

```
my @strings = < 1234 xyz abc 56789 >;
my @variable = <abc xyz 1234>;
my $pattern = rx/ || @variable /;

put "Before:";
for @strings {
    put "\t$_ matches" if $_ ~~ $pattern;
    }

# change the array after making the pattern
@variable[*-1] = 789;
```

```
put "After:";
for @strings {
    put "\t$_ matches" if $_ ~~ $pattern;
    }
```

The output shows that you matched with the current value of the variable instead of its value when you created the pattern. Different values match after you change the Array:

```
Before:
    1234 matches
    xyz matches
    abc matches
After:
    xyz matches
    abc matches
    56789 matches
```

Exercise 16.8

Output all the lines from the butterfly census file that have the genus *Lycaena*, *Zizeeria*, or *Hamadryas*. How many different species did you find?

Longest Token Matching

Some alternations might have "better" possibilities that could match. Rather than choosing the first specified possibility you can tell the match operator to try all of them, then choose the "best" one. This is generally called *longest token matching* (*LTM*), but it finds the best, not longest, match.

LTM alternation uses a single |. In this pattern all of the alternatives can match. The first possibility it could match is the single a. The "best" match is abcd, though. That's the match you see in the output:

```
my $pattern = rx/
    | a
    | ab
    | abcd
    /;

say 'abcd' ~~ $pattern;    # ⌈abcd⌋
```

An Array variable works just like it did in the || examples:

```
my @variable = <a ab abcd>;
my $pattern = rx/ | @variable /;

say 'abcd' ~~ $pattern;    # ⌈abcd⌋
```

What makes one possibility better than another? There are some rules that decide this. Better patterns have longer tokens, and that's where the confusion comes in. It's not actually about how much text it matches; it's about the pattern.

This next part will probably be more than you'll ever want to know. A pattern can have both *declarative* and *procedural* elements. In short, some parts of the pattern merely describe some text and other parts force the match operator to do something. The abc is declarative. The {} inline code is an action.

Consider this example. The longest text that might match is *Hamadry*. That alternative has the {True} inline code block in it, though. The second alternative is simply Hamad, and that is the one that matches:

```
say 'Hamadryas perlicus sixus' ~~ m/
    | Hama{True}dry
    | Hamad
    /;  # ⌜Hamad⌟
```

When the match operator is deciding which one has priority it looks for the pattern that has the longest declarative part. The first one has Hama; the second one has Hamad. That makes the second one the longer token. It's about the pattern, not the target text. (Ignore that you haven't read a definition of a token yet.)

Sometimes the two patterns can have the same size tokens, like these two alternatives. One has a character class and the other a literal *d*. The more specific one (the literal) wins:

```
$_ = 'Hamadryas perlicus sixus';

say 'Hamadryas perlicus sixus' ~~ m/
    | Hama<[def]>{put "first"}
    | Hamad      {put "second"}
    /;  # ⌜Hamad⌟
```

The code Blocks are only there to show which alternative was "best":

```
second
⌜Hamad⌟
```

Change that around to see it still choose the more specific one:

```
$_ = 'Hamadryas perlicus sixus';

say 'Hamadryas perlicus sixus' ~~ m/
    | Hamad      {put "first"}
    | Hama<[def]>{put "second"}
    /;  # ⌜Hamad⌟
```

Now the first alternative is more specific and it is "best":

```
first
⌜Hamad⌟
```

So what counts as a *token*? It's the longest stretch of things that aren't procedural. As I write this, however, the documentation avoids defining that. It requires deep knowledge of what happens in the guts of the language. It's a big ugly topic that I'll now ignore, although the book *Mastering Regular Expressions* by Jeffrey E.F. Friedl (O'Reilly) will tell you most of what you need to know. Perhaps the confusion will sort itself out by the time you read this.

All of that is to say that the match operator looks at each | alternative and can choose to do the one it thinks provides the best match. The match operator does not have to do them in the order that you typed them.

Summary

In this chapter you saw the common regex features that will solve most of your pattern problems. You can repeat parts of a pattern, capture and extract parts of the text, define alternate patterns that can match, and specify conditions within the pattern. There is much more that patterns can do for you. Practice what you've read here and delve into the documentation to discover more.

## CHAPTER 17

Grammars

Grammars are patterns on a higher plane of existence. They integrate and reuse pattern fragments to parse and react to complicated formats. This feature is at the core of Perl 6 in a very literal sense; the language itself is implemented as a grammar. Once you start using it you'll probably prefer it to regexes for all but the most simple problems.

A Simple Grammar

A grammar is a special sort of package. It can have methods and subroutines but mostly comprises special pattern methods called `regex`, `token`, and `rule`. Each of these define a pattern and apply different modifiers.

> Perl 6 tends to refer to `regex`, `token`, and `rule` declarations as "rules," which can be a bit imprecise at times. In this book, you can tell the difference between the language keyword and the general term by the typesetting. I'll try to not present an ambiguous situation.

Start with something simple (too simple for grammars). Define a `TOP` pattern that matches digits as the starting point. That name is special because `.parse` uses it by default. In this example, you declare that with `regex`:

```
grammar Number {
    regex TOP { \d }
    }

my $result = Number.parse( '7' );  # works

put $result ?? 'Parsed!' !! 'Failed!';  # Parsed!
```

This succeeds. .parse applies the grammar to the entire value of 7. It starts with the parts that TOP describes. It can match a digit, and the value you pass to .parse is a digit.

When .parse succeeds, it returns a Match object (it returns Nil when it fails). Try it with a different value. Instead of a single digit, try several digits:

```
my $result = Number.parse( '137' );  # fails (extra digits)

put $result ?? 'Parsed!' !! 'Failed!';  # Failed!
```

This time .parse doesn't succeed. It starts matching with the first character and ends matching on the last character. It asserts that the text starts, there is a single digit, and the text ends. If .parse sees that there are some characters before or after its match, it fails. It matches everything or not at all. It's almost the same thing as explicitly using anchors:

```
grammar Number {
    regex TOP { ^ \d+ $ }  # explicitly anchored
    }
```

But TOP is only the default starting point for a grammar. You can tell .parse where you'd like to start. This version defines the same pattern but calls it digits instead of TOP:

```
grammar Number {
    regex digits { \d+ }
    }
```

Tell .parse where to start with the :rule named argument:

```
my @strings = '137', '137 ', ' 137 ';

for @strings -> $string {
    my $result = Number.parse( $string, :rule<digits> );
    put "⌜$string⌟ ", $result ?? 'Parsed!' !! 'Failed!';
    }
```

The first element of @strings parses because it is only digits. The other ones fail because they have extra characters:

```
⌜137⌟ parsed!
⌜137 ⌟ failed!
⌜ 137 ⌟ failed!
```

Declare digits with rule instead of regex. This implicitly allows whitespace after any part of your pattern:

```
grammar Number {
    rule digits { \d+ }  # not anchored, and works
    }
```

Now the second `Str` matches too because the implicit whitespace can match the space at the end (but not the beginning):

```
⌈137⌋ parsed!
⌈137 ⌋ parsed!
⌈ 137 ⌋ failed!
```

The `rule` applies `:sigspace` to its pattern. It's the same thing as adding that adverb to the pattern:

```
grammar Number {
    regex digits { :sigspace \d+ }
    }
```

`:sigspace` inserts the predefined `<.ws>` *after* pattern tokens. Since there's a dot before the name `ws`, the `<.ws>` does not create a capture. It's the same as adding optional whitespace explicitly:

```
grammar Number {
    regex digits { \d+ <.ws> }
    }
```

Instead of showing `Parsed!`, you can on success output the `Match` object you stored in `$result`:

```
grammar Number {
    regex digits { \d+ <.ws> }
    }

my @strings = '137', '137 ', ' 137 ';

for @strings -> $string {
    my $result = Number.parse( $string, :rule<digits> );
    put $result ?? $result !! 'Failed!';
    }
```

The output isn't that different, but instead of its success status you see the text that matched:

```
⌈137⌋
⌈137 ⌋
Failed!
```

Modify the grammar to remove that dot from `<.ws>` so it captures whitespace and try again:

```
grammar Number {
    regex digits { \d+ <ws> }
    }
```

Now the output shows the nested levels of named captures:

```
⌈137⌋
 ws => ⌈⌋
```

```
⌜137 ⌟
ws => ⌜ ⌟
Failed!
```

This still doesn't match the `Str` with leading whitespace. The parser couldn't match that since `rule` only inserts `<.ws>` after explicit parts of the pattern. To match leading whitespace you need to add something to the front of the pattern. The beginning-of-string anchor does that, and now there's something that `<.ws>` can come after:

```
grammar Number {
    rule digits { ^ \d+ }    # ^ <.ws> \d+ <.ws>
    }
```

There's also the zero-width always-matches token, `<?>`:

```
grammar Number {
    rule digits { <?> \d+ }  # <?> <.ws> \d+ <.ws>
    }
```

Most of the time you don't want to play these games. If you want leading whitespace, you can note that explicitly (and you probably don't want to capture it):

```
grammar Number {
    rule digits { <.ws> \d+ }  # <.ws> \d+ <.ws>
    }
```

Use `token` instead of `rule` if you don't want any implicit whitespace:

```
grammar Number {
    token digits { \d+ }  # just the digits
    }
```

You'll see another feature of `rule` and `token` later in this chapter.

Exercise 17.1

Write a grammer to match octal digits, with or without a leading 0 or 0o. Your grammar should parse numbers such as 123, 0123, and 0o456, but not 8, 129, or o345.

Multiple Rules

Grammars wouldn't be useful if you were limited to one rule. You can define additional rules and use them inside other rules. In the first exercise you had only the TOP rule but you could separate the pattern into parts. Break up the pattern in TOP into rules for `prefix` and `digits`. It's this decomposability that makes it so easy to solve hard parsing problems:

```
grammar OctalNumber {
    regex TOP        { <prefix>? <digits>  }
    regex prefix     { [ 0o? ]  }
```

```
    regex digits       { <[0..7]>+ }
    }

my $number = '0o177';
my $result = OctalNumber.parse( $number );
say $result // "failed";
```

The stringified Match object shows the overall match and the named subcaptures:

```
⌜0o177⌟
 prefix => ⌜0o⌟
 digits => ⌜177⌟
```

You can access the pieces:

```
put "Prefix: $result<prefix>";
put "Digits: $result<digits>";
```

Exercise 17.2

Create a grammar to match a Perl 6 variable name with a sigil (ignore sigilless variables, because that's too easy). Use separate rules to match the sigil and the identifier. Here is a list of candidates to check if you don't come up with your own:

```
my @candidates = qw/
    sigilless  $scalar  @array  %hash
    $123abc    $abc'123 $ab'c123
    $two-words $two-    $-dash
    /;
```

You can suppress some of those named captures by prefixing the rule with a dot. You probably don't care about the prefix, so don't save it:

```
grammar OctalNumber {
    regex TOP          { <.prefix>? <digits> }
    regex prefix       { [ 0o? ]  }
    regex digits       { <[0..7]>+ }
    }

my $number = '0o177';
my $result = OctalNumber.parse( $number );
say $result // "failed";
```

The output doesn't include the prefix information:

```
⌜0o177⌟
 digits => ⌜177⌟
```

This doesn't make much of a difference in this small example, but imagine a complicated grammar with many, many rules. That brings you to the next big feature of grammars. Besides the grammar itself, you can specify an *action class* that processes the rules as the grammar successfully parses them.

Debugging Grammars

There are two modules that can help you figure out what's going on in your grammar. Both are much more impressive in your terminal.

Grammar::Tracer

The `Grammar::Tracer` module shows you the path through a grammar (and applies to any grammar in its scope). Merely loading the module is enough to activate it:

```
use Grammar::Tracer;

grammar OctalNumber {
    regex TOP           { <prefix>? <digits>  }
    regex prefix        { [ 0o? ]  }
    regex digits        { <[0..7]>+ }
    }

my $number = '0o177';
$/ = OctalNumber.parse( $number );
say $/ // "failed";
```

The first part of the output is the trace. It shows which rule it's in and the result. In this example each one matches:

```
TOP
| prefix
| * MATCH "0o"
| digits
| * MATCH "177"
* MATCH "0o177"
⌈0o177⌋
 prefix => ⌈0o⌋
 digits => ⌈177⌋
```

Changing the data to include invalid digits, such as `0o178`, means the grammar will fail. In the trace you can see it matches up to `0o17` but can't continue, so you know where in your `Str` things went wrong. It could be that the grammar should not match the text or the grammar is not as accommodating as it should be:

```
TOP
| prefix
| * MATCH "0o"
| digits
| * MATCH "17"
* MATCH "0o17"
digits
```

```
* FAIL
digits
* MATCH "0"
failed
```

Instead of adding `Grammar::Tracer` to your program you can load it from the command line with the -M switch. You probably don't mean to leave it in anyway:

```
% perl6 -MGrammar::Tracer program.p6
```

Grammar::Debugger

The `Grammar::Debugger` module does the same thing as `Grammar::Tracer` (they come together in the same distribution) but allows you to proceed one step at a time. When you start it you get a prompt; type h to get a list of commands:

```
% perl6 -MGrammar::Debugger test.p6
TOP
> h
    r                run (until breakpoint, if any)
    <enter>          single step
    rf               run until a match fails
    r <name>         run until rule <name> is reached
    bp add <name>    add a rule name breakpoint
    bp list          list all active rule name breakpoints
    bp rm <name>     remove a rule name breakpoint
    bp rm            removes all breakpoints
    q                quit
```

Typing Enter with no command single-steps through the parse process and gives you a chance to inspect the text and the state of the parser. The `rf` command will get you to the next failing rule:

```
> rf
|  prefix
|  * MATCH "0o"
|  digits
|  * MATCH "17"
* MATCH "0o17"
digits
* FAIL
>
```

A Simple Action Class

A grammar does its work by descending into its rules to take apart text. You can go the opposite way by processing each part of the parsed text to build a new `Str` (or data structure, or whatever you like). You can tell `.parse` to use an action class to do this.

Here's a simple action class, OctalActions. It doesn't need to have the same name as the grammar, but the method names are the same as the rule names. Each method takes a Match object argument. In this example, the signature uses $/, which is a variable with a few advantages that you'll see in a moment:

```
class OctalActions {
    method digits ($/) { put "Action class got $/" }
    }

grammar OctalNumber {
    regex TOP          { <.prefix>? <digits>  }
    regex prefix       { [ 0o? ]  }
    regex digits       { <[0..7]>+ }
    }
```

Tell .parse which class to use with the :actions named parameter. The name does not need to correspond to the grammar:

```
my $number = '0o177';
my $result = OctalNumber.parse(
    $number, :actions(OctalActions)
    );
say $result // "failed";
```

This action class doesn't do much. When the digits rule successfully matches it triggers the rule of the same name in the action class. That method merely outputs the argument:

```
Action class got 177
⌜0o177⌟
 digits => ⌜177⌟
```

Exercise 17.3

Implement your own action class for the OctalNumber grammar. When the digits method matches, output the decimal version of the number. The parse-base routine from Str may be useful. For extra credit, take one number per line from standard input and turn them into decimal numbers.

Creating an Abstract Syntax Tree

Actions shouldn't output information directly. Instead, they can add values to the Match object. Calling make in the action method sets a value in the *abstract syntax tree* (or .ast) slot of the Match. You can access that with .made:

```
class OctalActions {
    method digits ($/) {
        make parse-base( ~$/, 8 ) # must stringify $/
        }
```

```
        }

grammar OctalNumber {
    regex TOP            { <.prefix>? <digits>  }
    regex prefix         { [ 0o? ]  }
    regex digits         { <[0..7]>+ }
    }

my $number = '0o177';
my $result = OctalNumber.parse(
    $number, :actions(OctalActions)
    );
put $result ??
    "Turned ⌜{$result<digits>}⌟ into ⌜{$result<digits>.made}⌟"
    !! 'Failed!';
```

The make puts something into the .ast slot of the Match and .made gets it back out. You can make any value that you like, including containers, objects, and most other things you can imagine. You still get the original, literal match.

In the previous example, the digits action method handled the value. A TOP action method could do it, but it has to reach one level below the Match object:

```
class OctalActions {
    method digits ($/) {
        make parse-base( ~$/, 8 ) # must stringify $/
        }
    }

grammar OctalNumber {
    regex TOP            { <.prefix>? <digits>  }
    regex prefix         { [ 0o? ]  }
    regex digits         { <[0..7]>+ }
    }

my $number = '0o177';
my $result = OctalNumber.parse(
    $number, :actions(OctalActions)
    );
put $result.so ??
    "Turned ⌜{$number}⌟ into ⌜{$result.made}⌟"
    !! 'Failed!';
```

You don't have to use $/ in the signature; it's a convenience. There's nothing particularly magical about it. You could use some other variable if you are paid by the character:

```
class OctalActions {
    method TOP ($match) { make parse-base( ~$match<digits>, 8 ) }
    }
```

Exercise 17.4

Create a grammar to parse a four-part, dotted-decimal IP address, such as 192.168.1.137. Create an action class that turns the parse results into a 32-bit number. Output that 32-bit number in hexadecimal.

Ratcheting

The `rule` and `token` declarators have a feature that `regex` doesn't; they both prevent backtracking by implicitly setting the `:ratchet` adverb. Once one of those rules matches they don't backtrack to try again if there's a failure later in the grammar.

Here's a nonsense grammar that includes a rule `<some-stuff>` that matches one or more of any character. The TOP token wants to match digits surrounded by unspecified stuff:

```
grammar Stuff {
    token TOP { <some-stuff> <digits> <some-stuff> }
    token digits       { \d+ }
    token some-stuff   { .+  }
    }
```

This `Str` could satisfy that pattern. It has stuff, some digits, and more stuff:

```
my $string = 'abcdef123xyx456';
```

But, `Stuff` fails to parse it:

```
my $result = Stuff.parse( $string );
put "⌈$string⌋ ", $result ?? 'Parsed!' !! 'Failed!'; # Failed!
```

It's the `:ratchet` that makes it fail. Work out its path to see why. TOP has to first match `<some-stuff>`. That matches any character one or more times, greedily—it matches the entire text. TOP next needs to match `<digits>`, but there is nothing left to match because of that greediness. Without `:ratchet` the pattern might roll back some of the characters it already consumed. With `:ratchet` it doesn't do that. The grammar can't match the rest of TOP and it fails.

Without `:ratchet` the situation is different. If you use `regex` instead of `token`, you allow the grammar to give back characters it has already matched:

```
grammar Stuff {
    # regex does not turn on ratcheting
    regex TOP { <some-stuff> <digits> <some-stuff> }
    token digits       { \d+ }
    regex some-stuff   { .+  }
    }
```

That could match. The TOP matches `<some-stuff>` but realizes it's run out of text and starts backtracking. All parts of the grammar that want to allow backtracking have to use `regex`. It's not good enough for TOP to backtrack but not `<some-stuff>`.

Parsing JSON

In *Mastering Perl* I presented a JSON parser that Randal Schwartz created using some advanced features of Perl 5 regular expressions. In many ways his implementation was a grammar, but he was forced to inseparably combine the parsing and the actions. That made the regular expression almost impenetrable. It's much cleaner and more accessible to write it as a Perl 6 grammar.

JSON is actually quite simple with only a few weird things to handle, but it gives you the opportunity to see how `proto` rules can simplify actions:

```
grammar Grammar::JSON {
    rule TOP                  { <.ws> <value> <.ws> }

    rule object               { '{' ~ '}' <string-value-list> }
    rule string-value-list    { <string-value> * % ',' }
    token string-value        { <string> <.ws> ':' <.ws> <value> }

    rule array                { '[' ~ ']' <list> }
    rule list                 { <value> * % ',' }

    token value               {
        <string> | <number> | <object> | <array> |
        <true> | <false> | <null>
        }

    token true  { 'true'  }
    token false { 'false' }
    token null  { 'null'  }

    token string {
        (:ignoremark \" ) ~ \"
        [
            <u_char>                |
            [ '\\' <[\\/bfnrt"]> ] |
            <-[\\\"\n\t]>+
        ]*
        }

    token u_char {
        '\\u' <code_point>
        }

    token code_point { <[0..9a..fA..F]>**4 }

    token number {
```

```
            '-' ?
            [ 0 | <[1..9]><[0..9]>* ]
            [ '.' <[0..9]>+ ]?
            [ <[eE]> <[+-]>? <[0..9]>+ ]?
        }
    }
```

You may be surprised at how easy and short that grammar is. It's almost a straight
translation of the grammar from RFC 8259 (*https://trac.tools.ietf.org/html/rfc8259*).
Now, create an action class for that:

```
class JSON::Actions {
    method TOP ($/) { make $<value>.made }
    method object ($/) {
        make $<string-value-list>.made.hash.item;
        }
    method array ($/) {
        make $<list>.made.item;
        }

    method true        ($/) { make True }
    method False       ($/) { make False }
    method null        ($/) { make Nil }

    method value       ($/) { make (
        $<true> || $<false> || $<null> || $<object> ||
        $<array> || $<string> || $<number> ).made
        }

    method string-value-list ($/) {
        make $<string-value>>>.made.flat;
        }

    method string-value ($/) {
        make $<string> => $<value>
        }

    method list        ($/) { make ~$/ }
    method string      ($/) { make $<uchar>.made || ~$/ }

    method u_char      ($/) { make $<code_point>.made }
    method code_point ($/) { make chr( (~$/).parse-base(16) ) }
    method number      ($/) { make +$/ }
    }
```

Look at the clunky handling of value. Almost anything can be a value, so the action
method does some ham-handed work to figure out which thing just matched. It looks
into the possible submatches to find one with a defined value. Well, that's pretty stupid even if it's a quick way to get started (although there is some value in the immediate stupid versus the far-off smart).

A `proto` rule gets around this by making it easy for you to give different subrules the same name but different patterns. Instead of an alternation you have one token for each:

```
proto token value { * }
token value:sym<string> { <string> }
token value:sym<number> { <number> }
token value:sym<object> { <object> }
token value:sym<array>  { <array>  }
token value:sym<true>   { <sym>    }
token value:sym<false>  { <sym>    }
token value:sym<null>   { <sym>    }
```

The first `proto` rule matches *, which really means it dispatches to another rule in that group. It can dispatch to all of them and find the one that works.

Some of these use the special `<sym>` subrule in their pattern. This means that the name of the rule is the literal text to match. The `proto` rule `<true>` matches the literal text `true`. You don't have to type that out in the name and the pattern.

It doesn't matter which of those matches; the grammar calls each of them `$<value>`. The superrule only knows that something that is a value matched and that the subrule handled it appropriately. The action class `makes` the right value and stores it in the `Match`:

```
class JSON::Actions {
    method TOP      ($/) { make $<value>.made }
    method object ($/) { make $<string-value-list>.made.hash.item }

    method string-value-list ($/) { make $<string-value>>>.made.flat }
    method string-value       ($/) {
        make $<string>.made => $<value>.made
        }

    method array ($/) { make $<list>.made.item }
    method list  ($/) { make [ $<value>.map: *.made ] }

    method string     ($/) { make $<uchar>.made || ~$/ }

    method value:sym<number> ($/) { make +$/.Str }
    method value:sym<string> ($/) { make $<string>.made }
    method value:sym<true>   ($/) { make Bool::True  }
    method value:sym<false>  ($/) { make Bool::False }
    method value:sym<null>   ($/) { make Any }
    method value:sym<object> ($/) { make $<object>.made }
    method value:sym<array>  ($/) { make $<array>.made }

    method u_char     ($/) { make $<code_point>.made }
    method code_point ($/) { make chr( (~$/).parse-base(16) ) }
    }
```

Parsing CSV

Let's parse some comma-separated values (CSV) files. These are tricky because there's no actual standard (despite RFC 4180 (*https://tools.ietf.org/html/rfc4180*)). Microsoft Excel does it one way but some other producers do it slightly differently.

People often initially go wrong thinking they can merely split the data on a comma character—but that might be part of the literal data in a quoted field. The quote character may also be part of the literal data, but one producer might escape internal quote marks by doubling them, "", while another might use the backslash, \". People often assume they are line-oriented, but some producers allow unescaped (but quoted!) vertical whitespace. If all of that wasn't bad enough, what do you do if one line has fewer (or more) fields than the other lines?

 Don't parse CSV files like this. The Text::CSV module not only parses the format but also tries to correct problems as it goes.

Still willing to give it a try? You should find that grammars make most of these concerns tractable:

- The ratcheting behavior keeps things simple.
- You can easily handle balanced openers and closers (i.e., the quoting stuff).
- A grammar can inherit other grammars, so you can adjust a grammar based on the data instead of writing one grammar that handles all the data.
- You've seen action classes, but you can also have action instances that remember extra non-Match data.
- There's a .subparse method that lets you parse chunks so you can handle one record at a time.

Here's a simple CSV grammar based off the rules in RFC 4180 (*https://tools.ietf.org/html/rfc4180*). It allows for quoted fields and uses "" to escape a literal quote. If a comma, quote, or vertical whitespace appears in the literal data, it must be quoted:

```
grammar Grammar::CSV {
    token TOP       { <record>+ }
    token record    { <value>+ % <.separator> \R }
    token separator { <.ws> ',' <.ws> }
    token value     {
        '"'                  # quoted
            <( [ <-["]> | <.escaped-quote> ]* )>
        '"'
            |
        <-[",\n\f\r]>+  # non-quoted (no vertical ws)
            |
        ''                   # empty
    }

    token escaped-quote { '""' }
}

class CSV::Actions {
    method record ($/) { make $<value>».made.flat }
    method value ($/)  {
        # undo the double double quote
        make $/.subst( rx/ '""' /, '"', :g )
    }
}
```

Try this on entire files. The entire file either satisfies this grammar or doesn't:

```
my $data = $filename.IO.slurp;
my $result = Grammar::CSV.parse( $data );
```

You typically don't want to parse entire files, though. Let's fix the first part of that problem. You want to process records as you run into them. Instead of using .parse, which anchors to the end of the text, you can use .subparse, which doesn't. This means you can parse part of the text then stop.

You can deal with one record at a time. Using .subparse with the record rule gets you the first record and only the first record. The .subparse method always returns a Match, unlike .parse, which only returns a Match when it succeeds. You can't rely on the type of the object as an indication of success:

```
my $data = $filename.IO.slurp;
my $first_result = Grammar::CSV.subparse(
    $data, :rule('record'), :action(CSV::Actions)
    );
if $first-result { ... }
```

That works for the first line. Use :c(N) to tell these methods where to start in the Str. You have to know where you want to start. The Match knows how far it got; look in the .from slot:

```
my $data  = $filename.IO.slurp;
```

```
loop {
    state $from = 0;
    my $match = Grammar::CSV.subparse(
        $data,
        :rule('record'),
        :actions(CSV::Actions),
        :c($from)
        );
    last unless $match;

    put "Matched from {$match.from} to {$match.to}";
    $from = $match.to;
    say $match;
    }
```

This is most of the way to a solution—it fails to go through the entire file if `.sub` parse fails on one record. With some boring monkey work you could fix this to find the start of the next record and restart the parsing, but that's more than I want to fit in this book.

Adjusting the Grammar

You thought the problem was solved. Then, someone sent you a file with a slightly different format. Instead of escaping a " by doubling it, the new format uses the backslash.

Now your existing grammar fails to parse. You don't have a rule that satisfies that type of escape because you didn't need it for your grammar. As a matter of practice in both patterns and grammars, only match what you should match. Be liberal in what you accept in other ways, such as making a subgrammar to handle the new case:

```
grammar Grammar::CSV::Backslashed is Grammar::CSV {
    token escaped-quote { '\\"' }
    }

class CSV::Actions::Backslashed is CSV::Actions {
    method value ($/)  { make $/.subst( rx/ '\\"' /, '"', :g ) }
    }
```

With two grammars, how do you get the one that you need to use? The name interpolation `::($name)` comes in handy here:

```
my %formats;
%formats<doubled> = {
    'file'    => $*SPEC.catfile( <corpus test.csv> ),
    'grammar' => 'Grammar::CSV',
    };
%formats<backslashed> = {
    'file' => $*SPEC.catfile( <corpus test-backslash.csv> ),
    'grammar' => 'Grammar::CSV::Backslashed',
    };
```

```
for %formats.values -> $hash {
    $hash<data> = $hash<file>.IO.slurp;
    my $class = (require ::( $hash<grammar> ) );
    my $match = $class.parse( $hash<data> );
    say "{$hash<file>} with {$hash<grammar>} ",
        $match ?? 'parsed' !! 'failed';
}
```

The %formats Hash of Hashes stores the filenames and the grammars for them. You can load a grammar and use it to parse the data without the explicit grammar name:

```
corpus/test.csv with Grammar::CSV parsed
corpus/test-backslash.csv with Grammar::CSV::Backslashed parsed
```

That mostly solves the problem, although there are plenty of special cases that this doesn't cover.

Using Roles in Grammars

Roles can supply rules and methods that grammars can use. In the previous section you handled different sorts of double-quote escaping through inheritance, where you overrode the rule. You can do the same thing with roles.

A grammar can have methods and subroutines. The way you declare a name with sub, method, or rule tells the language parser (not your grammar!) how to parse the stuff in the Block.

First, adjust the main grammar to have a stub method for <escaped-quote>. This forces something else to define it:

```
grammar Grammar::CSV {
    token TOP       { <record>+ }
    token record    { <value>+ % <.separator> \R }
    token separator { <.ws> ',' <.ws> }
    token value     {
        '"'                   # quoted
            <( [ <-["]> | <.escaped-quote> ]* )>
        '"'
            |
        <-[",\n\f\r]>+  # non-quoted (no vertical ws)
            |
        ''                    # empty
    }

    # stub that you must define in a role
    method escaped-quote { !!! }
}
```

A role will fill in that stub method. There's one role for each way to escape the double quote:

```
role DoubledQuote     { token escaped-quote { '""'  } }
role BackslashedQuote { token escaped-quote { '\\"' } }
```

When it's time to parse a file you can choose which role you want to use. You can create a new object for Grammar::CSV and apply the appropriate role to it:

```
my $filename   = ...;
my $csv-data   = $filename.IO.slurp;
my $csv-parser = Grammar::CSV.new but DoubledQuote;
```

Use that object to parse your data:

```
my $match = $csv-parser.parse: $csv-data;
say $match // 'Failed!';
```

Doing this doesn't fix the double quotes in the data—a "" stays as a ""—but you can fix that in an action class.

Exercise 17.6

Adjust the CSV example to use roles instead of inheritance. Create an action class to adjust the escaped double quotes as you run into them. You can start with *Grammars/test.csv* from the downloads section of the book's website (*https://www.learning perl6.com/*) if you like.

Summary

Grammars are one of the killer features of the language. You can define complex relationships between patterns and use action classes to run arbitrarily complex code when something matches. You might find that your entire program ends up being one big grammar.

## CHAPTER 18

Supplies, Channels, and Promises

Supplies and *channels* provide ways to send data from one part of a program to another. A Supply is a direct line of communication from a source of data to possibly many consumers. A Channel allows any part of your program to add data to a queue that any part of your program can read.

A Promise allows code to run *asynchronously* (concurrently)—different bits of code can run in overlapping time frames. This is quite handy while employing either Supplys or Channels (or both).

Supplies

A Supplier emits a message to every Supply that has asked to receive its messages. This happens asynchronously; they do their work as your program does other things. You can process things in the background and handle the results as they come in rather than stopping the entire program to wait for all of the data. Other languages may call this "Publish–Subscribe" (or "PubSub").

Here's a useless example. Set up a Supplier and call .emit to send a message. Since you didn't define any Supplys that message goes nowhere; it's gone forever:

```
my $supplier = Supplier.new;
$supplier.emit: 3;
```

To receive that message ask the Supplier for a Supply (yes, the terminology is a bit thick) by calling .tap with a Block:

```
my $supplier = Supplier.new;
my $supply   = $supplier.Supply;
my $tap      = $supply.tap: { put "$^a * $^a = ", $^a**2 };
$supplier.emit: 3;
```

The Supply receives the 3 and passes that as the argument to the Block, which then outputs the message:

```
3 + 3 = 9
```

There are some useful builtin Supplys available. The .interval Supply *factory* automatically emits the next ordinal number at the number of seconds (possibly fractional) you specify. You don't specify the Supplier because that's handled for you:

```
my $fifth-second = Supply.interval: 0.2;
$fifth-second.tap: { say "First: $^a" };

sleep 1;
```

The output shows five lines. Why only five? There are five-fifths of a second until the program ends once the sleep finishes:

```
First: 0
First: 1
First: 2
First: 3
First: 4
```

Once you start the tap it continues to handle values asynchronously until the program ends (or you turn off the tap). Two things happen once your program reaches the sleep statement. First, the program waits the amount of time that you specified. Second, the Supplier emits values that the tap handles. Those two things happen concurrently. As you sleep the Supplier is still working. All that in a couple of lines of code!

 Concurrency isn't parallelism. Concurrency allows two different things to progress during overlapping time frames. Parallelism means that two different things happen at the exact same time. People tend to be fuzzy with their definitions, though.

If you took out the sleep statement you wouldn't get any output—the program would end right away. The Supplier doesn't keep the program going. If you increase the sleep time to make the program run longer you get more output.

Here's a counter that will loop forever but only makes one line. The carriage return goes back to the beginning of the line but doesn't advance the line (terminal buffering might interfere though):

```
my $fifth-second = Supply.interval: 0.2;
$fifth-second.tap: { print "\x[D]$^a" };

loop { }
```

Multiple Taps

You aren't limited to one tap; you can have as many as you like on the same `Supply`. This program will take two seconds to finish. The first tap will run for two seconds and the second tap will run for the last second:

```
my $supply = Supply.interval: 0.5;

$supply.tap: { say "First: $^a" };
sleep 1;

$supply.tap: { say "Second: $^a" };
sleep 1;
```

Each tap labels its output:

```
First: 0
First: 1
Second: 0
First: 2
First: 3
Second: 1
```

Notice anything strange here? The second tap started at 0 again instead of getting the same number as the first tap got at the same time. The `.interval` method creates an *on-demand supply*. It starts to produce values when a tap asks for them and it generates the interval fresh for each new tap. Each time a tap wants a value it gets the next one in line, independently of any other taps.

The code in a `tap` must completely finish before that code runs again with another value. This ensures that your code doesn't get confused when it has persistent variables. If this `Block` ran again before the first run finished then the value of `$n` would increment a couple of times before the first run could output its message:

```
$supply.tap: {
    state $n = 0; $n++;
    sleep 1;   # misses a couple of emitted values!
    say "$n: $^a"
    };
```

Exercise 18.1

Create a `Supplier` that emits lines of input. Tap that so that you output only the names you have not seen previously. You might use the butterfly census file from the Downloads section of the website (*https://www.learningperl6.com/*).

Live Supplies

A *live supply* is different from the *on-demand* ones you've encountered so far. It emits a single stream of values that all taps share. When a new value is available the old one is discarded even if no tap has read it. Each new tap starts with the current value from that single stream. Turn an on-demand supply into a live supply with `.share`:

```
my $supply    = Supply.interval(0.5).share;

$supply.tap: { say "First: $^a" };
sleep 1;

$supply.tap: { say "Second: $^a" };
sleep 1;
```

The output is different in two ways. First, the 0 value is missing. The Supply emitted that before the first tap had a chance to see it. After one second the second tap starts and the Supply emits 2; both taps see 2. After that both taps continue to see the same values until the end of the program:

```
First: 1
First: 2
Second: 2
First: 3
Second: 3
First: 4
Second: 4
```

When you no longer need a tap you can close it; it will no longer receive values:

```
my $supply = Supply.interval(0.4).share;

my $tap1 = $supply.tap: { say "1. $^a" };
sleep 1;

my $tap2 = $supply.tap: { say "2. $^a" };
sleep 1;

$tap2.close;

sleep 1;
```

At the start the first tap is handling everything. The second tap starts after the first `sleep` finishes. Then both taps handle things for a second, then the first tap closes and it's only the second tap still working:

```
First: 1
First: 2
First: 3
Second: 3
First: 4
Second: 4
```

```
Second: 5
Second: 6
Second: 7
```

So far this section has dealt with only `Supply`s that you created. Many other objects can provide a `Supply`. The `.lines` method returns a `Seq` which can turn into a `Supply`:

```
my $supply = $*ARGFILES.lines.Supply;  # IO::ArgFiles
$supply.tap: { put $++ ~ ": $^a" };

$supply.tap: {
    state %Seen;
    END { put "{%Seen.keys.elems} unique lines" }
    %Seen{$^a}++;
    };
```

Most things that are `List`s (or can turn into `List`s) can do this:

```
my $list = List.new: 1, 4, 9, 16;
my $supply = $list.Supply;
$supply.tap: { put "Got $^a" }
```

Even an infinite sequence will work:

```
my $seq := 1, 2, * + 1 ... *;
my $supply2 = $seq.Supply;
$supply2.tap: { put "Got $^a" }
```

Notice that these examples don't need a `sleep` to delay the end of the program. They aren't "on the clock" like `.interval`; they go through each of their values.

Exercise 18.2

Create a live `Supply` that emits a number every second. After three seconds, tap it and output the number it emitted. After another three seconds, tap it again to output the same thing. Wait three more seconds, then close the second tap. Finally, after another three seconds close the first tap.

Channels

`Channel`s are first-come, first-served queues. They ensure that something is processed exactly once. Anything can put thingys into the channel and anything can take thingys off the channel. The code on either side of the `Channel` doesn't need to know about the other. Several threads can share a `Channel`, but once something asks for the next thingy that thingy disappears from the `Channel` and can't be processed by other code.

Create a `Channel`. Add to it with `.send` and take a thingy with `.receive`. When you are done with the `Channel`, `.close` it:

```
my $channel = Channel.new;
$channel.send: 'Hamadryas';
put 'Received: ', $channel.receive;
$channel.close;
```

The output shows the value you added:

```
Received: Hamadryas
```

After the `.close` you can't send more values to the `Channel`. Anything you've already added is still in the `Channel` and available to process. You can `.receive` until the `Channel` is empty:

```
my $channel = Channel.new;
$channel.send: $_ for <Hamadryas Rhamma Melanis>;
put 'Received: ', $channel.receive;
$channel.close;  # no more sending

while $channel.poll -> $thingy {
    put "while received $thingy";
    }
```

The `while` uses `.poll` instead of `.receive`. If there is a thingy, `.poll` returns it. If there are no more thingys currently available it returns `Nil` (ending the looping):

```
Received: Hamadryas
while received Rhamma
while received Melanis
```

When `.poll` returns `Nil` you don't know if there will ever be more thingys available. If the `Channel` is still open something can add more thingys; if the `Channel` is closed there will never be anything more to `.receive`. Calling `.fail` closes the `Channel`, and `.receive` will throw an error if you call it again. You can CATCH the Exception to end the loop:

```
my $channel = Channel.new;
$channel.send: $_ for <Hamadryas Rhamma Melanis>;
put 'Received: ', $channel.receive;
$channel.fail('End of items');    # X::AdHoc

loop {
    CATCH {
        default { put "Channel is closed"; last }
        }
    put "loop received: ", $channel.receive;
    }
```

Instead of a loop you can `tap` the `Channel`; it calls `.receive` for you:

```
my $channel = Channel.new;
$channel.send: $_ for <Hamadryas Rhamma Melanis>;
put 'Received: ', $channel.receive;
$channel.fail('End of items');

$channel.Supply.tap: { put "Received $_" }
CATCH { default { put "Channel is closed" } }
```

The output is the same either way:

```
Received: Hamadryas
loop received: Rhamma
loop received: Melanis
Channel is closed
```

Exercise 18.3

Create a Channel and tap it. Send lines of input to the Channel but only print the ones with prime line numbers.

Promises

A Promise is a bit of code that will produce a result sometime later, and that later might not be soon. It schedules work to happen in another thread while the rest of your program moves on. These are the underpinnings of Perl 6's concurrency and they do most of the hard work for you.

Every Promise has a status. It might be waiting to run, currently running, or finished. How it finishes decides its status: a Promise is Kept when it succeeds or Broken when it fails. While it's working it's Planned.

A simple Promise is a timer. The .in method makes a Promise that will be kept after the number of seconds you specify:

```
my $five-seconds-from-now = Promise.in: 5;

loop {
    sleep 1;
    put "Promise status is: ", $five-seconds-from-now.status;
    }
```

At first the Promise is Planned. After five seconds (roughly) the Promise converts to Kept. At that point you know that five seconds have passed:

```
Promise status is: Planned
Promise status is: Planned
Promise status is: Planned
Promise status is: Planned
Promise status is: Kept
```

```
Promise status is: Kept
...
```

You don't need to continually check the Promise. Use .then to set up code to run when it is kept:

```
my $five-seconds-from-now = Promise.in: 5;
$five-seconds-from-now.then: { put "It's been 5 seconds" };
```

Nothing happens when you run this program; the Promise isn't kept before the program ends. Planned Promises don't prevent the program from ending.

You could give your program enough time for five seconds to elapse. A sleep extends the program time:

```
my $five-seconds-from-now = Promise.in: 5;
$five-seconds-from-now.then: { put "It's been 5 seconds" };

sleep 7;
```

Now you see the output from the code in .then:

```
It's been 5 seconds
```

Waiting for Promises

Instead of sleeping (and guessing the time you need to be idle), you can use await, which blocks your program until the Promise is either kept or broken:

```
my $five-seconds-from-now = Promise.in: 5;
$five-seconds-from-now.then: { put "It's been 5 seconds" };

await $five-seconds-from-now;
```

These examples use await because you need the program to keep running. In something more interesting your program is likely doing a lot of other work, so you might not need to keep the program alive.

Instead of a relative time you can use .at with an absolute time. That could be an Instant value or something that you can coerce to an Instant (or a Numeric value that represents an Instant):

```
my $later = Promise.at: now + 7;
$later.then: { put "It's now $datetime" };

await $later;
```

The start keyword creates a Promise. When the code completes the Promise is finished:

```
my $pause = start {
    put "Promise starting at ", now;
    sleep 5;
```

```
        put "Promise ending at ", now;
        };
    await $pause;
```

The output shows the start and end of the `Promise`:

```
Promise starting at Instant:1507924913.012565
Promise ending at Instant:1507924918.018444
```

A `Promise` is broken if it throws an `Exception`. You can return all the `False` values you like, but until you `fail` or throw an `Exception` with an error your `Promise` will be kept. This succeeds even though it returns `False`:

```
my $return-false = start {
    put "Promise starting at ", now;
    sleep 5;
    put "Promise ending at ", now;
    return False;  # still kept
    };
await $return-false;
```

This example breaks the `Promise` because you explicitly `fail`:

```
my $five-seconds-from-now = start {
    put "Promise starting at ", now;
    sleep 5;
    fail;
    put "Promise ending at ", now;
    };
await $five-seconds-from-now;
```

You get part of the output, but the `fail` stops that `Block` before you get the rest of the output:

```
Promise starting at Instant:1522698239.054087
An operation first awaited:
  in block <unit> at ...

Died with the exception:
    Failed
        in block  at ...
```

Waiting for Multiple Promises

The `Await` can take a list of `Promises`:

```
put "Starting at {now}";
my @promises =
    Promise.in( 5 ).then( { put '5 finished' } ),
    Promise.in( 3 ).then( { put '3 finished' } ),
    Promise.in( 7 ).then( { put '7 finished' } ),
    ;

await @promises;
```

```
put "Ending at {now}";
```

The program doesn't end until all of the Promises are kept:

```
Starting at Instant:1524856233.733533
3 finished
5 finished
7 finished
Ending at Instant:1524856240.745510
```

If any of the `Promises` are broken then the entire `await` is done and the planned `Promises` are abandoned:

```
put "Starting at {now}";
my @promises =
    start { sleep 5; fail "5 failed" },
    Promise.in( 3 ).then( { put '3 finished' } ),
    Promise.in( 7 ).then( { put '7 finished' } ),
    ;

await @promises;

put "Ending at {now}";
```

If the `.in( 3 )` Promise is kept then the one with `start` fails:

```
Starting at Instant:1524856385.367019
3 finished
An operation first awaited:
  in block <unit> at await-list.p6 line 9

Died with the exception:
    5 failed
      in block  at await-list.p6 line 4
```

Managing Your Own Promises

In the previous examples there was something else managing the `Promises` for you. You can do that all yourself. Start by making a bare `Promise`:

```
my $promise = Promise.new;
```

Check its status by smart matching against the constants from `PromiseStatus` (which you get for free):

```
put do given $promise.status {
    when Planned { "Still working on it" }
    when Kept    { "Everything worked out" }
    when Broken  { "Oh no! Something didn't work" }
    }
```

At this point `$promise` is planned and will stay that way. This will loop forever:

```
loop {
    put do given $promise.status {
        when Planned { "Still working on it" }
        when Kept    { "Everything worked out" }
        when Broken  { "Oh no! Something didn't work" }
        }

    last unless $promise.status ~~ Planned;
    sleep 1;
    }
```

You can use now to note the start time and to check that if it's five seconds later to make your own .at or .in. Some time after five seconds you call .keep to change the status:

```
my $promise = Promise.new;

my $start = now;
loop {
    $promise.keep if now > $start + 5;
    given $promise.status {
        when Planned { put "Still working on it" }
        when Kept    { put "Everything worked out" }
        when Broken  { put "Oh no! Something didn't work" }
        }

    last unless $promise.status ~~ Planned;
    sleep 1;
    }
```

Now the loop stops after five seconds:

```
Still working on it
Still working on it
Still working on it
Still working on it
Still working on it
Everything worked out
```

This Promise can still call code with .then:

```
my $promise = Promise.new;
$promise.then: { put "Huzzah! I'm kept" }

my $start = now;
loop { ... } # same as before
```

The output shows the output from the .then code:

```
Still working on it
Still working on it
Still working on it
Still working on it
Still working on it
```

```
Everything worked out
Huzzah! I'm kept
```

Or you might break the `Promise`. Either way your `.then` code runs, and you need to distinguish between those cases. The `.then` code has one argument; that's the `Promise` itself. If you don't name the argument it's in `$_`:

```
my $promise = Promise.new;
$promise.then: {
    put do given .status {
        when Kept { 'Huzzah!' }
        when Broken { 'Darn!' }
        }
    }

my $start = now;
loop {
    $promise.break if now > $start + 5;
    last unless $promise.status ~~ Planned;
    sleep 1;
    }
```

Promise Junctions

You can use `Junctions` to create an über-`Promise`. The `.allof` method creates a `Promise` that is kept if all of its included `Promises` are kept:

```
my $all-must-pass = await Promise.allof:
    Promise.in(5).then( { put 'Five seconds later' } ),
    start { sleep 3; put 'Three seconds later'; },
    Promise.at( now + 1 ).then( { put 'One second later' } );
put $all-must-pass;
```

The `.anyof` `Promise` is kept if any of its included `Promises` are kept. All except one of them can be broken and the larger `Promise` is still kept:

```
my $any-can-pass = await Promise.anyof:
    Promise.in(5).then( { put 'Five seconds later' } ),
    start { sleep 3; put 'Three seconds later'; fail },
    Promise.at( now + 1 ).then( { put 'One second later' } );
put $any-can-pass;
```

Both of these succeed. In the `.allof` case you see the output from all three `Promises`. Then you see the output from one of the `Promises` from `.anyof`. Not all of those `Promises` need to finish because the overall `Promise` already knows it can succeed:

```
One second later
Three seconds later
Five seconds later
True
One second later
True
```

Reactive Programming

A `react` `Block` allows you to run some code when new values are available. It keeps running until it runs out of values to handle. It's similar to an event loop. Here's a very simple example:

```
react {
    whenever True { put 'Got something that was true' }
    }

END put "End of the program";
```

You use `whenever` to supply values to the `Block` of code. In this case you have the single value `True`. This isn't a *conditional* expression or a test, as in `if` or `while`. The `Block` reacts to that single value and runs the `whenever` code. After that there are no more values and the `Block` exits:

```
Got something that was true
End of the program
```

You might be tempted to think of this as a looping construct, but it's not quite the same thing. It's not doing everything in the `react` `Block` then starting the `Block` again. The `whenever` for `True` only runs once, instead of running forever as you'd expect with a `loop`:

```
loop {
    if True { put 'Got something that was true'  }
    }
```

Change the `whenever` from `True` to a `Supply.interval` and you never see the end-of-program message:

```
my $supply = Supply.interval: 1;

react {
    whenever $supply { put "Got $^a" }
    }

END put "End of the program";
```

As long as the `Supply` has values for `whenever`, the `react` `Block` keeps going:

```
Got 0
Got 1
Got 2
...
```

You could have both the `Supply` and the `True` at the same time:

```
my $supply = Supply.interval: 1;

react {
```

```
    whenever $supply { put "Got $^a" }
    whenever True { put 'Got something that was true' }
    }

END put "End of the program";
```

The whenever with the Supply reacts immediately and outputs the first value in the Supply. The whenever with the True reacts next and exhausts its values (the single True). After that the Supply continues until you give up and interrupt the program:

```
Got 0
Got something that was true
Got 1
Got 2
...
```

If you reverse the whenevers the True will probably react first:

```
my $supply = Supply.interval: 1;

react {
    whenever True { put 'Got something that was true' }
    whenever $supply { put "Got $^a" }
    }

END put "End of the program";
```

The output is slightly different, but there's nothing that says this has to be the case. Perhaps future implementations will choose differently. This is concurrency; you can't depend on strict order of happenings:

```
Got something that was true
Got 0
Got 1
Got 2
...
```

Instead of interrupting the program to get the react to stop, you can do it from within the Block with done. You can use a Promise with .in to provide a value after some interval:

```
my $supply = Supply.interval: 1;

react {
    whenever $supply { put "Got $^a" }
    whenever True { put 'Got something that was true' }
    whenever Promise.in(5) { put 'Timeout!'; done }
    }

END put "End of the program";
```

After five seconds the Promise is kept and the whenever kicks in. It outputs the timeout message and uses done to end the react:

```
Got 0
Got something that was true
Got 1
Got 2
Got 3
Got 4
Got 5
Timeout!
End of the program
```

Add another react and the process starts over with a fresh Supply:

```
my $supply = Supply.interval: 1;

react {
    whenever $supply { put "Got $^a" }
    whenever True { put 'Got something that was true' }
    whenever Promise.in(5) { put 'Timeout!'; done }
    }

put "React again";

react {
    whenever $supply { put "Got $^a" }
    }

END put "End of the program";
```

The output for the Supply starts again, but at the beginning of the interval:

```
Got 0
Got something that was true
Got 1
Got 2
Got 3
Got 4
Timeout!
React again
Got 0
Got 1
```

Exercise 18.4

Modify the double react example to use a live Supply instead of an on-demand one. How does the output change?

Reacting in the Background

The react is a way that you can respond to values when they are available. So far you've seen the react as a top-level Block. It keeps running—and holds up the rest of the program—until it's done.

Instead, you most likely want your react to do its work in the background as your program does other things. You can wrap the react in a Promise with a start. That allows the react to work in a thread as the rest of the program continues:

```
my $supply = Supply.interval: 1;

my $promise = start {
    react {
        whenever $supply { put "Got $^a" }
        whenever True { put 'Got something that was true' }
        whenever Promise.in(5) { put 'Timeout!'; done }
        }
    }

put 'After the react loop';

await $promise;
put 'After the await';

END put "End of the program";
```

The first line of the output is from the put after the start block. The react is starting its work, but it's not blocking the rest of the program:

```
After the react loop
Got 0
Got something that was true
Got 1
Got 2
Got 3
Got 4
Timeout!
After the await
End of the program
```

Take it up a notch. Add a Channel into it. Move the Supply inside the whenever. When that Supply has a value it executes the Block to output the same thing it did before. It also sends the value to the Channel if it is a multiple of 2.

Add a second whenever to read the values available on the Channel. You need to convert the Channel to a Supply; that's easy because there's a .Supply method. The whenever taps that Supply:

```
my $channel = Channel.new;

my $promise = start {
    react {
        whenever Supply.interval: 1
            { put "Got $^a"; $channel.send: $^a if $^a %% 2 }
        whenever $channel.Supply
            { put "Channel got $^a" }
        whenever True
            { put 'Got something that was true' }
        whenever Promise.in(5)
            { put 'Timeout!'; done }
        }
    }

put 'After the react loop';

await $promise;
put 'After the await';

END put "End of the program";
```

The output is mostly the same as before with the Channel output inserted:

```
After the react loop
Got 0
Got something that was true
Channel got 0
Got 1
Got 2
Channel got 2
Got 3
Got 4
Channel got 4
Timeout!
After the await
End of the program
```

Exercise 18.5

Use IO::Notification to output a message every time there's a change to a file you specify on the command line.

Summary

Promises are the basis of concurrency, and there are various ways that you can create them to get what you what. Decompose your problem into independent bits and run them as Promises, which can run in separate threads (or maybe even on different cores). With those, Supplys and Channels provide a way to pass data between disconnected parts of your program. To get the most out of all of these you need to think differently from the procedural stuff you've seen so far. You'll get that with practice.

Controlling Other Programs

Sometimes you need to ask other programs to do some work for you. The Perl family of languages has been known as the "duct tape of the internet." Kicking off a well-known, stable, existing program can be easier and faster than reimplementing it yourself. This chapter shows many ways to start and control external programs to bend them to your will.

Quick and Easy

The `shell` routine is a quick way to run an external command or program. It takes the argument and runs it in the shell as if you had typed it out yourself. This example uses a Unix-like shell command to list all of the files:

```
shell( 'ls -l' );
```

If you were on Windows you'd use a different command. There's an implicit `cmd /c` in front of your command:

```
shell( 'dir' );   # actually cmd /c dir
```

The output from this command will go to the same place that your program's output will go (as long as you haven't lexically redirected standard output or error to something else).

You can choose between the commands by inspecting the `$*DISTRO` variable. The `Distro` object has an `.is-win` method that returns `True` if it thinks your program is running on that platform:

```
my $command = $*DISTRO.is-win ?? 'dir' !! 'ls -l';
shell( $command );
```

Be careful with variables as the argument to shell! Be sure you know what's in them. If a character is special in the shell then it's special in that value. More on that in a moment.

shell returns a Proc object. When you use that in sink context (where you do nothing with the result) and the command fails the Proc object throws an exception:

```
shell( '/usr/bin/false' );  # throws X::Proc::Unsuccessful
```

A command "fails" when it exits with something other than 0. That's a Unix convention where the nonzero numbers indicate various error conditions. Not all programs follow that convention, and where they don't you'll have to do more work.

You can save the result to avoid the exception. You can inspect the Proc object to see what happened:

```
my $proc = shell( '/usr/bin/false' );
unless $proc.so {
    put "{$proc.command} failed with exit code: {$proc.exitcode}";
    }
```

This still might not be what you want. If you expect it to return a nonzero value you might have to handle part of the process yourself:

```
my $proc = shell( '/usr/bin/true' );
given $proc {
    unless .exitcode == 1 {
        put "{.command} returned: {.exitcode}";
        X::Proc::Unsuccessful.new.throw;
        }
    }
```

If you don't care if the command fails you can call .so on the returned object. This "handles" the object and prevents the Proc from throwing the exception:

```
shell( '/usr/bin/false' ).so
```

Quoted Commands

Sometimes you want to capture the output of a command or save it in a variable. You can use quoting with the :x adverb to create a Str from the output of the command:

```
my $output = Q:x{ls -1};
my $output = q:x{ls -1};
my $output = qq:x{$command};
```

These have slightly shorter versions that do the same thing:

```
my $output = Qx{dir};
my $output = qx{dir};
my $output = qqx{$command};
```

These capture standard output only. If you want to merge standard error you need to handle that in the shell. This works in both Unix and Windows by using 2>&1. That merges the handles before they get to your program:

```
my $output = qq:x{$command 2>&1};
```

Safer Commands

The run routine allows you to represent your command as a list. The first item in the list is the command name, which Perl 6 executes directly without shell interaction. This command isn't as nasty as it looks because none of the characters are special to the shell. Those semicolons don't end a command and start another:

```
# don't do this, just in case
run( '/bin/echo', '-n', ';;;; rm -rf /' );
```

If you'd entered this as a single Str in shell you would have started a recursive operation to remove all files. Don't try this even in jest (or use a virtual machine with a saved snapshot!).

run returns a Proc object; handle it in the same way you saw for shell:

```
unless run( ... ) {
    put "Command failed";
    }
```

You might be tempted to use a bare command name with no path information:

```
run( 'echo', '-n', 'Hello' );
```

That's not particularly safe either. run will look for a matching file in the PATH environment variable. That's something people can set outside your program. Someone might be able to trick your program into running something else called *echo*.

You could clean out the PATH, forcing the program to always specify the full path to the command:

```
%*ENV{PATH} = '';  # won't find anything
run( '/bin/echo', '-n', 'Hello' );
```

Setting the PATH to the directories that you trust and will allow might be easier:

```
%*ENV{PATH} = '/bin:/sbin:/usr/bin:/usr/sbin'
run( 'echo', '-n', 'Hello' );
```

This doesn't mean that the command you find is the right one; someone might have tampered with that. No approach provides perfect security—but you don't have to make it too easy. Think about this whenever you interact with something outside your program.

Like shell, run returns a Proc object. The :out parameter captures standard output and makes it available through the Proc object. Use .slurp to extract it:

```
my $proc = run(
    '/bin/some_command', '-n', '-t', $filename
    :out,
    );
put "Output is ⌈{ $proc.out.slurp }⌋";
```

The :err parameter does the same thing for error output:

```
my $proc = run(
    '/bin/some_command', '-n', '-t', $filename
    :out, :err,
    );
put "Output is ⌈{ $proc.out.slurp }⌋";
put "Error is ⌈{ $proc.err.slurp }⌋";
```

If you don't want them as separate streams you can merge them:

```
my $proc = run(
    '/bin/some_command', '-n', '-t', $filename
    :out, :err, :merge
    );
put "Output is ⌈{ $proc.out.slurp }⌋";
```

You can also give it named arguments to control the encoding, environment, and current working directory (among other things).

Exercise 19.1

Use run to get a file listing of the current directory sorted by file size. Output that long file listing. The Unix command is ls -lrS and the Windows command is cmd /c dir /OS. Once you get that working, filter the lines to output only those with a 7. Finally, can you make one program work on both platforms?

Writing to a Proc

A process can receive data from your program. Including :in allows you to write to the process:

```
my $string = 'Hamadryas perlicus';

my $hex = run 'hexdump', '-C', :in, :out;

$hex.in.print: $string;
$hex.in.close;

$hex.out.slurp.put;
```

In this example you call .print once then close the output. That's fine for *hexdump*, but other programs may behave differently. Some may expect some input, give you some output, then expect more input after you've read it. How this works depends on the particular program and can be maddening at times:

```
my $string = 'Hamadryas perlicus';

my $hex = run 'fictional-program', :in, :out;
$hex.in.print: $string;
$hex.out.slurp;
$hex.in.print: $string;
...;
```

You can redirect the output from one external program into the input for another one. This example takes the output of perl6 -v and makes it the input of the next Proc:

```
my $proc1 = run( 'perl6', '-v', :out );
my $proc2 = run(
    'tr', '-s', Q/[:lower:]/,  Q/[:upper:]/,
    :in($proc1.out)
    );
```

That second run uses the external tr command to turn all the lowercase letters into uppercase letters:

```
THIS IS RAKUDO STAR VERSION 2018.04 BUILT ON MOARVM VERSION 2018.04
IMPLEMENTING PERL 6.C.
```

Procs

A Proc object handles both shell and run. Construct the object yourself to get more control. This happens in two steps; the Proc sets up something that will later run a command:

```
my $proc = Proc.new: ...;
```

Set up a general Proc that captures and merges the standard output and error streams:

```
my $proc =  Proc.new: :err, :out, :merge;
```

When you're ready to run the command, .spawn it. Your spawned process uses the setup that you've already established. The result is a Boolean based on the exit status of the program:

```
unless $proc.spawn: 'echo', '-n', 'Hello' {
    ... # handle the error
    }
```

Specify the current working directory and environment when you call .spawn if you want different settings:

```
my $worked = $proc.spawn: :cwd($some-dir), :env(%hash);
unless $worked {
    ... # handle the error
    }
```

Exercise 19.2

Create a `Proc` that captures the standard output and error. Spawn a command to get a directory listing.

Asynchronous Control

Executing a command through `Proc` (and `shell` and `run`) makes your program wait until the external program finishes its work. Using `Proc::Async` allows those programs to run in their own `Promise` while the rest of your program continues.

Running the external *find* and waiting for it to go through all of the filesystem could take virtually forever (at least it feels like it):

```
my $proc = Proc.new: :out;
$proc.spawn: 'find', '/', '-name', '*.txt';

for $proc.out.lines -> $line {
    put $++, ': ', $line;
    }

put 'Finished';
```

When you run this program you see all the lines of output from *find*. When that finishes, which might take a long time, you'll then see the `Finished` message. You can do this asynchronously instead.

You see the Unix *find* in these examples, but you also created a similar directory listing program in Chapter 8 that you can use as the external program to practice using `Proc`:

```
my $proc = Proc.new: :out;
$proc.spawn: 'perl6', 'dir-listing.p6';

for $proc.out.lines -> $line {
    put $++, ': ', $line;
    }

put 'Finished';
```

The interface to `Proc::Async` is a bit different than `Proc`'s. Once you have the object you can use the `Supply` and `Promise` features you saw in Chapter 18. This example

---

uses `.lines` to break the output into lines (instead of chunks of the buffer), then taps that `Supply` to process lines as they come in:

```
my $proc = Proc::Async.new: 'find', '/', '-name', '*.txt';

$proc.stdout.lines.Supply.tap: { put $++, ': <', $^line, '>' };
my $promise = $proc.start;

put 'Moving on';

await $promise;
```

This is a simple use of `Proc::Async`, but you can combine it with the concurrency features that you've already seen. Calling `.stdout` gets you the lines of output, but only after you call `.start`. Do both of those in a `Block`:

```
my $proc = Proc::Async.new: 'find', '/', '-name', '*.txt';

react {
    whenever $proc.stdout.lines { put $_;  }
    whenever $proc.start        { put "Finished"; done }
    };
```

That `.start` returns a `Promise` that isn't kept until the external program completes. Even though that `whenever` runs at the beginning of the program the `Promise` isn't kept until the end, and it's then that the `Block` does its work.

Exercise 19.3

Implement the asynchronous *find* program. Modify it so it stops after finding the number of files that you specify on the command line. Report the number of files it finds.

Summary

You can run programs and wait for their output or fire them off in the background and handle their output as it comes in. Expand this to handle several programs and your program becomes a fine handler of external resources. You've seen the mechanics of how it works, but it's up to you to design bigger and better things with it.

## CHAPTER 20

Advanced Topics

In such a short book I don't have enough pages to show you everything that you can do. This chapter is a brief survey of some of the features I would have liked to explain in more detail. You now know these exist and you can investigate them further on your own.

One-Liners

You can run *perl6 one-liners*. These are programs that you compose completely on the command line. The -e switch takes an argument that is the program:

```
% perl6 -e 'put "Hello Perl 6"'
Hello Perl 6
```

The -n switch runs the program once for each line of input. The current line is in $_. This one uppercases and outputs the line:

```
% perl6 -n -e '.uc.put' *.pod
```

You can load a module with -M:

```
% perl6 -MMath::Constants -e 'put α'
0.0072973525664
```

Declarator Block Comments

The parser doesn't discard all comments. It remembers special comments and attaches them to the subroutine. #| comments attach themselves to the subroutine after them and #= comments attach themselves to the subroutine before them. These comments are available through the .WHY meta-method:

```
#| Hamadryas is a sort of butterfly
class Hamadryas {
```

```
#| Flap makes the butterfly go
method flap () {

    }
}

Hamadryas.WHY.put;
Hamadryas.^find_method('flap').WHY.put;
```

The output is the combination of all the comments attached to that subroutine:

```
Hamadryas is a sort of butterfly
Flap makes the butterfly go
```

This is the sort of thing that's handy in an integrated development environment to grab a description of the thing you are trying to use. It's also useful when you are debugging something—that is, it's useful if the developer documented their code.

Feed Operators

The feed operators decide which way information flows. Here's a list-processing pipeline that has a .grep, a .sort, and finally a .map. What they do doesn't matter as much as their order:

```
my @array = @some-array
    .grep( *.chars > 5 )
    .sort( *.fc )
    .map( *.uc )
    ;
```

The final step is farthest away from the assignment. You might not like that. The leftward feed operator allows you to write this in a way where the data flows in one direction. This flows bottom to top into the new variable:

```
my @array <==
    map(  *.uc         ) <==
    sort( *.fc         ) <==
    grep( *.chars > 5  ) <==
    @some-array
    ;
```

Notice that the assignment operator disappeared because the feed operator took care of that.

The rightward feed operator goes the other way. The new variable is at the end this time. This is the same thing in the other direction:

```
@some-array
    ==> grep( *.chars > 5  )
    ==> sort( *.fc         )
```

```
==> map(  *.uc        )
==> my @array;
```

Destructuring Signatures

You can group parameters with square brackets to create a *subsignature*. Inside the [ ] you can break down the aggregate into a smaller signature:

```
sub show-the-arguments ( $i, [$j, *@args] ) {  # slurpy
    put "The arguments are i: $i j: $j and @args[]";
    }

my @a = ( 3, 7, 5 );
show-the-arguments( 1, @a );
```

With that, $i gets the first parameter and the [ ] gets the rest. The [ ] destructures the remaining arguments into $j and @args.

Defining Your Own Operators

You can create new operators. Almost all of the things that we call "operators" are methods.

The ↑ and ↑↑ represent Knuth arrows. These are higher levels of exponentiation:

```
multi infix:<↑> ( Int:D \n, Int:D \m  --> Int:D )
    is equiv(&infix:<**>)
    is assoc<right>
    { n ** m }

proto infix:<↑↑> ( Int:D \n, Int:D \m --> Int:D )
    is tighter(&infix:<↑>)
    is assoc<right>
    { * }
multi infix:<↑↑> ( \n,  0 ) { 1 }
multi infix:<↑↑> ( \n,  1 ) { n }
multi infix:<↑↑> ( \n, \m ) { [↑] n xx m }

put 2↑3;   # 2 ** 3 = 8
put 2↑↑3;  # 2 ** 2 ** 2 = 2 ** 4 = 16
```

Notice that the definitions allow you to set traits for precedence and associativity. As with other subroutines these are lexically scoped, so they won't affect other parts of your program.

Perl 5 Patterns

If you like Perl 5 patterns better, or already have some good ones that you'd like to reuse, you can do that. The :Perl5 adverb tells the match operator to interpret the pattern as a Perl 5 regular expression:

```
my $file = ...;
for $file.IO.lines {
    next unless m:Perl5/\A\s+#/;  # no quoting the # in Perl 5
    .put;
    }
```

Shaped Arrays

Want a multidimensional matrix? You can create a *shaped array* that knows how wide it is in any dimension. Use the ; to separate the dimensions:

```
my @array[2;2];
say @array; # [[(Any) (Any)] [(Any) (Any)]]

@array[1;0] = 'Hamadryas';
say @array; # [[(Any) (Any)] [Hamadryas (Any)]]

my $n = 0;
my $m = 1;

@array[$n;$m] = 'Borbo';
say @array; # [[(Any) Borbo] [Hamadryas (Any)]]
```

You can extend this to higher dimensions:

```
my @array[2;2;3];
```

The :shape adverb can describe the size in each dimension:

```
my @array = Array.new: :shape(3,3);
```

Once you set the limits in each dimension the size is fixed. This means that you can create fixed-size one-dimensional arrays. You won't be able to use operaters that increase or decrease the number of elements:

```
my @array[5];
```

Typed Containers

The container types (List, Array, Hash, and so on) can limit their elements to a particular type. There are a few ways that you can constrain these. Consider this example:

```
my Int @array = 1, 2, 3;
@array.push: 'Hamadryas';
```

Since a Str is not an Int the .push fails:

```
Type check failed in assignment to @array
```

That form types the @array variable. The type is actually Array[Int]. You can also bind to the object you construct directly:

```
my @array := Array[Int].new: 1, 3, 7;
```

You can create Hashes with objects for keys and many other interesting constraints.

NativeCall

There's a builtin foreign function interface named NativeCall. You use the is native trait to specify the external library. This one connects your program to the argumentless flap routine in *libbutterfly*:

```
use NativeCall;
sub flap() is native('butterfly') { * }
```

There are ways to tell NativeCall how to translate data structures to "native" types and the other way around.

The with Topicalizer

The with keyword sets the topic. In the postfix form you can use it so you don't have to repeat a long variable name:

```
put "$_ has {.chars}" with $some-very-long-name;
```

There's a Block form that's similar to if-elsif-else but sets the topic to the result of the condition. Instead of looking for True or False it tests for definedness. In each of these the topic inside the Block is the result of the respective .index:

```
my $s = 'Hamadryas';

   with $s.index: 'a' { $s.substr( $_, 2 ).put }
orwith $s.index: 'm' { put 'Found m' }
orwith $s.index: 'H' { fail "Why is there an H at $_?" }
```

## CHAPTER 21

Conclusion

Congratulations. You've made it to the end of the book. Some people estimate that only one-third of the readers of a technical book accomplish that feat. This book was only supposed to be 300 pages long, but I couldn't decide how to leave out anything still included. Sorry about that. The 80 pages of exercise answers really sent me over the limit. If you're reading this, send me an email noting your rarified status as a completist reader!

I wasn't able to teach you how to be a programmer. I only had the one book. I've been at it for several decades and I'm still learning. This book specifically avoided that goal, and I think I've succeeded there. Remember that what you've seen here to demonstrate and isolate concepts and syntax is not a prescription for good programming practices.

I hope you learned the basics of the language and that you can get simple programs to run. If you're at the start of your programming career, don't feel bad if you think you are taking longer than you should to get programs working. Writing programs is always the easy part. It's the debugging work that's hard. That takes practice. Every time you encounter a new problem you're adding to the list of things you've encountered. Eventually you encounter a problem often enough that you start to subconsciously avoid it. That merely makes space for new sorts of mistakes.

You aren't done learning the language. There's much more in the documentation. I noted some favorite excluded topics in Chapter 20, but even that was limited. I really wanted to talk more about those, but I couldn't go past that 500-page barrier. That list isn't nearly complete. There are so many other things I don't even mention. Explore those new topics as you become comfortable with what you've seen here.

Consider going back to the beginning and reading through the book again. Some of the things will make more sense now that you have a better overview of the major topics. You have more context for the design decisions you dealt with in the first few chapters.

Finally, read other books. Don't limit yourself to one author. I have a particular opinion about some things, and other people have their opinions. Sometimes those are at odds. You don't have to choose sides. As I write more extensively in *Mastering Perl*, your role is to take the best and most useful ideas from as many people as you can. Synthesize those into something that works in your world and for your tasks. Tell the world what decisions you made and what influenced them. Feed your ideas back into the milieu.

Glossary

When I italicize a word or phrase in this book it usually means you can find it defined in the glossary. Think of them as hyperlinks. You'll get used to these words the more you practice, but until then I provide this guide.

abstract method
A method that is defined but not implemented.

abstract syntax tree
A data structure a parser uses to translate its input into a usable form.

accessor method
A method that directly gets or sets a property of an object.

action class
A class used to generate side effects while a parser goes through a grammar.

adverb
A setting the modifies the action of a thingy. An adverb is often a colon pair like :out.

allomorph
A type that combines other types and can act as any of them. For example, an IntStr can act like an Int or a Str.

alternation
A pattern feature that allows different sub-patterns to possibly match at the same position.

Any
The base class for all types. Some things return Any on failure.

argument
The concrete value that fills in a parameter.

arity
The number of parameters a signature defines.

assertion
A pattern feature that matches a condition rather than a character.

assign
Store a value, typically in some sort of new container. This is different from binding.

Associative
A role that indexes its elements by strings.

associativity
The order in which operators of the same precedence decide which goes first.

asynchronous
Concurrent tasks can progress independently in overlapping time frames.

attribute
The label for data an object tracks.

autochomp
Automatically remove the line endings from input.

autothread
A feature that allows your program to apply the same operation to multiple thingys concurrently.

backreference
A reference to a previously captured value in a pattern.

backtrack
Part of a pattern can unmatch characters to allow a later part of the pattern to match.

bare block
A Block with no control keyword, such as loop or while.

binary assignment
The shortcut for a binary operator where the left operand is assigned back to itself. For example, $s += 1.

binary number
A base-2 number—a number represented by only the digits 0 and 1.

binary operator
An operator that takes two operands.

bind
Give a value a label without storing it in a new container. This is different from assignment.

block
Code contained in braces that has its own scope.

Boolean value
A value that is one of True or False. This is implemented as an enum of Ints.

branch
One path that code can follow. An if-else structure presents at least two branches.

callable
A thingy that can be called, possibly with arguments. Subroutines and things that act like them are callable.

camel case
The pattern of using capital letters to denote the start of words in an identifier.

Camelia
The name of the butterfly mascot of Perl 6. The Perl 5 camel is "Amelia."

candidate
A multi whose signature is compatible with the argument list.

capture
The remembered parts of the pattern match. The number variables $0 and so on are captures.

case insensitive
In comparisons or patterns, treat the uppercase and lowercase letters as the same thing.

case sensitive
In comparisons or patterns, treat the uppercase and lowercase letters as different things. This is the usual behavior.

catch
Intercept an Exception before it stops your program.

cat ears
A fanciful name for the exclusive Range operators, such as ^..^.

channel
A first-in, first out (FIFO) queue.

child class
A class based on (or that inherits from) another class (the parent).

circumfix

A bit of syntax that surrounds something else.

circumfix infix operator

An operator that surrounds something but also comes between other things. The hyperoperators like <<+>> are an example.

circumfix operator

An operator that surrounds its arguments, such as <...>.

class

The template that defines and creates objects. A class defines the attributes and methods for an object.

class method

A method available to the type object but not its objects. Constructors are typically class methods.

code (character)

A particular character in the Unicode Character Database (UCD). One or more codes make up a *grapheme*.

code point

An entry in the Unicode Character Database (UCD).

coercer

A method that turns a thingy into a different (and usually compatible) type. The .Str and .Bool methods are coercer methods. The ~ and ? operators do the same thing.

comment

A note that you include in your program but the compiler ignores.

comment out

Use commenting syntax to prevent code from being compiled. You can leave the code in the file and uncomment it later.

comparator

An operator that returns True or False based on the relationship of two thingys. The less-than operator < is a comparator for two numbers.

compile time

The phase of program operation where the code is being parsed and converted to something that can execute.

compile-time variables

Special variables that contain information about the operation of the compiler. The $?FILE variable, for instance.

complex number

The combination of a *Real* number and an *imaginary number*.

compunit

A loadable or compilable chunk of code. A module has zero or more compunits. The Perl 6 repository stores the compunits.

concatenation

The process of joining two things. Typically this is used to note the creation of a larger string from two distinct strings.

concurrency

Different parts of the program can be processed in any order without necessarily finishing them in order.

condition

An expression that must be satisfied before an operation can proceed.

conditional

One of the programming constructs that executes only if some assertion evaluates to True. The if and while constructs evaluate a condition to decide if they will execute their blocks.

constructor

A method that creates an object of the same type. Perl 6 typically uses .new for this but doesn't demand it.

container

Something that can hold a value. A container allows you to change the value.

control structure

A structure that decides the path of a program. Loop keywords such as while and conditionals such as `if` are control structures.

CURI

`CompUnit::Repository::Installation` —a thingy that knows how to install modules locally.

current working directory

The directory that a program uses to resolve relative paths. This is not necessarily the directory that contains the program. You can find this in the `$*CWD` variable.

CWD

The *current working directory*.

decimal number

A number represented with the digits 0 to 9 (or their equivalents in other languages). Sometimes this means a number with a decimal point, but computer people tend to use *floating point* in that case.

declarative (regex)

The part of a pattern that describes a string rather than instructing the operation to do something. The literal sequence of characters is declarative.

declare

Denote that you intend to use a variable name. The `my` keyword declares a variable.

decontainerize

Extract the values from a container.

directive (printf)

A placeholder in a `sprintf` template that describes how to format data.

double-quoted strings

Strings delimited by `"` (or its equivalent) that can interpolate special sequences, variables, or other things.

dual value

An object that can act like one of two other objects, such as `IntStr`, which can be an `Int` or a `Str`. This is also known as an *allomorph*.

DWIM

Do What I Mean. This is a design principle where the default behavior of something should be its most common use.

dynamic variable

A variable defined by its temporal (rather than lexical) scope. This definition is quite different from many other languages.

eager assignment

Assignment that forces a `Seq` to create all of its elements.

embedded comment

A comment made with `#`( ). These can appear in the middle of a statement.

empty list

A `List` with no elements.

empty string

A string that has no characters. It's defined but `False`.

escape

Note that the next character should be treated as special or literal depending on its unescaped interpretation.

escape character

The `\` is the escape character. In some string contexts it signals that the next character is literal (`\'`) or special (`\n`).

escaped string

A quoted string that allows some characters to represent something other than their literal selves (for instance, `\n`).

export

Define names and subroutines in the caller's scope. Normally these are defined in their own lexical scope.

extend

Define a method in a child class that calls the same method in the parent class but does additional work.

factory

A method that creates an object of a different type.

False

> A builtin Boolean value that does not satisfy a conditional. Many values can reduce to a Boolean value with the `.so` method.

fat arrow

> The =>. This constructs a `Pair`.

filehandle

> An object that connects your program to something that can accept input or give output.

flatten

> Treat a combination of values (like a `List`) that's normally a single thing as multiple things.

floating-point number

> A number that can have a fractional component. To the wider world that's often the same as a *decimal number*.

French quotes

> The fancier quotes « and ».

generalized quoting

> Creating a string with Q or one of its many forms.

gist

> The "human-readable" representation of an object. The `.say` method automatically calls `.gist` on its arguments.

gradual typing

> Enforcing the optional runtime type system only where you decide to use it.

grammar

> A special sort of package that has special syntax to create a parser.

grapheme

> A grapheme comprises one or more code points to represent a concept.

greedy

> A part of a regex that tries to consume as many characters as possible.

group

> Set apart some of an expression with parentheses or other delimiters.

Hamadryas

> The genus of the butterfly on the cover of this book.

Hamadryas perlicus

> The fictional species of butterfly used in the examples.

here doc

> A quoting mechanism for multiline strings.

hexadecimal number

> A base-16 number—a number represented by only the digits 0 to 9 and *A* to *F* (of either case).

hyperoperator

> An operator that applies another operator to corresponding elements of two `Positionals`.

identifier

> The name portion of the variable. An identifier can use letters, digits, underscores, hyphens, and apostrophes.

imaginary number

> A number that's a multiple of the *imaginary unit*.

imaginary unit

> The square root of –1. A *complex number* has a real and an imaginary part.

immutable

> A value that you can't change. Some types, such as `List` and `Map`, hold data that is fixed once created. A sigilless variable is immutable.

implicit parameter

> A parameter that is automatically included in the *signature*.

import

> Include in the current scope code or other features from other modules or libraries.

infinite loop

A *loop* that never exits. loop {} is such a beast.

infix

A bit of syntax that is between two other thingys.

infix operator

An operator that comes between its arguments, such as the + in $i + $j.

inherit

Use another class or object as the basis for a new class or object.

inheritance

The specialization of a class by basing a new class on it.

initialize

Give a variable its starting value.

instance

Another term for *object*.

integer

A whole number, positive or negative, and zero. The Int class represents these.

interpolated string

A quoting construct that interprets certain sequences as special. For example, an interpolated string may replace a variable with its value.

intersection

The new Set of elements that are in both Sets.

invocant

The thingy on which you call a method.

item assignment

Assignment into an item container. This sort of assignment has a different precedence than list assignment.

itemize

Interpret something as a single unit even though it may comprise multiple thingys.

iteration

The repetition of a set of operations for each element of a collection.

kebab case

The pattern of separating words in an identifier with hyphens. The -s appear to skewer the words.

key

A label for a value stored in an Associative type.

lazy

A Positional that doesn't generate its values until you need them.

Lazy (capital L)

One of the principle virtues of a programmer that causes them to do more work now in order to do less work later.

left associative

The leftmost operator goes first when two operators have the same precedence.

lexical scope

Scope that is defined by its position in the code rather than its order of execution. A Block defines a lexical scope.

lexicographic comparison

A character-by-character ordering or comparison of two strings. For the most part Perl 6 orders by the code number in the Unicode Character Database (UCD), although there are experiments in more sophisticated collation.

library

A file that comprises a collection of subroutines, classes, and other resources.

link

The connection between a filename and the data on the disk.

lisp case

The same as *kebab case*.

list

An immutable series of zero or more items.

literal value

A value that is exactly what is typed rather than a computed value. The values 137 and 'Hamadryas' are literal.

live supply

A Supply that provides only the current or future values. This is different from an on-demand *supply*.

logical operator

A bit of syntax that works on Boolean values (True and False).

longest declarative prefix

The part of a regular expression that is fixed when the pattern is compiled. This excludes procedural elements that aren't known until the pattern is applied.

longest token matching

The | in a match selects the "best" alternative of all possibilities by trying the one with the longest declarative part or most specificity.

loop

A Block of code that can run more than one time before the program moves on.

looser

The relative precedence of an operation is lower than another. The looser operation happens after the *tighter* operation.

LTM

Longest token matching. This applies to grammars and to the | regex alteration.

member

An element of a Set.

metacharacter

A character that has a meaning beyond its literal self. The * in a pattern is a metacharacter.

metadata

Additional data apart from the contents of a file. For example, file permissions are metadata.

method

Code that defines the behavior of an object.

method resolution order

The path through the inheritance tree to find a method. This matters in multiple inheritance.

mixin

Another name for a *role*.

module

A reusable code unit. Many modules provide classes, but they don't need to.

multiple inheritance

The process of basing one class on more than one other class. Perl 6 supports this, but think carefully before using it.

mutable

A value that you can change.

named parameter

A parameter with a label. These can appear anywhere in the parameter list, unlike *positional parameters* which must be specified in order.

negate

Make True into False and the other way around so you can specify that something is *not* something else.

NFG

Normal Form Grapheme. This is the special form Perl 6 uses to expose string data to the program.

Nil

The absence of value.

Normal Form Grapheme

The internal Perl representation of strings in its own normal form based on graphemes.

object

A concrete version of the class.

octal number

A base-8 number—a number represented by only the digits 0 to 7.

octet

The cool new name for byte. A sequence of 8 bits.

on-demand supply

A Supply that gives you the entire sequence of values. This is in opposition to a *live supply*.

one-liner

A program written and executed on the command line.

operand

A value used by an operator. It's the noun.

operator

Something that creates a new value from other values.

outer scope

The scope a level above the one you are in.

Pair

The grouping of a single key and value. Pair is a particular data type, but also forms the basis of other Associative data types. Adverbs and named arguments are also pairs.

paired delimiter

A delimiter with an opening and closing version, such as parentheses and braces.

parameter

The description of an expected argument to a callable.

parent class

The class another class bases itself on. This is sometimes called a base or superclass.

phaser

A special subroutine that runs at certain points during the program. The END phaser runs at the end of the program and the LAST phaser runs after the last iteration of a loop.

placeholder variable

An implicit parameter variable defined in the block. These have the ^ twigil, such as $^a.

positional parameter

A parameter defined by its position in the signature (as opposed to *named parameters*).

postcircumfix

Something that comes after one thing and surrounds another. The [] for a single-element array access (@array[$index]) comes after the array name and surrounds the index.

postcircumfix operator

An operator that surrounds something and comes before other things. The Positional index operator is an example.

postfix operator

An operator that comes after its argument, such as the ++ in $x++.

postfix rule

If an operator can be either infix or postfix, the infix version requires space around it. The postfix operators never have space before them.

precedence

The order of operations when several are involved in the same expression. Each operator knows its precedence.

precircumfix operator

An operator that surrounds something and comes before other things. The reduction operator is an example.

prefix operator

An operator that comes before the thing it works on.

private method

A method that is only visible inside the lexical scope of the class. It is not available to objects.

procedural (regex)

Part of a pattern that instructs the operation to do something instead of just match something. A Block in a pattern is a procedural element.

public attribute

An attribute available through the interface of the class rather than only within the class itself.

pun

Use a role as a class.

quantifier

A pattern feature that allows part of a pattern to repeat.

Rakudo Star

A distribution of Rakudo that includes documentation, extra modules, and tools. See *http://rakudo.org/how-to-get-rakudo/*.

recursion

Calling the same subroutine that is currently executing.

regex

A method that performs pattern matching.

regular expression

A pattern that describes a set of matching strings.

reify

Compute an actual value for a lazy construct. For example, to get the next position in a lazy list, Perl reifies it with the code that decides the next value.

REPL

The Read-Evaluate-Print-Loop interface. If you run the *perl6* command with no arguments, it starts its REPL and prompts you for a statement.

repository

A store for code units such as modules and libraries. Perl 6 can store these in files, databases, network stores, and so on.

return

Send a value to the thingy that called you.

return value

The result of a Routine available in the scope where it was called.

right associative

The rightmost operator goes first when two operators have the same precedence.

role

A class that provides features without using inheritance.

rule

A nonbacktracking regex.

satisfied

A conditional expression operator that evaluates to True.

scalar

A single thingy. That might be a literal value or an object.

scalar variable

A variable that holds a single thing.

set difference

The Set of elements in the second Set that aren't in the first.

shaped array

An Array that has multiple dimensions, such as my @array[3;2].

shebang

The #! line at the top of a program that specifies the interpreter that can interpret the program.

short-circuit operators

The &&, ||, and // (or equivalent) operators that evaluate to the last expression the operator examined.

sigil

A prefix on an identifier that denotes something about the variable.

sigilless variable

A variable without a sigil which doesn't automatically store its value in a container. These are useful for constants.

signature

Taken together, all of the parameters of a callable.

simple list

A flat List with no additional structure.

single argument rule

A single Iterable argument will fill a slurpy argument rather become one element of that slurpy.

single-quoted strings

Strings constructed with ' delimiters that are mostly literal.

sink context

The context where the evaluated value is not saved or used in any way. Typically this means the work is wasted.

slang

Slang for sublanguage.

slice

Multielement access to a Positional.

slurpy parameter

A part of the signature that takes the rest of the arguments.

smart match operator

The ~~. It decides how to compare items based on its operands.

snake case

The pattern of separating words in an identifier with underscores. The _s appear to crawl along the ground.

soft failure

An Exception that delays its action.

string

A series of characters taken as a single thingy.

structured list

A List that contains other Lists.

stub method

An unimplemented but defined method. These typically use ... or !!! to fail when run.

submethod

A noninheritable method or subroutine acting as a method.

subroutine

A noninheritable routine with a parameter list.

subset

A Set that is made up of elements in another Set.

subsignature

A part of a *signature* that further breaks down the structure of a parameter.

substring

A string contained inside another string. For example, Hamad is a substring of Hamadryas.

superset

A Set that is made up of all the elements of another Set, and possibly more.

supply

A receiver of values through a Supplier. A Supply can process and react to new values.

symbolic link

A file that stores a string that points to another file.

symmetric set difference

The Set of elements that aren't in both Sets.

syntax check

A way to compile the program without running it. If it compiles successfully there isn't a syntax error (although that does not mean the program is correct).

syntax error

A problem in a program because the code doesn't follow the rules of the language.

task distribution

A distribution that typically provides no code but uses the module installation process to install collections of modules. For example, the Task::Star module claims the Rakudo Star extras as dependencies.

term

The smallest unit of code. Literal values and variable names are examples of terms.

ternary operator

A disfavored but common name for the conditional operator ?? !!, because that operator has three parts.

thingy

A general term for something when you don't want to be particularly precise about its identity, behavior, or value.

throw

Cause an Exception to assert itself.

thunk

A piece of code that doesn't execute immediately. A thunk does not define a scope.

tighter

The relative precedence of an operation is higher than another one. A tighter operator does its work before a *looser* one.

token

A low-level, nonbacktracking regex.

topic

Another name for the default variable, $_. Methods without an explicit object use the one in $_, which leads to shorter code.

topicalization

The act of temporarily putting the value of a variable into $_. For example, given does this. This allows you to use the topic as the implicit object for method calls.

topical method

A method called on the implicit topic, $_.

True

A builtin Boolean value that satisfies a conditional. Many values can reduce to a Boolean value with the .so method.

twigil

A character added to a sigil to denote its scope. For example, the * in $*HOME.

type

The classification of a thingy that decides its behavior.

type object

An object that represents a type. This object knows its type but has no concrete value. It is always undefined.

UCD

The Unicode Character Database, sometimes (incorrectly) called just "Unicode."

unary

A thingy that takes one operand or argument.

unary operator

An operator that takes one operand. The operator can come before or after the operand.

union

The combination of two Sets into a potentially larger Set that contains all the elements of both sets.

unspace

Space inserted where it normally isn't allowed by prefixing it with \. You often use this to separate terms without using whitespace or to line up code.

UTF-8

A Unicode Tranformation Format using 8-bit code units. A UTF is a mapping of code points to byte sequences. Perl 6 assumes UTF-8 as the default encoding for input and output.

variable

A named value. These are not strictly "variable" because some are immutable.

Whatever

The token * that stands in for something decided by context, such as * - 1. This is shorthand for a closure, in this example { $^x - 1}.

yada yada

A placeholder operator (...) that compiles but is an error if it ever runs.

Exercise Answers

This appendix contains the answers to the exercises that appear throughout the book.

Answers to Preface Exercises

1. I don't really have an answer for you here other than what you read immediately before the exercise. The installation of Perl 6 is the hardest part of the problem.

   Once you have *perl6*, you can ask it for help. The -h and --help command-line switches tend to show you a list of the things you can do with a program. Here's an extract of the output:

   ```
   % perl6 -h
   perl6 [switches] [--] [programfile] [arguments]

       With no arguments, enters a REPL. With a "[programfile]" or
       the "-e" option, compiles the given program and, by default,
       also  executes the compiled code.

       -c          check syntax only (runs BEGIN and CHECK blocks)
       --doc       extract documentation and print it as text
       -e program  one line of program, strict is enabled by default
       -h, --help  display this help text
       ...
       -v, --version      display version information
       ...
   ```

   You see that *perl6* has -v and --version switches:

   ```
   % perl6 -v
   This is Rakudo version 2018.04 built on MoarVM version 2018.04
   implementing Perl 6.c.
   ```

At the top of that help message was a note about invoking *perl6* with no arguments. It drops into the REPL, where you can do the same things I showed you. At the prompt you type out a variable name and the REPL shows you its value:

```
% perl6
To exit type 'exit' or '^D'
> $*VM
moar (2018.04)
> $*PERL
Perl 6 (6.c)
```

There! You've completed your first exercise! You know that you have Perl 6 and that it works. You also know how to get some of the details you may need to report a problem.

2. There isn't much to say about this exercise. Most of the job is interacting with the *Learning Perl 6* website. Now that you know it's there, look around to see what else I've left there.

Answers to Chapter 1 Exercises

1. I haven't told you about these methods, but you know to look at the Int class to find out what you can do. I tend to go right to the online documentation.

   If you didn't know the value was an Int you could use the .^name method to find out:

   ```
   % perl6
   > 137.^name
   Int
   ```

   Looking through the Int documentation, you should discover the .sqrt and .is-prime methods. Call those on the value:

   ```
   > 137.sqrt
   11.7046999107196
   > 137.is-prime
   True
   ```

   You could also put these in a program file. You have to output the values yourself though:

   ```
   put 137.^name;
   put 137.sqrt;
   put 137.is-prime;
   ```

   Now I'll expect that you can find the documentation for a class and discover methods you can use for that class.

2. This variable isn't important for this exercise. The point is to know where to find out what it is. Look in the documentation for variables (*https://docs.perl6.org/ language/variables*). $*CWD is the current working directory. That's the default directory when you read or write files with a relative path (Chapter 8). You can try it in the REPL:

```
% perl6
> $*CWD
"/Users/hamadryas".IO
```

If you started *perl6* in a different directory you should get a different value:

```
% cd work/perl6-files/ch-01
% perl6
> $*CWD
"/Users/hamadryas/work/perl6-files/ch-01".IO
```

3. There's not much of an answer for this. Steal the program from the chapter and put it in a file:

```
#!/usr/local/bin/perl6
put 'Hello World!';
```

Run the program:

```
% perl6 hello-world.p6
```

Now the rest of the book is easy; it's merely different text in the file!

Answers to Chapter 2 Exercises

1. The programs are the same ones that you've seen in the chapter. Here's the one-line version:

```
put 'Hello Perl 6!';
```

The MAIN program is the same with a little extra:

```
sub MAIN {
    put 'Hello Perl 6!'
    }
```

2. This exercise is more about getting a program to run than understanding everything in it. The answer is a slight extension of the two-parameter program:

```
sub MAIN ( $thingy1, $thingy2 = 'perlicus', $thingy3 = 'sixus' ) {
    put '1: ', $thingy1;
    put '2: ', $thingy2;
    put '2: ', $thingy3;
    }
```

Here are several runs with different numbers of arguments. With no arguments you get a help message that shows you need to specify at least one argument:

```
% perl6 three-args.p6
Usage:
  three-args.p6 <thingy1> [<thingy2>] [<thingy3>]

% perl6 three-args.p6 Hamadryas
1: Hamadryas
2: perlicus
2: sixus

% perl6 three-args.p6 Hamadryas amphinome
1: Hamadryas
2: amphinome
2: sixus

% perl6 three-args.p6 Hamadryas amphinome fumosa
1: Hamadryas
2: amphinome
2: fumosa
```

3. This program is a variation on the favorite number example in the chapter:

```
my $name = prompt 'What is your name? ';
put 'Hello ', $name;
```

Inside the description for MAIN you can use prompt to set the default value:

```
sub MAIN ( $name = prompt( 'What is your name> ' ) ) {
    put 'Hello ', $name;
    }
```

Now you can run the program in two ways:

```
% perl6 name.pl
What is your name> Gilligan
Hello Gilligan

% perl6 name.pl Roger
Hello Roger
```

4. All of the examples in different bases are the same number. The base is merely a different representation of the same idea. The REPL echoes its results in base 10 though:

```
% perl6
> 137
137
> 0b10001001
137
> 0o211
137
```

```
> 0x89
137
```

5. Simply type the examples into the REPL to see their decimal representation:

```
% perl6
> :7<254>
137
> :19<IG88>
129398
> :26<HAL9000>
5380136632
> :36<THX1138>
64210088132
```

6. You can create a MAIN subroutine that has a single parameter. Each line in the routine outputs the same number in a different base. You could add a prefix to some of the bases:

```
sub MAIN ( $number ) {
    put '0b', $number.base:  2;
    put '0o', $number.base:  8;
    put      $number;
    put '0x', $number.base: 16;
    }
```

When you run the program with a decimal number you should see that number in four representations:

```
% perl6 formats.p6 343
0b101010111
0o527
343
0x157
```

If you specify something other than a decimal number you get an error from the .fmt method. Don't worry about the meaning of that error right now:

```
% perl6 formats.p6 BEEF
Directive b not applicable for type Str
```

With Eastern Arabic digits it still works:

```
% perl6 formats.p6 ١٣٧
0b10001001
0o211
137
0x89
```

7. Add one more step at the top of the block. Turn the argument into a number with .parse-base, then format that into the different bases:

```
sub MAIN ( $thingy ) {
    my $number = $thingy.parse-base: 16;
```

```
put '0b', $number.base:  2;
put '0o', $number.base:  8;
put $number;
put '0x', $number.base: 16;
}
```

8. When you use the postfix ++ you output the original value, then update it. Your output starts at 0 because that's the current value when you enter the loop:

```
0
1
2
...
```

When you use the prefix ++ you first update the value and then output the new value. The first time through the loop the value starts at 0. You update it to 1, then output that:

```
1
2
3
...
```

9. You only need to replace the expression that you output. Add three to it each time:

```
loop {
    state $sum = 0;
    put $sum += 3;
    }
```

This is the same as using $sum on each side of the assignment operator:

```
loop {
    state $sum = 0;
    put $sum = $sum + 3;
    }
```

Make this program slightly better by moving the interval out of the loop. Use a variable to hold the number that you want to add each time:

```
my $interval = 3;
loop {
    state $sum = 0;
    put $sum += $interval;
    }
```

Later in this chapter you'll read how to take it to the next step with a MAIN routine:

```
sub MAIN ( $interval = 3 ) {
    loop {
        state $sum = 0;
```

```
    put $sum += $interval;
    }
}
```

You still don't know how to stop the loop, though. Keep reading!

10. You evaluate the `last` when `$sum` is 5. Since you are using the postfix autoincrement, you updated `$sum` *after* you used the value. When you outputted 4 you also updated the value to 5. When you test `$sum` after you output 4 the current value is 5. The `==` evaluates to `True`, and the `last` stops the loop. The output stops at 4:

```
0
1
2
3
4
```

11. There are many ways that you could solve this problem, although not many of them are limited to what you've already seen in this book. Here's one possible solution:

```
loop {
    state $n = 1;
    put do if $n %% 3 and $n %% 5 { 'FizzBuzz' }
        elsif $n %% 3            { 'Fizz' }
        elsif $n %% 5            { 'Buzz' }
        else                    { $n }

    $n += 1;
    last if $n > 100;
    }
```

It might look like a tangled mess, but break it down. First there's the stuff to go through the numbers. That's easy enough. That `state` declaration defines a persistent variable in the scope of `loop`. At the end of the loop you add one to that number:

```
loop {
    state $n = 1;
    ...
    $n += 1;
    last if $n > 100;
    }
```

Then the middle part outputs some value. That's just put:

```
loop {
    state $n = 1;
    put ...;
    $n += 1;
    last if $n > 100;
    }
```

Finally, the meat of the problem is deciding the text to output. The `%%` is `True` if the first number is evenly divisible by the second one. Use that (and combinations of that) to choose the value:

```
if $n %% 3 and $n %% 5 { 'FizzBuzz' }
        elsif $n %% 3              { 'Fizz' }
        elsif $n %% 5              { 'Buzz' }
        else                      { $n }
```

The `do` in front of the `if` makes the chosen value available to the `put`:

```
put do if ...;
```

This may seem overwhelming now, but by the end of the book it should seem simple. The more code you read the easier a time you'll have picking it apart.

12. Instead of hardcoding 100 you can use the variable `$highest`. Set that to 100 unless there's a command-line argument:

```
sub MAIN ( $highest = 100 ) {
    my $number = $highest.rand.Int;
    put 'Number is ', $number;

    if $number > 50 {
        put 'The number is greater than 50';
        }
    elsif $number < 50 {
        put 'The number is less than 50';
        }
    else {
        put 'The number is 50';
        }
    }
```

Add a second parameter, `$pivot`, and give it a default value. Use `$pivot` wherever you saw the literal 50 in the program:

```
sub MAIN ( $highest = 100, $pivot = 50 ) {
    my $number = $highest.rand.Int;
    put 'Number is ', $number;

    if $number > $pivot {
        put 'The number is greater than ', $pivot;
        }
    elsif $number < $pivot {
        put 'The number is less than ', $pivot;
        }
    else {
        put 'The number is exactly ', $pivot;
        }
    }
```

This still has a problem. What if the first argument is less than 50? No number would be greater than the pivot in that case. You'll fix that in a moment.

13. You can steal the line from the chapter to set the pivot to half the highest number:

```
sub MAIN ( $highest = 100, $pivot = $highest / 2 ) {
    my $number = $highest.rand.Int;
    put 'Number is ', $number;

    if $number > $pivot {
        put 'The number is greater than ', $pivot;
        }
    elsif $number < $pivot {
        put 'The number is less than ', $pivot;
        }
    else {
        put 'The number is exactly ', $pivot;
        }
    }
```

14. I'll take extra care to go through this answer step by step. It's easier to build up programs incrementally than to try to get everything working at the same time. First, you need to take a command-line argument and set a default. Start with that part of the program:

```
sub MAIN ( $maximum = 100 ) {
    put 'Maximum is ', $maximum;
    }
```

You know how to make the secret number. Add that step next:

```
sub MAIN ( $maximum = 100 ) {
    my $secret-number = $maximum.rand.Int;
    put 'Secret number is ', $secret-number;
    }
```

Get a guess with prompt. You don't have to do anything with it other than check that you assigned what you answered:

```
sub MAIN ( $maximum = 100 ) {
    my $secret-number = $maximum.rand.Int;
    put 'Secret number is ', $secret-number;

    my $guess = prompt 'Enter a guess: ';
    put 'Your guess was ', $guess;
    }
```

Now give the person a hint based on their guess. Use if and elsif to compare the guess to the secret number. This only works for one pass and then it's done; there's no chance for a second guess:

```
sub MAIN ( $maximum = 100 ) {
    my $secret-number = $maximum.rand.Int;
```

```
        put 'Secret number is ', $secret-number;

        my $guess = prompt 'Enter a guess: ';

        if $guess == $secret-number {
            put 'You guessed it!';
            }
        elsif $guess < $secret-number {
            put 'Guess higher!';
            }
        elsif $guess > $secret-number {
            put 'Guess lower!';
            }
        }
```

Add a `loop` around the prompt and the hints. Use `last` in the branch where the person guesses the number correctly. That ends the `loop` and there's nothing left to do in the program:

```
sub MAIN ( $maximum = 100 ) {
    my $secret-number = $maximum.rand.Int;
    put 'Secret number is ', $secret-number;

    loop {
        my $guess = prompt 'Enter a guess: ';

        if $guess == $secret-number {
            put 'You guessed it!';
            last;
            }
        elsif $guess < $secret-number {
            put 'Guess higher!';
            }
        elsif $guess > $secret-number {
            put 'Guess lower!';
            }
        }
    }
```

I took the time to go through this process so you can see what real programming looks like. Often you'll start without knowing what the entire program will look like. Even then, you can start by getting the outer parts in place and then work your way toward the middle.

Answers to Chapter 3 Exercises

1. Here are the values from Table 3-1 so the `.^name` applies to the entire thing. Most are straightforward:

```
% perl6
> 137.^name
Int
> (-17).^name
Int
> 3.1415926.^name
Rat
> 6.026e34.^name
Num
> (0+i).^name
Complex
> i.^name
Complex
```

In these examples the complex numbers and negative integers need grouping parentheses. The - and the + have lower precedence than the method call dot, so they need grouping parentheses too.

2. Writing a program that takes two command-line arguments is easy:

```
sub MAIN ( $one, $two ) {
    put $one.^name;
    put $two.^name;
    }
```

When you enter one number and one text argument you get two different types:

```
% perl6 args-types.p6 1 two
IntStr
Str
```

If you make the second argument a fractional number you'll see a different type, RatStr:

```
% perl6 args-types.p6 4 3.5
IntStr
RatStr
```

There's also ComplexStr, which you'll see when you specify text that looks like a complex number:

```
% perl6 args-types.p6 4 1+3i
IntStr
ComplexStr
```

Each of the number type names you see here ends in Str. You'll read more about these after the exercise.

3. Wrap a MAIN around the given example but don't specify a type for the argument:

```
sub MAIN ( $arg ) {
    put 'Saw ', do given $arg {
        when Int     { 'an integer' }
        when Complex { 'a complex number' }
```

```
when Rat     { 'a rat! Eek!' }
default      { 'something' }
    }
}
```

Run it with different types of arguments:

```
% perl6 what-is-it.p6 17
Saw an integer
% perl6 what-is-it.pl 17.0
Saw a rat! Eek!
% perl6 what-is-it.pl 17i
Saw a complex number
% perl6 what-is-it.pl Hamadryas
Saw something
```

4. The program is simple. Perl 6 automatically creates the fraction for you. Take a number from the command line and output the fraction using the `.numerator` and `.denominator` methods:

```
sub MAIN ( $number ) {
    put $number.numerator, ' / ', $number.denominator;
    }
```

It's a little cleaner with a postfix `given`:

```
sub MAIN ( $number ) {
    put .numerator, ' / ', .denominator given $number;
    }
```

When you try it on a few numbers you'll see the fractions:

```
% perl6 fraction.p6 3.1415926
15707963 / 5000000

% perl6 fraction.p6 2.71828182845905
54365636569181 / 20000000000000
```

5. You can adjust the example to create a new series. This time you have to start with $n at 1. Get rid of the power of two and you have it:

```
my $n   = 1;
my $sum = 0.FatRat;
loop {
    $sum += FatRat.new: 1, $n++;
    put .numerator, '/', .denominator, ' = ', $_ given $sum;
    last if $n > 100;
    }
```

The sum slowly diverges:

```
1/1 = 1
3/2 = 1.5
11/6 = 1.833333
```

```
25/12 = 2.083333
137/60 = 2.283333
49/20 = 2.45
...
```

6. Use `.Rat`. For the reciprocal, you swap the numerator and denominator:

```
my $number = 7.297351e-3;
put 'Number is a ', $number.^name;

my $rat = $number.Rat;
put 'Fraction is ', $rat.perl;

my $reciprocal = Rat.new: $rat.denominator, $rat.numerator;
put 'Reciprocal is ', $reciprocal;
put 'Reciprocal fraction is ', $reciprocal.perl;
```

The output shows a number close to one you have already seen in this book:

```
Number is a Num
Fraction is <27/3700>
Reciprocal is 137.037037
Reciprocal fraction is <3700/27>
```

7. This like your basic number-guessing program, but you have to make two sets of comparisons. It seems like you'd have to make twice as many guesses but you can home in on both parts at the same time:

```
sub MAIN ( $maximum = 100 ) {
    my $secret = Complex.new:
        $maximum.rand.Int,
        $maximum.rand.Int;

    put 'Secret number is ', $secret;

    my $re = $secret.re;
    my $im = $secret.im;

    loop {
        my $guess =
            prompt( 'Enter your guess (n+mi): ' ).Complex;

        if $guess == $secret {
            put 'You guessed it!';
            last;
            }

        given $guess {
            put "Real part is ",
                do if $re > .re { 'too small' }
                elsif $re < .re { 'too large' }
                else            { 'just right' }
```

```
            put "Imaginary part is ",
                do if $im > .im { 'too small'  }
                elsif $im < .im { 'too large'  }
                else            { 'just right' }
            }
        }
    }
```

Note a few features in this solution. First, you create $re and $im so you can make the comparison lines shorter. That's the only reason for that.

You convert the result of prompt to a complex number. If it's not a value you'll get an error. You'll see how to handle that in Chapter 7.

The given puts the guess in $_ so you can use it as the topic. That's the default object for method calls. You can type .im instead of $guess.im.

Answers to Chapter 4 Exercises

1. Prompt for some text and get the count with .chars:

```
my $string = prompt 'Enter a string: ';
put 'There are ', $string.chars, ' characters';
```

Run it a couple of times with different answers:

```
% perl6 char-count.p6
Enter a string: Hamadryas perlicus sixus
There are 24 characters

% perl6 char-count.p6
Enter a string: W 🦋 🐛 éåü
There are 6 characters
```

2. Add a loop and use last to break out of it if there are no characters:

```
loop {
    my $string = prompt 'Enter a string: ';
    last if $string.chars == 0;
    put 'There are ', $string.chars, ' characters';
    }
```

This continues to run until you have an empty answer:

```
% perl6 char-count-loop.p6
Enter a string: Hello
There are 5 characters
Enter a string: Perl 6
There are 6 characters
Enter a string:
```

3. This answer is much like the character-counting answer but looking at a different aspect of the Str:

```
loop {
    my $string = prompt 'Enter a string: ';
    last if $string.chars == 0;
    put 'Found Hamad!' if $string.contains: 'Hamad';
    }
```

You only get more output when the substring is present and has the same capitalization:

```
% perl6 test.p6
Enter a string: Hamadryas
Found Hamad!
Enter a string: Hamad is in the house
Found Hamad!
Enter a string: hamad
Enter a string: Koko likes Kool-Aid
Enter a string:
```

To make this work regardless of the capitalization you can lowercase the starting Str and substring with .lc (or use .fc, which you'll see later):

```
loop {
    my $string = prompt( 'Enter a string: ' ).lc;
    last if $string.chars == 0;
    put 'Found Hamad!' if $string.contains: 'Hamad'.lc;
    }
```

Now the capitalization doesn't matter:

```
% perl6 test.p6
Enter a string: Hamadryas
Found Hamad!
Enter a string: hamadryas
Found Hamad!
Enter a string:
```

4. Here's a simple program. The $first and $second variables start off as Str objects. You don't need to convert them yourself because the numeric operations do that for you implicitly and without warnings:

```
my $first  = prompt( 'First number:  ' );
my $second = prompt( 'Second number: ' );

put 'Sum is ',        $first + $second;
put 'Difference is ', $first - $second;
put 'Product is ',    $first * $second;
put 'Quotient is ',   $first / $second;
```

Run this and reply with two numbers and it works out nicely:

```
% perl6 two-numbers.p6
First number:  12
Second number: 34
Sum is 46
Difference is -22
Product is 408
Quotient is 0.352941
```

When you enter something that is not a number you get a conversion error:

```
% perl6 two-numbers.p6
First number:  Two
Second number: Three
Cannot convert string to number: base-10 number must
begin with valid digits or '.'
```

I haven't shown you how to avoid that just yet. You'll have to wait until Chapter 7.

5. You can modify the previous exercise answer into two paths. In the `if` condition, use `val` to check that each `Str` can convert to a number. If each successfully smart matches against the `Numeric` role, the math operations should work. If one of them fails you note that:

```
my $first  = prompt( 'First number:  ' );
my $second = prompt( 'Second number: ' );

if val($first) ~~ Numeric and val($second) ~~ Numeric {
    put 'Sum is ',        $first + $second;
    put 'Difference is ', $first - $second;
    put 'Product is ',    $first * $second;
    put 'Quotient is ',   $first / $second;
    }
else {
    put 'One of the values isn\'t numeric.';
    }
```

That isn't a very Perly way to write this, though. You have to type the smart match operator and the role twice. You don't know this yet, but with a `Junction` (Chapter 14) you can use `all` to denote that every thingy should satisfy the match:

```
if all( val($first), val($second) ) ~~ Numeric {
```

Another possibility is a program with three paths. You can check each `Str` to show which one is the problem:

```
my $first  = prompt( 'First number:  ' );
my $second = prompt( 'Second number: ' );

if val($first) !~~ Numeric {
    put 'The first string is not numeric.'
    }
```

```
    elsif val($second) !~~ Numeric {
        put 'The second string is not numeric.'
        }
    else {
        put 'Sum is ',        $first + $second;
        put 'Difference is ', $first - $second;
        put 'Product is ',    $first * $second;
        put 'Quotient is ',   $first / $second;
        }
```

6. Instead of giving multiple things to put you do it all inside the interpolated Str to handle the input and the number of characters:

```
loop {
    my $string = prompt( 'Enter a string: ' ).lc;
    last if $string.chars == 0;
    put "'$string' has {$string.chars} characters";
    }
```

Now you see the text and its count on the same line:

```
% perl6 interpolate.p6
Enter a string: Hamadryas
'hamadryas' has 9 characters
Enter a string: hamad
'hamad' has 5 characters
Enter a string: perl6
'perl6' has 5 characters
```

7. You can use the conditional operator to select the command based on the operating system and then interpolate that into the qqx:

```
my $command =
    $*DISTRO.is-win
        ??
    'C:\Windows\System32\hostname.exe'
        !!
    '/bin/hostname';

print qqx/$command/;
```

Instead of interpolation you can run the shell Strs directly:

```
print do
    if $*DISTRO.is-win { qx/C:\Windows\System32\hostname.exe/ }
    else               { qx|/bin/hostname| }
```

Answers to Chapter 5 Exercises

1. Define a variable with `state` and assign it the starting value. Use `last` to stop the loop if the value is over 75. Otherwise, output the current value, then add three to it:

```
loop {
    FIRST { put 'Starting' }
    state $n = 12;
    last if $n > 75;
    put $n;
    $n += 3;
    }
```

The C-style loop looks a little more organized:

```
loop ( my $n = 12; $n <= 75; $n += 3 ) {
    FIRST { put 'Starting' }
    put $n;
    }
```

In either style use the `FIRST` phaser to output the starting message the first time (and only the first time) through the loop.

2. The most obvious way to use `while` probably declares the variable outside of the Block. Otherwise it looks similar to the answers with `loop`:

```
my $n = 12;
while $n <= 75 {
    FIRST { put 'Starting' }
    LAST  { put 'Stopping' }
    put $n;
    $n += 3;
    }
```

A more clever (or *Lazy*) approach could replace `loop` with `while True` without changing anything else. The condition is always satisfied, and you use the `last` to end the loop:

```
while True {
    FIRST { put 'Starting' }
    LAST  { put 'Stopping' }
    state $n = 12;
    last if $n > 75;
    put $n;
    $n += 3;
    }
```

3. The `$trim-and-lower` code uses `$_`, so it expects a single argument. Call `.trim` and assign it back to `$_`, then do the same with `.lc`:

```
my $trim-and-lower := {
    $_ = $_.trim;
    $_ = $_.lc;
    };

my $string = ' HaMaDrYaS   ';
$trim-and-lower( $string );
put "[$string]";
```

Notice that the output surrounds $string with brackets. This way you can see any leading or trailing whitespace:

```
[hamadryas]
```

That $trim-and-lower isn't very Perly. Since $_ is the default object you can omit it in the method call:

```
my $trim-and-lower := {
    $_ = .trim;
    $_ = .lc;
    };
```

You could also use the . operator with binary assignment. This does the same thing (with the same amount of typing):

```
my $trim-and-lower := {
    $_ .= trim;
    $_ .= lc;
    };
```

But you can also chain methods and assign back to $_:

```
my $trim-and-lower := {
    $_ = .trim.lc;
    };
```

For this to work the argument must be a container so you can change it. If you give it a Str directly you'll get an error:

```
$trim-and-lower( 'Perlicus   ' );
```

The error tells you that it's immutable:

```
Cannot assign to an immutable value
```

You don't need to worry about that for now.

4. The max subroutine takes multiple thingys and evaluates what it thinks the biggest one is. With all numbers or Strs that's easy to figure out. With a mix of types max compares them all as Strs:

```
my $block := { max $^a, $^b, $^c };

put $block( 1, 2, 19 );                    # 19
put $block( 'a', 'b', 'c' );               # c
```

```
put $block( 9, 'Hamadryas', 'perlicus' );   # perlicus
put $block( 'a', 'b' );          # Error! Too few parameters
```

5. Use a where and a thunk to limit the denominator variable to anything that's not zero:

```
subset NotZero of Int where * != 0;
sub divide ( $num, NotZero $dem ) { $num / $dem }

put divide 1, 137; # 0.007299
put divide 5, 0;   # Error: Constraint type check failed
```

You can do that directly inside the signature too:

```
sub divide ( $num, $dem where * != 0 ) { $num / $dem }

put divide 1, 137; # 0.007299
put divide 5, 0;   # Error: Constraint type check failed
```

Answers to Chapter 6 Exercises

1. This MAIN routine takes a Str and a number, and uses the xx to replicate that Str into a List of $n items. The parentheses group that so you can call .join to connect them all with a newline:

```
sub MAIN ( Str $s, Int $n ) {
    my $list = $s xx $n;
    put $list.join: "\n";
    }
```

The output has five copies of the Str:

```
B<% perl6 repeat.p6 'Hello' 5
Hello
Hello
Hello
Hello
Hello
```

You could skip the $list variable:

```
sub MAIN ( Str $s, Int $n ) {
    put ( $s xx $n ).join: "\n";
    }
```

2. The answer is very similar to the code you saw in this same section. lines() provides the input line by line. Output a count and the line as you process each element:

```
for lines() {
    put $++, ": $_";
    }
```

The anonymous scalar $ is useful there because you need it in one place. It's automatically a persistent variable. You can do that explicitly:

```
for lines() {
    state $line-number = 1;
    put $line-number++, ": $_";
    }
```

Use .words to break up the line then .elems to count the number of things you got:

```
for lines() {
    put $++, ": $_ ({ .words.elems })";
    }
```

3. Outputting the lines is easy. Use next to skip any that don't have the substring—the .contains method you saw in Chapter 4 is handy for this (although the regexes you'll see in Chapter 15 are useful too):

```
for lines() {
    next unless .contains( 'Pyrrhogyra' );
    .put;
    }
```

Counting them is a little more work. Create a persistent variable to count each time you make it past the next. The LAST phaser outputs its message at the end of the last time through the loop:

```
for lines() {
    state $count = 0;
    next unless .contains( 'Pyrrhogyra' );
    .put;
    $count++;
    LAST { put "Found $count lines" }
    }
```

4. Try these in the REPL:

```
% perl6
> ('aa'..'zz').elems
676
> ('a'..'zz').elems
702
```

The alphabetic ranges get to the end of the English alphabet and start again. After 'z' comes 'aa' (like a spreadsheet).

5. Try it in the REPL. A Range magically works here:

```
> ('b5'..'f9').List
(b5 b6 b7 b8 b9 c5 c6 c7 c8 c9 d5 d6 d7 d8 d9
e5 e6 e7 e8 e9 f5 f6 f7 f8 f9)
```

You can flip the number and letter columns:

```
> ('5b'..'9f').List
(5b 5c 5d 5e 5f 6b 6c 6d 6e 6f 7b 7c 7d 7e 7f
8b 8c 8d 8e 8f 9b 9c 9d 9e 9f)
```

Can you envision some easy matrix math with this?

6. This will cycle through a `Seq` of colors. Each time through the `loop` the `take` gets the next element in the `Array`. It increments the anonymous scalar `$` and divides by the number of elements in the `Array` to keep the computed index in the right range:

```
my @colors = lazy gather {
    state @array = <red green blue>;
    loop { take @array[ $++ % * ] }
    }

put @colors[$++] for ^10
```

The output shows the first 10 colors:

```
red
green
blue
red
green
blue
red
green
blue
red
```

That uses `gather`, which was the point of the exercise. There's another idiom I didn't expect you to know: using `xx` with the `Whatevers` list infinitely replicates the thing you give it. It's lazy so it doesn't exist all at once:

```
my @colors = |<red green blue> xx *;
put @colors[$++] for ^10;
```

7. Using 0 as the first square number at position 0, the next square is *0 + 2(1) – 1*. That's 1. The pattern continues like that. Once you define the `Seq` you can ask for any position that you want. The persistent variable `$n` stores the position and `$^a` is the previous value in the `Seq`:

```
my $squares := 0, { state $n; $^a + 2*(++$n) - 1 } ... *;
say $squares[25];    # 625
```

8. The program is simple and similar to what you've done in previous exercises:

```
for @*ARGS {
    put $_;
    }
```

When you run this program you get each argument on a separate line:

```
% perl6 args.p6 Hamadryas perlicus sixus
Hamadryas
perlicus
sixus
```

You can number the command-line arguments:

```
for @*ARGS {
    put ++$, ': ', $_;
    }
```

Now each line shows the position in the arguments:

```
% perl6 args.p6 Hamadryas perlicus sixus
1: Hamadryas
2: perlicus
3: sixus
```

You can also assign to @*ARGS. For MAIN to be able to work with it the thingys need to be Strs:

```
BEGIN @*ARGS = <4 5>;   # allomorphs
say @*ARGS;

sub MAIN ( Int $n, Int $m ) {
    put "Got $n and $m";
    }
```

9. Since .shift takes an element off the front of an Array and .unshift puts an element on the front of one, using those together means that the first element of the first Array ends up being the last element of the new Array:

```
my @array = @( 'a' .. 'f' );
my @new-array = Empty;

while @array.shift {
    @new-array.unshift: $^a;
    }

say @new-array;   # [f e d c b a]
```

The .pop and .push operators do the same thing from the opposite sides of the Array:

```
my @array = @( 'a' .. 'f' );
my @new-array = Empty;

while @array.pop {
    @new-array.push: $^a;
    }

say @new-array;   # [f e d c b a]
```

Either of these are possible with `.splice`. There's a slight change because `.splice` doesn't simply fail on an empty `Array`—you need to avoid the error. You won't see `try` until Chapter 7, but otherwise this one works like `.pop` and `.push`:

```
my @array = @( 'a' .. 'f' );
my @new-array = Empty;

try {
    while @array.splice: *-1, 1, Empty {
        put $^a;
        @new-array.splice: @new-array.end + 1, 0, $^a;
        }
    }

say @new-array;  # f e d c b a
```

You needn't do any of this work, though. Use `.reverse`, then clean out the original `Array`:

```
my @new-array = @array.reverse;
@array = Empty;
```

10. You can mimic the `.shift`, `.unshift`, `.pop`, and `.push` methods with `.splice` if you get the starting index and the length right. The `*-1` stands in for the last index of the object:

```
my @letters = 'a' .. 'f';
put @letters.elems;

# shift - start at beginning and replace one with nothing
put 'shift ', '-' x 10;
my $first-element = @letters.splice: 0, 1;
say $first-element;
say @letters; # [b c d e f]

# pop - start at end and replace one with nothing
put 'pop ', '-' x 10;
my $last-element = @letters.splice: * - 1, 1;
say $last-element;
say @letters; # [b c d e]

# unshift - start at beginning and replace none
put 'unshift ', '-' x 10;
@letters.splice: 0, 0, 'A';
say @letters; # [A b c d e]

# push - start at end and replace none
put 'push ', '-' x 10;
@letters.splice: *, 0, 'F';
say @letters; # [A b c d e F]
```

Notice that in the `.push` version the starting index is one greater than the last index. The `*` is the number of elements in the array, but there's not an index with that number yet.

11. Apply `.rotor` to `lines` to get chunks of lines from the files you specify on the command line or from standard input. The value in the `Block` is a `List` and you can extract any element you like from it:

```
for lines.rotor(3) {
    put $^a.[2];
    }
```

A slightly more general form gets the middle index from the chunk size. If it's an odd number `.Int` truncates it (selecting on the side closer to zero):

```
my $chunk-size = 5;
my $index = ( $chunk-size / 2 ).Int;

for lines.rotor($chunk-size) {
    say $^a.^name;
    say $^a.[$index];
    }
```

12. Create two `Array`s for the letters and positions. Zip those with Z:

```
my @letters = 'a' ..'z';
my @positions = 1 .. 26;
my @tuples = @letters Z @positions;
say @tuples;
```

The output shows you the `Array` and its sublists:

```
[(a 1) (b 2) (c 3) (d 4) (e 5) (f 6) (g 7) (h 8) (i 9) (j 10)
(k 11) (l 12) (m 13) (n 14) (o 15) (p 16) (q 17) (r 18) (s 19)
(t 20) (u 21) (v 22) (w 23) (x 24) (y 25) (z 26)]
```

You can make that a bit shorter by getting the length of the alphabet by looking at `@letters`:

```
my @letters = 'a' ..'z';
my @tuples = @letters Z 1 .. @letters.end;
say @tuples;
```

13. It's easy to cross the two `List`s:

```
my $ranks = ( 2, 3, 4, 5, 6, 7, 8, 9, 10, 'J', 'Q', 'K', 'A' );
my $suits = < ♣ ♡ ♠ ◇ >;

my $cards = ( @$ranks X @$suits );
say $cards;
put "There are {$cards.elems} cards";
```

Putting the ranks first means that the same ranks in different suits show up next to each other:

```
((2 ♣) (2 ♡) (2 ♠) (2 ◇) (3 ♣) (3 ♡) (3 ♠) (3 ◇)
(4 ♣) (4 ♡) (4 ♠) (4 ◇) (5 ♣) (5 ♡) (5 ♠) (5 ◇)
(6 ♣) (6 ♡) (6 ♠) (6 ◇) (7 ♣) (7 ♡) (7 ♠) (7 ◇)
(8 ♣) (8 ♡) (8 ♠) (8 ◇) (9 ♣) (9 ♡) (9 ♠) (9 ◇)
(10 ♣) (10 ♡) (10 ♠) (10 ◇) (J ♣) (J ♡) (J ♠) (J ◇)
(Q ♣) (Q ♡) (Q ♠) (Q ◇) (K ♣) (K ♡) (K ♠) (K ◇)
(A ♣) (A ♡) (A ♠) (A ◇))
There are 52 cards
```

If you reversed the ranks and suits in the code all the cards from the same suit would show up next to each other. To print all the cards of the same suit on one line go through each suit and cross it with the ranks. Since you're using the $ sigil you need to turn it into its elements so `for` can iterate through them. The `@` coercer will work:

```
my $ranks = ( 2, 3, 4, 5, 6, 7, 8, 9, 10, 'J', 'Q', 'K', 'A' );
my $suits = < ♣ ♡ ♠ ◇>;

for @$suits {
    say $_ X @$ranks;
    }
```

Each suit is now on one line (with some output hidden to fit it on the page):

```
((♣ 2) (♣ 3) (♣ 4) ... (♣ 10) (♣ J) (♣ Q) (♣ K) (♣ A))
((♡ 2) (♡ 3) (♡ 4) ... (♡ 10) (♡ J) (♡ Q) (♡ K) (♡ A))
((♠ 2) (♠ 3) (♠ 4) ... (♠ 10) (♠ J) (♠ Q) (♠ K) (♠ A))
((◇ 2) (◇ 3) (◇ 4) ... (◇ 10) (◇ J) (◇ Q) (◇ K) (◇ A))
```

This version is slightly trickier. Cross all the suits with the entire weights list as a single item. Notice the lack of the `@` in front of `$ranks`:

```
for @$suits X $ranks {
    say [X] @$_
    }
```

The value in `$_` is a list of two elements. The first is a `Str` representing the suit and the second is a list of all the ranks:

```
(♣ (2 3 4 5 6 7 8 9 10 J Q K A))
```

The reduction operator does a cross of all the sublists:

```
[X] @$_;
```

That cross give the `List` of `List`s for that suit (slightly modified here to fit the page):

```
((♣ 2) (♣ 3) (♣ 4) ... (♣ 10) (♣ J) (♣ Q) (♣ K) (♣ A))
```

14. A `MAIN` subroutine that lets you pick the number of hands and their size will work. Once you make the cards use `.pick` to choose as many of them as you need. The `.rotor` method divides them into hands:

```
sub MAIN ( Int $hands = 5, Int $hand-size = 5 ) {
    my @ranks = <2 3 4 5 6 7 8 9 T J Q K A>;
    my @suits = <♣ ♡ ♠ ◇>;
    my $ranks-str = @ranks.join: '';

    my @cards = @ranks X @suits;

    for @cards.pick( $hands * $hand-size ).rotor: 5 {
        .sort( { $ranks-str.index: $^a.[0] } ).say
        }
    }
```

The `.sort` Block is a bit clever. It uses the position in the `Str` of all the ranks concatenated. This sorts the numbered cards, the face cards, and the ace appropriately:

```
((4 ♡) (5 ♠) (J ♠) (Q ♠) (A ♠))
((6 ♡) (T ♠) (Q ♡) (Q ◇) (Q ♣))
((2 ♣) (2 ♡) (5 ♡) (6 ◇) (A ♣))
((3 ◇) (5 ◇) (7 ♣) (9 ♠) (J ♣))
((8 ♠) (9 ♡) (T ◇) (K ♠) (A ♡))
```

You may have come up with other ways that work.

15. The crux of this approach is the sorting technique. From the `Lists` of the ranks and suits the Block creates two `Strs`. The position in those `Strs` from `.index` is the sort order of the elements. This is handy to sort the ace, 10, and face cards along with the numbered cards. It also works for the nominal data of the ranks where you can choose any order you like.

The next part of the program creates the hands as in the previous exercise. Then you go back to the middle of the code, which has the Block to do the `.sort`. That's the same as the last name/first name sorting:

```
sub MAIN ( Int $hands = 5, Int $hand-size = 5 ) {
    my @ranks = <2 3 4 5 6 7 8 9 T J Q K A>;
    my @suits = <♣ ♡ ♠ ◇>;
    my $block = {
        state $r = @ranks.join;
        state $s = @ranks.join;

        $r.index( $^a.[0] ) <=> $r.index( $^b.[0] )
            or
        $s.index( $^a.[0] ) <=> $s.index( $^b.[0] )
        };

    my @cards = @ranks X @suits;

    for @cards.pick( $hands * $hand-size ).rotor: $hand-size {
        .sort( $block ).say
```

```
            }
        }
```

The output shows five sorted hands:

```
((2 ♡) (9 ◇) (T ♠) (K ◇) (A ♣))
((4 ♣) (9 ♣) (9 ♠) (Q ♡) (A ♡))
((5 ♣) (5 ♡) (5 ♠) (Q ♠) (K ♣))
((7 ♣) (8 ♠) (9 ♡) (T ◇) (Q ♣))
((5 ◇) (6 ♣) (8 ◇) (J ♡) (A ◇))
```

Answers to Chapter 7 Exercises

1. Use the `try` block you've already seen, but change the problematic code:

```
try {
    CATCH {
        default { put "Caught {.^name} with ⌈{.message}⌋" }
        }
    say 137 / 0;
    }

put "Got to the end.";
```

You get this error:

```
Caught X::Numeric::DivideByZero with
    ⌈Attempt to divide 137 by zero using div⌋
Got to the end.
```

2. The first program doesn't handle the error:

```
sub top { stubby() }
sub stubby { ... }  # the yada yada operator

top();
```

The error output shows the `Backtrace`:

```
Stub code executed
  in sub stubby at /Users/brian/Desktop/test.p6 line 4
  in sub top at /Users/brian/Desktop/test.p6 line 3
  in block <unit> at /Users/brian/Desktop/test.p6 line 6
```

You can catch the error by wrapping the problem code with `try`:

```
sub top { stubby() }
sub stubby { ... }  # the yada yada operator

try {
    CATCH {
        default { put "Uncaught exception {.^name}" }
        }
```

```
    top();
    }
```

The output tells you the Exception type:

```
Uncaught exception X::StubCode
```

You can have it both ways by outputting the Backtrace too. The Exception type has a `.backtrace` method that extracts that:

```
sub top { stubby() }
sub stubby { ... }

try {
    CATCH {
        default { put "Uncaught exception {.^name}\n{.backtrace}" }
        }
    top();
    }
```

3. From the previous exercise, replace the ... with die:

```
sub top { stubby() }
sub stubby { die "This method isn't implemented" }

try {
    CATCH {
        default { put "Uncaught exception {.^name}" }
        }
    top();
    }
```

Now the error type is different. The X::AdHoc stands in for everything that doesn't have a more specific type:

```
Uncaught exception X::AdHoc
```

You can choose another type. Construct that object and use it as the argument to die. Change your stubby implementation:

```
sub stubby {
    die X::StubCode.new( payload => "This method isn't implemented" );
    }
```

The error isn't X::AdHoc this time:

```
Uncaught exception X::StubCode
```

You don't need the die because you can throw the Exception directly:

```
sub stubby {
    X::StubCode
        .new( payload => "This method isn't implemented" )
        .throw;
    }
```

4. One way to handle a nonnumeric addition is to attempt it then catch it. Inside the CATCH you can use `fail`:

```
sub add-two-things ( $first, $second ) {
    CATCH {
        when X::Str::Numeric {
            fail q/One of the arguments wasn't a number/
            }
        }

    return $first + $second;
    }

my @items = < 2 2 3 two nine ten 1 37 0 0 >;

for @items -> $first, $second {
    my $sum = add-two-things( $first, $second );

    put $sum.defined ??
        "$first + $second = $sum" !!
        "You can't add $first and $second";
    }
```

You can test that `$sum` is defined to handle the case where it is zero:

```
2 + 2 = 4
You can't add 3 and two
You can't add nine and ten
1 + 37 = 38
0 + 0 = 0
```

If you wanted to work harder you could test each argument individually to report which one wasn't a number.

5. Check each argument with `val` and a smart match against `Numeric`. If that doesn't work out, use `warn` to complain about it:

```
sub add-two-things ( $first, $second ) {
    CATCH {
        when X::Str::Numeric {
            fail q/One of the arguments wasn't a number/
            }
        }

    for $first, $second {
        warn "'$_' is not numeric"  unless val($_) ~~ Numeric;
        }

    return $first + $second;
    }

my @items = < 2 2 3 two nine ten 1 37 0 0 >;
```

```
for @items -> $first, $second {
    my $sum = add-two-things( $first, $second );

    put $sum.defined ??
        "$first + $second = $sum" !!
        "You can't add $first and $second";
    }
```

The `quietly` will ignore any errors:

```
my $sum = quietly add-two-things( $first, $second );
```

Answers to Chapter 8 Exercises

1. Go through the command-line arguments and test each one individually:

```
for @*ARGS {
    unless .IO.e {
        put "'$_' does not exist";
        next;
        }

    .put;
    put "\treadable"   if .IO.r;
    put "\twritable"   if .IO.w;
    put "\texecutable" if .IO.x;
    }
```

Using `given` gets rid of the multiple `.IO` calls but complicates the code in other ways:

```
for @*ARGS -> $file {
    given $file.IO {
        unless .e {
            put "'$file' does not exist";
            next;
            }

        put $file;
        put "\treadable"   if .r;
        put "\twritable"   if .w;
        put "\texecutable" if .x;
        }
    }
```

The output reports different things depending on the file:

```
% perl6-latest file-test.p6 hamadryas /etc/hosts /usr/bin/true
'hamadryas' does not exist
/etc/hosts
```

```
        readable
/usr/bin/true
        readable
        executable
```

2. Here's a start:

```
put "Home dir is $*HOME";

unless chdir $*HOME.IO.add: @*ARGS[0] {
    die "Could not change directories: $!"
    }

put "Current working dir is now $*CWD";
```

The surrounding put statements are easy. They output the values of the special variables. But what about that hardcoded subdirectory? Part of the exercise was to try it with a directory that does not exist. You could grab the first command-line argument instead:

```
put "Home dir is $*HOME";

unless chdir $*HOME.IO.add: @*ARGS[0] {
    die "Could not change directories: $!"
    }

put "Current working dir is now  $*CWD";
```

You could also wrap all this in a MAIN subroutine:

```
sub MAIN ( Str $subdir ) {
    put "Home dir is ", $*HOME;

    unless chdir $*HOME.IO.add: @*ARGS[0] {
        die "Could not change directories: $!"
        }

    put "Current working dir is now $*CWD";
    }
```

3. Here's a short program. This one uses CATCH to handle the Failure that might be in $file. The program simply exits if there's a problem, but you could do something fancier:

```
sub MAIN ( $subdir = '/etc' ) {
    state $count = 1;
    CATCH { default { exit } }
    for dir( $subdir ).sort -> $file {
        put "{$count++}: $file";
        }
    }
```

The output counts the files:

```
1: /etc/afpovertcp.cfg
2: /etc/afpovertcp.cfg~orig
3: /etc/aliases
4: /etc/aliases.db
5: /etc/apache2
...
```

4. Here's an iterative (nonrecursive) solution. Use `@queue` to maintain the list of directories to process. Output the name of each file. If it's a symbolic link skip the rest of the block—this is important because symlinks can take you back to parts of the filesystem that are above where you started. You'll only make that mistake several times in your career. If you get past all of that add the file to the queue if it's a readable directory:

```
sub MAIN ( Str:D $dir where *.IO.d = '/' ) {
    my @queue = $dir;

    while @queue.elems > 0 {
        for dir( @queue.shift ) {
            next if ($_ eq '.' or $_ eq '..'); # virtual dirs
            # next if $_ ~~ any( <. ..> )  # junction
            .put;
            next if .IO.l; # do not follow symlinks
            @queue.unshift($_) if .IO.d and .IO.r;
            }
        }
    }
```

Here's a recursive solution. It's less typing but it also creates many layers of subroutine calls:

```
sub MAIN ( Str:D $dir where *.IO.d = '/' ) {
    show-dir( $dir.IO );
    }

sub show-dir ( IO::Path:D $dir where *.IO.d ) {
    for dir( $dir ) {
        next if ($_ eq '.' or $_ eq '..'); # virtual dirs
        .put;
        next if .IO.l; # do not follow symlinks
        &?ROUTINE( $_ ) if .IO.d and .IO.r;
        }
    }
```

Even though the default `:test` argument excludes the . and .. directories, you still might like to skip them explicitly. If someone changes the filter you still want to avoid those. It's like wearing a belt *and* suspenders.

There are some other examples in the documentation for dir, including a gather-take if you don't want to output the files as you go.

5. Here's a program to simply make a directory:

```
sub MAIN ( $subdir ) {
    CATCH {
        when X::IO::Mkdir
            { put "Failed to make directory $subdir" }
    }

    mkdir $subdir.IO.mkdir;
}
```

Your argument can be an absolute or relative path:

```
% perl6 mkdir.p6 Butterflies
% perl6 mkdir.p6 Butterflies/hamadryas
```

If you specify a directory that you aren't allowed to make you catch the error:

```
% perl6 mkdir.p6 /Butterflies
Failed to make directory /Butterflies
```

You might try it with a directory that you can't create but that already exists. In that case you get no error:

```
% perl mkdir.p6 /etc
```

6. The trick to this program is to treat the template like any other Str. You can interpolate the width into it:

```
sub MAIN ( Int $width, Str $s ) {
    put '123456789.' x ($width + 10) / 10;
    printf "%{$width}s", $s;
}
```

```
% perl6 right.p6 18 Hamadryas
123456789.123456789.
        Hamadryas
```

7. The %f directive handles floating-point numbers. Use .3 to specify that you want only three decimal places. Double up the % to get a literal percent sign. Don't limit yourself to directives in your template:

```
sub MAIN ( Int $n, Int $m ) {
    printf "$n/$m = %.3f%%", 100 * $n / $m;
}
```

The output shows your formatted percentage:

```
% perl6 percentages.p6 15 76
15/76 = 19.737%
```

8. Create a template that has 12 directives and make each one wide enough for the largest number you'll encounter (144) along with some space to separate the numbers:

```
my $template = [~] '% 4d' x 12, "\n";
for 1 .. 12 -> $row {
    printf $template, (1..12) <<*>> $row;
    }
```

Here's the formatted table:

```
% perl6 multiplication-table.p6
 1   2   3   4   5   6   7   8   9  10  11  12
 2   4   6   8  10  12  14  16  18  20  22  24
 3   6   9  12  15  18  21  24  27  30  33  36
 4   8  12  16  20  24  28  32  36  40  44  48
 5  10  15  20  25  30  35  40  45  50  55  60
 6  12  18  24  30  36  42  48  54  60  66  72
 7  14  21  28  35  42  49  56  63  70  77  84
 8  16  24  32  40  48  56  64  72  80  88  96
 9  18  27  36  45  54  63  72  81  90  99 108
10  20  30  40  50  60  70  80  90 100 110 120
11  22  33  44  55  66  77  88  99 110 121 132
12  24  36  48  60  72  84  96 108 120 132 144
```

9. The program can be simple:

```
put 'Hello Perl 6';
```

Run the program normally. You should see the output in the terminal:

```
% perl6 hello.p6
Hello Perl 6
```

Run it again and redirect the output to a file. The same message should show up in the file:

```
% perl6 hello.p6 > output.txt
```

Redirecting to the null device completely ignores the output:

```
% perl6 program.p6 > /dev/null
C:\ perl6 program.p6 > NUL
```

10. Here's a short program that outputs to both filehandles. The message isn't important:

```
put 'This is standard output';
note 'This is standard error';
```

On the command line you can redirect either one of the filehandles. When you send that output to the null device you don't see any of it:

```
% perl6 out-err.p6 2> /dev/null
This is standard output
```

```
% perl6 out-err.p6 > /dev/null
This is standard error
```

11. Here's the first program. Take the first element off @*ARGS to use as the substring you want to find. Use the rest of the thingys in @*ARGS as the filenames to read:

```
my $string = @*ARGS.shift;

for lines() {
    next unless .contains: $string;
    .put;
    }
```

Try it to ensure it does what you want:

```
% perl6 put.p6 for *.p6
for @*ARGS -> $file {
        for lines() {
for 1 .. 12 -> $row {
for lines() {
for lines() { .uc.put }
```

Here's the second. It reads the lines and uppercases each one. You can run this one on a file to ensure it does what it should, but I'll skip that here:

```
for lines() { .uc.put }
```

Now pipe the output of one program into the input of another:

```
% perl6 put.p6 for *.p6 | perl6 uc.p6
FOR @*ARGS -> $FILE {
        FOR LINES() {
FOR 1 .. 12 -> $ROW {
FOR LINES() {
FOR LINES() { .UC.PUT }
```

And that's Unix in a nutshell: a collection of small utilities that each do their job very well and that you join together like pieces of garden hose. Research the history of Doug McIlroy's contributions to the world to learn more.

12. Use a FIRST phaser to tell .on-switch to print a file banner at the start of each file. That only works when you switch files, so you'll need to do it separately for the initial file:

```
for lines() {
    FIRST {
        my $code = { put join( "\n", '=' x 50, $^a, "-" x 50) };
        $code( $*ARGFILES );

        $*ARGFILES.on-switch = -> $handle {
            $code( $*ARGFILES ) if $handle.is-open;
            };
        }
```

```
        .put;
        }
```

You get output like this, but it has an extra banner after the last file. The filehandle switches from the last one to nothing (although that's a bit annoying):

```
=======================================================
line-banner.p6
- - - - - - - - - - - - - - - - - - - - - - - - - - - - - - - - - - - - - - -
#!/Users/brian/bin/perl6s/perl6-latest


    for lines() {
        FIRST {
            my $code = { put join( "\n", '=' x 50, $^a, "-" x 50) };
            $code( $*ARGFILES );

            $*ARGFILES.on-switch = {
                $code( $*ARGFILES );
                };
            }

        .put;
        }
=======================================================
<closed IO::CatHandle>
- - - - - - - - - - - - - - - - - - - - - - - - - - - - - - - - - - - - - - -
```

To suppress that you can test if the handle is open (and not closed as it says in that filename). The `.is-open` method returns `False` in that case, so you can use that to skip the banner code:

```
$*ARGFILES.on-switch = -> $handle {
    $code( $*ARGFILES ) if $handle.is-open;
    };
```

13. Here's a simpleminded solution (which is completely adequate for what you are practicing here).

Go through `@*ARGS` one item at a time. Try to open that file. Output a warning if you can't and move on to the next one. Get the lazy list from `.lines`. Output the line in index 0 and the one in index `*-1`. Use `.elems` to figure out how many lines you left out:

```
for @*ARGS {
    my $fh = .IO.open;
    put '=' x 20, ' ', $_;
    unless $fh {
        warn "Could not open $_: {$fh.exception.message}";
        next;
```

```
        }
    my $lines = $fh.lines;
    put $lines.[0];
    put "... { $lines.elems - 2 } lines hidden ...";
    put $lines.[*-1];
    }
```

There are a few cases that cause problems here. If the file has two or fewer lines you want to do something else. In those cases you'll hide no lines:

```
for @*ARGS {
    my $fh = .IO.open;
    put '=' x 20, ' ', $_;
    unless $fh {
        warn "Could not open $_: {$fh.exception.message}";
        next;
        }
    my $lines = $fh.lines;

    given $lines.elems {
        when 0 { next }
        when 1 { put $lines.[0] }
        when 2 { .put for @$lines }
        default {
            put $lines.[0];
            put "... { $lines.elems - 2 } lines hidden ...";
            put $lines.[*-1];
            }
        }
    }
```

That given might be a bit too much. You can change the first example to conditionally output some of the lines based on the number of elements:

```
for @*ARGS {
    my $fh = .IO.open;
    put '=' x 20, ' ', $_;
    unless $fh {
        warn "Could not open $_: {$fh.exception.message}";
        next;
        }
    my $lines = $fh.lines;

    next if $lines.elems == 0;

    put $lines.[0];
    put "... { $lines.elems - 2 } lines hidden ..." if $lines.elems > 2;
    put $lines.[*-1] if $lines.elems > 1;
    }
```

14. The first part of the problem isn't that difficult:

```
my $file = 'primes.txt';
sub MAIN ( Int:D $low, Int:D $high where * >= $low ) {
    unless my $fh = open $file, :w {
        die "Could not open '$file': {$fh.exception}";
        }

    for $low .. $high {
        $fh.put: $_ if .is-prime;
        }
    }
```

The second part deals with a file that already exists. There are various things that you can do. One approach is to refuse to keep going. Use the :exclusive adverb to only open the file if it doesn't exist:

```
my $file = 'primes.txt';
sub MAIN ( Int:D $low, Int:D $high where * >= $low ) {
    unless my $fh = open $file, :w, :exclusive {
        die "Could not open '$file': {$fh.exception}";
        }

    for $low .. $high {
        $fh.put: $_ if .is-prime;
        }
    }
```

This is slightly better than checking if the file exists before you do something. Here, there's a little bit of time between your check and the open when something else might create that file (a "race condition"):

```
my $file = 'primes.txt';
sub MAIN ( Int:D $low, Int:D $high where * >= $low ) {
    die "File exists" if $file.IO.e;
    ...
    }
```

Another option is to append to the existing file:

```
my $file = 'primes.txt';
sub MAIN ( Int:D $low, Int:D $high where * >= $low ) {
    unless my $fh = open $file, :a {
        die "Could not open '$file': {$fh.exception}";
        }

    for $low .. $high {
        $fh.put: $_ if .is-prime;
        }
    }
```

15. Here's a simple hex dump program that shows the numeric octet values. First try to open the file, and if you can't do that catch the exception and exit immediately. If you can, you loop until you can't read any more from the file.

For each buffer that you read, use `.map` to format it into a two-digit hexadecimal number and join these with a space. That goes to the output. If you're at the end of the file, break out of the `loop` and close the filehandle:

```
sub MAIN ( $file ) {
    # values that may be configurable later
    my $octets-per-line  = 16;
    my $column-separator = ' ';

    my $fh = try {
        CATCH {
            when X::AdHoc { put "Could not open $file"; exit }
            default { put .^name; exit }
            }
        open $file, :bin;
        }

    loop {
        my Buf $buffer = $fh.read: $octets-per-line;

        put $buffer
            .map( *.fmt: '%02x' )
            .join( $column-separator )
            ;

        last if $fh.eof;
        }

    $fh.close;
    }
```

16. Here's the program taken from the chapter:

```
my $path = 'buf.txt';
unless my $fh = open $path, :w, :bin {
    die "Could not open file";
    }

my $buf = Buf.new: <52 61 6b 75 64 6f 0a>.map: *.parse-base: 16;
$fh.write: $buf;
```

Once you run it, look in the file; you should find the text "Rakudo\n".

Answers to Chapter 9 Exercises

1. Here's a way that you can do it. The `value-to-ordinal` subroutine uses `if` branches to transform the numbers to `Pair`s. There's the special case of the num-

---

bers ending in 11 to 19. All of those get th. In the remaining cases, numbers ending in 1, 2, and 3 get st, nd, and rd. The default block gives everything else th:

```
for 1 .. 120 {
    my $ordinal = value-to-ordinal( $_ );
    put $ordinal.value ~ $ordinal.key;
    }

sub value-to-ordinal ( Int $n where * > 0 ) {
        if $n % 100 ~~ 11..19 { 'th' => $n }
    elsif $n %  10 == 1     { 'st' => $n }
    elsif $n %  10 == 2     { 'nd' => $n }
    elsif $n %  10 == 3     { 'rd' => $n }
    else                    { :th($n)   }
    }
```

Remember that the subroutine returns the last evaluated expression, so you get
the value from the block for whichever branch you followed.

2. The first part of this solution is the same as that for the previous exercise:

```
for 1 .. 10 {
    my $ordinal = value-to-ordinal( $_ );
    put $ordinal.value ~ $ordinal.key;
    }
```

The value-to-ordinal subroutine is different, though. The Map stores the pre-
computed values, but only for the key of the Pair that you will return. You can
see why by looking at the if block. You can check the numbers that end in 11 to
19 mod 100 to look up the ordinal suffix. If that isn't a key in $ordinals try the
same thing mod 10. This way you can handle 1 and 101 with the same rule to get
st as well as 11 and 111 to get th:

```
sub value-to-ordinal ( Int $n where * > 0 ) {
    state $ordinals = Map.new:
        '1' => 'st',
        '2' => 'nd',
        '3' => 'rd',
        map { $_ => 'th' }, 11 .. 19;


        if $ordinals{$n % 100}:exists { $ordinals{$n % 100} => $n }
    elsif $ordinals{$n %  10}:exists { $ordinals{$n %  10} => $n }
    else                             { :th($n)   }
    }
```

Isn't that simpler? Instead of several branches of checks, it's either in $ordinals
or it isn't.

When you finish that program, someone throws a new rule at you. If it ends in 5 (but not 15), you should use the suffix ty. Since you are using a Map, simply add another key:

```
sub value-to-ordinal ( Int $n where * > 0 ) {
    state $ordinals = Map.new:
        '1' => 'st',
        '2' => 'nd',
        '3' => 'rd',
        '5' => 'ty',
        map { $_ => 'th' }, 11 .. 19;

        if $ordinals{$n % 100}:exists { $ordinals{$n % 100} => $n }
    elsif $ordinals{$n %  10}:exists { $ordinals{$n %  10} => $n }
    else                             { :th($n)     }
    }
```

Had you done this with Pairs you would have had to add another branch to your if statement.

3. You can call .map on a Range. Since the key and the value both need to use the current value, you can't use a thunk here. You can create a block that returns a Pair:

```
my $squares =
    Map.new: (1..10).map: { $^a => $^a ** 2 };

loop {
    my $number = prompt 'Enter a number: ';
    last unless $number;

    if $squares{$number}:exists {
        put "$number squared is $squares{$number}";
        }
    else {
        put "$number is an invalid number";
        }
    }
```

4. This first part of the problem is simple. Change the object from a Map to a Hash. Everything else works the same because a Hash works the same:

```
for 1 .. 120 {
    my $ordinal = value-to-ordinal( $_ );
    put $ordinal.value ~ $ordinal.key;
    }

sub value-to-ordinal ( Int $n where * > 0 ) {
    state $ordinals = Hash.new:
        '1' => 'st',
        '2' => 'nd',
```

```
                     '3' => 'rd',
                     '5' => 'ty',
                     map { $_ => 'th' }, 11 .. 19;


          if $ordinals{$n % 100}:exists { $ordinals{$n % 100} => $n }
       elsif $ordinals{$n %  10}:exists { $ordinals{$n %  10} => $n }
       else                             { :th($n) }
       }
```

The second part of the problem is a bit trickier. First, check the $ordinals with :exists. If the key is not there, figure out what the suffix should be and add it to $ordinals. At the end of the subroutine, create the Pair from the values in the Hash:

```
for 1 .. 10 {
    my $ordinal = value-to-ordinal( $_ );
    put $ordinal.value ~ $ordinal.key;
    }

for 10 .. 15 {
    my $ordinal = value-to-ordinal( $_ );
    put $ordinal.value ~ $ordinal.key;
    }

sub value-to-ordinal ( Int $n where * > 0 ) {
    state $ordinals = Hash.new:
        '1' => 'st',
        '2' => 'nd',
        '3' => 'rd',
        map { $_ => 'th' }, 11 .. 19;

    unless $ordinals{$n}:exists {
        # only see this message once
        put "Trying new suffix for $n";
        $ordinals{$n} = do
                if $ordinals{$n % 100}:exists { $ordinals{$n % 100} }
            elsif $ordinals{$n %  10}:exists { $ordinals{$n %  10} }
            else                             { 'th' }
        }

    return $ordinals{$n} => $n;
    }
```

There's another way you can create that Pair in the return statement. The :p adverb returns the key-value as a Pair:

```
return $ordinals{$n}:p;  # almost
```

But you've stored the number as the key and the suffix as the value, which is the opposite of what you want to return. You can turn that around with .antipair:

```
return $ordinals{$n}:p.antipair;
```

Perhaps by the time you read this answer, a certain experimental feature won't be experimental. You can set a trait on your subroutine so it caches return values. If your subroutine is a function, which means that it always returns the same thing for the same input, you don't have to cache it yourself.

The is cached trait handles it all for you, although you need to declare you want to use an experimental feature. This one doesn't have to use :exists because it doesn't care about adding new entries:

```
use experimental :cached;

for 1 .. 10 {
    my $ordinal = value-to-ordinal( $_ );
    put $ordinal.value ~ $ordinal.key;
    }

for 10 .. 25 {
    my $ordinal = value-to-ordinal( $_ );
    put $ordinal.value ~ $ordinal.key;
    }

sub value-to-ordinal ( Int $n where * > 0 ) is cached {
    state $ordinals = Hash.new:
        '1' => 'st',
        '2' => 'nd',
        '3' => 'rd',
        map { $_ => 'th' }, 11 .. 19;

    # take the first one that's defined
    my $suffix =
        $ordinals{$n}        //
        $ordinals{$n % 100} //
        $ordinals{$n %  10} //
        'th';

    return $suffix => $n;
    }
```

If you don't cache it your program still works, and it's a bit simpler than the previous solution. It might seem silly to cache such a simple result. Looking up something in a Hash is very quick (that's the point), but when you do some real work you might have something meaty. When that happens, you don't want to compute it again if it doesn't change.

5. This program is actually much simpler than its description. There are two for loops. The first gets the input and counts the words. The second outputs the keys and values in descending order by value. That's the basic structure of many accumulation tasks:

```
my %Words;
for lines.words { %Words{ .lc }++ }

for %Words.keys.sort( { %Words{$^k} } ).reverse {
    put "$^key: %Words{$^key}";
    }
```

In the first loop the current word is the topic. Inside the Hash index, call .lc on the word to normalize it. That way you don't get separate entries that differ only in capitalization.

The second loop is a pipeline. Get the keys but sort them by their value. By default the lower values are closer to the front of the List, but a .reverse takes care of that.

Using the *Butterflies_and_Moths.txt* file gets you these counts:

```
% perl6 count-words.p6 Butterflies_and_Moths.txt
the: 9434
of: 4991
and: 3828
a: 2952
in: 2327
is: 2253
to: 2162
are: 1547
it: 1326
with: 1261
on: 1168
be: 1056
that: 1007
or: 892
this: 853
as: 747
for: 697
by: 676
may: 659
```

But what if two words have the same count? You can sort those on the word as a secondary sort like you saw in Chapter 6:

```
my $block := {
    %Words{$^a} <=> %Words{$^b}  # count
        or
    $^a leg $^b                  # word
    };

for %Words.keys.sort( $block ).reverse {
    put "$^key: %Words{$^key}";
    }
```

Many of the words in that list are not that interesting. You could filter those out by keeping a list of stopwords and skipping those. Creating a Hash from a List then checking with :exists works nicely:

```
my %Stop-Words = map { $_ => 1 } <
    a an the this that ...
    >;

my %Words;
for lines.words { %Words{ .lc }++ }

for %Words.keys.sort( { %Words{$^k} } ).reverse {
    next if %Stop-Words{ .lc }:exists;
    put "$^key: %Words{$^key}";
    }
```

That's a bit more than you needed to do for this exercise though.

6. You can easily read lines from a file with $file.IO.lines, and you can use .words to break up the lines based on whitespace. After that, you use those words as the keys for the Hash. You don't have to create the structure beforehand —just specify the keys and levels you want:

```
my $file = @*ARGS[0] // 'butterfly_census.txt';

my %census;
for $file.IO.lines -> $line {
    my ( $genus, $species ) = $line.words;

    %census{$genus}{$species}++;
    }

for %census.keys.sort( {%census{$_}.elems} ).reverse -> $genus {
    put $genus;
    my $seq := %census{$genus}.keys.sort( {%census{$genus}{$_}} );
    for $seq.reverse -> $species {
        ( "\t", $species, %census{$genus}{$species} )
            .join( ' ' ).put
        }
    }
```

That long list of methods in the for loop might look tricky. You go through the list of keys and sort them by the number of second-level keys, %census{$_}.elems. That returns the list sorted in ascending order. The .reverse turns that around so the first key has the most second-level keys.

Instead of iterating over the keys yourself, you can use something like Pretty Dump to do it for you:

```
my $file = @*ARGS[0] // die 'Specify a butterfly list file';

my %census;
for $file.IO.lines -> $line {
    my ( $genus, $species ) = $line.words;

    %census{$genus}{$species}++
}

use PrettyDump;
say PrettyDump.new.dump: %census;
```

7. This solution is similar to the previous exercise, but it writes its output to a file:

```
my $file = 'census-tabs.txt';

for lines() {
    state %Animals;
    LAST {
        my $fh = try open $file, :w;
        die "Could not open file: $!" if $!;
        for %Animals.keys -> $genus {
            for %Animals{$genus}.keys -> $species {
                $fh.put: join "\t",
                    $genus, $species, %Animals{$genus}{$species};
            }
        }
    }
    my ( $genus, $species ) = .words;

    %Animals{$genus}{$species}++;
}
```

You could have gone a different direction with this by outputting to standard output and redirecting that on the command line. That might be a better solution for real work, but then you don't get to practice making a file inside your program.

Answers to Chapter 10 Exercises

1. These answers aren't that tough as long as the modules don't develop errors or bad tests that don't let them install. By name it's quite simple:

   % zef install Inline::Perl5

   Installing Grammar::Debugger by its repository URL is a bit trickier since you need to discover that. You could start by searching GitHub, but you could also look at *https://modules.perl6.org*. Follow the link to its GitHub page, then find the clone URL:

```
% zef install https://github.com/jnthn/grammar-debugger.git
```

2. It's easy to see the repository locations for the environment and command-line switch options. The program is the same as the one in the chapter:

```
for $*REPO.repo-chain -> $item {
    say $item;
    }
```

Run this on its own to see what's there. Some are paths and some are CompUnit::Repository objects:

```
% perl6 repo.p6
inst#/Users/hamadryas/.perl6
inst#/Applications/Rakudo/share/perl6/site
inst#/Applications/Rakudo/share/perl6/vendor
inst#/Applications/Rakudo/share/perl6
CompUnit::Repository::AbsolutePath.new(...)
CompUnit::Repository::NQP.new(...)
CompUnit::Repository::Perl5.new(...)
```

When you add libraries you should see them show up in the list:

```
% perl6 -I/usr/local/lib show-repo.p6
file#/usr/local/lib
inst#/Users/hamadryas/.perl6
inst#/Applications/Rakudo/share/perl6/site
inst#/Applications/Rakudo/share/perl6/vendor
inst#/Applications/Rakudo/share/perl6
```

```
% export PERL6LIB=/opt/lib
% perl6 show-repo.p6
file#/opt/lib
inst#/Users/hamadryas/.perl6
inst#/Applications/Rakudo/share/perl6/site
inst#/Applications/Rakudo/share/perl6/vendor
inst#/Applications/Rakudo/share/perl6
```

On Windows:

```
C:\ set PERL6LIB=C:\MyPerl6
C:\ perl6 show-repo.p6
inst#C:\MyPerl6
inst#C:\Users\hamadryas\.perl6
inst#C:\rakudo\share\perl6\site
inst#C:\rakudo\share\perl6\vendor
inst#C:\rakudo\share\perl6
CompUnit::Repository::AbsolutePath.new(...)
CompUnit::Repository::NQP.new(...)
CompUnit::Repository::Perl5.new(...)
```

3. To check that a module is installed, create the dependency specification and pass that to $*REPO.resolve. If that returns something that is True, then the module is installed:

```
sub MAIN ( Str $module-name ) {
    my $ds = CompUnit::DependencySpecification.new:
        :short-name($module-name);

    put "$module-name is{
        $*REPO.resolve( $ds ) ?? '' !! ' not'
        } installed";
}
```

Running it shows what's installed and what's not:

```
% perl6 module-installed.p6 Number::Bytes::Human
Number::Bytes::Human is installed

% perl6 module-installed.p6 Does::Not::Exist
Does::Not::Exist is not installed
```

You don't need to do this from inside a program. *zef* can list all the available modules:

```
% zef list
```

Using the info command tells you about a particular module:

```
% zef info Does::Not::Exist
!!!> Found no candidates matching identity: Does::Not::Exist

%  zef info Number::Bytes::Human
- Info for: Number::Bytes::Human
- Identity: Number::Bytes::Human:ver<0.0.3>
- Recommended By: /Applications/Rakudo/share/perl6/site
- Installed: Yes
Description:    Converts byte count into an easy to read format.
License:    MIT
Source-url:  git://github.com/dugword/Number-Bytes-Human.git
Provides: 1 modules
Depends: 0 items
```

4. This answer combines two programs from the chapter. Create a subroutine that takes a list of candidate modules and yields the ones that are installed. In MAIN, use gather to collect those and use the first one that you find:

```
my %dumper-adapters = %(
    'Data::Dump::Tree' => 'ddt',
    'PrettyDump'       => 'dump',
    'Pretty::Printer'  => 'pp',
    );

sub installed-modules ( *@candidates ) {
```

```
        for @candidates -> $module {
            my $ds = CompUnit::DependencySpecification.new:
                :short-name($module);
            if $*REPO.resolve: $ds {
                take $module;
                }
            }
        }

    sub MAIN (
        Str $class = (
            gather installed-modules( %dumper-adapters.keys )
            ).[0]
        ) {
        put "Dumping with $class";
        CATCH {
            when X::CompUnit::UnsatisfiedDependency {
                note "Could not load $class";
                exit 1;
                }
            }
        require ::($class);

        my $method = %dumper-adapters{$class};
        unless $method {
            note "Do not know how to dump with $class";
            exit 2;
            }

        put ::($class).new."$method"( %dumper-adapters );
        }
```

5. Most of this answer is the same code you saw in the chapter, but with a MAIN wrapped around it. At the end you output the $data. If you fetch an image file or other sort of binary data this might mess up your terminal. You could inspect the content type and decide to do something differently, but that's not the point of this exercise:

```
    sub MAIN ( $url ) {
        use HTTP::UserAgent;

        my $ua = HTTP::UserAgent.new;
        $ua.timeout = 10;

        my $response = $ua.get( $url );

        my $data = do with $response {
            .is-success ?? .content !! die .status-line
            }
```

```
put $data;
}
```

6. You might have to install these modules first. Since you want to use a Perl 5 module you must have that installed.

This program does it in a MAIN sub that uses the program name itself as the default filename. It slurps the data and stores that so it passes the same thing to each version of Digest::MD5. You'll read more about slurp in Chapter 10.

The code inside the dos is taken from the documentation examples for each of the modules:

```
sub MAIN ( $file = $*PROGRAM ) {
    my $data = slurp $*PROGRAM;
    unless $data {
        note "Could not read $file";
        exit;
    }

    my $digest-p5 = do {
        use Digest::MD5:from<Perl5>;
        my $ctx = Digest::MD5.new.add( $data );
        put $ctx.hexdigest;
    }

    my $digest-p6 = do {
        use Digest::MD5;
        my $d = Digest::MD5.new;
        put $d.md5_hex( $data );
    }

    put join "\n", "p5: $digest-p5", "p6: $digest-p6";
    die "Digests do not match!"
        unless $digest-p5 eq $digest-p6;
}
```

The particular form of the program isn't important as long as you were able to use both modules.

Answers to Chapter 11 Exercises

1. MAIN takes the arguments, passes them to the subroutine, and saves the result. That path of the data is the entire point of this exercise. Once you know how to structure it you can put anything you like in the subroutine:

```
sub MAIN ( Int $n, Int $m ) {
    my $lcm = least-common-multiple( $n, $m );
    put "The least common multiple of $n and $m is $lcm";
```

```
    }
sub least-common-multiple ( Int $n, Int $m ) {
    return $n lcm $m
    }
```

You can also define the subroutine inside MAIN (although why would you in this case?). Only the code inside MAIN can see this subroutine:

```
sub MAIN ( $n, $m ) {
    sub least-common-multiple ( $n, $m ) {
        $n lcm $m
        }
    my $lcm = least-common-multiple( $n, $m );
    put "The least common multiple of $n and $m is $lcm";
    }
```

2. Here's a simple recursive implementation. If the argument is 1 it returns 1 right away. Otherwise it returns the argument multiplied by the factorial of the next smaller positive number:

```
sub factorial ( $n ) {
    return 1 if $n == 1;
    $n * &?ROUTINE( $n - 1 );
    }

put factorial(5);   # 120
```

If you want to write this as a command-line program you can wrap it in MAIN:

```
sub MAIN ( $n ) { put factorial($n) }

sub factorial ( $n ) {
    return 1 if $n == 1;
    $n * &?ROUTINE( $n - 1 );
    }
```

The easy Perl 6 way uses the reduction operator with * on the inside. It's so simple you probably don't even want to define a subroutine:

```
sub MAIN ( $n ) { put factorial($n) }

sub factorial ( $n ) { [*] 1..$n }
```

How big a number did you get? With arbitrary precision you can get as big a number as you care to wait for. I was able to generate results with tens of thousands of digits in less than a tenth of a second (although outputting them takes time, so I skip that part):

```
sub factorial ( $n ) { [*] 1..$n }

sub MAIN ( $max-duration = 2 ) {
    loop {
```

```
        state $n = 0;
        my $start = now;
        my $f = factorial( ++$n );
        my $duration = now - $start;
        put "$n: {$f.chars} ($duration)";
        last if $duration > $max-duration;
        }
    }
```

I used .chars because .log10 started failing at the factorial of 171 (just where 64 bits would give up).

3. One way to check random-between is to run it repeatedly and see if you get all the values that you expect. In this case, a for running 100,000 times should do the job:

```
sub random-between ( $i, $j ) {
    ( $j - $i ).rand.Int + $i;
    }

my %results;
for ^100_000 {
    %results{ random-between( 5, 14 ) }++;
    }

say %results.keys.sort( {$^a <=> $^b} ).join: " ";
```

When you output the results, you see that 14 doesn't show up. The subroutine doesn't actually do its job if you expect both endpoints to be in the results. Without testing the subroutine you may have never noticed this:

```
5 6 7 8 9 10 11 12 13
```

4. The answer has a little new code. You can add the MAIN subroutine to the *random-between.p6* code. That handles the command-line arguments:

```
# random-between.p6
use lib $*PROGRAM.IO.parent;

use MyRandLibrary;

sub MAIN ( $i, $j ) {
    say random-between( $i, $j );
    }
```

MyRandLibrary.pm6 stays the same:

```
# MyRandLibrary.pm6
sub random-between ( $i, $j ) is export {
    ( $j - $i ).rand.Int + $i;
    }
```

No matter which order you give it arguments you get an answer in the range between the smallest and largest numbers:

```
% perl6 random-main.p6 99 4
55
% perl6 random-main.p6 4 99
33
```

You get an error if you give it something other than a decimal number:

```
% perl6 random-main.p6 4 Hamadryas
Cannot convert string to number: base-10 number must begin
with valid digits or '.' in '⏛Hamadryas' (indicated by ⏛)
```

You'll fix that in a moment.

5. Implement your subroutine and pass it the arguments from the exercise. The idea is to see how a basic subroutine treats them differently:

```
count-and-show( 1, 3, 7 );
count-and-show( 1, 3, ( 7, 6, 5 ) );
count-and-show( 1, 3, ( 7, $(6, 5) ) );
count-and-show( [ 1, 3, ( 7, $(6, 5) ) ] );

sub count-and-show {
    put "There are ", @_.elems, " arguments";
    for @_ -> $thing {
        print "\t";
        say $thing;
        }
    }
```

The output shows different ways that the subroutines see these arguments:

```
There are 3 arguments
    1
    3
    7
There are 5 arguments
    1
    3
    7
    6
    5
There are 4 arguments
    1
    3
    7
    (6 5)
There are 3 arguments
    1
    3
    (7 (6 5))
```

6. You already know how to make a library that exports subroutines. For these functions you need to use a slurpy parameter to flatten the arguments. The `head` returns the first thing and the `tail` returns everything else. The signature is the same for both subroutines and both use the `is export` trait to define them in the scope that loaded the library:

```
# HeadsTails.pm
sub head ( *@args ) is export { return @args[0] }
sub tail ( *@args ) is export { return @args[1..*-1] }
```

You may have discovered that you don't need to do this. There are already `.head` and `.tail` methods.

Answers to Chapter 12 Exercises

1. Define the classes before you use them. You don't need anything in the braces. You should be able to create objects from them even though they look empty:

```
class Butterfly {}
class Moth {}
class Lobster {}

my $number = Butterfly.new;
my $str    = Moth.new;
my $set    = Lobster.new;
```

2. Your program is similar to the one from previous exercise. Instead of defining the classes you load them with use:

```
use Butterfly;
use Moth;
use Lobster;

my $number = Butterfly.new;
my $str    = Moth.new;
my $set    = Lobster.new;
```

Create separate *Butterfly.pm6*, *Moth.pm6*, and *Lobster.pm6* classes in the same directory as your program:

```
# Butterfly.pm6
class Butterfly {};
```

You can use `unit` instead since the entire file is devoted to that class:

```
# Butterfly.pm6
unit Butterfly;
```

When you run your program you can add the current directory to the module search path with `-I`:

```
$ perl6 -I. butterfly.pm6
```

3. Steal the basic `Butterfly` class from the text, then add a `$!color` attribute that
   follows the pattern:

```
class Butterfly {
    has $!common-name = 'Unnamed butterfly';
    has $!color       = 'White';

    method common-name is rw { $!common-name }
    method color       is rw { $!color }
    }

my $butterfly = Butterfly.new;
$butterfly.common-name = 'Perly Cracker';
$butterfly.color = 'Vermillion';

put "{.common-name} is {.color}" with $butterfly;
```

4. You can do most of this problem with just the details from the chain of inheritance. The class names already have the information about the animal's classification. To generate the full names you simply use the class names (except for `Any`
   and `Mu`, hence the `[0..*-3]`):

```
class Animalia                   { }
class Arthropodia is Animalia    { }
class Insecta     is Arthropodia { }
class Lepidoptera is Insecta     { }
class Nymphalidae is Lepidoptera { }
class Hamadryas   is Nymphalidae {
    has $.genus   = 'Hamadryas';
    has $.species;
    method full-name {
        my @classes = map { .^name }, (self.^mro)[0..*-3].reverse;
        say @classes;
        join ' ', @classes, $.species
        }
    method Str { "$.genus $.species" }
    }

my $butterfly = Hamadryas.new: :species('perlicus');
put $butterfly.full-name;
```

If you were actually representing species in your program this probably wouldn't
be a good way to do it. But maybe it is. It depends on your task. With the names
as classes you could use smart matching to distinguish things:

```
given $thingy {
    when Monera   { ... }
    when Protista { ... }
    when Fungi    { ... }
```

```
    when Plantae  { ... }
    when Animalia { ... }
    }
```

5. Create a `Meta` class inside `Butterfly`. Declare it with `my class` to make it private.

   Inside `Meta` track when the object was created and modified. Also keep a counter of the number of updates. None of this is available outside of `Butterfly`. It's convenient to wrap it in its own class because none of this has anything to do with something being a butterfly. If you were interested in doing this for your objects you'd probably have this as a separate class available to everyone, but then you wouldn't be able to try private classes for this exercise:

```
class Butterfly {
    has $!meta;
    my class Meta {
        has $.created = now;
        has $.modified;
        has $.update-count;
        method update {
            $!modified = now;
            $!update-count++;
            }
        }

    submethod TWEAK { $!meta = Meta.new }

    method update { $!meta.update }
    method show-meta {
        put $!meta.update-count, ': ', $!meta.modified;
        }
    }

my $b = Butterfly.new;

for ^4 {
    $b.update;
    sleep 1;
    $b.show-meta;
    }
```

To set up the `Meta` object, use the `TWEAK` submethod to initialize it. At that point the object has been completely constructed and you can initialize it without worrying about arguments and so on.

The particular output from `show-meta` isn't as important as your ability to store and retrieve data from it:

```
1: Instant:1528856314.611059
2: Instant:1528856315.616867
```

```
3: Instant:1528856316.623853
4: Instant:1528856317.625833
```

Answers to Chapter 13 Exercises

1. The code for `ScientificName` is the same as for `CommonName`. Both of them store a `Str`:

   ```
   role ScientificName {
       has $.scientific-name is rw = 'Thingus anonymous';
       }

   class Butterfly does ScientificName {}

   my $name = Butterfly.new: :scientific-name('Hamadryas perlicus');
   put $name.scientific-name; # Hamadryas perlicus
   ```

2. Here's a role that fills in the taxonomy for butterflies. It's the same as `Scientific Name` but with fixed values for some of the levels:

   ```
   role Lepidoptera {
       # these are fixed
       has $.kingdom = 'Animalia';
       has $.phylum  = 'Arthropoda';
       has $.class   = 'Insecta';
       has $.order   = 'Lepidoptera';

       # these are changeable
       has $.family is rw;
       has $.genus is rw;
       has $.species is rw;
       }

   class Butterfly does Lepidoptera {}

   my $butterfly = Butterfly.new:
       :family(  'Nymphalidae' ),
       :genus(   'Hamadryas' ),
       :species( 'perlicus' ),
       ;

   say $butterfly;
   ```

   The output shows that all the levels in the taxonomy show up in the object:

   ```
   Butterfly.new(kingdom => "Animalia", phylum => "Arthropoda",
   class => "Insecta", order => "Lepidoptera",
   family => "Nymphalidae", genus => "Hamadryas",
   species => "perlicus")
   ```

From there you can add `CommonName`:

```
class Butterfly does Lepidoptera does CommonName {}

my $butterfly = Butterfly.new:
    :family(     'Nymphalidae'  ),
    :genus(      'Hamadryas'    ),
    :species(    'perlicus'     ),
    :common-name( 'Perly Cracker' )
    ;

say $butterfly;
```

The output includes the common name:

```
Butterfly.new(common-name => "Perly Cracker",
kingdom => "Animalia", phylum => "Arthropoda",
class => "Insecta", order => "Lepidoptera",
family => "Nymphalidae", genus => "Hamadryas",
species => "perlicus")
```

3. The `Lepidoptera` role is the same except for a method that constructs a `Str` based on the genus and species. The class `Butterfly` then has that method and you can call it on objects of that class:

```
role Lepidoptera {
    # these are fixed
    has $.kingdom = 'Animalia';
    has $.phylum  = 'Arthropoda';
    has $.class   = 'Insecta';
    has $.order   = 'Lepidoptera';

    # these are changeable
    has $.family is rw;
    has $.genus is rw;
    has $.species is rw;

    # this is the difference in this exercise
    method binomial-name () { "$.genus $.species" }
    }

role CommonName {
    has $.common-name is rw;
    }

class Butterfly does Lepidoptera does CommonName {}

my $butterfly = Butterfly.new:
    :family(  'Nymphalidae' ),
    :genus(   'Hamadryas' ),
    :species( 'perlicus' ),
    ;
```

```
put $butterfly.binomial-name;
```

The output is the two-part name:

```
Hamadryas perlicus
```

4. You aren't writing much new code to satisfy this exercise. You need to create four files: two for the roles, one for the class, and one for your program. The roles each get their own files. The Lepidoptera role goes into *Lepidoptera.pm6*:

```
role Lepidoptera {
    # these are fixed
    has $.kingdom = 'Animalia';
    has $.phylum  = 'Arthropoda';
    has $.class   = 'Insecta';
    has $.order   = 'Lepidoptera';

    # these are changeable
    has $.family is rw;
    has $.genus is rw;
    has $.species is rw;

    # this is the difference in this exercise
    method binomial-name () { "$.genus $.species" }
    }
```

The CommonName role goes into *CommonName.pm6*:

```
role CommonName {
    has $.common-name is rw;
    }
```

The Butterfly class goes into a file named *Butterfly.pm6*. The code is short. You load the two roles, then use them when you define the empty class:

```
use Lepidoptera;
use CommonName;

class Butterfly does Lepidoptera does CommonName {}
```

You might have to adjust your library search path to find your modules. You already know the rest of the program file:

```
use lib <.>; # The current working directory
use Butterfly;

my $butterfly = Butterfly.new:
    :family(  'Nymphalidae' ),
    :genus(   'Hamadryas' ),
    :species( 'perlicus' ),
    ;
```

```
put $butterfly.binomial-name;
```

5. In Chapter 12 you did a similar exercise with inheritance. That's probably the better way to approach a taxonomy like this since each level is a more specific thingy, but in this chapter you're practicing your use of roles. This exercise isn't a demonstration of how you should organize real-world complexity.

Here's the program you want to work. You need to create the infrastructure to support it:

```
use lib <.>;
use Hamadryas;

my $cracker = Hamadryas.new:
    :species( 'perlicus' ),
    :common-name( 'Perly Cracker' ),
    ;

put $cracker.binomial-name;
put $cracker.common-name;
```

Create the Hamadryas class that will be a more specific Butterfly (so, inheritance). You can pull in roles for CommonName and BinomialName. The next higher taxonomic order is the family *Nymphalidae*, which gets its own role. Each level only knows the level above it. The Hamadryas class knows the genus and adds a species attribute that you can set yourself:

```
use Nymphalidae;
use CommonName;
use BinomialName;

class Hamadryas
    does Nymphalidae
    does CommonName
    does BinomialName
    {
    has $.genus = 'Hamadryas';
    has $.species is rw;
    }
```

You might as well start with a role for the binomial name. Previously you'd put that in the Lepidoptera class. It's more appropriate for its own role:

```
role BinomialName {
    method binomial-name { join ' ', $.genus, $.species }
    }
```

The Nymphalidae role is in its own file named *Nymphalidae.pm6*. This role sets the family attribute and does the next taxonomic role above it—the order *Lepidoptera*:

```
use Lepidoptera;
role Nymphalidae does Lepidoptera { has $.family = 'Nymphalidae' }
```

The Lepidoptera role is similar and lives in *Lepidoptera.pm6*:

```
use Insecta;
role Lepidoptera does Insecta { has $.order = 'Lepidoptera' }
```

This continues through Insecta in *Insecta.pm6*:

```
use Arthropodia;
role Insecta does Arthropodia { has $.class = 'Insecta' }
```

And Arthropodia in *Arthropodia.pm6*:

```
use Animalia;
role Arthropodia does Animalia { has $.phylum = 'Arthropodia' }
```

And ultimately Animalia in *Animalia.pm6*:

```
role Animalia { has $.kingdom = 'Animalia' }
```

If you included methods in any of these roles they would be in your Hamadryas class, but not through inheritance. After you've set up your roles and classes the initial program should output the binomial name.

Answers to Chapter 14 Exercises

1. For what it's worth, the fastest way to tell if something is a prime is to already know the answer (and you already know a lot of primes). Here's a simple solution:

```
my $primes = any( 2, 3, 5, 7 );

for 1 .. 10 {
    put "$_ is { $_ == $primes ?? '' !! 'not' } prime";
    }
```

This outputs:

```
1 is not prime
2 is  prime
3 is  prime
4 is not prime
5 is  prime
6 is not prime
7 is  prime
8 is not prime
9 is not prime
10 is not prime
```

Perl 6 mostly has this built in. You could have easily done this without the Junction:

```
for 1 .. 10 {
    put "$_ is { $_.is-prime ?? '' !! 'not'  } prime";
    }
```

This has to decide if a number is prime. For really big numbers, that might be quite the task. But storing all those primes is a big task too.

You may have done something slightly different. You might have created your Junction without knowing which numbers are prime. You can let .is-prime and grep figure that out:

```
my $primes = any( grep { $_.is-prime }, 1 .. 100 );

for 1 .. 100 {
    put "$_ is { $_ == $primes ?? '' !! 'not'  } prime";
    }
```

2. Here it is with a MAIN subroutine and a slurpy parameter. It requires at least one argument:

```
sub MAIN ( *@args where @args.elems > 0 ) {
    put all(@args).is-prime ??
        "All of <@args[]> are prime"
            !!
        "Some of <@args[]> are not prime";
    }
```

3. The first part is straightforward and much like the answers to the previous exercises:

```
sub MAIN ( *@args where @args.elems > 0 ) {
    put none(@args).is-prime ??
        "None of <@args[]> are prime"
            !!
        "Some of <@args[]> are prime";
    }
```

The second part of the problem seems tricky at first, but that's just the second branch of the ?? !!. If the none is False then you know that one of the numbers must be prime.

4. Here's how you might have done it. Start with a way to create the secret numbers then show yourself them so you don't drive yourself crazy guessing while you debug your program:

```
my @secret-numbers = map { 100.rand.Int }, 1 .. 3;
put "The secret numbers are @secret-numbers[]";
my @guessed;
```

Create the various `Junctions` all at once. This simplifies the conditions later:

```
my $any  = any  @secret-numbers;
my $all  = all  @secret-numbers;
my $one  = one  @secret-numbers;
my $none = none @secret-numbers;
```

Inside a `loop`, use `given-when` to figure out what to do. Get a guess, but give up if the user didn't enter anything. Check their guess to see if it is *not* an integer or if they've already guessed it. In those cases, use `next` to skip the rest and get another guess.

Use the `any` `Junction` to see if they guessed another number. You've already skipped previous correct guesses, so this should be a new number. Add that to `@guesses`. End the game if `@guesses` has the same number of elements as `@secret-numbers`. The `proceed` at the end of the block lets the `given` try more of the `when`s.

If the guess is larger than any of the secret numbers, decide how much more information you want to give. If the guess is larger than all of them, say so. If it's larger than only one of them or some (i.e., two) of them, tell them that. That way they have more hints. Do the same if the guess is smaller than all, one, or some of the numbers. Finally, tell them if their guess is larger or smaller than *none* of the numbers (although you can leave that off since larger than all is also smaller than none):

```
loop {
    last if @guessed.elems == @secret-numbers.elems;

    my $guess = prompt "=== ( @guessed[] ) Guess> ";
    last unless $guess;

    given $guess {
        when .Numeric !~~ Int    {
            put "You didn't guess a number!"; next }
        when @guessed.grep: $guess {
            put "You already guessed $_!"; next }
        when $_ == $any {
            put "$_ was one!";
            @guessed.push: $_;
            put "So far you have guessed @guessed[]!";
            last if @guessed.elems == @secret-numbers.elems;
            proceed;
            }

        when $_ > $any {
            if    $_ > $all { put "$_ is larger than all" }
            elsif $_ > $one { put "$_ is larger than one" }
            else            { put "$_ is larger than some" }
```

```
            proceed;
            }
        when $_ < $any {
            if $_ < $all    { put "$_ is smaller than all" }
            elsif $_ < $one { put "$_ is smaller than one" }
            else            { put "$_ is smaller than some" }
            proceed;
            }
        when $_ > $none {
            put "$_ is larger than none";
            proceed;
            }
        when $_ < $none {
            put "$_ is smaller than none";
            proceed;
            }
        }
    }
```

If you did this without the given you might think it's a bit cleaner (I do). You could have used $_ instead of $guess (or a shorter variable name). With a series of ifs you don't need the proceeds to move on to the next when:

```
my @secret-numbers = map { 100.rand.Int }, 1 .. 3;
put "The secret numbers are @secret-numbers[]";
my @guessed;

my $any  = any  @secret-numbers;
my $all  = all  @secret-numbers;
my $one  = one  @secret-numbers;
my $none = none @secret-numbers;

loop {
    last if @guessed.elems == @secret-numbers.elems;

    my $guess = prompt "=== ( @guessed[] ) Guess> ";
    last unless $guess;

    if $guess.Numeric !~~ Int    {
        put "You didn't guess a number!"; next }
    if @guessed.grep: $guess {
        put "You already guessed $_!"; next }
    if $guess == any( @secret-numbers ) {
        put "$guess was one!";
        @guessed.push: $guess;
        put "So far you have guessed @guessed[]!";
        last if @guessed.elems == @secret-numbers.elems;
        }

    if $guess > $any {
```

```
            if $guess > $all { put "$guess is larger than all"  }
        elsif $guess > $one { put "$guess is larger than one"  }
        else                { put "$guess is larger than some" }
        }
    if $guess < $any {
            if $guess < $all { put "$guess is smaller than all"  }
        elsif $guess < $one { put "$guess is smaller than one"  }
        else                { put "$guess is smaller than some" }
        }
    if $guess > $none { put "$guess is larger than none"  }
    if $guess < $none { put "$guess is smaller than none" }
    }
```

5. Get the answer from the prompt routine, lowercase it with .lc, break it up with .words, and coerce it into a Set. With a Map you used :exists to check that a color is a key. With a Set use ∈ to check if an element is a member:

```
my $colors = prompt "Enter some colors on one line: ";
my $color-set = $colors.lc.words.Set;

loop {
    my $color = prompt( "Try a color: " ).trim.lc;
    last unless $color;
    put $color ∈ $color-set ??
        "\t$color is in the set"
        !!
        "\t$color is not in the set"
        ;
    }
```

When you input some colors the spacing and capitalization don't matter:

```
% perl6 color-set.p6
Enter some colors on one line: red green blue
Try a color: blue
    blue is in the set
Try a color: Blue
    blue is in the set
Try a color:    Blue
    blue is in the set
Try a color: green
    green is in the set
Try a color: gray
    gray is not in the set
```

6. The hardest part of this problem is probably constructing the Sets. There are many ways that you could have done this. This solution uses a subroutine that creates a Range, picks 10 elements from it, and turns it into a Set. After that it's a matter of using the right operators:

```
sub make-set (Int:D $a, Int:D $b where $a < $b ) {
    ($a .. $b).pick(10).Set
    }

my $set-a = make-set( 1, 50 );
my $set-b = make-set( 1, 50 );

my $union        = $set-a ∪ $set-b;
my $intersection = $set-a ∩ $set-b;

put qq:to/END/;
set A: $set-a
set B: $set-b

union: $union
intersection: $intersection
END
```

To check that it's actually working you can output the two starting Sets:

```
% perl6 set-operations.p6
set A: 12 18 41 32 5 46 3 35 25 22
set B: 30 18 11 40 21 10 49 2 24 8

union: 30 41 18 12 11 40 32 21 46 5 10 3 49 22 25 35 8 24 2
intersection: 18
```

If you wanted to improve this you could get a List of their keys and sort those:

```
my $set-a = make-set( 1, 50 );
my $set-b = make-set( 1, 50 );

my $union        = $set-a ∪ $set-b;
my $intersection = $set-a ∩ $set-b;

put qq:to/END/;
set A: {$set-a.keys.sort}
set B: {$set-b.keys.sort}

union: {$union.keys.sort}
intersection: {$intersection.keys.sort}
END

sub make-set (Int:D $a, Int:D $b where $a < $b ) {
    ($a .. $b).pick(10).Set
    }
```

This output might be easier to read:

```
% perl6 set-operations-sorted.p6
set A: 1 3 4 9 15 21 22 35 45 50
set B: 2 3 13 14 21 31 34 38 42 44
```

```
union: 1 2 3 4 9 13 14 15 21 22 31 34 35 38 42 44 45 50
intersection: 3 21
```

Answers to Chapter 15 Exercises

1. An easy solution is a for that skips the nonmatching lines:

   ```
   for lines() {
       next unless /Hamadryas/;
       .put
       }
   ```

   For a simple pattern like this you might have also used `.contains`.

2. This answer is like the one for the first exercise, but with a different pattern:

   ```
   my $pattern = rx/ \d\d\d /;

   for lines() {
       next unless $pattern;
       .put;
       }
   ```

   This is a bit longer than it needs to be because I haven't shown you quantifiers yet.

3. Here's one way to do it. The tricky part of the program is the pattern, but you've already seen it:

   ```
   / <:Letter + :Number> /
   ```

   The `.chr` method turns a number into the code point it represents. Once you have the character you can match against it. If it doesn't match, skip the rest of the block. Accumulate the count for anything you didn't skip.

   The LAST phaser outputs a message after the last time the block executes. This is a nice construct for keeping all of the variables and values inside the same block. Otherwise you'd need to define everything outside the block so you could access it after the for loop finished:

   ```
   my ($lower, $upper) = ( 0x0001, 0xFFFD );

   for $lower .. $upper {
       state $count = 0;
       next unless .chr ~~ / <:Letter + :Number> /;
       $count++;
       LAST {
           printf "There are %d characters that are letters or numbers\n" ~
           "That's %.1f%% of the characters between %#x and %#x\n",
           $count, 100*$count / ( $upper - $lower ), $lower, $upper;
   ```

```
    }
  }
```

This outputs:

```
There are 49483 characters that are letters or numbers
That's 75.5% of the characters between 0x1 and 0XFFFD
```

4. Use a character class that matches all the letters but knocks out the vowels. If that pattern matches, skip the line. Output what makes it past that. You might find that many blank lines match this, so skipping lines that don't have something other than whitespace might be useful:

```
for lines() {
    next if / <:Letter - [aeiou]> /;
    next unless / \S /;
    .put;
    # a e i
    }
```

Adding a line that only has letter characters that are vowels can help your testing.

5. Here's one way to do it:

```
my $pattern = rx/ ei /;

for lines() {
    next unless $pattern;
    .put;
    }
```

You can also use an explicit variable:

```
my $pattern = rx/ ei /;

for lines() -> $line {
    next unless $line ~~ $pattern;
    $line.put;
    }
```

You might have used m// instead:

```
for lines() -> $line {
    next unless $line ~~ m/ ei /;
    $line.put;
    }
```

You can run this by specifying files as arguments:

```
% perl6 matching_lines.p6 file1 file2
```

You can redirect input:

```
% perl6 matching_lines.p6 < file1
```

Or pipe input:

```
% ls | perl6 matching_lines.p6
```

If you don't have your own file to search, you can use one of the files in the Downloads section of this book's website (*https://www.learningperl6.com/*).

6. The answer is simpler than the exercise makes it out to be. Take each line of input and break it up by tabs. Select the column that you want:

```
for lines() {
    put .split( /\t/ ).[2]
    }
```

A more sophisticated solution lets you pick the column from the command line. This one loses the feature of multiple files (not hard to fix but left up to you):

```
sub MAIN ( Str:D $file, Int:D $column = 2 ) {
    for $file.IO.lines() {
        put .split( /\t/ ).[$column]
        }
    }
```

But what happens when a line doesn't have the column number that you request? Break the line into parts and check how many parts you got before you try to extract the column. If you track the line number you can give the person a hint about where the file has a problem:

```
sub MAIN ( Str:D $file, Int:D $column = 2 ) {
    for $file.IO.lines() {
        state $line = 0;
        $line++;
        my @parts = .split( /\t/ );
        if $column > @parts.end {
            $*ERR.put: "Column out of range at line $line";
            next;
            }
        put .split( /\t/ ).[$column]
        }
    }
```

Previously you did this exercise and used `.words` to break up the line. That would accidentally work for this exercise because the data doesn't have significant spaces in it. If a species was `perlicus sixus`, for instance, `.words` would make two elements out of that.

Answers to Chapter 16 Exercises

1. The *butterfly_census.txt* file is in the Downloads section of the book's website (*https://www.learningperl6.com/*) (Preface). This file has a long list of species

names with repetitions. Your task is to find the ones that have a repeated *ii* and output the number of distinct names.

Use a for loop to read a file line by line and add the lines with one or more consecutive *i*'s to a Hash. The Hash acculumator can use the keys to create a distinct list, then output that list:

```
my $file = 'butterfly_census.txt';
my %ii-census;

for $file.IO.lines -> $line {
    if $line ~~ /ii+/ {
        %ii-census{$line}++
        }
    }

%ii-census.keys.sort.join( "\n" ).put;
```

This doesn't count them, but it allows you to see what it will count. When you know you have it right you can output the number of keys:

```
%ii-census.keys.elems.put;
```

Wrapping that in a MAIN subroutine allows you to specify a file on the command line:

```
sub MAIN ( $file = 'butterfly_census.txt' ) {
    my %ii-census;

    for $file.IO.lines -> $line {
        %ii-census{$line}++ if $line ~~ /ii+/;
        }

    %ii-census.keys.elems.put;
    }
```

Perhaps you went for the count directly but you still need a way to discard previously encountered names:

```
sub MAIN ( $file = 'butterfly_census.txt' ) {
    my %ii-census;
    my $count;

    for $file.IO.lines -> $line {
        $count++ if ($line ~~ /ii+/ and %ii-census{$line}++ == 0);
        }

    put $count;
    }
```

You could forget about for and use .grep with your pattern to find the ones that match, then use .unique to make a list of distinct values:

```
sub MAIN ( $file = 'butterfly_census.txt' ) {
    put $file.IO.lines.grep( /i+/ ).unique.elems
    }
```

2. This answer is much like any of the answers for the previous exercise, but with a different pattern:

```
sub MAIN ( $file = 'butterfly_census.txt' ) {
    put $file.IO.lines.grep( /a <[ n s ]>* a/ ).unique.join: "\n";
    }
```

Your pattern has two *a*'s with some stuff in the middle. That's a character class that will match an *n* or an *s*.

3. Here's a basic counting program. The pattern part is the line with next; you'll skip everything that doesn't match. After that you use the line as the key for the Hash. The LAST phaser outputs a summary at the end:

```
for lines() {
    state %Count;
    next unless /  <[aeiou]> ** 4 /;
    %Count{$_}++;
    LAST {
        for %Count.keys.sort( { %Count{$^a} } ).reverse {
            printf "%4d  %s\n", %Count{$_}, $_;
            }
        }
    }
```

There are two species that have four vowels in a row:

```
923  Chorinea octauius
235  Diaeus variegata
```

4. The program is almost the same as the one from the previous exercise:

```
for lines() {
    state %Count;
    next unless /  [a <-[aeiou]>] ** 4 /;
    %Count{$_}++;
    LAST {
        for %Count.keys.sort( { %Count{$^a} } ).reverse {
            printf "%4d  %s\n", %Count{$_}, $_;
            }
        }
    }
```

The pattern groups two things. There's the literal *a*, then a character class that subtracts the vowels:

```
[a <-[aeiou]>]
```

Repeat that exactly four times:

```
[a <-[aeiou]>] ** 4
```

Using the butterfly census file as input finds some interesting matches. Sometimes a space is the character that comes after the *a*:

```
892  Vanessa atalanta
682  Potamanaxas laoma
623  Paralasa jordana
552  Matapa aria
378  Protogoniomorpha anacardii
359  Potamanaxas effusa
334  Potamanaxas paralus
247  Potamanaxas andraemon
166  Potamanaxas melicertes
```

5. Use this pattern to find the text between underscores. The .+? won't go past the next underscore:

```
/ '_' .+? '_' /
```

The rest of the program goes through each line. To get all the matches on a line use the :global adverb:

```
for lines() {
    my @matches = m:global/ '_' .+? '_' /;
    say @matches if @matches.elems > 0;
    }
```

Here are a few lines at the end of the output:

```
(「_Pieris_」)
(「_Mamestra_」)
(「_Bombyx_」)
(「_Thecla_」)
(「_The Small Copper_」 「_Polyommatas Phlaeas_」)
(「_Brunneata_」)
```

Try this without the ? to see how the output changes.

6. Use a global match to extract all the text between underscores. Capture the entire text, but also define subcaptures for the genus and species. There's some extra data between underscores (italicized words), but you know a little more about scientific names: the genus is capitalized and the species isn't. For the input data they are also limited to the Latin alphabet:

```
for lines() {
    my $matches =
        m:global/

            _
            (
            $<genus>=(<[A..Z]><[a..z]>+)
            \s
            $<species>=(<[a..z]>+)
            )
            _
```

```
    /;
  next unless $matches.elems > 0;
  say $matches;
  }
```

You'll see another way to write this in a couple of sections. You can keep the starting and ending text together and specify the middle part at the end:

```
my $matches =
  m:global/ _ ~ _
    (
    $<genus>=(<[A..Z]><[a..z]>+)
    \s
    $<species>=(<[a..z]>+)
    )
    /;
```

It's often a good idea to start small to make sure the meat of your program is doing what you think it is. After that you can solve the other parts. The rest of the program is counting and outputting things:

```
for lines() {
  state %Found;
  my $matches =
    m:global/

        _
        (
            $<genus>=(<[A..Z]><[a..z]>+)
            \s
            $<species>=(<[a..z]>+)
        )
        _
        /;
  next unless $matches.elems > 0;
  for @$matches -> $m {
    put ~$m[0];
    %Found{$m[0]<genus>}{$m[0]<species>}++;
    }

  LAST {
    my @species-count =
      %Found
        .keys
        .map( {$^k => %Found{$^k}.keys.elems} )
        .sort( *.value )
        .reverse;
    for @species-count {
      last if $++ > 5;
      printf "%2d %s\n", $^p.kv.reverse;
      }
```

```
        }
    }
```

The end of the output looks something like this:

```
4 Populus
3 Eupithecia
3 Salix
3 Crambus
3 Trifolium
3 Melanippe
```

7. Go through all of the characters to match. This answer only goes up through those with ordinal values between 0 and 0xFFFF. Turn each number into a character with `.chr` then match against that:

```
for 0 .. 0xFFFF -> $ord {
    my $char = $ord.chr;
    next unless $char ~~ /\w/;
    next if $char ~~ / <:Alpha> /;
    put "[$ord] $char";
    }
```

When I ran this exercise I found 371 "word" characters that are not letters. Almost all of them are numbers, but there is also the underscore character. Everything else is a nonword character, with the inclusion of the beginning and the end of a Str.

8. Here's a quick way to do it. Put the names in an `Array` and combine those with `||`:

```
my @genus = < Lycaena Zizeeria Hamadryas >;
for lines() {
    state %Species;
    LAST { put "Found {%Species.keys.elems} species" }
    next unless m/ || @genus /;
    %Species{$_}++;
    .put;
    }
```

You could have put those directly in the pattern:

```
next unless m/
    || < Lycaena Zizeeria Hamadryas >
    /;
```

Or even spread out the options:

```
next unless m/
    || Lycaena
    || Zizeeria
```

```
|| Hamadryas
/;
```

Answers to Chapter 17 Exercises

1. Here's a first stab at this. This one uses `regex` for `TOP` so there's no significant whitespace:

```
grammar OctalNumber {
    regex TOP          { [ 0o? ]? <[0..7]>+  }
    }

my @numbers = qw/
    123 0 0123
    8 129
    0o456 o345
    /;

for @numbers -> $number {
    put "⌈$number⌋ ",
        OctalNumber.parse( $number ) ?? "matched" !! "failed";
    }
```

The output is:

```
⌈123⌋ matched
⌈0⌋ matched
⌈0123⌋ matched
⌈8⌋ failed
⌈129⌋ failed
⌈0o456⌋ matched
⌈o345⌋ failed
```

2. Here's a simple grammar. The tricky part is the inclusion of the ' and - characters; in an identifier those have to come before an alphabetic character:

```
grammar Variable {
    token TOP          { <sigil> <identifier> }
    token alpha        { <:Letter> }
    token number       { <:Number> }
    token other        { <['-]> }

    token sigil        { <[$@%]> }
    token identifier   {
        <alpha> [ <alpha> | <number> | <other><alpha> ]*
        }
    }

my @candidates = qw/
    sigilless   $scalar  @array   %hash
```

```
$123abc     $abc'123 $ab'c123
$two-words $two-     $-dash
/;

for @candidates -> $candidate {
    my $result = Variable.parse( $candidate, );
    say "⌜$candidate⌟ ", $result ?? 'Parsed!' !! 'Failed!';
    }
```

Here's the output:

```
⌜sigilless⌟ Failed!
⌜$scalar⌟ Parsed!
⌜@array⌟ Parsed!
⌜%hash⌟ Parsed!
⌜$123abc⌟ Failed!
⌜$abc'123⌟ Failed!
⌜$ab'c123⌟ Parsed!
⌜$two-words⌟ Parsed!
⌜$two-⌟ Failed!
⌜$two'⌟ Failed!
⌜$-dash⌟ Failed!
```

3. Here's a simple way to turn an octal number into its decimal representation. It's mostly the same as the code in the chapter:

```
class OctalActions {
    method digits ($/) {
        put "⌜$/⌟ is ⌜{ parse-base( ~$/, 8 ) }⌟"; # or $/.Str
        }
    }

grammar OctalNumber {
    regex TOP           { <.prefix>? <digits>  }
    regex prefix        { [ 0o? ]  }
    regex digits        { <[0..7]>+ }
    }

my $number = '0o177';
my $result = OctalNumber.parse(
    $number, :actions(OctalActions)
    );
```

The output shows the decimal version of 0177:

```
⌜177⌟ is ⌜127⌟
```

If you did the extra credit work, you might have done it like this:

```
class OctalActions {
    method digits ($/) {
        put "⌜$/⌟ is ⌜{ parse-base( ~$/, 8 ) }⌟"
        }
```

```
    }

grammar OctalNumber {
    regex TOP        { <.prefix>? <digits>  }
    regex prefix     { [ 0o? ]  }
    regex digits     { <[0..7]>+ }
    }

loop {
    my $number = prompt("octal number> ");
    last unless try $number.chars;
    my $result = OctalNumber.parse(
        $number, :actions(OctalActions)
        );
    put "Failed on ⌈$number⌋" unless $result.so;
    }
```

The output shows that it handles octal numbers, fails on nonoctal numbers, and quietly exits when there's no number:

```
octal number> 177
⌈177⌋ is ⌈127⌋
octal number> 0177
⌈177⌋ is ⌈127⌋
octal number> 0o177
⌈177⌋ is ⌈127⌋
octal number> 198
⌈1⌋ is ⌈1⌋
Failed on ⌈198⌋
octal number> 777
⌈777⌋ is ⌈511⌋
octal number> 377
⌈377⌋ is ⌈255⌋
octal number>
```

The prompt routine was quite handy there.

4. Here's a possible grammar for a dotted-decimal IP address. It uses the <?{}> to look at the matched digits and assert something about the number:

```
grammar DottedDecimal {
    token TOP { <digits> ** 4 % '.' }
    regex digits { ( <[0..9]> ** 3 ) <?{ 0 <= $0 <= 255 }> }
    }
```

The action class isn't that hard. Each digits capture shows up in an Array. The high octet is the first element, so shift up those bits 24 places, and shift the next two elements in the Array 16 and 8 places (leave the last one alone, although you could shift it 0 places). Add all of those results with the [+] reduction operator. That sum is the value you make:

```
class DottedDecimal::SimpleActions {
    method TOP ($/) {
        # get the list of digits and shift each octet over the
        # right number of bits
        make [+] (
            $<digits>.[0] +< 24,
            $<digits>.[1] +< 16,
            $<digits>.[2] +<  8,
            $<digits>.[3]
            );
    }
}

my $string = '192.168.1.137';
my $match = DottedDecimal.parse(
    $string,
    :actions(DottedDecimal::SimpleActions)
    );
say $match;
say $match.made.fmt('%X');
```

If you like the hyper- and cross operators, you might have done something more like this:

```
class DottedDecimal::Actions {
    method TOP ($/) {
        # get the list of digits and shift each octet over the
        # right number of bits
        make [+] (
            $<digits>                   # the octets, as an Array
                »+<«                     # hyper bit shift +<
            ( (0 .. $<digits>.end) X* 8 ).reverse
            );
    }
}
```

5. I won't reproduce the code here because it would be the same as in the chapter.

6. The first part of the solution fetches the file over the web, but you could save it locally and slurp its contents instead:

```
use HTTP::UserAgent;

my $ua = HTTP::UserAgent.new;
$ua.timeout = 10;

my $url = 'https://goo.gl/sPUwjp';   # or go to GitHub directly
my $response = $ua.get( $url );

my $data = do with $response {
    .is-success ?? .content !! die .status-line
    }
```

The grammar and the roles are the same examples from the chapter:

```
grammar Grammar::CSV {
    token TOP       { <record>+ }
    token record    { <value>+ % <.separator> \R }
    token separator { <.ws> ',' <.ws> }
    token value     {
        '"'                 # quoted
            <( [ <-["]> | <.escaped-quote> ]* )>
        '"'

            |
        <-[",\n\f\r]>+  # non-quoted (no vertical ws)
            |
            ''                  # empty
    }

    token escaped-quote { '""' }
}

role DoubledQuote     { token escaped-quote { '""' } }
role BackslashedQuote { token escaped-quote { '\\"' } }
```

It's the action class that's new. To handle the double-quote escaping you can process the `value` to substitute a single double quote for any form of the escaped version:

```
class UnescapeDoubleQuote {
    method TOP      ( $/ ) { make $<record>».made.flat }
    method record   ( $/ ) { make [ $<value>».made.flat ] }
    method value    ( $/ ) {
        make $/.Str.subst: / [ '\\' || '"' ] '"' /, '"', :g;
        }
    }
}

my $csv-parser = Grammar::CSV.new but DoubledQuote;

my $match = $csv-parser.parse:
    $data,
    :actions(UnescapeDoubleQuote);

say $match.made // 'Failed!';
```

Answers to Chapter 18 Exercises

1. You need two things to make this work, a `Supplier` to emit the values and a tap to read them:

```
my $supplier = Supplier.new;
my $tap = $supplier.Supply.tap:
```

```
        { state %Seen; ! %Seen{$^a}++ ?? put $^a !! False };
    $supplier.emit( $_ ) for lines();
```

This solution uses `lines()` to read input from the files on the command line:

```
% perl6 emitter.p6 butterfly_census.txt
```

You've reimplemented the *uniq* program!

2. This program is a series of steps where you wait three seconds between each. The first tap runs during most of the program and the second tap runs for a short period in the middle:

```
my $interval = 3;
my $supply = Supply.interval(1).share;

sleep $interval;
my $first-tap = $supply.tap: { put "First got $^a" };

sleep $interval;
my $second-tap = $supply.tap: { put "Second got $^a" };

sleep $interval;
$second-tap.close;

sleep $interval;
$first-tap.close;

put 'Done';
```

The output shows that the first tap starts at 3 because the live `Supply` has already emitted some numbers. When the second tap runs, it gets the same number as the first tap:

```
First got 3
First got 4
First got 5
First got 6
Second got 6
First got 7
Second got 7
First got 8
Second got 8
First got 9
First got 10
First got 11
Done
```

3. Here's a simple `Channel`. Each time through the loop it gets a `Pair` of line number and text. It checks if the line number is a prime number. If so it outputs that line:

```
my $channel = Channel.new;
$channel.Supply.tap: -> Pair:D $p {
```

```
    put "{$p.key}: {$p.value}" if $p.key.is-prime
};
```

```
for lines() { $channel.send: $++ => $_ }
```

Using the program file as its own input gives this result:

```
2:      put "{$p.key}: {$p.value}" if $p.key.is-prime
3:      };
5:  for lines() { $channel.send: $++ => $_ }
```

4. The change is slight in typing and large in effect. By calling .share you turn the Supply into a live one. Additional taps start at the current value instead of starting over:

```
my $supply = Supply.interval(1).share;
```

```
react {
    whenever $supply { put "Got $^a" }
    whenever True { put 'Got something that was true' }
    whenever Promise.in(5) { put 'Timeout!'; done }
}
```

```
put "React again";
```

```
react {
    whenever $supply { put "Got $^a" }
}
```

```
END put "End of the program";
```

The output changes in two ways. There's no Got 0 because the Supply is already running and has supplied its first value by the time a whenever can tap it. The second react taps the Supply again and picks up where the interval left off:

```
Got something that was true
Got 1
Got 2
Got 3
Got 4
Got 5
Timeout!
React again
Got 6
Got 7
...
```

If you inserted a sleep between the two reacts you'd skip values in the interval.

5. You don't need to install anything because IO::Notification is part of the language. .watch-path returns a Supply which you can use in a react. This program runs forever:

```
sub MAIN ( Str:D $s where *.IO.e, $timeout = 10 ) {
    my $supply = IO::Notification.watch-path( $s );

    react {
        whenever $supply { put "{.path}: {.event}" }
        }
}
```

If you give this a file it watches only that file. If you give it a directory it checks the directory and anything in it (but it doesn't look inside subdirectories—install `IO::Notification::Recursive`) for that.

There are various things you could do to stop the program. You might want it to run for a certain time and then stop. An `.in` `Promise` would work for that:

```
sub MAIN ( Str:D $s where *.IO.e, $timeout = 10 ) {
    my $supply = IO::Notification.watch-path( $s );

    react {
        whenever $supply { put "{.path}: {.event}" }
        whenever Promise.in( $timeout ) { put "Stopping"; done; }
        }
}
```

Or you could use an interval to periodically check if enough changes have been made:

```
sub MAIN ( Str:D $s where *.IO.e ) {
    my $supply = IO::Notification.watch-path( $s );
    my $changes = 0;

    react {
        whenever $supply { put "{.path}: {.event}"; $changes++ }
        whenever Supply.interval(1) {
            if $changes > 10 {
                put 'Stopping';
                done;
                }
            }
        }
}
```

Finally, you can create a `Supply` that handles a signal (although you did not see that in the chapter). `SIGINT` is the signal that Control-C sends. Intercept that so you can run your code to clean up and exit the program:

```
sub MAIN ( Str:D $s where *.IO.e ) {
    put "PID is $*PID";
    my $supply = IO::Notification.watch-path( $s );
    my $changes = 0;

    react {
```

```
        whenever $supply { put "{.path}: {.event}"; $changes++ }
        whenever signal(SIGINT) {
            put 'Stopping';
            done;
            }
        }
    }
```

Answers to Chapter 19 Exercises

1. Here's a simple program that chooses a list of strings based on the current operating system. Whatever ends up in @command becomes the argument to run:

    ```
    my @command = $*DISTRO.is-win ??
        < cmd /c dir /OS >
        !!
        < ls -lrS >
        ;

    my $proc = run @command, :out;
    ```

    To filter those use .grep:

    ```
    for $proc.out.lines.grep( rx/7/ ) -> $line {
        put $++, ': ', $line;
        }
    ```

    Here's the output on a Unix machine (with some columns elided for space):

    ```
    % perl6 ls-exercise.p6
    0: -rwxrwxr-x@    72 Jan  6 19:36 shell-perl6-exit1.p6
    1: -rw-r--r--@   162 Apr 25 20:27 find.p6
    2: -rw-rw-r--@   177 Apr 26 13:35 ls-exercise.p6
    3: -rw-r--r--@   217 Apr 25 21:42 write-to-proc.p6
    4: -rwxrwxr-x@   277 Jan  6 19:36 channels.p6
    5: -rw-rw-r--@   667 Jan  6 19:36 respawn.p6
    ```

    And the same on Windows:

    ```
    C:\ perl6 ls-exercise.p6
    > perl6 ls-exercise.p6
    0: 01/20/2018  10:22 AM                 75 shell-perl6-exit1.p6
    1: 01/20/2018  10:22 AM                687 respawn.p6
    2: 01/20/2018  10:22 AM                700 search.p6
    3:               2 Dir(s)  37,557,620,736 bytes free
    ```

2. This answer is similar to what you've already done with run but with an extra .spawn step involved:

    ```
    my $is-win = $*DISTRO.is-win;
    my @command = $is-win ?? < cmd /c dir> !! < ls >;
    ```

```
    my $proc = Proc.new: :out;
    $proc.spawn: @command;
    $proc.out.slurp.put;
```

3. Start with the program from the chapter. Wrap a MAIN around it to accept the command-line argument.

   In the react Block, intercept the output and count the lines. Call done when you've seen enough input. You can add a signal handler and a timeout too:

```
sub MAIN ( Int:D $max-files = 100 ) {
    my $proc = Proc::Async.new: 'find', '/', '-name', '*.txt';

    react {
        my $count;
        whenever $proc.stdout.lines {
            done if ++$count > $max-files;
            put "$count: $_";
            }
        whenever signal(SIGINT)     {
            put "\nInterrupted! $count files"; done
            }
        whenever $proc.start        {
            put "Finished: $count files"; done
            }
        whenever Promise.in(60)     {
            put "Timeout: $count files"; done
            }
        }
    }
```

Index

Symbols

! (exclamation point)
    adverbs and, 198
    pattern matching with, 254
    private methods and, 205
    unary operators and, 28
!= (numeric inequality operator), 30
" (double quote), 63
(hashtag), 9, 148
#! (shebang), 345
$ (end-of-string anchor), 275
$ sigil, 12, 18
$! variable, 124
$$ (end-of-line anchor), 275
$/ variable, 247, 269
$_ variable (topic), 42, 79, 245, 347
% (percent sign), 146, 274
% sigil, 12, 166
%% operator, 31
%() variable, 165
%_ variable, 198
& (all junction operator), 237
& sigil, 12, 78, 192
&& (logical AND operator), 27
() (parentheses)
    allomorphic quoting and, 160
    as grouping operator, 78, 89
    changing precedence with, 7
    literal quoting and, 52
    program arguments and, 19
    whitespace and, 34
* prefixing array parameter, 188
* quantifier, 264
* twigil, 14

** quantifier, 266
+ (plus sign)
    hyperoperators and, 115
    pattern matching using, 254
    unary operators and, 61
+ quantifier, 263
+& (bitwise AND operator), 139
+> (bitwise right shift operator), 139
, (comma), 20
- (minus sign)
    pattern matching using, 254
    unary operators and, 39
-> (pointy arrow), 81
-I switch, 175
. (dot), 251
.. (range operator), 96
... (triple-dot sequence operator), 100-102
// (defined-or operator), 29
: (colon)
    in adverb syntax, 53, 160, 337
    in method arguments, 11
    in named parameters, 197
    quantifiers and, 267
    representing numbers and, 23
    searching substrings, 56
::() (interpolated module names), 177
:= (binding operator), 17, 78
; (semicolon), 8, 84, 111, 332
< (less than), 31
<<>> (double angle brackets), 91, 115, 277
<> (angle brackets), 91, 118, 160, 248
= (item assignment operator), 17
=> (fat arrow notation), 159, 162, 341
> (greater than)

about, 159, 337
exercise answers, 388-395
hashes and, 165-170
key/value pairs, 159-161
maps and, 162-165
sigil associated with, 12
associativity, 7, 337
asynchronous execution, 303, 326, 337
at method, 310, 313
attributes
about, 203, 338
private, 207-209
public, 209-210
autochomp, 94, 338
autothread, 234, 338

B

%b directive, 146
:b adverb, 70
\b escape sequence, 65
backreferences, 272-273, 338
backslash (\)
as escape character, 53-54, 340
as unspace, 10
naming terms, 205
backtracing exceptions, 126
backtracking, 265, 267-268, 294, 338
bare block, 71, 338
base method, 23
basename method, 136
beginning-of-line anchor (^^), 275
behavior, adding to classes, 223-225
:bin adverb, 155-156
binary assignment, 26, 338
binary files
about, 155
moving around, 156
writing, 156
binary numbers, 22, 338
binary operators, 5, 117, 338
binding operator (:=), 17, 78
binding values, 17-18, 161, 338
bitwise AND operator (+&), 139
bitwise right shift operator (+>), 139
<blank> pattern, 249
bless method, 215
blocks
about, 8, 71-72, 338
bare, 71, 338

control structures, 73-75
exercise answers, 366-368
gathering values with, 102-103
lexical scope, 9, 72, 342
named subroutines, 84-84
phasers, 75-77
simple subroutines, 82-83
special rule for, 72
storing, 78-79
Whatever code, 85-86
with parameters, 79-82
Bool method, 32
Boolean values, 27-30, 338
branches
about, 34, 338
conditional, 33-35
BUILD method, 207, 209, 215-219
BUILDALL method, 215

C

:c adverb, 69-70, 161, 299
\c escape sequence, 64-65
cache method, 99, 102
callables
about, 338
sigils associated with, 12, 78
callsame routine, 213
camel case, 12, 338
candidate, 193, 338
captures
about, 268, 338
backreferences to, 272-273
capture tree, 271-272
named, 269-270
caret (^)
anchors and, 275
as one junction operator, 238
as placeholder variable, 80
range operator and, 96
case insensitivity, 56, 338
case sensitivity, 56, 58, 257, 338
cat ears, 96, 338
CATCH block, 125-130, 133
catching exceptions, 124-126, 338
chained comparison operators, 32
changed method, 140
channels
about, 303, 307-309, 338
exercise answers, 428-431

poll method, 308
pop method, 109
positional parameters
    about, 81, 344
    arguments and, 191
    named parameters and, 199
    parameter constraints, 192
    parameter traits, 191
    single argument rule, 189
    slurpy parameters and, 188, 190
positionals
    about, 89
    arrays and, 106-113
    combining lists, 113-117
    constructing lists, 89-95
    creating maps from, 163-164
    exercise answers, 368-376
    filtering lists, 117
    lazy, 342
    ranges and, 96-98
    sequences and, 98-103
    sigil associated with, 12
    single-element access, 103-106
    sorting lists, 119-122
    transforming lists, 118
postcircumfix, 344
postcircumfix operator, 6, 103, 344
postfix operator, 6, 344
postfix rule, 344
precedence
    about, 344
    evaluating expressions, 7
    logical operators and, 27
    string comparisons, 58
precircumfix operator, 6, 344
predefined variables, 14
prefix operator, 6, 344
PrettyDump module, 394
<print> pattern, 249
print routine, 13, 67
printf subroutine, 147
private attributes, 207-209
private classes, 220
private methods, 205, 344
Proc::Async class, 326
procedural element (regex), 282, 345
processes, writing to, 324-325
$*PROGRAM variable, 174
programs

asynchronous control and, 326
capturing command output, 322
controlling other, 321-327
exercise answers, 351-358, 432
interrupting, 73
MAIN subroutine, 18-21
making and running, 15-16
number-guessing, 17-37
representing commands as lists, 323
running external, 321-325
writing to processes, 324-325
promises
    about, 303, 309-310
    exercise answers, 428-431
    junctions and, 314
    managing, 312-314
    waiting for, 310-311
    waiting for multiple, 311
prompt routine, 21, 59, 151
public attributes, 209-210, 345
<punct> pattern, 249
puns, 224, 345
push method, 109
put routine, 13

Q

:q adverb, 53, 70, 161
\q escape sequence, 65
Q quoting form
    about, 52, 70
    adverbs modifying, 53, 160
    interpolated strings and, 65
:qq adverb, 65, 69-70
\qq escape sequence, 65
qqx construct, 67
quantifiers
    about, 263, 345
    backtracking and, 265, 267-268
    controlling, 267
    greediness and, 265
    minimal and maximal, 266
    summarized list of, 268
    zero or more, 264
    zero or one, 265
question mark (?), 129, 191
quoting in strings
    fancier quoting, 69
    generalized quoting, 52, 341
    literal quoting, 51-52

as unary prefix operator, 61
in pattern matching, 273
title case, 55
:to adverb, 66, 70
token declarator, 285, 288, 294, 347
topic ($_ variable), 42, 79, 245, 347
topical method, 347
topicalization, 211, 333, 347
tr command, 325
transforming lists, 118
trim method, 60
trim-leading method, 61
trim-trailing method, 61
triple-dot sequence operator (...), 100-102
True value, 347
try block, 124-130, 133
TWEAK method, 216, 219
twigil, 14, 347
type objects, 3, 11, 347
types
    about, 3, 347
    container-supported, 332
    inheriting, 212-215
    integer constraints, 40-42
    junction, 233-239
    number, 39-50
    parameter constraints, 82

U

%u directive, 147
UCD (Unicode Character Database)
    about, 23, 254, 347
    code point properties, 254
    graphemes and, 57, 339
    set comparators, 240-242
UCS (Universal Character Set), 119
unary operators
    about, 5, 347
    exclamation point, 28
    minus sign and, 39
    plus sign and, 61
    tilde and, 61
underscore (_), 40, 346
Unicode Character Database (UCD)
    about, 23, 254, 347
    code point properties, 254
    graphemes and, 57, 339
    set comparators, 240-242
union

of character class properties, 254
    of sets, 242, 347
Universal Character Set (UCS), 119
unless statement, 34
unlink method, 141, 143
unlinking files, 140-141
unshift method, 109
unspace, 10, 47, 252, 347
<upper> pattern, 249
use routine, 172
user-defined character classes, 255-256
UTF-8, 16, 347

V

:v adverb, 70, 118
\v character class shortcut, 253
\V character class shortcut, 253
value method, 160
values
    assigning, 17-18, 337
    binding, 17-18, 161, 338
    Boolean, 27-30, 338
    checking allowed for maps, 164-165
    checking in sets, 240
    decontainerizing, 112, 340
    literal, 22, 193-194
    mapping keys to, 162-165
    prompting for, 21
    simple output of, 13
variables
    about, 11, 347
    declaring, 12, 340
    initializing, 13, 342
    lexical scope, 13, 72
    output values of, 13
    placeholder, 80, 344
    predefined, 14

W

:w adverb, 91
\w character class shortcut, 253
\W character class shortcut, 253
w method, 137
Wall, Larry, xiv, 179
warn subroutine, 132, 150
warnings, 132-133
<|w> pattern, 276
<|wb> pattern, 249
Whatever class, 85-86, 348

WhateverCode class, 85
when statement, 42
whenever statement, 315-319
where clause, 85-86
while statement, 77
whitespace
    match operator and, 246
    parentheses and, 34
    pattern matching and, 252
    prompt routine accepting, 60
    statement considerations, 8
    syntax considerations, 10
WHY meta-method, 329
with keyword, 333
word boundaries, 276
<word> pattern, 249
words method, 260
writing binary files, 156
writing output, 154-155
writing to processes, 324-325
<ws> pattern, 249
<ww> pattern, 250

X

X (cross) operator, 114
%x directive, 146
x (replication operator), 54
:h adverb, 70

:x adverb, 67, 70, 322
%X directive, 147
\x escape sequence, 64, 66
x method, 138
X::AdHoc class, 130, 377
X::IO::Chdir class, 143
X::IO::Copy class, 142
X::IO::Link class, 141
X::IO::Mkdir class, 145
X::IO::Rename class, 142
X::IO::Rmdir class, 146
X::IO::Unlink class, 141
X::Method::NotFound class, 129
X::NYI class, 131
X::Str::Numeric class, 125
X::StubCode class, 131
<xdigit> pattern, 250
xx (list replication operator), 91

Y

yada yada, 9, 348

Z

Z (zip operator), 113
z method, 138
zef module manager, 171, 173
zip routine, 114

About the Author

brian d foy is a prolific Perl trainer and writer, and runs The Perl Review (*https://www.theperlreview.com/*) to help people use and understand Perl through education, consulting, code review, and more. He's a frequent speaker at Perl conferences. brian is the coauthor of *Learning Perl*, *Intermediate Perl*, and *Effective Perl Programming* (Addison-Wesley), and the author of *Mastering Perl*. He was an instructor and author for Stonehenge Consulting Services from 1998 to 2009 and has been a Perl user since he was a physics graduate student and a die-hard Mac user since he first owned a computer. He founded the first Perl user group, the New York Perl Mongers, as well as the Perl advocacy nonprofit Perl Mongers, Inc., which helped form more than 200 Perl user groups across the globe. He maintains the *perlfaq* portions of the core Perl documentation, several modules on CPAN, and some standalone scripts.

Colophon

The animal on the cover of *Learning Perl 6* is a Hamadryas butterfly. *Hamadryas* is a genus that includes several related species of butterfly. Hamadryas butterflies live throughout South and Central America, with some species found as far north as Arizona. Nine different species can be found in Costa Rica alone.

Hamadryas butterflies are commonly known as cracker butterflies for the distinctive noise made by males during territorial displays. Males wait in plant and tree branches for females to arrive, and emit clicking sounds to ward off predators and rival males.

Hamadryas butterflies usually feature coloring that allows them to blend in with their surroundings. Unlike other types of butterflies, they do not feed on nectar. Rather, they feed on rotting fruit, sap, and animal dung.

Many of the animals on O'Reilly covers are endangered; all of them are important to the world. To learn more about how you can help, go to *animals.oreilly.com*.

The cover image is from *Insects Abroad*. The cover fonts are URW Typewriter and Guardian Sans. The text font is Adobe Minion Pro; the heading font is Adobe Myriad Condensed; and the code font is Dalton Maag's Ubuntu Mono.

Learn from experts.
Find the answers you need.

Sign up for a **10-day free trial** to get **unlimited access** to all of the content on Safari, including Learning Paths, interactive tutorials, and curated playlists that draw from thousands of ebooks and training videos on a wide range of topics, including data, design, DevOps, management, business—and much more.

Start your free trial at:
oreilly.com/safari

(No credit card required)

Lightning Source UK Ltd.
Milton Keynes UK
UKHW03f2135300818
327990UK00003B/3/P